DIANA, WILLIAM AND HARRY

A list of titles by James Patterson appears
at the back of this book

DIANA, WILLIAM AND HARRY

JAMES PATTERSON
& CHRIS MOONEY

CENTURY

1 3 5 7 9 10 8 6 4 2

Century
20 Vauxhall Bridge Road
London SW1V 2SA

Century is part of the Penguin Random House group of companies
whose addresses can be found at global.penguinrandomhouse.com.

Copyright © James Patterson 2022

Excerpt from *James Patterson by James Patterson:
The Stories of My Life* © James Patterson 2022

James Patterson has asserted his right to be identified as the author of this
Work in accordance with the Copyright, Designs and Patents Act 1988.

First published in the UK by Century in 2022

www.penguin.co.uk

A CIP catalogue record for this book is available from the British Library.

Part opener photographs courtesy of – Part 1: Central Press/Getty Images; Part 2: Terry Fincher/
Princess Diana Archive/Getty Images; Part 3: Tim Graham Photo Library via Getty Images;
Part 4: Jayne Fincher/Getty Images; Part 5: Tim Graham Photo Library via Getty Images;
Part 6: UK Press/Getty Images; Part 7: Mark Cuthbert/UK Press/Getty Images;
Part 8: Chris Jackson/Getty Images; Part 9: Max Mumby/Indigo/Getty Images.

ISBN 978–1–529–12553–5 (hardback)
ISBN 978–1–529–12554–2 (trade paperback)

Printed and bound in Great Britain by Clays Ltd, Elcograf S.p.A.

The authorised representative in the EEA is Penguin Random House Ireland,
Morrison Chambers, 32 Nassau Street, Dublin D02 YH68.

Penguin Random House is committed to a sustainable future
for our business, our readers and our planet. This book is made
from Forest Stewardship Council® certified paper.

Contents

Prologue

She grips her seat as the driver opens the throttle. The black Mercedes S280 is built for speed.

As the two-ton sedan pulls away from the Ritz Paris hotel, photographers' flashbulbs explode in the night like gunfire. More cameramen, on motorcycles and scooters, are in pursuit.

Earlier this month, pictures of her and her boyfriend kissing while on a yacht in the Mediterranean sold to the tabloids for millions. The couple has only been in Paris a few hours, but the photographers following her won't stop until they get another image worth a fortune.

It's after midnight, but she's still dressed for a summer dinner in white jeans and a dark Armani jacket, her red lipstick bright against skin tanned from a season in the sun.

She looks around at the three men in the car: her boyfriend, Egyptian film producer Dodi Fayed, is beside her in the back seat; their British bodyguard, Trevor Rees-Jones, is directly in front of her.

At the wheel is Henri Paul, the hotel's deputy chief of security. Paul is an experienced tactical driver, trained at a Mercedes-Benz course in Germany.

When her boys, William and Harry, were younger, they played with toy cars and once waved from a BMW motorbike that a kind policeman let them pretend to drive.

Henri Paul is driving too fast.

There's an established route from the hotel to Dodi's apartment, over a Cartier store on rue Arsène Houssaye near the Arc de Triomphe, but Paul doesn't take it. He turns sharply onto Cours Albert 1er.

Only a few hours ago, she spoke with her sons, a few quick words between games with their cousins at Balmoral Castle. At twelve and fifteen, they're still young enough to need her.

Henri Paul shields his eyes with a visor against the bright lights of the cameras. As the driver glances at the rearview mirror, she turns in her seat to look out the back window.

They're traveling away from City Center, west along the north bank of the Seine. Across the river, the sky around the Eiffel Tower shines midnight blue with pockets of red and purple reflected by the lights of the monument.

Men on motorbikes are trying to overtake them.

She looks at the speedometer: 160 kilometers per hour and climbing.

If the boys were here with her, the three of them would be traveling together with a lead car and a tail car, the kind of first-rate protection afforded to the queen and those in immediate line to succeed her.

But since she divorced, she's refused the royal protection squad.

She's got a flight back to London tomorrow. She'll see William and Harry at home, at Kensington Palace. *I'm going to give Harry the PlayStation I bought for his birthday.*

The Mercedes swerves to the right, toward the entrance of the tunnel under the Pont de l'Alma. The burst of speed whirls her surroundings into a dizzying, kaleidoscopic blur.

The bodyguard shouts and points.

Out the front window, she sees a white car that has stopped short of the tunnel.

Henri Paul loses control. He hits the Mercedes's brakes, sending it skidding wildly into the white car's left rear quarter panel, then spins out, crashing first into a concrete pillar and then into an embankment wall.

As her body lurches forward, there's a sensation of dropping headfirst from a great height.

Like when she rode Disney World's Splash Mountain, Harry in the front, screaming with delight at the speed of the descent.

She's alive. Somehow, she's still alive—and fighting for breath. The pain inside her head—she's never felt anything like it. A concussion? Has to be.

Like that awful time when William's skull was accidentally fractured by a golf club.

William survived, and I will, too. I'm going home, and I'm going to hold them in my arms and smother them with kisses and tell them again and again just how much I love them.

PART 1
Lady Diana

Chapter 1

April 20, 1978
London

Lady Diana Spencer takes a deep breath.

She clutches her bouquet of roses and ducks her head, aware that all eyes are on her. She straightens her spine, then steps lightly, the way her ballet teachers have taught her.

Diana spots the beaming faces of wedding attendees, including the Duchess of Kent, the Duke and Duchess of Gloucester—and the Queen Mother, standing beside Diana's own maternal grandmother, Lady Ruth Fermoy.

Slowly, she begins her walk down the aisle, moving through the nave toward the chancel as she glides to her place at the altar.

Inside Guards' Chapel, a few hundred yards from Buckingham Palace, attention shifts from her to the bride: her sister Jane, lovely in her form-fitting high-necked long-sleeved embroidered lace gown and veil.

The real eye-catcher of Jane's bridal ensemble is an heirloom: the Spencer Tiara, which has been in the family for more than a century. A wedding present from a Spencer cousin to Lady Cynthia Hamilton, their paternal grandmother, the tiara is an ornate diamond headpiece embellished with a flower-shaped centerpiece. Diana dreams of wearing it on *her* future wedding day.

On this bright Thursday afternoon, though, sixteen-year-old Diana is in a floor-length ruffled pinafore-style pink gingham dress with cream-colored puffed sleeves. Even though she's chief bridesmaid, her gown is identical to those worn by the little flower girls. At least she's wearing pearls and has her shoulder-length fair hair fashionably clipped up on one side.

From her spot at the front of the church, Diana casts an eye over the congregation. Jane is marrying Robert Fellowes, the queen's assistant private secretary. Both the bride's and groom's sides are closely tied to the royal family. Queen Elizabeth is even godmother to Diana's thirteen-year-old brother, Charles. And while Robert possesses a courtier's prestige, it's the Spencer earldom that commands an uncommon fortune of $140 million, including the magnificent Althorp estate.

The newlyweds will be moving into the Old Barracks, a cottage on the grounds of Kensington Palace.

Oh, I would love to live at KP, Diana thinks, glancing again over pews filled with the elegantly dressed members of the royal inner circle.

She spots James Whitaker of the *Daily Mirror*. He's been reporting on a romance between the eldest Spencer sister, Sarah, and Prince Charles.

All the talk of "a potential match" has really gone to her twenty-three-year-old sister's head. Diana's seen the way Sarah revels in the attention, pasting into a scrapbook all the articles and photos about herself and His Royal Highness.

Just before today's ceremony began, Diana had bounced up to the reporter.

"You're the wicked Mr. Whitaker, aren't you?" she asked.

"Who are you, and how do you know me?" he volleyed back.

"I am Diana, the little sister, and I know all about you from Sarah," she said with a laugh. She stops short of telling the reporter what she's told friends, which is that she actually feels "desperately sorry" for Prince Charles having Sarah "wrapped around his neck because she's quite a tough old thing."

Diana may be the youngest Spencer daughter, but she is the most romantic. She remembers Jane confiding about her new husband: *We have known each other all our lives and have gradually grown closer.*

Diana breathes a quiet sigh, already looking forward to the reception, where she can't wait to tuck into all the good food and sweets.

Chapter 2

April 20, 1978
London

Inside St. James's Palace, the Queen Mother stands with Ruth Roche, Lady Fermoy, her confidante and lady-in-waiting.

The Queen Mother is rather taken with Lady Fermoy's teenage granddaughter. Though still a little pudgy, the youngest Spencer girl is quite tall, with flashing eyes and a captivating smile.

Diana has told the family that she only wants "to be with people and have fun and look after people."

Today, she shows it, moving easily among the party crowd, charming her elders and enthralling the children.

Diana was only a child herself when her mother, Ruth's daughter Frances, caused a public scandal by leaving her husband, the soon-to-be eighth Earl Spencer, for married wallpaper heir Peter Shand Kydd. Even after Frances and Peter divorced their spouses and married each other, young Diana had clung desperately to the hope that her mother would one day return home.

The Queen Mother is less impressed with Johnnie Spencer's second wife, Raine Legge, Countess of Dartmouth. Is it true that the earl's children call the woman Acid Raine?

Gazing across the hall now, the Queen Mother feels compelled to compliment the father of the bride, Lord Spencer, on young Lady Diana's warmth and grace.

The earl gratefully acknowledges her kindness.

"But now you have the most difficult part," she advises him. "You must think about her future settlement in life."

The family *has* been thinking about Diana's future. They see a fine match for her with the Queen Mother's second grandson—in fact they're so sure of it that Diana's close friends and family already call her "Duch," for Duchess.

Won't it be perfect if Sarah Spencer marries Prince Charles and Diana marries his younger brother Andrew?

Chapter 3

November 15, 1978
London

P rince Charles stands in front of his mirror, buttoning his dress shirt.

It's the day after his thirtieth birthday. Tonight, his parents are hosting a private family dinner, followed by a party for 350 guests at Buckingham Palace, "the big house."

Charles relishes his reputation as "The Playboy Prince" as well as his moniker of "Action Man." His military service and his pursuit of daredevil stunts, surfing, and polo prove his boasts that "I believe in living life dangerously." And if his love of pranks and jokes has also gotten him called "The Clown Prince," well, at least it's proof that he's not dull company.

He's been dubbed "the most popular man in Britain." And there's no question that he's the most eligible bachelor in the empire these days.

When Charles was twenty-one and visiting the White House, President Nixon's daughter called him an "excellent dancer." That's when Charles realized, as he later said, "They were trying to marry me off to Tricia Nixon." The American matchmaking didn't take.

"A man should sow his wild oats before settling down," Charles's "Uncle Dickie," Lord Mountbatten, once counseled, though he advised discretion in any such affairs. "But for a wife, he should choose a suitable and sweet-charactered girl before she meets anyone else she might fall for."

Charles agrees. He's of the opinion that marriage is "a much more important business than just falling in love." It's about "creating a secure family unit" to give children a happy upbringing. "That is what marriage is all about, creating a home."

"I personally feel," he said at age twenty-five, "that a good age for a man to get married is around thirty."

Now that he *is* thirty, his father insists, "You'd better get on with it, Charles, or there won't be anyone left." It's an unavoidable fact that three hundred years have passed since a Prince of Wales—Charles II, the Merry Monarch—remained unmarried at the age of thirty.

But the current Charles, Prince of Wales, really does enjoy the falling-in-love part.

He tugs on his cuffs, straightens, picks up his 50/50 martini. *I've fallen in love with all sorts of girls, and I fully intend to go on doing so.*

Chapter 4

G etting an invitation to Prince Charles's birthday party is simply the most exciting thing that's happened to seventeen-year-old Diana in ages.

"I hated going to the finishing school except for the skiing," she writes to her former nanny Mary Clarke of her one term at Institut Alpin Videmanette, in Switzerland. Since leaving, back in the spring, she's been "at a loose end," living mainly with her mother in London's Cadogan Square. Poor Daddy suffered a stroke in September, just as Diana was starting a cooking class, but thank goodness he's stabilized. She enjoyed the class, but now that it's finished, she's still casting about for what to do next.

She's the first to admit that she's not "academically interested at all" and hadn't much liked West Heath, her school in Kent, always feeling unable to live up to the strong academic standard set by her clever older sisters—though it is awfully nice that the school awarded her the Leggatt Cup for Helpfulness and noted her as the sort of "girl who notices what needs to be done, then does it willingly and cheerfully."

Even housework.

I've always loved cleaning, she thinks. Her sisters, Jane and Sarah, are willing to pay her a little to do some chores. Diana also adores children and has done some nannying for a family friend. But these are only temporary solutions.

At boarding school, she'd slip out of bed and go to the performance hall to "dance for hours and hours." Being a professional ballerina is unlikely because she's too tall, she's been told, but she *could* teach dance to children. At Mummy's suggestion, she's taken the initiative to contact the Vacani School of Dancing and inquire about teaching positions.

I might become a famous dancer, Diana still dreams.

As she crosses the immense red-carpeted Ballroom at Buckingham Palace, she intends to dance all night.

She finds her place at the 175-foot-long dining table, lavishly set with the queen's gilt-edge porcelain and centuries-old pieces from King George IV's Grand Service. Her dinner companion is Luis Basualdo, a handsome, well-dressed man with thick black hair parted razor-sharp.

Diana knows all about the dashing Argentinian playboy, whom the *Daily Mail* has nicknamed "the Bounder," but asks him polite questions about the polo pony he's giving Prince Charles as a birthday gift.

Luis finds her "very shy, very naive but rather nice," and makes small talk as they read over the elegant program detailing tonight's four-course menu, guest list, and entertainment.

Diana feels perfectly at ease in the palace. "I'm not at all intimidated by the surroundings," she says. "Amazing place."

After dinner, Luis accompanies Diana to the Picture Gallery, with its full view of the crowded dance floor and of Prince Charles jumping on stage to dance with the Three Degrees, a girl group from Philadelphia. She knows all the words to the group's number one single, "When Will I See You Again."

A man who enthusiastically dances! What fun.

Diana watches as His Royal Highness moves from one glamorous partner to the next, from lead singer Sheila Ferguson to actress Susan George to Lady Jane Wellesley.

He even dances with Diana's sister Sarah, who's mucked up her chances with him.

It's her sister's own fault. Sarah knew that talking to the tabloids would be unforgivable in the eyes of the royal family, yet seduced by the publicity, she gave an extended interview to *Women's Own* magazine in which she coyly claimed that the prince is "a romantic who falls in love easily," whereas she herself "wouldn't marry anyone I didn't love whether he were the dustman or the King of England."

"There's no question of me being the future Queen of England," Sarah told reporters. "I don't think he's met her yet."

It was a gamble, acting so modest—a gamble Sarah lost.

Tonight, Prince Charles seems especially taken with a sporty-looking blond woman who keeps leaning over to him and whispering, making him roar with laughter.

Diana notices that the woman doesn't seem the slightest bit intimidated by the prince. She doesn't fawn all over him the way Sarah did, nor does she act upset when other women compete for his attention. She seems completely relaxed in his company. It's as if the woman knows His Royal Highness will always return to her, again and again.

Who could she be?

Chapter 5

Summer 1980
London

Diana steps back to admire her handiwork: a sign reading CHIEF CHICK that she's affixed to her bedroom door.

She couldn't be happier about having her own place, a three-bedroom flat at 60 Coleherne Court, a few miles southwest of central London. She's been living here since last year, shortly after her eighteenth birthday, when she received two significant coming-of-age gifts—a three-strand pearl choker with a flower-shaped clasp in the front, and an inheritance from her mother's paternal grandmother, the American heiress Frances "Fanny" Work, which allowed Diana to purchase the flat.

Diana's been charging rent—eighteen pounds a week—to three other girls and enforcing the cleaning, but it's been such fun living with her friends. "You'd be amazed how many times ABBA goes round the turntable in this flat," flatmate Anne Bolton comments.

What with having easy work she "could do blindfolded" (as an assistant at Young England Kindergarten), attending classes at Dance Centre in Covent Garden, and having a laugh with others in her set, Diana is enjoying her life immensely.

One weekend in July, friends invite her out to their country estate in Sussex, where she knows she'll spot a familiar face: Prince Charles.

She hasn't seen him in ages. They've been friendly enough in the past but the effect he has on her now is unexpected.

"I sat there and this man walked in and I thought, *Well I am quite impressed this time round.*"

So is Charles. Diana's flattered when he compliments her on how much she's grown up.

"No more puppy fat," he teases.

"I'm just taller now," Diana replies. "I've stretched the puppy fat."

The prince laughs.

Sparks fly between them over the weekend, and to Diana's delight, when she's back home in London a few days later, Charles rings to ask if she'd like to join him for a performance at the Royal Albert Hall—and dinner afterward at Buckingham Palace.

It's absolutely thrilling to have the older man's attentions. Charles escorts her to the opera, invites her to watch him race and hunt and play polo, and takes her aboard the 412-foot royal yacht, *Britannia,* to the Cowes Week regatta, near the Isle of Wight.

The prince does blow a bit hot and cold, calling her every day for a week, then going silent. Diana tries to play it cool, hoping to project an air of *He knows where I am if he wants me.*

Her flatmates are unable to maintain that same level of detachment.

"The thrill when he used to ring up was so immense and intense. It would drive the other three girls in my flat crazy," Diana says of them.

"We'll help you plot your strategy," they promise. "It'll be great fun, a bit of a game!"

When Diana's friend Simon Berry asks about her life plans, the nineteen-year-old replies, "It would be nice if I could be a dancer—or the Princess of Wales."

But that's just a dream. This has all happened so fast that it doesn't seem quite real.

Chapter 6

November 1980
London

I n 1906, the Ritz was the first hotel in London to welcome unmarried women, unchaperoned—and on November 4, 1980, Diana attends a party there, solo. It's a belated fiftieth birthday for the queen's younger sister, Princess Margaret.

Photographers are lined up outside the Ritz, some of them on ladders, documenting the glamorous guests. The object of Charles's rumored affections has been of particular interest since the *Sun* declared on September 8, "He's in love again" and "Lady Di is the new girlfriend for Charles."

"We must not be photographed together," Charles has told her, and he's quite rigid about it. Photographer Jayne Fincher waits until three in the morning before spotting Lady Diana walking alone in her long pink dress and green wool coat.

"Oh, excuse me, can I get through?" Charles's young girlfriend asks sincerely. Diana's still getting used to being targeted by the press.

I know it's just a job they have to do, but sometimes I do wish they wouldn't.

Diana's invited to celebrate Charles's thirty-second birthday—on Friday, November 14—at Sandringham, the royal family's country estate. A frenzy of speculation has the prince proposing to her at the party, but the event passes without a hint of "anything imminent."

Amid newspaper talk of "Lady Diana's lovely weekend," the "fresh, friendly and unsophisticated, well-bred, well-spoken and well liked" nineteen-year-old drives a red Austin Mini Metro back to London under police escort.

Charles remains in Sandringham, telling a cluster of reporters, "I know you were expecting some news Friday, and I know you were disappointed."

With a hint of mystery, he adds, "You will be told soon enough."

But the engagement that didn't happen is not the biggest story of the weekend.

On November 16, while Diana was still at Sandringham, the *Sunday Mirror* led with an explosive front-page headline: ROYAL LOVE TRAIN.

According to the article, on the evening of November 5, a woman—blond, like Diana—was seen boarding the Royal Train, where Charles had been staying, and remained there until the early hours of the morning. The following day, the article claims, the woman—presumed to be Diana—hid out in "the country home of the Prince's close friend and confidant" Camilla Parker Bowles before supposedly dashing off to the train for a second tryst on November 6. An unnamed person on Camilla's staff even goes on record, adding ominously, "I dare not say anything more about this."

The Palace's reaction is swift. That same day, the queen's press secretary denies the story and demands an apology from the *Mirror*'s editor, Robert Edwards.

Edwards refuses, standing by his source.

Privately, Charles—who's about to embark on a multiweek trip to India—says the story is "rubbish and it has put Lady Diana in such a bad light."

Diana herself tells the *Daily Mail* shortly after, "I was sooo shocked.

I simply couldn't believe it. I've never been anywhere near the train, let alone in the middle of the night."

She also reaches out to royal reporter James Whitaker, now features editor at the *Daily Star,* telling him she'd had a quiet night at home that Wednesday. After all, her 3 a.m. exit from Princess Margaret's party the night before was documented by photographers.

"I was feeling very frail" after the late-night party, Diana says, so on the fifth, "I had some supper and watched television before going to bed early."

It's all so upsetting that Diana doesn't even have a chance to wonder whether it might've been a *different* blond woman—someone other than she—who was going between the Royal Train and Camilla's home.

The trouble is, people do believe what they read.

Chapter 7

November 1980
India

Y ou've got to be bloody kidding me, Harry. With my back?"

"Listen Arthur, it was this or trekking a mile on foot. There wasn't a taxi to be found in all of Delhi. Now if you want off, we're going to have to jump!"

What on earth is going on here?

Prince Charles is attending a cocktail party at the British High Commission in New Delhi, India—but as his limousine pulls up to the compound, there's an elephant blocking the security gate.

He leans out the window, recognizing the two well-dressed men squabbling with each other from atop the giant mammal as reporter Harry Arnold and photographer Arthur Edwards from the *Sun*. Charles knows the men well. They were the ones who first broke the story of his budding romance with Diana Spencer.

It's the second day of His Royal Highness's tour. Even here in India, he can't escape the constant questions about his relationship with Diana.

Up ahead, Arnold manages to slide off the elephant, his trademark pin-striped Savile Row suit relatively unscathed, but Edwards collapses in the gutter with a dramatic groan, calling out for a restorative gin and tonic.

Later that evening at the reception, Charles turns to Harry Arnold. "I understand you've been asking my friend if I'm going to marry Lady Diana Spencer," he says conversationally. "Why do you think she is the one?"

Arnold looks flustered and caught out, but he admits, "Well, I think we could be forgiven, Sir, for saying that you do treat her in a rather different manner from your usual cavalier approach to your girlfriends."

That may be true. There is something intriguing and different about his feelings for Diana. What does it mean? Can he imagine himself having a wonderful marriage with her? *She is exquisitely pretty, a perfect poppy . . . but she doesn't look old enough to be out of school, much less married.*

If given a choice, he would prefer to remain single. But the future king of England must have a bride. Obligation before emotion, always.

"You mustn't rush me," Charles chides the press group. "I mustn't get it wrong or you lot will be the first to criticize me in a few years' time."

Charles walks away. He's recently had a letter from his father urging him to either propose, "pleasing his family and the country," or end the relationship before he causes "lasting damage to Diana Spencer's reputation."

Charles detects in Philip's letter a grave personal risk—being cut off from his family.

He confides in a friend. "To have withdrawn, as you can no doubt imagine, would have been cataclysmic. Hence I was permanently trapped between the devil and the deep blue sea."

Chapter 8

T he queen asks Elton John to dance.

A mobile discotheque has been installed for the one thousand guests attending Prince Andrew's twenty-first birthday party on February 19 at Buckingham Palace. The palace's exterior, made of Bath stone, is awash in psychedelic lights.

The thirty-three-year-old rock superstar, who will celebrate his own birthday next month, has been invited to entertain the younger set—though the music is playing at such low volume that the dancers' footfalls sound louder than the music.

Elton John is dancing with Princess Anne to Elvis Presley's "Hound Dog" when the queen joins them. It's upon Diana's arrival in the ball-room, though, that he recognizes in her a "kindred spirit," and the two are soon laughing uproariously and soft-shoeing the Charleston.

As the older guests leave the party, the playlist amps up. So does Diana, who whirls from partner to partner, even after Charles goes to his rooms to sleep.

Diana dances on until five in the morning, when the music plays for her alone.

Back in her room, energized by the evening, she picks up a pen and writes a note to John. He's a new friend, one she wants to know better.

The party is a success, especially as a cover for a much bigger event—Diana and Charles's engagement.

A few days earlier, Crown Jeweller David Thomas had arrived at the palace carrying a briefcase. Its alleged contents: a selection of signet rings that Prince Andrew might choose as a birthday gift. It was a ruse. The velvet-lined case was filled with ladies' diamond and sapphire rings.

⊶⊷

"With Prince Charles beside me I can't go wrong," Diana says, standing with her new fiancé on palace grounds.

Queen Elizabeth has announced "with greatest pleasure" the couple's engagement, and journalists from ITV (Independent Television News), the Press Association, and the BBC have arrived to cover the breaking news.

Outside the palace gates, a British mother and her ten-year-old daughter are among the euphoric crowds. "God bless that pretty young couple," they tell the *New York Times*. "We'll be lucky to have them for our king and queen, won't we?"

Commenting on their twelve-year age gap, Charles is quick to self-deprecate. He tells reporters that "I think Diana will keep me young," adding, "I think I shall be exhausted."

Diana brushes off questions with an easygoing reply: "I mean, it's only twelve years, and lots of people have got married with that sort of age difference." Like her own mother and father, who were eighteen and thirty when they wed in 1954.

Diana faces the cameras wearing a cobalt-blue Cojana skirt suit purchased from the racks at Harrods—and her engagement ring. Inside an eighteen-carat white gold setting and surrounded by fourteen solitaire diamonds is the ring's central stone: a twelve-carat oval Ceylon sapphire the same deep blue as her eyes.

In response to comments on the sapphire's size, Diana jokes, "I can't get used to wearing it yet. The other day I even scratched my nose with it, because it's so big—the ring, I mean."

The queen and Prince Charles chose it.

The ring is inspired by the wedding brooch Prince Albert commissioned from the House of Garrard for Queen Victoria in 1840.

"A splendid brooch," Queen Victoria wrote in her diary. "A large sapphire set round with diamonds, which is really quite beautiful." Albert gave it to her shortly before they married, and she proudly wore it pinned to her white wedding dress. She appointed Garrard Crown Jeweller in 1843.

"Prince Charles had always seen this beautiful sapphire brooch," a spokesperson for Garrard says, so when he saw that ring, he "thought it was perfect."

Diana doesn't mention that she would have preferred a more "elegant and simple" ring.

Later, when Diana and Charles watch the recorded broadcasts, Diana stares intently at the screen.

"My God, I look so fat!"

"It's just the television. Don't worry about it. You look fine." Charles puts a hand around her waist. "Oh, a bit chubby here, aren't we?"

That's it. *I'm not walking up the aisle waddling like a duck.*

She goes on a crash diet, reluctant to eat anything at all. "I might not lose all the weight I need to," she protests when others say it's too extreme.

But by day three, her self-control weakens.

At a souvenir shop across the street from Buckingham Palace, she buys a supply of candy bars.

She peels off one wrapper, then finds herself taking bite after bite, wolfing down the chocolate.

It gives you a feeling of comfort. It's like having a pair of arms around you, but it's . . . temporary.

Diana stares in disgust at the empty candy wrappers. She's eaten every last chocolate bar.

I can't believe what I've done.

But she knows what she has to do next.

Chapter 9

Spring 1981
London

T he headlines blare DARING DI when Diana wears a floor-length
strapless black satin gown with a plunging neckline, trimmed
in sequins and ruffles, to her first public appearance post-
engagement, a March 3 recital at Goldsmiths' Hall.

In the weeks since Charles proposed, there's been a flurry of mother-
daughter shopping for "six of everything" to enhance Diana's minimal
personal wardrobe, which she admits previously consisted only of "one
long dress, one silk shirt, one smart pair of shoes, and that was it."

In the Brook Street showroom of couture label Emanuel, Diana is
enchanted by the black gown, a "real grown-up dress"—though the
amount of cleavage it exposes earns her a stern message from the Queen
Mother to "never again wear a dress that reveals the royal jewels."

Despite the criticism she receives for the evening gown, Diana chooses
the Emanuel designers, David and Elizabeth Emanuel—a couple in
their late twenties, not much older than the bride-to-be—to design her
wedding dress. When the news breaks, the Emanuels outfit their studio
with privacy blinds so that the place is "a sanctuary without anyone
spying on her."

Diana is "always open and spirited, as if she was chatting in the hairdressers," but the Emanuels take every precaution, nightly storing sketches and swatches in a safe, and tearing up their designs after showing them to Diana and her mother.

"It sounds a bit over-the-top, but it really did seem like people would go to any lengths to find out what the dress looked like," Elizabeth says. "The British press were rooting through our rubbish," reveals David.

They take wide-ranging inspiration from lavish costumes in films like *Gone with the Wind* to historic royal wedding gowns. They even incorporate into their design a sixteenth-century square of Carrickmacross lace that once belonged to Queen Mary, Queen Elizabeth's grandmother.

"It was a big adventure for us all," Elizabeth Emanuel says, booking the dress fittings under Diana's code name, "Deborah," with the expectation that Palace officials will eventually give them royal parameters.

It never happens. Diana takes her fittings alone.

Chapter 10

May 3, 1981
En route from London to Aberdeen

D iana sits in her window seat, working a piece of embroidery. Dressed in a burgundy sweater over tan corduroys tucked into black boots, she's aboard a British Airways Boeing 737 flight from London to Aberdeen, Scotland.

She's more than willing to brave the stormy weather in the flight path. Charles has been away on a six-week tour, first to Australia and New Zealand, and then to the United States, where the College of William & Mary, in Virginia, held a special convocation to award him their first honorary fellowship.

Tonight, the engaged couple will reunite at Balmoral Castle. Their July 29 wedding is less than three months away.

"Are you enjoying your engagement, Lady Diana?" a well-meaning woman asks her at a palace garden party.

"Oh no! I absolutely hate the engagement," Diana confesses. "But I shall adore being married to Charles."

To one of her husband-to-be's cousins, she likewise confides, "There can be nothing more desirable in the world than being the Princess of Wales."

The cousin may have thought her ambitious, but he misunderstood. She's marrying for love.

Outside the plane, bright light flashes in quick succession followed by a resounding *crack*.

"What on earth was that?" Diana exclaims. She looks around at the other bewildered passengers, which include her personal bodyguard, forty-year-old detective Paul Officer.

Charles worried about her being lonely while he was away on his trip and instructed his staff to "look after Lady Diana." It's been an adjustment, having a bossy bodyguard around all the time. Paul Officer was assigned to her immediately upon the engagement and oversaw her move from her three-bedroom flat into Clarence House, near Buckingham Palace.

"This is the last day of freedom you'll have for the rest of your life. Enjoy it," he told her that day. A bit ominous.

She didn't realize just how serious he was about it until a few days later, when she went to get in her car and he hopped in beside her.

"It's all right," she told him. "I can manage."

"Sorry, we're part of your life now," was his reply.

Rather irritating to the nineteen-year-old bride-to-be. But Diana is secure in her future. "This is the life for me," she's told friends, serene, though she leaves behind a note for her former Coleherne Court flat-mates when she moves out, declaring: "For God's sake, ring me up—I'm going to need you."

Captain Charles Pack makes an announcement over the plane's loudspeaker. "The noise you just heard was lightning striking the plane twice." He continues, "There is no damage and we'll be continuing to Aberdeen as normal."

If "normal" is traveling to a castle purchased by Prince Albert for Queen Victoria in the mid-nineteenth century and now owned by her future in-laws.

The plane flies on for the next uneventful hour, and when they land, Diana is met by a royal Range Rover on the tarmac. Charles is waiting for her at Balmoral. Soon they'll be together again.

Chapter 11

Charles and Diana will wed at St. Paul's Cathedral, the highest point in the City of London. Holding a royal wedding anywhere but Westminster Abbey breaks centuries of tradition—but it was here at St. Paul's that a previous Prince of Wales, Tudor prince Arthur, married Catherine of Aragon in 1501. The date was November 14—Prince Charles's birthday.

The vast Renaissance-style church can host a congregation of 3,500 among its vast network of pillars, and the nave runs more than five hundred feet in length and more than two hundred feet at the transepts. The wedding gown's train, the Emanuels insist, must "fill the aisle and be quite dramatic." They decide on a length of twenty-five feet—the longest bridal train, by five feet, in royal wedding history. Because the train is longer than their studio, they take it to Buckingham Palace to lay it out correctly.

"Do you think it should be bigger?" the bride jokes.

Diana invites the Spencer family housekeeper, Maudie Pendry, to the wedding ceremony. Mrs. Pendry will recognize that the dress also honors a Spencer ancestral portrait hanging in the picture gallery at Althorp, the family home.

Mrs. Pendry inquires, "Will I be able to see you in St. Paul's?"

"I promise," Diana says, "you'll be able to see all of me."

On July 28, 1981, the day before the wedding, London police seal off St. Paul's Cathedral. As Diana and Charles plus their officiants and attendants all gather inside the great church to rehearse the ceremony, security experts and terrorism specialists lock it down.

Today, Diana makes her entrance from a guarded underground parking lot. Tomorrow, she'll pass through the Great West Door, which stands nine meters tall at the westernmost end of the nave and opens only for occasions as special as her and Charles's wedding.

Diana, who on July 1 turned twenty, stands arm in arm with Charles. Princess Margaret's seventeen-year-old daughter, Lady Sarah Armstrong-Jones, and thirteen-year-old India Hicks, Charles's goddaughter and the granddaughter of the late Lord Mountbatten, have been entrusted with carrying the train of Diana's wedding gown. They're practicing with white sheeting precisely cut to the train's dimensions while the Emanuels study the way the fabric flows down the wide aisle of black-and-white paving.

White is for patience. Black is for humility. A strong foundation for every marriage.

Charles steps away to confer with Sir David Willcocks, director of the Royal College of Music. St. Paul's is large enough to accommodate a full orchestra, and Charles and Willcocks have chosen three, in addition to the Bach choir and soprano soloist Kiri Te Kanawa.

Diana looks up at the ceiling soaring thirty meters overhead, adorned with intricate mosaics representing the Evangelists and the Prophets in the style of Roman art.

Tomorrow, she'll be Princess of Wales.

Chapter 12

July 28, 1981
London

Half a million people gather in Hyde Park, within sight of Buckingham Palace. The King's Troop Royal Horse Artillery fires a salute to the Prince of Wales, carrying on royal tradition.

The guns sound. Charles lights a ceremonial bonfire.

And then the first-ever royal wedding fireworks begin.

Charles retreats inside the palace. He stands at a window, watching and listening as the lights flare. When the crowd choruses "Rule, Britannia," he can't hold back his tears.

How fortunate he feels that "someone as special as Diana seems to love me so much," as he writes to a friend. How honored he is that his grandmother the Queen Mother has welcomed Diana into the family with precious gifts of royal jewels, including a diamond-and-emerald necklace worth millions. The design of the necklace includes three feathers arranged inside a crown, the traditional heraldic symbol for the Prince of Wales. Charles has chosen a coordinating diamond-and-emerald bracelet as his own wedding gift to Diana.

When their engagement is announced, Charles says, "I feel positively delighted and frankly amazed that Di is prepared to take me on." He emphasizes, "Delighted and happy."

And in love?

"Of course!" Diana scoffs.

"Whatever 'in love' means," Charles demurs, mumbling about its being open to one's "own interpretation."

His take is, "I want to do the right thing by my country. I want to do the right thing by my family." He keeps repeating those words until he believes them.

Despite the millions of people who will be watching tomorrow, the Prince of Wales—heir apparent to the British throne—considers the vows he's about to take intensely private.

Now, on the night before his wedding day, Charles asks himself a question no one else can answer for him.

"Is it possible to love two women at the same time?"

Chapter 13

July 29, 1981
London

P rince Charles and Lady Diana's Wednesday wedding is a British national holiday.

Along the processional route to St. Paul's Cathedral are more than six hundred thousand people hoping to catch a glimpse of the bride and groom. Some of these spectators claimed their roadside positions two days earlier.

Police with explosive-sniffing dogs are checking and rechecking the streets along the Mall, where manhole covers are open for maximum safety. Sharpshooters are in place on strategically chosen rooftops. The media coverage is likewise massive: Fleet Street reporters are planning to use ambulances to cut through traffic along the two-mile route between the church and their offices.

At Clarence House, bridal preparations begin at six thirty in the morning. The place quickly fills with bridesmaids, palace attendants, and a continual stream of fresh floral arrangements. At eight, under police escort, Longmans Florist delivers the forty-two-inch all-white bridal bouquet, a cascade of orchids, freesias, gardenias, and lilies of the valley.

Diana, dressed comfortably in jeans, sits at a dressing table watching on a small TV the images of crowds gathering. As hairdresser Kevin Shanley and makeup artist Barbara Daly do their work, Diana turns to them with a giggle and says, "Gosh, it's a lot of fuss for a wedding, isn't it?"

Shanley's been cutting Diana's hair since she was seventeen and is responsible for her much-copied feathered hairdo. Diana met Daly—a professional artist who did the makeup for *A Clockwork Orange*, *The Shining*, and *Barry Lyndon*—when *Vogue* brought her in, and they bonded immediately over both being five feet ten inches tall. "Ah, somebody I can look right in the eye!" Diana gushed.

It's time for the bridal tiara. Diana straightens her head.

Instead of the pearl-and-diamond Cambridge Lover's Knot Tiara offered by the queen from her private collection, Diana's chosen her family heirloom Spencer Tiara. Diana is the third Spencer sister (after Jane and then Sarah, who was married last May) to wear the diamond star-and-flower scrollwork set in silver and gold around a central heart motif. The headpiece has to be carefully and firmly affixed, without the use of any styling products near the delicate jewels.

Hair and makeup complete, the Emanuels are ushered in to begin dressing the bride.

First is a petticoat fashioned from three hundred feet of tulle. Layered atop is the taffeta gown of ivory silk spun at England's only silk farm, in Lullingstone. Its flounced lace scoop neckline is secured with a taffeta bow and the puffed three-quarter sleeves are gathered at the elbow with more lace and taffeta frills. The bodice and full skirt are hand-embroidered with ten thousand micro pearls and mother-of-pearl sequins.

Sewn into the dress's label is a small diamond-studded eighteen-carat-gold horseshoe, for good luck.

Diana's dieting has narrowed her waist substantially, from twenty-nine to twenty-three and a half inches. But it means that the nipped-waist style of the wedding dress's bodice now sags where it should be taut.

Oh, no.

The Emanuels have a last-minute fix. They'll sew her into the dress.

Diana picks up a bottle of her favorite scent, Quelques Fleurs, but fumbles it.

She turns to makeup artist Daly. "I've just put my perfume on and I've spilled some on the front of the dress. They'll kill me."

Daly suggests Diana cover the stained fabric with her hand.

"Do you think if I just tuck the front in they'll never notice?" Diana asks.

"Yes absolutely—you and every bride in the country has done that."

She's the only bride Charles is waiting for at the altar. *I am so proud of you,* he wrote in the note he left for her last night. *Just look 'em in the eye and knock 'em dead.*

Shanley and the Emanuels fit the tiara with a tulle veil embellished with thousands of tiny translucent mother-of-pearl sequins that sparkle in the light, "creating a fairy dust effect," Elizabeth Emanuel says.

Diana descends to the ground floor of Clarence House, where her father, Earl Spencer, is waiting to escort her to the ceremony.

He's been unsteady on his feet since recovering from his stroke, but when he takes her hand, his grip is gentle yet strong.

Chapter 14

July 29, 1981
London

A t 10:22 a.m., the queen leaves Buckingham Palace by horse-drawn carriage for the twenty-minute two-mile procession route to St. Paul's Cathedral.

At 10:40, a team of four gray horses steps out, pulling an open coach with a lone passenger: Prince Charles, looking dashing in his Royal Navy commander's uniform, his service medals and the gold epaulets on both shoulders shining brightly in the morning light.

Diana's carriage makes a late departure from Clarence House. Her bridesmaids have practiced properly folding the wedding train inside the Glass Coach, but the sheer volume of the fabric and the substantial presence of Earl Spencer have cost precious minutes.

Her arrival at the cathedral is greeted by thunderous applause and cries from the adoring crowds.

Diana smiles and, arm in arm with her father, begins to climb the first of the twenty-four granite steps to the Great West Door of St. Paul's. Not trusting her feet in the sequin-and-pearl, satin-and-lace wedding slippers, Diana grips her father's arm fiercely. The shoes, hand-painted beneath each low heel with the initials *C* and *D* conjoined by a red heart, point her toward the eastern reach of the nave, where Charles waits at the marble-and-carved-gilded-oak altar.

The walk to the altar, Diana knows from rehearsals, takes a little over three minutes.

All eyes are upon her. She can't take her eyes off him.

Standing next to Charles, she feels deeply that he will always look after her.

The music stops. The archbishop of Canterbury speaks.

"Here is the stuff of which fairy tales are made—prince and princess on their wedding day."

Chapter 15

K iss! Kiss!"

Thousands of well-wishers have gathered outside Bucking-ham Palace to welcome the newly married couple.

As Diana and Charles wave from the balcony, the crowd happily repeats the command.

Could it be the start of a royal wedding tradition, to make up for the missed kiss after they exchanged vows?

"I am not going to do that caper," the prince says. "They are trying to get us to kiss."

"Well, how about it?" his bride asks.

Charles pauses to reconsider. "Why ever not?"

The new husband and wife exchange a sweet kiss, to thunderous applause.

Photographer Lord Patrick Lichfield hovers nearby, working his camera. Lichfield, Queen Elizabeth's cousin, is the only photographer granted access to the wedding party. A referee's whistle hangs around his neck, and he uses it to choreograph group shots.

Diana moves over to where six-year-old Catherine Cameron, wearing a flower crown that matches her bouquet, is standing. The little girl keeps touching her petticoat to her runny nose. Her eyes are puffy and red. As Diana nears, Cameron looks up at the bride and explains that she is allergic to horses.

Diana comforts the girl while more royals gather on the balcony.

Then she hears another child wailing. The youngest member of her bridal party, five-year-old Clementine Hambro—Winston Churchill's great-granddaughter and one of Diana's favorite students from Young England Kindergarten—is sitting on the floor.

Diana picks her up. "Did you bump your bottom?"

"No," Hambro whimpers, "I bumped my head."

Diana consoles the girl.

While scanning for Charles, she touches the gold band on her finger, engraved with a message from her new husband: I LOVE YOU, DIANA. The ring is made of a nugget from the Clogau St. David's gold mine. Queen Elizabeth the Queen Mother, Princess Margaret, and Queen Elizabeth II all wear wedding rings of the same pure Welsh gold.

The queen never removes her wedding ring.

What a romantic notion. Diana vows she'll follow suit.

PART 2
Charles and Di

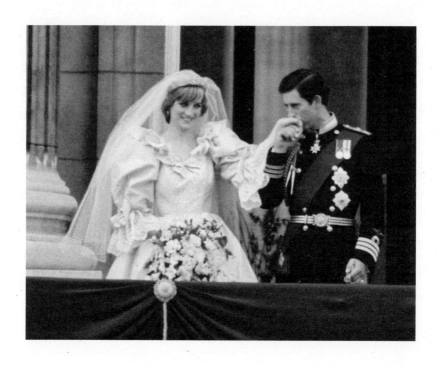

Chapter 16

February 1982
Windermere Island, Bahamas

M r. and Mrs. Hardy" have travel plans.

So do Harry Arnold and Arthur Edwards of the *Sun*.

Using a pseudonym while on a ten-day winter holiday in the Bahamas would seem a sensible precaution—if Charles and Diana hadn't failed to take into account the fervor of tabloids on the hunt for lucrative photos of royals on vacation.

Prince Charles's Mountbatten cousin Lord Romsey is hosting the royal couple at his holiday home on Windermere Island, and the Fleet Street reporters have followed them, packing their long-range lenses. Edwards hides on the private beach, snapping exclusive photos of the Princess of Wales in a red strapless bikini that fully exposes her pregnant belly.

The oblivious parents-to-be frolic on the shore, Diana rubbing lotion on Charles's shoulders.

His skin is kissable.

After sunbathing, she runs into the waves, playfully shouting, "Ships, I see no ships!"

The royal baby is expected in June. News broke last November, the day after Diana's first official engagement as princess—the State Opening of Parliament. The white gown and tiara she wore to the event had the *Times* of London pronouncing Diana "a glamorous concoction almost beyond description, shimmering from head to toe."

Today's tiny bikini and straw hat are a far cry from that previous angelic look. The photographers on the beach are hidden enough to escape notice, but soon everyone sees the pictures under the *Sun*'s front-page headline: DI-LAND IN THE SUN. Additional photos inside dub her BAHAMA MAMA!

A distressed queen calls the press corps to Buckingham Palace and makes a protective order. "You simply have to leave Princess of Wales alone."

No one listens. The princess is too important. Her child-to-be will soon be second in succession to the monarchy.

Twenty-year-old Diana takes it in stride, later teasing Edwards when he claims not to have made much money off of the sneaky photos. "Oh pass me the Kleenex," she chides with a laugh.

As winter turns to spring and summer, Diana's maternity style turns more traditional. She's photographed wearing brightly colored long jackets or flowing dresses that hide her bump at the Cheltenham Gold Cup steeplechase race and in the stands during Charles's polo matches at the Guards Polo Club.

On June 21, 1982, barely a month before Charles and Diana's first anniversary, the palace gates bear the news: Diana has delivered a healthy son, heir to the House of Windsor.

They'll name him William, after William the Conqueror. Diana overrules Charles's preference for the name Arthur, but it's added as a middle name, along with Philip, for his father, and Louis, for Lord Louis Mountbatten, his beloved "Uncle Dickie."

While Diana is recovering from a sixteen-hour labor she later says left her "sick as a parrot," Charles ventures out from the private Lindo Wing of St. Mary's Hospital to take questions from throngs of reporters ringed by crowds of well-wishers.

"Is your son the prettiest baby in the world?" one asks.

"Well, he's not bad," Charles says.

He's elated but saves his innermost thoughts until he can get them down on paper.

I am so thankful I was beside Diana's bedside the whole time because by the end of the day I really felt as though I'd shared deeply in the birth and as a result was rewarded by seeing a small creature which belonged to us even though he seemed to belong to everyone else as well.

Charles's father-in-law, Johnnie, Earl Spencer, joins in the celebration.

"The baby is lucky to have Diana as a mother," Johnnie says of his daughter. Then he adds, "I'm off to have a beer."

Chapter 17

September 18, 1982
Monte Carlo

P rincess Diana arrives in Monte Carlo for her first solo royal appearance.

She's here to pay her last respects to Princess Grace of Monaco.

Five days ago, fifty-two-year-old Princess Grace—former actress Grace Kelly—had been driving with her younger daughter, Stephanie, when their British Rover 3500 took a particularly sharp and dangerous turn on Cap-d'Ail and plunged down a 120-foot embankment.

Diana's heard conflicting reports: the princess may have suffered a stroke behind the wheel, or the car may have experienced mechanical failure. Seventeen-year-old Stephanie, who couldn't stop the Rover even after pulling the hand brake, cracked a vertebra and remains in the hospital.

Princess Grace could not be saved.

At twenty-one, Diana's closer in age to Stephanie than to her mother (and is younger than Princess Grace's two older children), but she's felt a kinship to the American woman since they met last March at Goldsmiths' Hall, during Diana's first public appearance as Charles's fiancée.

While Diana was feeling ill at ease in her chosen black dress "two sizes too small," Grace looked ethereal in a blue iridescent gown with leg-of-mutton sleeves, her blond hair woven into a pearl-strewn crown of braids.

During the reception, Diana and Grace spoke in the ladies' room, the only private place at Buckingham Palace. Diana confided her feelings of isolation, her fear of failing to meet royal standards.

"Don't worry, dear," Princess Grace had told her, placing a comforting hand on Diana's cheek and adding wryly, "It'll only get worse."

She'd been speaking from experience. *How wonderful and serene she was,* Diana observes of the late Princess of Monaco (one of the 140 titles Grace earned upon her 1956 marriage to Prince Rainier III), *but there was troubled water under her, I saw that.*

"Even in Hollywood," Princess Grace once reflected, "my private life was pretty much my own. When I married, my private life became public and I really had no privacy at all—and that was an adjustment to make."

Less than fourteen months after becoming Princess of Wales, Diana's already learning just how right the older woman had been.

It wasn't easy for Diana to convince Charles that she can act as the royal family's representative at the funeral. And she's had to leave their three-month-old son, William, back in England for the trip. Charles deferred to his mother, saying, "We'll have to ask Mama, but I doubt she'll let you go."

He's wrong. When Diana makes her appeal, the queen says, "If you want to do this, you can."

She does want to go. Diana feels "psychically connected" to Princess Grace, who "was an outsider who married into a big family, and I've done the same."

Now in Monaco, Diana exits her chauffeured Rolls-Royce and climbs the flower-strewn steps of the Cathedral of Our Lady Immaculate, where the American actress and the Monegasque prince wed twenty-six years earlier. Straightening her demure black dress and veiled black straw hat, Diana passes through the congregation of European and Holly-wood royalty—among them Cary Grant, Grace Kelly's costar in the 1955 thriller *To Catch a Thief*—and is seated in a front pew beside the American First Lady, Nancy Reagan, who hides her tears under the wide brim of her own black hat.

As the Grand Organ sounds its seven thousand pipes, Prince Rainier III and his two eldest children, Princess Caroline and Prince Albert, approach the coffin that rests in front of the high altar adorned with pink "Princesse de Monaco" roses.

Diana touches a hand to the diamond necklace at her throat. Its centerpiece is heart-shaped, a gift from Charles to celebrate William's birth and the start of their family.

With the loss of Princess Grace, Monaco's royal family is forever changed.

No one could have anticipated that the Princess of Monaco would leave them so soon. But by coincidence, when recently asked a question about how she'd like to be remembered, Grace replied: "I suppose I think mostly in terms of my children," adding, "I would like to be remembered as trying to do my job well, of being understanding and kind."

Princess Diana feels exactly the same.

Diana returns to London on the Queen's Flight. The luxuriously modified BAe 146 of the Royal Air Force's historic 32 Squadron is equipped with a full bar, monogrammed china, and crystal glasses, but she's too exhausted to appreciate it. "Will Charles be there to meet us?" she asks her staff as they prepare to land.

He is not. Nor is he waiting at apartments 8 and 9, the home they share at Kensington Palace. He's away in Portsmouth with his parents, celebrating the return of his younger brother Prince Andrew, recently home after serving five months as a Sea King helicopter pilot aboard the HMS *Invincible* in the Falkland Islands.

When Diana wakes the following morning, members of the house staff hand her the morning papers, which praise her for representing Great Britain in Monaco. "They say you did brilliantly."

Did she? Nobody from the Palace has mentioned it.

While Diana awaits official word from "the Establishment"—as she calls the royals and the network that keeps them firmly atop the world—she pours out her feelings on a piece of monogrammed stationery.

"It's quite amazing," Diana writes to a friend, "the change that is going on inside me—the Diana bit wanting to go and hide rather than be out in the public eyes and the Princess who is here to do a job to the best of her ability. The second lady was winning, but at what cost to the first?"

The Establishment's answer is silence.

Chapter 18

Autumn 1982
London

I t's early morning, still dark.

Diana jolts awake from a recurring dream about Charles's coronation as king of England: His crown is a perfect fit, while the one meant for her is the wrong size.

She's disturbed by the dream, fears it can have only one meaning. *She'll never be queen.*

Rising from the mahogany four-poster bed, she puts on her white bathrobe and climbs barefoot up to the cozy nursery suite, with its strawberry-print carpet and baby crib adorned with the Prince of Wales's Feathers.

Diana enters the nursery to find the senior royal nanny, forty-two-year-old Barbara Barnes, cradling William as he sniffles. The narrow corridors in the Kensington Palace apartments carry sound, and there is precious little privacy.

The nanny is quick to assure the young mother that her son is fine.

"Are you sure?" Diana asks, eyeing the nearby cot where she sleeps when concerned about her baby.

As the wife of one future king and the mother of a second, she worries about them constantly. Even when Charles is close to home, she panics anytime he's late.

Her concerns are intense but not unfounded.

Threats against the royal family are part of their lives. It was only a few years ago that an Irish Republican Army bomb killed Charles's great-uncle Lord Mountbatten, and now, following a recent stretch of IRA bombings around London, William has been named a potential kidnapping target.

To protect the Prince of Wales's family, the "men in gray suits"—the Establishment's male courtiers—are heightening security at KP, installing panic buttons in hidden locations and posting guards around the clock.

Diana's private secretary, Oliver Everett, inundates her with detailed reports that never stop, never let up, to the point that when he calls her over the bedroom's squawk box, she piles several pillows on top of the intercom to mute the sound of his voice.

No, she hasn't done the reading. It's too overwhelming.

But she does do the training.

Diana is escorted to intensive sessions with the Special Air Service (SAS), the British Army's elite special forces unit.

These rigorous exercises are nothing like reading Everett's reports. The lessons are high-stakes, frightening.

Diana drives an obstacle course arranged to train people in offensive and defensive driving maneuvers. If a vehicle rams into her while she's driving, she must control her car, prevent it from spinning out. If a vehicle follows her, she must evade it, analyze routes to avoid dangerous choke points such as bridges and streams.

Suddenly, a car veers in front of her, and a man jumps out and points a semiautomatic weapon at her. She quickly shifts into reverse, slams on the gas, executes a quick turn, and drives away safely.

The exercise ends. Her heart is pounding, her skin slick with sweat.

The instructors immediately throw her into a different scenario. This time, as she drives the obstacle course, smoke bombs are flung in front of her car—and men dressed in camouflage and ski masks, gloved hands holding automatic weapons, shoot at her.

The bullets are blanks, but the weapons are real.

Chapter 19

September 1983
Gloucestershire

Fifteen-month-old Prince William bursts inside Highgrove House, Charles and Diana's gray stone country retreat, 113 miles from London.

"Look, Mummy!"

William is waving at her, but there's something in his hand.

It's a dead rabbit.

While Diana has been taking pictures of the gardens for her photo albums, her toddler son has been off exploring.

Now the little boy is as filthy as the rabbit he's holding. He swings the dead rabbit, then chases after his mother until she persuades him to place the rabbit outside in a compost pile.

Then her mini tornado is off and running again, this time chasing after Harvey, his father's beloved yellow Labrador.

"Whirlwind Will," Charles says of his son, "is a spindly little character with a good sense of humor." But the young prince "can be very destructive." Worse than a puppy, William has chewed up antique books in the library and tried—without success—to flush his father's Gucci loafers down the loo, although he did succeed with his own booties.

"He's quite a handful," Diana agrees. So does the queen, though William is affectionate with his grandmother. On a recent visit to Buckingham Palace, he spotted Queen Elizabeth standing next to a guest and took off running in her direction.

"Gary!" William cried as he tripped and fell. "Gary!"

"Who's Gary?" the guest asked.

"I'm Gary," the queen replied, picking up her grandson. "He hasn't learned to say 'Granny' yet."

Diana misses London—she prefers city life—but appreciates that Highgrove is as secure as a fortress.

Until her and Charles's wedding, the nine-bedroom, six-bathroom Georgian home was protected only by dilapidated iron gates. Local residents installed strong new gates as a wedding gift to the couple. The estate's surveillance center operates inside a cottage containing the closed-circuit automatic television cameras that scan every single inch of the walled property.

Diana hopes she'll never need to shelter in the indestructible, impenetrable twenty-by-twenty-foot panic room that's also been added, stocked with provisions to sustain the young family for weeks.

I hate it when I'm not in control. And I hate being watched.

But this is her life now. Her blood type is on file, vials of it stored for emergency use. Officers from the Gloucestershire Constabulary on continuous patrol, coming and going from an on-site police lodge. Existing under constant surveillance.

Chapter 20

October 1983
Aberdeenshire, Scotland

B y tradition, a lone bagpiper plays "The Royal Salute" to greet the queen as she arrives at her favorite residence, Balmoral.

The queen is at her liveliest when she's on the fifty-thousand-acre Scottish Highlands estate, enjoying her favorite gin-and-Dubonnet cocktails, but Diana finds the temperatures in the old castle uncomfortably cold and the routines rigid. It's the kind of place where "the minute you went out of a room there was always somebody switching off a light behind you," she complains.

But she does have some pleasant associations. For example, when she and Charles honeymooned here, the prince delighted her by placing gifts and affectionate notes under her pillow.

William is a curious toddler at sixteen months, too young to hunt grouse or picnic on the shores of freshwater Loch Muick with the extended family. His parents take him on walks by the River Dee.

The elder royals are surprised by Charles and Diana's devotion to hands-on parenthood. Becoming a father, Charles tells a cousin, is "the most wonderful thing that's ever happened to me," yet his own father retorts, "You'd think the Prince of Wales could find more gainful ways of employing himself than bathing his son, when the boy already has a nanny to do such monumental tasks for him."

And while Diana holds that "having a child is a miracle," the queen is astonished at her daughter-in-law's enthusiasm for stepping in when William's nanny goes on holiday. "I don't understand why Diana has to do this," the queen says. "There are millions of housemaids around."

Yet when Charles and Diana travel from Balmoral to London in early October for an appearance, it feels only natural to leave William in the care of his grandparents.

Until the prince's senior royal protection officer hustles the prince and princess out of the event. A signal is sounding at Aberdeen police headquarters.

A panic button has been triggered inside Balmoral.

Buckled into the soundproof cabin of the red-and-dark-blue Westland Wessex, Diana wills the Royal Air Force helicopter pilot to fly faster, faster. More than five hundred miles stretch between London and Balmoral.

Royal security and local police seal off the grounds. As the copter prepares to land, blinking emergency lights flash across the ivy-covered granite face of the castle up to the turreted clock tower, which will soon strike midnight.

A grave-faced senior policeman makes his report to Charles and Diana. There is no need for concern. Upon being left momentarily alone in his nursery, their son had discovered the security alarm button on the wall and decided to push it.

William and his grandparents are now safely tucked inside their rooms, under heavy guard.

Two months later, at Kensington Palace, William presses another alarm. Engineers reinstall the buttons well out of the toddler's reach.

William relishes all the commotion, innocently unaware that there are people in the world who wish him dead.

Chapter 21

Spring 1984
Gloucestershire

I have to get used to being here, there and everywhere," Diana writes to a friend. "Charles is being wonderful, so understanding when I sometimes feel a bit bemused and sad with the pressure. I never realized what a support he could be to me."

Diana stops writing and taps her fountain pen against the desk, wondering if she should confess the lonely state of her marriage. She quickly decides against it. To her friends and the public, her life with Prince Charles is a storybook romance.

She's in her sitting room at Highgrove. Charles is downstairs in his library, where he goes when he wants to be alone. She hears Verdi's *Aida*, one of her husband's favorite pieces of music, playing on the custom-made stereo. He's also been sleeping in a single bed in his dressing room, his only companion his much-loved childhood teddy bear.

Diana turns back to her letter. "I am trying to support Charles too and be a mother. Strange to know which should come first."

Diana carefully gets to her feet. She's pregnant with their second child, due in September.

Buckingham Palace announced the news of her pregnancy—along with Queen Elizabeth and Prince Philip's "delight"—to the public in mid-February. The front page of the *Daily Express* cheers, "Valentine's Day Joy for Charles and Diana," noting that "the royal couple have no preference whether it is a boy or girl."

But that's not entirely true. Charles is happily convinced that William is going to have a sister.

Diana treads lightly across the wooden floors. The pale yellow walls are hung with Charles's watercolors, and the furniture is upholstered in light green. Diana chose decorator Dudley Poplak for Highgrove and Kensington Palace because he promised their homes wouldn't look as if a decorator had even been near them.

She likes Poplak's strategy. The invisible touch.

From the hallway outside Charles's library, Diana hears her husband speaking in hushed tones.

The music stops. Diana inches closer.

Who could he be talking to?

She has her suspicions.

Not long before his and Diana's wedding, Charles was asked why he'd bought Highgrove the year before. His reply was, "I fell in love with the garden." He has planted beds fragrant with lilacs and roses. Diana rejects red and purple flowers, instructing the estate gardeners that she prefers pastel shades of pink, white, and yellow.

Charles also keeps a walled vegetable garden. Only one person is allowed inside: Camilla Parker Bowles.

Diana knows that Camilla is the real reason that Charles bought Highgrove. The woman lives only fifteen miles away, at Bolehyde Manor.

Charles exits his library and takes a sharp turn toward the front door, nearly crashing into Diana. He's dressed to join the Duke of Beaufort's Hunt, where for years he and Camilla have been riding to hounds.

"What am I supposed to do all day while you're off enjoying yourself?" Diana asks. "Die of boredom? You call yourself a husband? Some husband you are."

Her husband detests confrontation, but his expression softens slightly when he sees she's crying.

"What is it now, Diana?" His tone is compassionate, but she can hear the undercurrent of impatience beneath his words. "What have I said now to make you cry?"

She's unable to express her concerns and Charles gives up and heads off to the hunt. Diana has overheard people calling her "deranged and paranoid" for suspecting her husband of cheating. What she needs is proof.

She goes into his study, where a towering pile of papers is pinned with a note: "Do not move anything on this desk." Diana picks up the phone and presses the Redial button.

"Hello, Bolehyde Manor."

Diana recognizes the voice of one of Camilla's staff. She hangs up.

In the organized chaos that only Charles claims to understand, Diana finds private letters addressed to her husband. She brings them upstairs, puts a kettle on to boil in her sitting room, and switches on her own stereo. As Dolly Parton's "I Will Always Love You" spins, Diana steams open the sealed envelopes, searching for evidence that her husband has been unfaithful.

Chapter 22

Summer 1984
London

O n July 1, 1984, Diana wakes to a headline on the cover of the *News of the World*'s Sunday magazine: HAPPY BIRTHDAY DI. Inside, there is a two-page photo spread: "She's more than a priceless jewel in the crown of England, she's our very own darling Di."

Diana can't help but smile. Today, she is twenty-three.

And hopeful. *Charles and I are the closest we've ever, ever been.*

Her husband has given her the greatest, most amazing gift. He has postponed all his overseas royal engagements for the summer.

On July 5, Charles puts on a gray suit and Diana dons a sparkly emerald-green maternity dress before joining a crowd of twelve thousand to hear Neil Diamond perform in Birmingham at a benefit for the Prince's Trust. During the second set, Diamond plays "Forever in Blue Jeans," Diana's favorite of his songs, and she's delighted backstage when he and his family present her with a gift for two-year-old William: an oversize plush Garfield, the cartoon cat.

Back at Kensington Palace, Charles and Diana sit together on the floor of the nursery watching William ride his white wooden rocking horse. Their second child is due in six weeks.

"I'm having a boy," Diana has confided in Paul Burrell, her butler.

She hasn't told Charles, who's hoping for a girl. She's afraid that when he learns the truth, the renewed closeness in their marriage will vanish.

She doesn't want to lose her husband. Not now, not ever.

—❧—

On September 15, 1984—a week earlier than expected—Diana enters the Lindo Wing at St. Mary's Hospital, where she labors for nine hours, Charles by her side. She delivers a healthy son.

A crowd of hundreds waits outside for news.

"Did you expect a boy?" a reporter asks Charles when he emerges.

"No," Charles admits, adding, "It doesn't matter what it was as long as it's alright... I couldn't be more delighted."

He goes on to describe "a lovely baby" with "pale blue eyes" and hair of "a sort of indeterminate color."

The following morning, when Diana hears Charles and William coming down the hall, she moves to the bassinet, telling the nurse, "It's important that the first time William sees his brother, I'm holding him in my arms."

William barrels into the room but gently takes the newborn baby's hand.

Charles studies his new son's features. "How different a character he is from William. His fingers are long and slender instead of the sausage ones William inherited from me."

Outside the hospital, photographers snap pictures of toddler William waving at the crowds with one hand, the other holding on to nanny Barbara Barnes. Cheers grow louder still when Charles and Diana appear, Diana holding the infant prince, whom they name Henry Charles Albert David.

"It will be lovely for William to have a companion and a playmate, and someone to fight with," Diana's father, Earl Spencer, says. "I'm sure Harry will be a very good chap."

Charles takes his family home in a Daimler, then plays in a polo match in honor of "just plain Harry," as the prince will be known. Afterward, in the back of a Land Rover at Guards Polo Club, Smith's Lawn, Windsor, Charles joins his teammates in a Champagne toast to his son.

He doesn't even like Champagne.

Chapter 23

Winter 1984
London

T he royals gather in the queen's private chapel at Windsor Castle. Diana, in a blue dress and cloche, an ensemble set off by an heirloom Spencer pearl choker, holds baby Harry, who's wearing a historic christening gown made for Queen Victoria's eldest daughter.

But one senior royal is notably absent: Charles's sister, Princess Anne, who has decided to go game shooting at her country estate. She's been passed over as godmother first to William, and now to Harry, and the family row leaves Charles and his father "not on speaking terms."

Charles has also offended his mother-in-law, Frances Shand Kydd, by lamenting of Harry, "We were so disappointed—we thought it would be a girl."

So did the British public. Prince William had received 4,500 baby gifts, and the new baby is similarly deluged with hand-knitted clothing and layette items. After Harry's birth, Diana writes that "The reaction to our small son's arrival has been totally overwhelming—having been sent millions of pink (!) clothes for the last nine months."

From the start, the brothers are exceptionally close. Diana delights in watching them together, observing, "William has totally taken over his brother and Charles and I are hardly allowed near as he covers Harry in an endless supply of hugs and kisses."

Not that William has given up seeking out his own attention. During the formal portrait session following Harry's christening ceremony, he breaks away from his place between Diana and the queen. His childish antics allow the assembled adults an opportunity to relax their stiff poses and indulge in broad and loving smiles.

But William is temperamental.

Diana is an indulgent mother, but even she can see that her son "knows he is different, and that he is treated with more respect than his friends."

"Any child would take advantage—and yes, William does," she admits.

After a long day of travel to Balmoral, William ruins the Queen Mother's tea, yanking a tablecloth and smashing valuable cups and saucers, screaming at servants who try to intervene. "I tell *you* what to do. Go away!"

———— ∞ ————

In April of 1985, Scotland Yard elevates Sergeant Barry Mannakee from backup to prime duty as Diana's personal protection officer. The six-foot-tall, ruggedly handsome former police dog handler is compassionate, kind, and funny.

At Balmoral, he rescues Diana.

She's sitting on a riverbank while her husband joins a party for fly-fishing. A hook lodges in her eyelid.

Mannakee drives her to the hospital and makes sure she is safe. Charles leaves Diana in the officer's care.

Charles is often leaving his lonely wife in the care of other people.

When Diana's feeling insecure, Mannakee compliments her.

"Barry, how do I look?"

"Sensational, as you know you do. I could quite fancy you myself."

I'm only happy when he's around, she decides.

She thinks nothing of inviting him to tea in her drawing room at KP. It doesn't occur to her to wonder who will protect her protector.

Chapter 24

September 1985
London

On September 24, 1985, Diana and William walk the five minutes between Kensington Palace and a Victorian row house newly fitted with bulletproof glass windows. Inside is Mrs. Mynors' Nursery School, where all the proper security protocols are in place, from an armed bodyguard constantly stationed beside the prince to a panic button installed in William's classroom.

At age three years and three months, William will be the first future king of England to attend nursery school outside the palace.

Diana can't help feeling a little sad, "because it's opening up another chapter in my life, and certainly William's," but she's advocated for him to go to school and knows it's the right thing to do. "He's ready for it. He's a very independent child."

"He was so excited about it all," she reflects, that William even picked out his own clothes that morning. "He just adores other children."

In a curriculum geared toward "a happy start," William is given a lunch box and a finger puppet and lessons in art and drama. Aside from the precautions taken to protect him, William is largely treated the same as any of the school's thirty-six other pupils. He has little idea there's anything unusual about his family until a classmate comes up and asks him if he knows the queen.

William looks at the other child, slightly confused. "Don't you mean Granny?"

Still, he starts to understand and explore the power of his lineage. And his tendency toward tantrums is not quickly overcome. He roughhouses and fights on the playground, earning him the nicknames "Basher Wills" and "Billy the Basher."

At a classmate's birthday party, he throws a plate on the floor, raging, "When I'm king, I'm going to send all my knights around to kill you!"

In the schoolyard, William taunts other children: "My daddy's a real prince, and my daddy can beat up your daddy."

In the classroom, he asks a classmate to be his wife and threatens to put her in jail if she refuses.

In the school play, he criticizes the appearance of a girl in the cast, adding, "You have to look like my mum to be a princess."

"He's a typical three-year-old," his mother, a former nursery teacher, says in his defense. "He's not at all shy, and very polite, extraordinarily enough." But Diana can barely look at the papers once they call her son "William, Prince of Wails."

Chapter 25

A merica is gripped by royal fever.

Time magazine announces Charles and Diana's imminent arrival in America's capital with the headline HERE THEY COME!

Diana is greeted by crowds hoping to catch a glimpse of her. "Princess! Princess!" they shout.

Frenzied socialites are willing to pay ridiculous sums of money to meet the world's most glamorous couple, in town as patrons of the National Gallery of Art's largest-ever exhibition, *The Treasure Houses of Britain*.

At seven thirty on the evening of November 9, a Rolls-Royce belonging to the British embassy delivers Charles and Diana to the North Portico of the White House, where they're welcomed by the First Lady and President Reagan. Nancy Reagan is in a beaded white Galanos gown that Diana recognizes from inaugural balls for the president's second term, earlier this year.

Diana has chosen a marvelous off-the-shoulder gown: a bespoke Victor Edelstein creation in midnight-blue velvet. It's enhanced by a seven-strand pearl choker newly set with an enormous sapphire-and-diamond-cluster centerpiece, originally Queen Victoria's brooch—the same one that had inspired Diana's engagement ring design and that the

Queen Mother had given her as a wedding gift. Though Diana doesn't favor gloves for daytime occasions, she dons a dark-blue satin pair that stretch above the elbow for this evening's reception with the American president and his eighty guests.

She is seated for the three-course dinner in the State Dining Room between President Reagan and her hero, Mikhail Baryshnikov.

"As a teenager," she confesses to the world-renowned ballet dancer, "I stood in the rain outside the stage door at Covent Garden when you were dancing because I was such an admirer and I wanted to get your autograph."

Throughout dinner, Diana hopes Baryshnikov will ask her onto the dance floor, but the famous dancer has injured his ankles. Instead, he's the one who asks for *her* autograph tonight.

After the guests adjourn to the East Room for entertainment, Neil Diamond takes the stage, accompanied by a military band. Diana approaches the singer after his performance of "September Morn" and "You Don't Bring Me Flowers," certain the cameras will pick up her visible blush.

"Is it proper in America for a lady to ask a gentleman to dance?"

Diana removes her satin gloves. Her dance card is full. In addition to Diamond, she dances with President Reagan and actors Tom Selleck and Clint Eastwood. At midnight, she feels someone touch her elbow. She turns and sees the star of *Saturday Night Fever* and *Grease*.

John Travolta is a bit awestruck but all smiles as he makes his way through the unfamiliar process of a royal greeting. Then he asks, "Would you care to dance with me?"

"Absolutely," she replies.

He bows; she curtsies.

The floor clears for the Princess of Wales and the actor. Travolta looks her in the eye and says, "We're good. I can do this."

The two dance together for fifteen minutes to a medley of music from Travolta's films.

"Maybe some day we'll get to do this in a less watched situation," Travolta says as they spin across the floor.

"That would be great," Diana agrees. With every turn, she can see the faces of famous guests watching her as if she were once again a fairy-tale bride.

Shortly before the royal couple arrived in Washington, a construction worker asked Charles, "You gonna have more kids?"

"Certainly—maybe sooner than you think," he'd answered cheekily.

Tonight, the spell is broken.

Diana doesn't dance with her husband.

Chapter 26

Spring 1987
Gloucestershire

P lans are under way for a tree house at Highgrove. Princes William and Harry, ages five and three, have design notes.

"I want it to be as high as possible," William says, "so I can get away from everyone, and I want a rope ladder which I can pull up so no one can get at me."

No one...except the "Big Bad Wolf."

It's a game the boys play with their father. Their goal is to find a way past him and to escape the top-floor nursery. They position themselves on chair cushions spread across the nursery floor, while Charles remains in the doorway. He leans forward, hands on his knees.

Growls.

William, older and faster, reaches Charles first. Charles scoops up the future king and throws him toward a nearby sofa, then picks up Harry and tosses him onto one of the cushions.

The boys can't stop laughing. They keep coming after him.

Just as they keep coming after Ken Wharfe, the family's chief protection officer.

Wharfe is always immaculately dressed in his plainclothes uniform. Under his Turnbull & Asser suit, he carries his Scotland Yard–issued 9mm Glock pistol.

"Ken, do you want to fight?" the brothers are forever asking him, delivering blows before Wharfe can even answer.

Charles checks in when the roughhousing seems to get out of control. "They're not being too much trouble, are they, Ken?" His Royal Highness asks.

That's the boys' cue to stop. And they do.

Charles is pleased to see that their new nanny, Ruth Wallace, a.k.a. Nanny Roof, has restored discipline and order to the family. Wallace has royal experience—she applied to the Waleses from Princess Michael of Kent's household—but because she is a Cordon Bleu–certified chef who has also deejayed at London's exclusive Raffles nightclub, her training's been largely unconventional.

While Diana likes Wallace's flair, Charles is impressed by the woman's results. He's especially proud of the transformation in William and delights in hearing Diana say that Wallace has "ended William's tantrums and Harry started to come out of his shell."

There's been another staff change—the replacement of the thirty-nine-year-old married father of two Barry Mannakee. Word is, Diana's former bodyguard had become overly familiar. His duty transfer came down to a case of what the Queen Mother calls "red carpet fever."

On May 16, Charles and Diana are in the royal limousine en route to RAF Northolt, where they'll take the Queen's Flight to the fortieth Cannes Film Festival, a tribute to Sir Alec Guinness.

"Barry Mannakee died last night in a motorbike accident," Charles tells his wife.

It's a cruel blow.

But by the time they arrive in France, Diana has composed herself.

Photographers in Cannes await the Prince and Princess of Wales's arrival. The journalists snap Diana in a double-breasted white blazer over a "puffball" striped dress by Catherine Walker, one of her favorite British designers. One film director has complained about the royals attending Cannes, saying that "the unfortunate thing about them is the hysteria they create."

Diana keeps the hysteria to a minimum until she steps out of the limo. Her evening gown—which had had its own seat on the plane—is another Catherine Walker design, a powder-blue strapless silk chiffon dress accessorized with a stole of identical fabric knotted backward around her neck, reminiscent of a gown Grace Kelly wore in Alfred Hitchcock's *To Catch a Thief*.

It's a brilliant homage and an unplanned disguise.

No one suspects Diana's heart is broken.

Chapter 27

Spring 1988
London

Every morning when William and Harry wake up, they rush into Diana's bedroom. Filled with gratitude, she hugs her sons as tightly as she can. *I've got two very healthy, strong boys. I realize how incredibly lucky I am.*

Diana wants her sons to know they're loved, to understand the importance of having feelings and *sharing* them, openly.

Even the difficult ones.

Five-year-old William is struggling to learn a new lesson: be nice to the people with cameras.

Dozens of paparazzi line the streets to catch glimpses of the royals as Diana drives the prince to his new school in Notting Hill, under the watch of their royal protection officer Ken Wharfe. "Wharfie" is a solid man who keeps Diana laughing with his perfect impression of Charles, but he'll never replace Barry Mannakee.

Inside the car, Diana turns to her son and says, "Now listen, William, there's going to be a lot of photographers at your new school, so you need to behave yourself."

"I don't like 'tographers," he says.

Diana calmly tells him what will happen next. "You're going to go to school today, there's going to be all these people who want to take your picture, and if you're a good boy and you let them take your picture, then I'll take you to Thorpe Park next week."

As it would for most little children, the promise of a visit to an amusement park works wonders.

———◦∞◦———

Diana is spending the night in the Great Ormond Street Hospital for Children. Three-year-old Harry is having emergency surgery to treat a protruding abdominal hernia.

"He is well enough in the circumstances," the Palace tells the press, but Diana cancels her appearance schedule, saying, "I wouldn't let him stay on his own." She sleeps on a mattress on the floor next to Harry's hospital bed.

Doctors clear Harry for release by noon the next day, and Diana takes him home to Kensington Palace. Soon he's strong enough to put on a leather bomber jacket and striped Bermuda shorts and walk five minutes in the May sunshine to Mrs. Mynors' Nursery School, the same one William once attended.

Charles, vacationing in Europe, learned of Harry's condition and treatment plan while en route from France to Italy. Though he's telephoning every half hour to check in on his son, the prince doesn't return from his travels.

Diana suspects that Charles is not alone—that "the Rottweiler," as she refers to Camilla, is with him.

Diana now has further evidence that her husband's been spending time with Mrs. Parker Bowles. In the butler's pantry at Highgrove, she's found the staff's desk diary, color-coded to mark the days when Charles is in the country and Diana is in London. On those days, Camilla has been a frequent guest.

Suddenly, the color-coded lists of names change to an anonymous "4 for lunch."

Chapter 28

February 1989
London

L ady Annabel Goldsmith, who describes herself as an "incredible mother, rather a good mistress, but not a very good wife" to billion- aire financier Sir James Goldsmith, is hosting a birthday party.

The guest of honor is Camilla Parker Bowles's younger sister, who's turning forty.

Diana stares at the invitation. She knows it's a mere formality. It would be strange, not to mention rude, to invite the Prince of Wales and not his wife. But no one is expecting her to actually attend. Especially not Charles.

Diana is about to toss out the invitation when an inner voice says, *Go for the hell of it.*

She does. But once face-to-face with Camilla at the party, Diana experiences a spike of fear.

Instead of kissing the woman hello, she shakes Camilla's hand. The action emboldens her, strengthens her bravery.

Diana feels a calmness sweep through her, a feeling that lasts through- out dinner.

Afterward, Diana notices that her husband and Camilla are nowhere to be found. More than an hour passes, and still there is no sign of them.

She decides to investigate.

Downstairs, in the basement, Diana spots Charles and Camilla in a children's playroom.

Diana returns upstairs and seeks out Ken Wharfe.

"I am not going to be shown up in this way," Diana tells him. "I want to talk to her—now."

Wharfe is uneasy in the knowledge that there's no dissuading Diana. Last summer, while vacationing with the boys at her mother's home off the west coast of Scotland, the princess insisted on ironing her body-guard's shirts.

"I enjoy it," she told him.

"Ma'am, you really can't."

She didn't listen then, and it will be the same tonight.

Diana needs a witness. Wharfe will do nicely.

A guest sees where she's going and intervenes. "Diana, don't go down there."

"I'm just going to find my husband," she replies.

Wharfe reluctantly follows.

Diana finds Camilla and Charles sharing a sofa, locked in intimate conversation.

The two of them look uncomfortable. Guilty.

As if one, they stand. Wharfe turns to leave.

"Please don't go, Ken," Diana says, but Wharfe excuses himself so that Diana, Charles, and Camilla can address this private matter.

"Camilla, I'd like to have a word with you, if it's possible," says Diana. She waits for her husband to leave her alone with his mistress.

"Camilla, would you like to sit down?"

They sit on the sofa. The princess has always been terrified of this woman, the power she holds; but when Diana speaks, her voice is calm.

"I know about you two."

Camilla tries to shift the blame. "Don't think it's my fault. Charles and I had a pact that I wouldn't contact him for five years after the wedding."

"I'm sorry I'm in the way, and it must be hell for the both of you," Diana says icily. "But I do know what's going on. Don't treat me like an idiot."

"You've got everything you ever wanted," Camilla states. "You've got two beautiful children. What more could you want?"

"I want my husband."

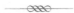

In March, Charles and Diana travel together on an official visit to Kuwait and the United Arab Emirates.

They stay in separate suites.

Diana's feelings toward Charles have turned. *There comes a time when you just don't care anymore. That time has come. I just don't care anymore,* she's decided. *If I could write my own script I would have my husband go away with his woman and never come back.*

But there are William and Harry to think of, always.

The first time I experienced true happiness was when I held William in my arms. I'd never been that happy before. And I've never been that happy since, except when I had Harry.

Diana opens her suitcase and finds an envelope. Inside is a letter from William wishing her and Charles a "lovey time" on their tour.

"But come home soon," he writes. "I miss you."

PART 3
Mummy

Chapter 29

September 1989
London

W hen I grow up, I want to be a policeman and look after you,
Mummy," seven-year-old William announces.

He and Harry are in the car with their mother, along with
their nanny and Ken Wharfe. Diana smiles at her older son, but Harry
jumps in.

"Oh no you can't," he teases his big brother. "You've got to be king."

"I don't really want to be king," William says.

Harry, nearly five years old, is gleeful. "If you don't want the job,
I'll have it!"

The nanny tries to intervene as the boys argue. Harry delivers a parting
blow. "*You'll* be king one day, I won't. So *I* can do what I want."

Diana's gaze darts between the nanny and Wharfe. "Where the hell did
he get that from?" she says under her breath.

───────⊗⊗⊗───────

This morning, it's just Diana and Ken Wharfe in the car on the way to
the Passage Day Centre, a homeless shelter in central London.

London's increasing homeless population is not a glamorous cause, but it's drawn her in over the months she's spent conversing with people who "sleep rough" on the streets. She's been listening and learning about their troubled mental and physical circumstances, their struggles to steer clear of problems with drugs, alcohol, and/or abusive relationships.

Royals, she has been warned repeatedly, do not get involved in controversial matters. But Diana has plans to become a different kind of royal—one who can act as an agent of change for real people.

On occasion, she's even snuck out from KP in the evenings to secretly put coats and clothing in rubbish bins where homeless people could find them. "They are human beings like us," Diana says. "They have [a] right to clothing and to be warm. It's an obligation of the welfare state."

Diana wonders how the royal family would react if they discovered how she's broken the unspoken rules of royal charity work. Her efforts could be met with disapproval, possibly even contempt—the kind Charles expressed this past March during a tour of the Persian Gulf States. When asked about her schedule, Diana had been about to share her plans to tour a clinic for immigrant women and a day-care center catering to mentally handicapped children when Charles cut her off, saying, "Shopping, isn't it, darling?"

Her husband's prevailing attitude is that she isn't smart enough to join his conversations. That her passions aren't important.

That *she* isn't important.

But that's an issue for another day. As she and Ken Wharfe pull up to the Passage Day Centre, Diana spots Cardinal Hume, the archbishop of Westminster, and Sister Barbara Smith, the center's director, both awaiting her arrival.

Diana exits the car, feeling slightly apprehensive, though Wharfe has assured her the building is safe. Police sniffer dogs have already searched for knives and drugs, and undercover officers are inside.

Even though she is dressed down, people instantly recognize the princess. She shakes hands, then approaches a woman combing a doll's hair and muttering to herself.

The situation is not far different from Diana's volunteer work at

Darenth Park Hospital when she was a teenager. Whereas her West Heath classmates would hesitate to engage with the residents of the mental health center, Diana immediately connected, sharing a laugh that warmed people to her.

Sister Barbara makes the introductions. "Your Royal Highness," she says, "this is Margaret."

Margaret stands. Princess Diana doesn't hesitate to shake the woman's hand. The two chat easily for a few minutes—until a disheveled middle-aged man jumps in.

"It's all right for the likes of you to come down here just for half an hour," he yells, pointing a finger at Diana. "You want to try living on the streets..."

The man's clothes are soiled, and alcohol scents his breath. Wharfe is already moving to intercept, but Diana holds him off.

"It's okay, Ken," she whispers calmly. "I'm fine."

As the man continues his profanity-laced diatribe, Diana maintains eye contact.

"Well," she says when he finishes speaking, "the reason I am here is to see exactly what it is like, so that I can help in any way I can."

Her words soothe his anger, and Diana continues her visit for more than an hour.

On the way home, she defends the angry man who confronted her. "Perhaps he's right, Ken," she says.

"Ma'am, you must be true to yourself," Wharfe replies. "Follow your instincts and you won't go wrong."

His words help solidify something inside Diana.

"This is the work I want to get involved in from now on," she declares. "If I can make something positive happen for these unfortunate people, and people like them, then there is a place for me."

Chapter 30

September 1989
London

H arry sees all the photographers and TV cameras and nearly comes to a full stop.

His mother gently urges him to keep walking. She has explained that these people would be waiting here today outside of Wetherby, the all-boys pre-preparatory school in Notting Hill, which his older brother has been attending since January of 1987.

It's Harry's first day. The boys are both dressed in the school uniform, a double-breasted red-trimmed gray blazer with a gray cap, navy-blue shorts, and buckled shoes with gray socks. Harry grips a sack of his belongings, and William sports a leather satchel on his shoulders.

Harry's already much more relaxed than William, who seems to want to turn and run away. Even at five years old—well, nearly; his birthday is coming up later this week, on September 15—Harry recognizes that although William must be on his best behavior in public, the same rules don't always apply to the little brother.

People say that William is "incredibly confident for a little boy his age" and that talking to the seven-year-old is "a bit like talking to another adult," but Harry still hangs back a bit. He'd sometimes even stay home from nursery school just to have an excuse to spend the day alone with Mummy.

But today, he's thrilled to go to school. When they meet the head-master outside, Harry turns to the cameras, smiling and waving, then glances up at William, face beaming. It's *so* exciting to be going to Wetherby like his big brother. But William doesn't look nearly as happy. His brother dislikes the media, all the questions, everyone always watching him. He stares at the camera, lips pursed, then forces a smile before disappearing inside.

At least the photographers can't follow them to class.

Chapter 31

December 31, 1989
Sandringham, Norfolk

Diana shuts the door to her bedroom. She needs a break from Charles and his family, their incessant talk about tomorrow's New Year's Day horse riding and pheasant hunt. *They're always out killing things.*

Last year, she'd escaped to the Caribbean with her mother and sisters, plus all their children, shortly after Christmas. It had been a relief to leave Charles behind at Sandringham with "the Germans," as she calls her dreary in-laws.

This year has been even worse.

All she wants is to talk to James.

She turns on the TV and raises the volume high enough to muffle her voice should someone decide to listen outside her door. Sandringham is considerably smaller than Windsor. There are eyes and ears everywhere.

Diana picks up the landline phone and makes the call.

——— ⌘⌘ ———

Nearly a decade into her and Charles's relationship, it's chillier than ever. Her bold confrontation with Camilla barely caused a blip. If anything, the affair feels even more flagrant now.

Diana's had to find happiness for herself where she could. For a while, she thinks she's found it with cavalry officer Captain James Hewitt. The two of them met at a party three years earlier, and the tall, handsome redhead later helped her overcome her fear of horses, giving her riding lessons at Knightsbridge Barracks, in central London.

When Charles is away, Hewitt visits Highgrove. William and Harry adore Hewitt, call him Uncle James. He enjoys pillow fights with the boys and reads *Winnie-the-Pooh,* Harry's favorite book, to them at night. He has taken them to the army barracks, where William and Harry spend hours examining and playing on armored vehicles—the tanks especially.

Diana feels confident and at ease in Hewitt's presence and has even spent time visiting him at his mother's place in Devon, happily doing the domestic chores that she has always enjoyed, and though she insists to Ken Wharfe that she and Hewitt are simply close friends, Wharfe's simple reply is: "You know my only concern is for your safety."

Wharfe never judges her, and Diana confides in him. "After Harry was born, my marriage to Charles just died," she says. "I tried, I honestly tried, but he just did not want me. We haven't slept in the same bed for two years."

Diana feels safe with Hewitt. She feels she's finally met a man she can trust.

Even more, she confesses, she needs him.

"You give me strength," Diana tells Hewitt. "I can't stand it when I'm away from you. I want to be with you. I've come to love you."

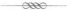

It's not James Hewitt she calls now, though—it's James Gilbey, a child-hood sweetheart she reconnected with this past summer at a friend's thirtieth birthday party. Hewitt's job has taken him to Germany, and in his place, Gilbey has quickly become a trusted confidant. He even has a special nickname for Diana: Squidgy.

Gilbey is on his way to a dinner party, but he always makes time for her. Diana vents to him her frustration over how her Christmas gifts of cashmere sweaters and mohair scarves go unappreciated. The royal family only likes to receive—and give—joke gifts, like the white leather toilet seat Charles got from his sister, Anne. He thought it was hilarious and roared with laughter.

Gilbey sympathizes, then asks, "And so, darling, what other lows today?"

"I was very bad at lunch and I nearly started blubbing," Diana admits. The state of her marriage and the way she's treated by Charles and his family despite all her hard work often sets her off. "I felt really sad and empty, and I thought, 'Bloody hell, after all I've done for this fucking family.'"

It all comes pouring out of her—the sadness and frustration and resentment, especially regarding Charles. "He makes my life real, real torture, I've decided," Diana says. "I can't stand the confines of this marriage."

She can't quite tell how the others regard her. The Queen Mother, for example, is "always looking at me with a strange look in her eyes," she says. "It's not hatred, it's sort of interest and pity mixed into one. I am not quite sure. Every time I look up she's looking at me then smiles and looks away... I don't know what's going on."

They chat awhile longer. It's such a relief to unburden herself to Gilbey, who says the sweetest things. "You don't mind it, darling, when I talk to you so much?" he asks.

Someone who *wants* to talk to her? It's heaven. "Oh no, I love it," Diana assures him. "I've never had it before."

She doesn't match his ardor, but she absolutely appreciates it.

"Oh, Squidgy," Gilbey announces, "I love you, love you, love you." To which Diana responds, "You are the nicest person in the whole wide world."

It's coming up on 8:00 p.m. when Diana hangs up. She won't join the others for New Year's Eve dinner, she's decided. She'll eat alone in her room. *Just some salad with yogurt. Like when I was ill in bed.*

Not exactly the way a princess—the world's most famous woman—ought to be ringing in the new year.

Chapter 32

April 8, 1990
Necker Island, British Virgin Islands

A s owner of Virgin Atlantic Airways, Richard Branson can fly his
friends anywhere he likes—including over Windsor Castle. Sitting as his guest in the cockpit of one of Branson's planes, with
William on her lap, Diana speaks into the microphone.

"If you look out to the left, you will see Granny's house!" she announces
over the intercom, earning laughs from her fellow passengers.

In the spring of 1990, Branson invites Diana to spend the pre-Easter
holidays at Necker Island, his seventy-four-acre retreat in the British Virgin
Islands. It's her second visit; Branson also hosted Diana and family on his
private island fifteen months earlier, welcoming them with a lobster barbecue and popping open Champagne he's had bottled exclusively for guests.
Diana is eager to return this year, having found the seclusion exactly what
she's longed for, "some peace and quiet within this mad life we lead."

She travels to Necker with a party of seventeen—herself and the young
princes, her sisters and their children, her brother and his new wife, her
mother, and a few bodyguards. The main building on Necker is the Great
House, situated on the island's highest point, every room offering sweeping
views of crystal-blue Caribbean water and pristine white beaches. The children rush inside with barely a glance at the Balinese-style beamed ceiling,
going straight for the billiard table set up by a deck overlooking the ocean.

After their arrival, Ken Wharfe and Diana review the security measures arranged with local police and officials. Flights over the island are banned, and no one is allowed within a mile of the shoreline.

Diana soaks in the gorgeous view and the soft steel drum music, relaxing with her family, feeling completely at peace.

It's paradise.

But it's not long before she spots a small fleet of boats on the horizon, floating outside the legal boundaries.

The press has found her.

Wharfe makes no promises, but he sets out toward the press boats to attempt a negotiation.

Hours later, he returns and tells Diana that the *Daily Mail* has offered to broker a deal with the paparazzi to leave her alone. The trade-off is that she first allow them a photo shoot.

"But can you guarantee it, Ken?" Diana levels her gaze at the protection officer. "Can they be trusted?"

A question they both know he can't answer. But the *Daily Mirror's* photographer, Wharfe says, passed along a message: "Tell the Princess she looks like a million dollars, and I'll make sure the pictures of her in the *Daily Mirror* do her justice. She'll knock 'em dead back home."

It's an intriguing offer. Diana weighs the chances of these Fleet Street reporters—the same fellows who once told Charles, "We may be scum, sir, but we are la crème de la scum"—keeping their end of the bargain. She briefly wonders whether seeing photos of her enjoying a sun-kissed holiday with the children will spark any feeling in her husband.

Jealousy? Regret? Shame? She rather hopes so, unlikely as it may be.

She agrees to do the photo call.

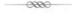

Harry and William have been enjoying themselves immensely. Since they've been to the island before, they already know all the fun things to do here—rolling the billiard balls as if they were giant marbles, going snorkeling, exploring the island's undergrowth, digging in the white sand with red plastic shovels.

They investigate the three massive catapults that the house manager has recently brought to the island, using them to engage in intense water balloon fights between themselves, their cousins, and their protection officers—until boats full of photographers, dozens of them, line up offshore and start snapping away at the family gathering on the beach.

Diana sits in the sand, with Harry between her legs and William nearby with their cousins. They're meant to pretend that the photographers aren't there, but even from a distance, they can all hear the rapid machine-gun *click-click-click* of the cameras echoing in the cool sea air.

William peers at the boats, but Harry bows his head and covers his eyes. Mummy's eyes are hidden behind a pair of dark-lensed sunglasses. Granny Frances frowns directly at the cameras.

Soon enough, though, the children do rather forget they're being watched and join together to bury Diana's legs in the sand, up to her waist.

Twenty minutes later, it's over. The boats motor away.

The next few days are absolutely peaceful. Then Wharfe tells Diana that the French paparazzi are planning on returning. They want more photos.

The boys are irate. So is Diana, who complains when Wharfe suggests allowing another brief photo session. "You said that if I did the first one they would leave us alone, so why have I got to do another one?"

But seven-year-old William, who shares his mother's mischievous streak, has a plan.

"He hates the press even more than I did when I first got into this family," Diana told a friend about William's antagonistic attitude toward photographers—made even worse after a photo of him taking a leak outdoors was published last December under the headline THE ROYAL WEE. "He sees them as the enemy, but he's going to have to learn that they can be handled."

This time, William's ready. He strategizes with Harry and his cousins, then approaches Ken Wharfe.

His mother, he says, *should* tell the French photographers to come. And then, "when the photographers come back in their boats, why don't we catapult them from the house?"

William knows the perfect spot.

"We can go to the top of the cliff," he says, "and when Mummy does the photo call, we can fire the balloons at the press."

Wharfe regards William seriously and says he'll inform Her Royal Highness of this important development. Shortly after, he returns with news of Diana's wholehearted endorsement.

When the press boats appear, the boys are fully equipped. They've mounted the catapults in trees and other strategic locations overlooking the shore, and they have filled hundreds of colorful melon-size balloons with water.

Even Diana has been helping out, readying the ammunition. Wharfe calls her their "chief loader."

The journalists are told they have ten minutes to snap photos. As soon as the time is up, the counterattack begins.

For the next twenty minutes, the press boats are pelted with water balloons. The children are in charge, but the grown-ups are delighted, calling it "a wonderful assault on the invading paparazzi."

When the boats depart, William runs to his mother to celebrate their heroic success.

The paparazzi don't return.

Press attention begins as soon as Diana and Prince Charles are linked, in November 1980. (*Jayne Fincher/Princess Diana Archive/Getty Images*)

Charles gives Diana a stunning sapphire-and-diamond engagement ring in February 1981. (*Tim Graham Photo Library via Getty Images*)

The smiling couple poses with Queen Elizabeth, four months before their wedding. (*Fox Photos/Hulton Archive/Getty Images*)

The newlyweds pose for a wedding day portrait at Buckingham Palace on July 29, 1981. (*Lichfield Archive via Getty Images*)

Diana comforts her youngest bridesmaid, Clementine Hambro, Winston Churchill's great-granddaughter. (*Lichfield Archive via Getty Images*)

Diana and Charles share a tender moment, not long after their first wedding anniversary. (*Gavin Kent/ Mirrorpix/Getty Images*)

Dressed in white and wearing the Spencer Tiara, as she did on her wedding day, Princess Diana accompanies Queen Elizabeth. (*Terry Fincher/Princess Diana Archive/Getty Images*)

Prince William, age two, upstages the christening of his infant brother, Prince Harry. (*Lord Snowdon via Anwar Hussein/Getty Images*)

Princess Diana's gown at the Cannes Film Festival is a tribute to the late Princess Grace of Monaco. (*Anwar Hussein/Getty Images*)

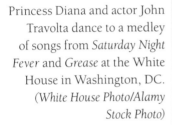

Princess Diana and actor John Travolta dance to a medley of songs from *Saturday Night Fever* and *Grease* at the White House in Washington, DC. (*White House Photo/Alamy Stock Photo*)

Charles and Diana pose with their sons, William and Harry, in the wildflower meadow at their country estate, Highgrove. (*Tim Graham Photo Library via Getty Images*)

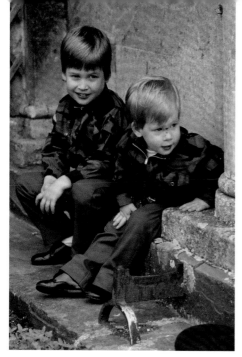

Princes William and Harry grow up fascinated by all things military. *(Tim Graham Photo Library via Getty Images)*

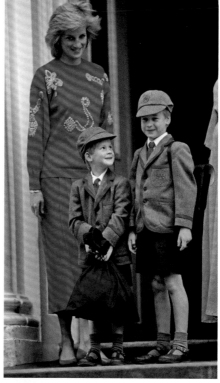

Diana enjoys taking her sons to school like an ordinary mother. *(Tim Graham Photo Library via Getty Images)*

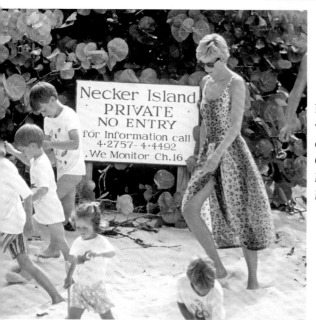

Photographers find Diana wherever she goes, even on a private island in the Caribbean. *(Tim Graham Photo Library via Getty Images)*

Diana runs the mothers' race at the school Sports Day. (*Anwar Hussein/WireImage*)

Amusement parks are a favorite outing for the Princess of Wales and her sons. (*Julian Parker/UK Press via Getty Images*)

The warm relationship between William and Harry always makes Diana smile. (*Antony Jones/Julian Parker/ UK Press via Getty Images*)

Princess Diana has a special connection with children. *(Tim Graham Photo Library via Getty Images)*

Fellow humanitarians Mother Teresa and Diana, Princess of Wales, together in New York in June 1997. *(Anwar Hussein/WireImage)*

Newly divorced Diana auctions off dozens of her couture dresses for charity at the suggestion of teenage Prince William. *(Tim Graham Photo Library via Getty Images)*

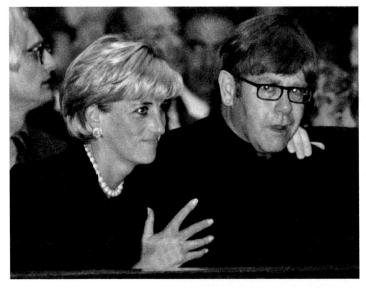

Diana comforts singer Elton John at the funeral of their mutual friend, designer Gianni Versace. *(Stefano Rellandini/Alamy Stock Photo*

In August 1997, Diana vacations in the Mediterranean on the Fayed family's private yacht, the *Jonikal*. *(Stephane Cardinale/Sygma via Getty Images)*

That same month, Prince Charles brings William and Harry to Balmoral for the royal family's annual holiday. *(Tim Graham Photo Library via Getty Images)*

Chapter 33

June 28, 1990
Gloucestershire

T here's an ambulance on standby at every polo match.

All the Windsor men are obsessed with polo, but it's Charles who can't seem to keep his mount. When he was engaged to Diana, he fell three times in six weeks.

"Accident prone," Philip and the queen pronounced the prince, whose sporting pursuits left Diana "in a fair tizz."

Nearly a decade has passed, and Action Man is still taking a beating.

Skiing in Switzerland two years earlier, the forty-year-old prince survived a deadly avalanche that exploded in a "terrifying matter of seconds."

"We don't want our royals to be wimps," said the *Star*, but as the *Sun* demanded, "Why was he there?" the *Daily Mail* appealed to the queen: "Please, Your Majesty, can you ask your offspring, for the nation's sake, to show just a little more care?"

Diana is even more blunt. "For heaven's sake, Charles, why don't you give up polo? You're just too old now."

It's true that his injuries have taken a toll. Sometimes the muscle spasms in his lower back get so bad he can barely move. Neither the demanding exercises he's been doing off the field nor the special orthopedic cushion he sits on inside the car can help loosen the tension.

Yet the prince continues to live dangerously, especially on the polo field, where he's determined to keep playing "as long as I bounce when I fall off." It's a point of pride to play through the pain.

Today he's with his team, Windsor Park, up near Highgrove at Cirencester Park Polo Club. Diana's down in London, attending a school play. They haven't been spending much time together lately—and both prefer it that way. Diana always manages to pull all the attention when she comes to watch polo anyway. She'll be the one on the front pages the next day. *Quite the glamour girl,* Charles sneers. He's been informed of his wife's relationship with Captain Hewitt, but frankly it's a relief to have her attentions occupied elsewhere.

The only time he feels a rivalry with the tank commander is when he faces off against the younger man on the polo field.

Half an hour into today's match, Charles lines up a shot, swings his arm back to go for it—and loses his balance, tumbling from his horse.

He hits the ground and lies stunned, unable to move as his horse trots away.

The entire polo field goes silent. Have they just witnessed the death of the Prince of Wales? Author Jilly Cooper exclaims from the audience, "It looked for a moment as though he might have bought it."

A stretcher is quickly brought onto the field. At the emergency room of nearby Cirencester Memorial Hospital, the prince recovers enough to laugh and joke with the hospital staff and other patients.

"A silly thing to do," he says, downplaying his injury.

But it's a bad break: a double fracture above his right elbow that will require extensive surgery to repair. At least they're able to reset it without using pins. Among those in his retinue who rush to his side are his royal chef and press secretary...and Camilla, who manages to slip by the journalists outside the hospital, all waiting for Diana to show up.

Charles is touched by Camilla's concern yet aware of the PR disaster that will ensue if anyone—especially his wife—realizes that she is here. He instructs his staff to listen in on the police radios and give notice before Diana arrives, so Camilla will have time to remove herself.

It's annoying how popular his wife continues to be. *He's* the royal-born future king of England, a man with serious ideas. No matter where they go, Diana eclipses him, even now as they leave the hospital together, smiling for pictures as husband and wife.

On the way to Highgrove, Diana suggests that she stay there to take care of him, which irritates Charles immediately. He senses she has some sort of romantic notion about aiding him through his convalescence.

He refuses her help, telling her that he doesn't want to be nursed.

At least not by her.

Disappointed, Diana drops him off at Highgrove and returns to her life at Kensington Palace.

After his wife leaves, Camilla appears within the hour.

Chapter 34

Autumn 1990
Berkshire

William tucks away his latest note from Mummy.

"My darling Wombat. It was lovely to catch a kiss and a hug from you this morning, even though I would like to run away with you," she writes.

"Wombat" is one of Mummy and Papa's nicknames for William, ever since their royal family trip to Australia when he was a baby. A beloved wombat toy is one of the items William has brought with him from home to Ludgrove, an all-boys boarding school.

He and his parents had smiled and waved for the cameras on September 10, when he started at the school, though Mummy cried a bit in private. Papa tried cheering him up with funny stories, putting a happy spin on his own boarding-school memories, but William could read between the lines. At least Ludgrove isn't too far away—not like Gordonstoun, the boarding school Grandpa Philip and Papa attended, located in a remote corner of northeast Scotland.

Though the eight-year-old prince was initially nervous, he's liking it here at Ludgrove rather a lot, actually. He's settled in quickly, and the Barbers, the headmaster and his wife, are really kind.

He's far away from his parents and his little brother but also from the complicated feelings he sometimes has at home.

The sights and sounds of his parents quarreling can make him shout out loud. "I hate you, Papa. I hate you so much. Why do you make Mummy cry all the time?" he'd once yelled when his parents got into a particularly nasty argument. He passed tissues under the bathroom door to his weeping mother while telling her, "I hate to see you sad," but also admitted to a friend, "Papa never embarrasses me but Mummy sometimes does." For Harry, though, William puts on a brave face. "Mummies and daddies fight all the time," he assures his little brother. "It doesn't mean they don't love each other."

But here at Ludgrove, he's shielded from all that. The press isn't allowed anywhere on the 120-acre school grounds, which include a nine-hole golf course, tennis courts, a swimming pool, cricket and football pitches, and woods where students can camp out—completely secluded from the prying eyes of tabloids and TV programs.

When William returns home on the weekends, he's full of stories about his life at school: how after breakfast, he plays sports before it's time for class, with more downtime for games or television between dinner, at six, and bedtime, at eight.

Students aren't allowed to make phone calls, but Mummy comes up to visit all the time and writes letters constantly. She's always slipping him contraband sweets, tucking them into his socks.

"You can be as naughty as you want, just don't get caught," she says, teasing him.

It's not as if William can get into *too* much trouble—he's got two royal protection officers, Sergeants Reg Spinney and Graham Craker, watching over him at Ludgrove, though they do their best to keep their distance and allow him some normalcy.

It will be even better when Harry's old enough to come here, too.

Chapter 35

Winter 1990
London

D iana's running a little late. As she heads up the stairs to the East London studio at around 3:00 p.m., she hears voices.

"Who is it we're shooting next, Mary?" a man with a faint Scottish accent asks. "We were told we had one more to do."

"I've no idea," a woman's voice replies. "It's all been very hush-hush. All I was told was that it was for British *Vogue,* but 'we can't tell you who the client is, so just look smart that day.'" She sounds almost offended when she adds, "As I normally would do, of course."

"I hear it is someone very important, very high-profile. Maybe Margaret Thatcher?" a man with a heavy French accent suggests. "Do you know who it is, Anna?"

Diana doubles her speed, bounding up the remaining steps and fairly bursting through the doors. "I'm Diana, how are you?" she says brightly, sticking out her hand and giving them all a huge smile. The only person in the room she already knows is Anna Harvey, her stylist, an editor at British *Vogue.* The other woman, she learns, is Mary Greenwell, the makeup artist. The Scot is hairstylist Sam McKnight, and the Frenchman is photographer Patrick Demarchelier.

Right away, she can tell this will be fun. Patrick Demarchelier is a dream, even if she can barely understand him. "He's incredibly flirtatious and not remotely deferential," Anna Harvey comments. Diana trusts his skill, since she knows his work—she actually contacted him once after admiring other *Vogue* covers he's shot.

As long as he doesn't drop a light on her head, as photographer David Bailey's assistant once did during a shoot for the National Portrait Gallery.

"Don't think about it," she'd insisted at the time. "It was a terrible accident."

"You're very magnanimous," he'd told her.

Besides, the joke was that her hairdo was sprayed and shellacked "solid as a plastic dummy."

She feels immediately comfortable with Mary Greenwell, even when the makeup artist criticizes her beloved Elizabeth Arden Blue kohl 636 electric-blue eyeliner and mascara.

"Blue eyes should never wear blue pencil or shadow—it dulls your eyes!" Greenwell chides. "I think beiges and browns are just so much prettier. Simple as that."

It's the first time she hasn't used blue eyeliner in ages, and Diana loves the new look. *What a difference!*

Diana picks up a nearby newspaper as Sam McKnight pins her hair under the Cambridge Lover's Knot Tiara, which she's brought with her for the shoot—one of her favorites, alongside the one she wore at her wedding, the Spencer Tiara.

"Oh, those velvet headbands are at it again," she says with a laugh, flipping through a tabloid that labels her "*Dynasty* Di," after the TV show famous for its 1980s power outfits and shoulder pads.

It still stings a little bit, though.

"Velvet headbands" are the stodgy women who prefer Diana's preppy Sloane Ranger look over her more fashion-forward outfits. But even if she's made a few fashion faux pas—she won't be wearing leather trousers again anytime soon; *that* was a real balls-up—on balance, Diana's still got millions of women around the globe emulating her style.

But it's the nineties now, and she wants a new one.

Plus, Charles banned all aerosols in their houses two years ago, and she hasn't found a decent hairspray since. Addressing environmentally minded businesses, Charles joked that for the sake of husbands every-where, "if anybody can come up with a really good answer, an alternative to hairsprays, then for God's sake do so."

It's all very well, Charles making light of it—he's not the one whose hairstyles are scrutinized in the media. Ever since becoming Princess of Wales, she's had to make changes excruciatingly slowly. "One-fourth of an inch at a time over several weeks" is as quickly as her longtime hairdresser, Richard Dalton, will cut her heavily feathered long bob. Anything more drastic risks becoming front-page news and upsetting the senior royals.

"I'll show this family," she'd complain to Dalton as he soothed her frustrations with treats of white chocolate and the Opal Fruits candy she loves.

"Could you come sit down on the floor?" Demarchelier asks now. On the floor? Gosh, it's frightfully nice to try something less stuffy than the typical poses she's used to. Diana is loving this relaxed, informal photo shoot. George Michael's new song, "Freedom! '90," is on heavy rotation—that stunning video with all the supermodels? George took the idea from a January British *Vogue* cover!—and it's been just the most amazing day spent laughing, chatting about the latest episodes of *Brookside* and *The Golden Girls,* and gossiping. (Is it true that Diana had an incognito night out with Freddie Mercury at the Royal Vauxhall Tavern? She'll neither confirm nor deny.)

Most important, the photos are turning out to look spectacular. It's given her a much-needed confidence boost.

As the shoot wraps and she's nearly ready to head back out, Diana makes a spontaneous decision.

"Sam, what would you do with my hair if I just said, 'Do anything'?" Diana asks McKnight.

"I'd cut it all off and just start again," he replies immediately.

"Do it then," she says. After a moment to check whether she's serious, he jumps to work.

No surprise: the media goes absolutely crazy over her chic new cut. Well, no surprise to Diana, but hairstylist McKnight's unprepared for the coverage. Journalists even swarm all over his parents, to the point where they decamp from their home for two weeks until the fervor dies down.

But the princess has no regrets.

It's liberating.

Chapter 36

T he Princess of Wales is having lunch with a friend at San Lo-
renzo, a family-run Italian restaurant close to Harrods
department store. It's one of her favorite spots and is becoming
a celebrity hangout: Jack Nicholson and Joan Collins have been spotted among the patrons recently. Diana's shared many meals here with
close friends, and William even made reservations on her behalf once
when he sensed his mother was feeling blue, noting that it'd be "just
the thing to cheer you up."

She has been feeling a bit blue lately, reflecting on her upcoming
thirtieth birthday and tenth wedding anniversary—two occasions the
public seems more excited about than she does.

Today, Diana's just finished her seafood pasta and is about to order the
fresh mangoes for dessert when Ken Wharfe approaches the table. He
looks shaken.

"What is it?" Diana asks.

It's William. He's being rushed to the hospital.

His skull has been fractured.

⸺∞⸺

Wharfe speeds Diana to Royal Berkshire Hospital, in Reading, six miles from Ludgrove, where William's personal protection officers have already brought him, per preestablished "contingency plans" for any serious medical event involving the second in line to the throne.

During a lunch break at Ludgrove, William and some friends had been messing around on the putting green when one of the other boys swung his golf club, a 7 iron, and delivered a serious blow to William's forehead above his left eye.

A school spokesman insists it was a complete accident. "No one was being nasty or unkind to Prince William. He is a very much liked boy here at the school."

It's a significant but not life-threatening injury, and by the time an agonized Diana arrives at the hospital, eight-year-old William is "chirpy and chatting away."

Charles is already there. He was at Highgrove when his protection officer informed him about the accident. "My heart went cold," he tells her.

London's Great Ormond Street Hospital for Children is the nation's best children's hospital. It's where three-year-old Harry had his hernia surgery—and where Princess Diana has been president since 1989. Diana travels with William in the ambulance, holding his hand the entire ride. Charles follows in his Aston Martin.

Neurologists determine that the blow to William's skull has left him with a "depressed fracture." In the operating room, surgeons work for seventy minutes to repair the dented bone, leaving him with a long scar and twenty-four stitches.

The longest seventy minutes of my life, Diana thinks.

Charles decides to carry on with his royal duties—hosting a black-tie performance of *Tosca* at Covent Garden—while Diana sits by William's bed, continuing to hold his hand overnight while nurses come in every twenty minutes to check his blood pressure and reflexes.

William's first visitor the next morning is six-year-old Harry, who comes to see his brother before heading off to school. For two days, Diana stays by William's side. Charles checks in regularly, but Fleet Street is aghast.

On its front page, the *Sun* declares: 42 MINS: THAT'S ALL CHARLES CAN SPARE FOR WILLS, adding: "What kind of dad are you?"

The Palace is unprepared for the public's dismay. Once again, the nation's loyalties oppose the future king.

Chapter 37

June 11, 1991
London

D iana kicks off her shoes and hitches her long tan skirt to knee level.

How delicious the grass feels on her bare feet.

With William safely out of the hospital, she's eager for some fun with Harry at Wetherby's end-of-term Sports Day. He's been doing the sack races, and she's lined up with around half a dozen other mums for the mothers' race. Her competitive spirit is kicking in. She placed first in this race in 1987 and '88 and second in '89. Last year was her worst showing—third place. She's not about to let *that* happen again.

There's always a pleasure in the feeling speed brings. She's chased it on the ski slopes, on roller skates, in go-karts, even on bicycles. She used to love zipping around London on her beloved blue Raleigh Traveller—it was a sad day when the Palace insisted she stop before the wedding, deeming bike riding unsuitable and unseemly for a princess. The *Evening Standard* even called it her "shame bicycle."

Ridiculous. But she did as she was told and gave it up, selling it to her friend's father for a little over £200.

She also has something of a heavy foot when she's behind the wheel of a car.

"Diana only married me so she could go through red traffic lights," her husband told reporters earlier this year. And that's without Charles knowing that she's been pulled over for speeding—once going one hundred miles per hour!

Ken Wharfe was riding with her at the time. "Ken, you'll have to sort this out," Diana pleaded as the intimidating traffic officer began walking toward them. When Wharfe refused, Diana knew what she had to do.

She turned on the charm.

Angling her head in classic "Shy Di" fashion and widening her eyes to their most innocent and beguiling, she managed to stun the poor traffic officer with the sheer force of her personality.

No ticket, just a simple warning. And probably a story the officer will tell at the pub for years to come.

The footrace about to begin, Diana considers ditching her blazer, but a look at the other mums shows they're all still wearing their sweaters and cardigans—part of the fun is how daft they'll all look, running flat-out in their respectable clothes.

She shares a quick grin with her competitors as they ready for the race. Then—*crack!*—they're off, and she's running as fast as her long legs will carry her, laughing and enjoying every minute.

In the end, it's a close race, but she comes in second.

There's always next year.

Chapter 38

August 1991
Aberdeenshire, Scotland

T he whole royal family's up in Scotland at Balmoral Castle. The queen enjoys tromping the estate on foot, on horseback, or via Range Rover—and doing the washing up herself after meals. Harry and William have the run of the place, with its fifty-two bedrooms, and go fly-fishing on the River Dee with their grandfather. Afterward, Prince Philip mans the barbecue grill, laughing and affectionately calling his wife "Cabbage" and "Sausage." Meanwhile Charles braves the swarms of midges to indulge in solo hiking or painting.

Attendance at Balmoral is mandatory, and there are rules—spoken and unspoken—that everyone is meant to follow. Still, when a call comes through on August 19 that a dear friend of Diana is dying of AIDS, she doesn't wait for royal permission to return to London. When someone she loves is in trouble, Diana moves quickly. And there isn't much time.

Last rites have already been administered to her friend, Adrian Ward-Jackson, a forty-one-year-old art dealer, director of the Royal Opera House Trust, governor of the Royal Ballet, and deputy chairman of the AIDS Crisis Trust. Diana races through the night to St. Mary's Hospital, praying she'll cover the 550 miles in time to say goodbye in person, as she's promised him she would.

The princess has been at the forefront of HIV/AIDS awareness for years, to the disapproval of her husband—who calls her efforts "inappropriate"—and her mother-in-law, the queen, who suggests, "Why don't you get involved with something more pleasant?"

Diana disagrees. Ever since 1987, when she accepted an invitation from Middlesex Hospital to open the UK's first ward dedicated to treating patients with HIV/AIDS, Diana has felt an ever-growing connection to the campaigns to find a cure.

And to AIDS patients.

Although Queen Elizabeth always wears gloves in public to protect her health, Diana refuses, rejecting gloves as too impersonal. "It's all about touching," she says, grasping the hands of the ill, skin to skin, wanting them to feel her love.

It's a powerful move. She's not scared by the stigma of the disease. She publicly embraces patients. Where others are often at a loss, Diana offers comfort.

"What do you say to a little girl with AIDS?" Darren McGrady, Diana's personal chef at Kensington Palace, once asked her as she stopped in the kitchen on her way to tour a hospital.

"Well, there is not a lot I can do or say," she admits, "but if by sitting with her and chatting with her, perhaps making her laugh at my bad jokes, I can take her mind off her pain for just that short time, then my visit will have been worth it."

This past April, Diana gave a speech at the Children and AIDS Conference, sponsored by the National Children's Bureau and the National AIDS Trust. The speech highlighted her scientifically backed position: "HIV does not make people dangerous to know, so you can shake their hands and give them a hug. Heaven knows they need it."

When she returned to visit the Middlesex AIDS ward last month, a man began crying as she held his hand. The princess yearned to console him.

Diana, do it, just do it, she told herself. So she did. She gave him "an enormous hug."

She does the same now for her friend Adrian when she arrives at his bedside with hours to spare.

Diana's starting to find her voice, her actions growing braver as her compassion is sparked.

Two months later, in late October, Diana and Charles embark on a weeklong tour of Canada, bringing along seven-year-old Harry and nine-year-old William. It's the first time the children have come with them on a trip abroad, but the couple makes few joint appearances and is basically on "two tours in one."

With little emotional value left in Diana's marriage, her children and her social causes come first. In Toronto, Diana makes time to visit a small AIDS hospice, sitting with dying residents and holding their hands.

As she's leaving, she stops—the mother of a former patient has signed to her, and Diana pauses to reply in kind. Many people seem to forget that she's also a patron of the British Deaf Association, and she's worked hard to learn some sign language.

No such skills are needed to interpret the frosty distance between the Prince and Princess of Wales.

Chapter 39

March 29, 1992
Lech, Austria

S ki in, ski out. The five-star Hotel Arlberg, in Lech, offers access to snow runs in a mountain pass of the Austrian Alps.

Diana, in a white hotel robe and wet hair, leans over the balcony despite the chill to wave at Harry and William, having a snowball fight down below.

It's the boys' spring holidays, and Diana has decided to take them skiing.

Her one requirement is that it be someplace *other* than Klosters, their father's favorite ski resort, in Switzerland. She's adamantly refused to return there since 1988, when their friend Major Hugh Lindsay died in a terrible avalanche that nearly killed Charles, too.

Lech is perfect—it is charming and luxe and has hosted many a celebrity and royal looking to avoid glitzier ski areas. Last year, Diana was delighted to join chart-topping British musician Cliff Richard at his après-ski late-night sing-alongs in the hotel bar.

"I believe you sing on a Friday night in the bar. Could you do it for the boys?" she asks him. "But they go to bed early, can we do it before dinner?"

Richard happily agrees to perform several of his hit songs for the young princes in a private performance. As Harry starts to yawn, however, Richard changes tactics and asks what they'd like to hear.

"Do you know 'Great Balls of Fire'?" Harry asks. "That's one of Mummy's favorites, she plays it all the time."

When Richard launches into it, Harry and William jump to their feet, grabbing Toblerone chocolate bars to use as makeshift microphones while gyrating energetically to the song.

This year, Diana intends to invite Cliff and his band out to dinner with her—and with Charles.

Given the state of their relationship, eyebrows are raised when Diana announces that she's invited her estranged husband to join her and the boys. Equally surprising is that Charles, an avid and admittedly far better skier than Diana, has accepted.

"Extraordinary," remarks Ken Wharfe. "I would never have predicted it."

Is a reconciliation in the works? Diana is always open to that prospect, but there are other issues at play as well. Always on her mind is her own parents' divorce.

She's highly sensitive to the unhappiness she felt as a little girl, "when Mummy decided to leg it." Diana's relationship with her mother has occasionally been rocky, but even though Frances blames the end of her second marriage on the nonstop media frenzy over "Princess Diana," the two women are currently on good terms. Diana's mother is well positioned to offer counsel—and caution. When Frances "bolted" from her unhappy marriage to Johnnie, the future Earl Spencer, she lost custody of her four children.

That would be Diana's worst nightmare.

She's got to stay on good terms with Charles for the children's sake.

Besides, she knows just how difficult it can be to feel pulled between two parents.

"I come from a divorced background and I didn't want to get into that again," she says. Even now, it's a balancing act.

Things have recently been tense with her father, mostly because of complaints she and her siblings have over the way Johnnie's second wife, Raine, is handling the family estate. He's currently in the hospital, but it's not serious—Diana and William went to visit him the day before their ski trip, and Johnnie told her brother that he'd be out "in a day or two."

It takes a moment for Diana to hear the knock on her suite door over the sounds of the boys laughing and taunting each other as she cheers them on from the balcony.

She nips back inside to answer the door. Wharfe stands there and gently delivers devastating news.

Her father has had a heart attack and died.

"Oh my God. What am I to do?" Diana sobs, keenly aware even in her grief that it's her protection officer, and not her husband, who's here to comfort her.

Charles has gone out to join the boys in the snow, declining to come to her in her hour of need.

Chapter 40

May 1992
Studland Bay, Dorset

F or the next few months, Diana combats her loneliness with a busy schedule.

But what she truly craves is an opportunity to be alone, free of everyone—including her twenty-four-hour security detail.

Her personal protection officer Ken Wharfe agrees to drive her 120 miles from London, in an unremarkable car, to the vintage Sandbanks Ferry at Poole. They have no backup.

On the westernmost point of Studland Bay, Diana stands alone on the sandy beach holding a two-way radio and a map. Ahead she can see the Isle of Wight, a guidepost on her walk to the Old Harry Rocks. The cliffs, made of chalk, have stood for millions of years. No one knows whether they're named for a local pirate or the devil.

Diana's Harry is only seven years old. He and his brother are too young to have to cope with the failure of their parents' marriage, but there's no turning back.

Walking toward a fixed destination is sure to steady her. Ken Wharfe, who grew up on the nearby Isle of Purbeck, will meet her at the far end of the bay.

Wharfe drives the car to the parking lot of the Bankes Arms, a sixteenth-century pub overlooking the beach. He watches and waits until he hears Diana's voice on the radio.

"How is it going?" he asks.

"Ken, this is amazing," she says. "I can't believe it."

The princess is over and out, but only for a moment.

"You never told me about the nudist colony," Diana calls, laughing and laughing.

She's giddy with freedom.

Chapter 41

October 1992
Berkshire

T he boys are well and enjoying boarding school a lot, although Harry is constantly in trouble!" Mummy reads aloud the note she's writing to her friend, and Harry laughs because it's true.

He's not at all sorry about it, either. None of the trouble has been serious, and part of him enjoys being treated like all the other boys at school and taken to task when he misbehaves. It's so wonderfully ordinary.

Sure, Harry was rather homesick when he started at Ludgrove, last month, but he's been quick to make friends and settle in. Plus, William's here with him.

It's the weekends that can be tricky now. There's been an upsetting book about Mummy published, and all the grown-ups seem at odds. It's altogether preferable being away at school.

Mummy has taken them on some cracking outings, though. One of Harry's favorites was when Wharfie took them to a shooting range.

It was the coolest day ever! An absolute dream come true.

On the day, Wharfie brings Harry, William, Mummy, and a few friends to a real police range over in Lippitts Hill, Essex. Of course, they first must pay close attention to all the safety warnings. Harry is mesmerized.

"He's too young to understand things," William started whining, but Mummy put a stop to it right away.

"Oh shut up, William, we'll see who's been concentrating in a minute," she says.

That's nearly the best part. The *actual* best part is that when Harry finally gets his hands on a weapon, he hits the bull's-eye. Again and again and again. He's the best of all of them. Afterward, he gets to keep his target sheet.

It's so exciting to earn first at something. He's used to coming in second—at least to William—and he's learning that certain things will simply stay that way. Even when they took their family trip to Canada last year and Harry did his first "walkabout," greeting the crowds of people there to see them, Mummy had to hold his hand and keep him back a little so that William could walk ahead, since his older brother's closer in line to the throne.

Harry and William and Mummy also do a training session in which they act as if baddies have taken over the cars and tried shooting at them or blowing them up, then Wharfie and some of the other officers throw themselves across the seats. It's brilliant.

He's already looking forward to the time when it'll be his turn to serve in the military, like Grandpa and Papa, who were both in the Royal Air Force and the Royal Navy. Harry's been dressing up for the role since he was a little boy, always fascinated with the uniforms, the tanks, the helicopters, the weaponry, and all the rest. He especially likes the army.

Harry can't wait to be a soldier.

Chapter 42

November 1992
Paris

I t's time to spread my wings," Diana tells the *Sun's* Arthur Edwards in November. There's a mystery behind her smile.

On Friday the thirteenth, she flies to Paris.

Charles's forty-fourth birthday is tomorrow. He'll spend the day at Highgrove, but Diana has plans with another man—the French president, François Mitterrand.

Emerging onto the Paris tarmac in a bright green skirt suit adorned with a double row of gold buttons, accented by pearl-and-gold Chanel earrings, Diana's welcomed to Élysée Palace. Mitterrand's home is larger than both the White House and the Palace of Versailles, a scale as grand as today's achievement. Diana's solo talks with France's head of state mark a first for a Princess of Wales.

On Saturday, Diana visits the cultural complex at Parc de la Villette to reconnect with her first love: ballet. Her pink skirt suit is several shades brighter than the pale ensembles of the Paris Conservatory dancers performing *The Nutcracker*. Afterward, she joins them onstage, longing to dance *en pointe* again. Eyeing the cameras trained on her, she decides against taking the risk.

She's facing a fresh challenge as keynote speaker on November 17 during European Drug Prevention Week back in London. Diana is patron of the Institute for the Study of Drug Dependency, and the organizers have given her a prepared speech, but the text is dry, filled with policy minutiae.

Diana wants to talk about people, not programs. She throws the speech away and writes a new one, all her own.

As she steps up to the podium in the conference center at the London Metropole Hotel, the crowd applauds, then settles in to listen. She's dressed in a sharply tailored navy-blue pin-striped suit over a round-necked cream-colored blouse, with the same Chanel pearl-and-gold earrings she wore to meet President Mitterrand.

Diana is widely known for her compassion and for choosing causes she connects to personally. Today she launches into a passionate call to action that comes straight from the heart.

"Hugging has no harmful side effects," she says. "There are *potential* huggers in every household."

Diana elaborates on her central theme. All of us are responsible for the care of others, for family, especially the youngest members.

"Children who have received the affection they deserve will usually continue to recognize how good it feels, how right it feels, and will create that feeling around them. We've all seen the families of the skilled survivors. Their strength comes from within and was put there by means of learning how to give and receive affection, without restraint or embarrassment, from their earliest days."

The words come pouring out of her, the speech stretching into one of the longest she's ever made.

"If the immediate family breaks up, the problems created can still be resolved, but only if the children have been brought up from the start with the feeling that they are wanted, loved, and valued. Then they are better able to cope with such crises."

Carried by the energy of conviction and emotion, Diana closes out her talk. She's bared her soul to a ballroom full of strangers. It's a powerful feeling.

Chapter 43

Winter 1992
London

I t's becoming impossible to avoid the specter of separation, possibly even divorce, despite warnings from the *Daily Mail* that "if there's a divorce, that's the end of the royal family."

But things are too far gone to repair.

On November 25, Charles visits Diana at Kensington Palace. He comes straight to the point.

He wants a separation. Immediately.

Diana agrees to it. She changes the locks on apartments 8 and 9 and gets a new number for her private telephone line.

In the dark of night, Charles's house staff transfers his possessions from KP to the prince's new London address, St. James's Palace. Diana won't miss his ceremonial uniforms, mahogany desk, and library of leather-bound history books. Nor will she miss the painting of Charles, her husband of more than eleven years, wearing a kilt.

It takes a convoy of moving vans to collect Diana's belongings from Highgrove, but there is much she's happy to leave behind. It's especially easy to part with the king-size bed made "to last a lifetime," a wedding gift from a West Midlands firm.

The most valuable of their more than ten thousand wedding gifts, worth more than $15 million altogether—including hundreds of uncut diamonds from the king of Saudi Arabia—will be stored at Windsor Castle.

A different fate awaits the lesser but unwanted reminders of married life.

In the gardens at Highgrove, a bonfire is lit.

Diana makes a special contribution—articles of Charles's clothing. She's always hated the "fuddy-duddy" way he dresses.

Notepaper headed CHARLES AND DIANA is consigned to the flames, along with figurines and keepsakes now fully stripped of sentimental value.

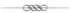

At 3:30 p.m. on December 9, the prime minister stands before the House of Commons. His words add smoke to the fire.

"It is announced from Buckingham Palace that, with regret, the Prince and Princess of Wales have decided to separate.

"The Royal Highnesses have no plans to divorce, and their constitutional positions are unaffected."

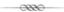

At Middlewick House, Camilla faces the press.

"If something has gone wrong, I'm very sorry for them. But I know nothing more than the average person on the street. I only know what I see on television."

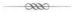

Diana listens to the news on her car radio—in Vail, Colorado.

At last the world knows her secret.

"Oh well," she says, resigned. "I suppose that's that!"

Jenni Rivett, her personal trainer and friend, suggested that Diana come skiing with her in Vail when the princess mentioned how much she's dreading being away from William and Harry. She won't be joining the royal family at Sandringham for the holidays, and it'll be the first one that her sons, now eight and ten, will be spending without her.

"Well, I'd love to, Jenni," she'd said when her friend invited her to a place nearly five thousand miles away from London, where headlines put mounting pressure on her elder son. Isn't it enough that he's losing the stability of the only family he's ever known without predictions of the separation forever altering his future? "MPs Say Charles Won't Be King, Di Won't Be Queen," the *Sun* insists. "It's Down to Wills."

It might be snowing in Sandringham today, but it's nothing compared to Vail.

From the top of a secluded trailhead, Diana skis off into the powder.

PART 4
Princess of Wales

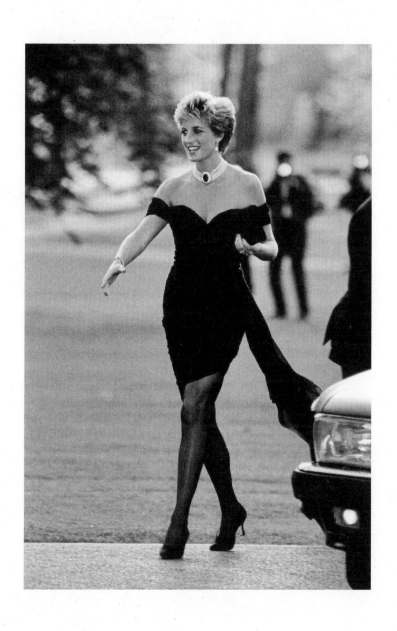

Chapter 44

March 1993
Lech, Austria

I n the last days of March, heavy snow is falling. It's a skier's paradise. But Diana, William, and Harry can't get to the slopes. European paparazzi are blocking their way.

"Ken, I want you to keep them away from me," Diana tells her personal protection officer.

Ken Wharfe can't control the pack of photographers, so he tries reasoning with the most aggressive of the bunch.

"Where are you from?" Wharfe asks.

"Italy," the cameraman says.

"Well, it's not your country either. Now just back off!"

Instead, the photographer pushes even closer to Diana. Too close. Wharfe takes him down, one-handed, then faces off against the Italian's buddy.

"Do it again, Ken," William says. He's smiling, waiting for the detective's next move.

"Go away! Go away!" Diana screams at the photographers.

The mood shifts. The boys pick up on their mother's fear, and she puts her arms around them protectively.

"They're only eight and 10, and I was worried they would get injured in all the chaos," Diana explains to a British cameraman. "Well, it's all over now. I'm really looking forward to a happy holiday. The boys are really enjoying themselves, and I want it to be special."

So do the owners of a nearby ski shop, who present Diana with personalized racing skis designed for speed.

"They are the very best," one of them says. "She will ski much faster and more safely, and it gives her the edge over the photographers. We are delighted to help out."

An edge is exactly what Diana wants. She's happy to be back in Lech but is still feeling tightly wound. There's no escaping the sad memories of last year's trip, cut short by the terrible news of her father's death.

Her suite at the Arlberg is on a wing that extends from the first floor of the hotel. She waits until she's sure the boys' nanny, Olga Powell, has them settled for the night and that her protection officers are in their rooms. Then she steps onto her balcony, takes in the view of the surrounding snowdrifts.

It must be twenty feet to the ground, but the fresh snow is piled high.

She jumps.

Landing on her back cushions the blow. She gets up and walks into town.

In the morning, Wharfe is alerted that his team can't account for the princess's whereabouts overnight. He embarks on a solo investigation of the hotel grounds and uncovers the clues she's left behind—the impression in the snow where her body fell and the footprints leading into Lech.

Wharfe enters the sitting room of Diana's suite.

"Ma'am, it's about last night," he begins. "What on earth were you thinking when you jumped off the balcony? Anything could have happened."

Diana's face flushes at the reminder of Wharfe's skill as a detective. She answers with confidence. "Yes, I did jump from the balcony. I knew it was okay—it was deep, soft snow and I knew it would be all right."

"Do you want to tell me where you went?" her protection officer asks.

"I know what I'm doing."

"No, ma'am, I really don't think you do" is Wharfe's terse reply.

But that's all Diana will say about her few precious hours alone.

She lavishes attention on William and Harry. They ski out from the Arlberg, and after a few runs on the slopes—the new Austrian skis are ready to race—she watches their spirited snowball fights. Then it's time for a winter adventure.

They climb into a sleigh and bundle together under a rug that will keep them warm. The sleigh skims over the snow at high speed. The feeling of moving fast is the best part of all.

Chapter 45

June 1993
London

D
iana signs her name in bold dark ink. She rounds her vowels and dots the *i* she makes from the downstroke of her capital *D*. This first day of June marks a solemn occasion—the making of her will in the presence of a solicitor from the Lawrence Graham firm.

Here in her private apartments at Kensington Palace, Diana surrounds herself with flowers—especially freesias, one of her favorites, alongside forget-me-nots—and possessions she treasures not only for their beauty but also for their sentimental value and humor. The furniture is upholstered in dusty pink, and her rooms are full of books and artwork as well as tchotchkes and embroidered silk pillows emblazoned with amusing sayings.

Her sons take pride of place, of course. Even when they're away at school rather than watching television by the fireplace, she can see the princes' faces smiling from framed photos on every shelf and surface. There's also a series of five black-and-white mother-and-sons portraits taken by French fashion photographer Patrick Demarchelier. Diana keeps those dear photos, her favorites, in the nursery.

She reads over the document fresh with her signature. "I express the wish that should I predecease my husband he will consult with my mother with regard to the upbringing, education and welfare of our children."

Granny Frances, or "Super Gran," as William and Harry call her, will take care of the boys if ever she can't.

And they are to inherit not only her belongings, including her personal jewelry, couture gowns, and wedding dress, but also the lucrative copyright, trademarks, and royalty rights to her name and likeness. It's not inconsiderable.

Her sister Sarah once joked that Diana's "face is on the tea towels," and it's been said that "Diana's face will wash your hands, dry your dishes, pour you a drink, warm a teapot, hold a pan. You can have her with your tea, on your biscuit, and as an after-dinner mint."

Income from any future mementos will stay largely with William and Harry.

From KP, it's fewer than five miles to Somerset House, where wills are recorded, then another 120 or so miles to Birmingham, where more than forty million wills—including Charles Darwin's—are stored in a secret warehouse.

There Diana's wishes will rest, hidden from view.

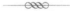

Not a single head turns as the world's most recognizable woman walks up the busy thoroughfare.

"Meet you on the High Street," Diana told her friend and voice coach Stewart Pearce over her private phone line. "I'll be wearing a black trench coat."

Pearce waits on the corner. Minutes later, he's joined by Diana, disguised in a long blond wig and sunglasses.

The pair, giddy with success, hurries to their destination, a dark movie theater. The princess has once again slipped past the royal watchers.

More than ever, she's feeling the weight of constant surveillance. Kensington Palace is filled with electronic security cameras and the roving eyes of Diana's neighbors—her in-laws—who are as quick to judge as the domestic staff is to talk about what they see in apartments 8 and 9. And though truly grateful for her security staff, Diana's only half joking when she calls them her jailers. Ever since her separation went public, she's been looking for a more private place to call home.

"The Garden House seems to suit your needs perfectly," her brother, Charles, whom Diana playfully calls Carlos, writes to her in June.

With their father's death, ownership of Althorp, their family's ancestral home, has passed to Charles, the ninth Earl Spencer. The one-hundred-thousand-square-foot main house sits on fourteen thousand acres in Northamptonshire and has thirty-one bedrooms, but Diana is eyeing the freestanding four-bedroom Garden House.

"I see your clear need for a country retreat," her brother says, "and I am happy to help provide it as long as there is not too much disruption to us or the estate."

Living on the Spencer property would be ideal and would help ease her concerns about public opinion turning on her if she overspends. It's what Diana's father always wanted for her as well—during her engagement, Johnnie told reporters, "There are times I wish she was marrying an ordinary chap, so I could have her and my son-in-law living here with me in the park."

Diana sends Ken Wharfe to determine whether the house is suitable for security. It is—the brick structure lies a discreet distance from every other building on the property, and there's an annex where Diana's protection officers can work. She hires a designer to remodel the interiors with fresh designs and colors.

Two weeks later, there's an abrupt turnaround.

"Dearest Duch," Charles writes, "I am sorry but I have decided that the Garden House is not a possible move. There are many reasons, most of which center on the inevitable police and press interference that will follow."

The loss of the house is a sharp setback. "I know you will be disappointed but I know I am doing the right thing for my wife and children," he says, adding a feeble, "I am just sorry I cannot help my sister!" He doesn't even reply to her follow-up letter, sending it back unopened with a cover note that reads, "Knowing the state you were in the other night when you hung up on me, I doubt whether reading this will help our relationship." The postscript wishing her a happy birthday is hardly celebratory.

It's one more sign of her total isolation—from family, friends, everyone but her boys.

Perhaps he has a point. Why would anyone want all the fuss that goes with me?

Chapter 46

August 1993
Orlando, Florida

P rince Harry, nearly nine, is holding hands with a princess.

Princess Aurora, a.k.a. Sleeping Beauty, never leaves his side, even accompanying him on a semiprivate boat ride to watch a dazzling fireworks show.

If there's any kingdom under the sun sure to deliver on its promises of royal treatment, even for actual royals, it's Walt Disney World's Magic Kingdom.

It doesn't take much to convince Harry or his eleven-year-old brother, Will, that Disney World is indeed "the most magical place on earth." Mummy's brought them and a few friends here on a three-day trip, and she's rented the entire fifth floor of Disney's Grand Floridian Beach Resort. Even more impressive than their massive hotel suite are the underground tunnels, through which a private escort secretly whisks them to the best rides: Country Bear Jamboree, the Jungle Cruise, Big Thunder Mountain Railroad, and, of course, Splash Mountain, where resort photographers catch them all screaming with delight even as Mummy ducks her head to try to keep her hair dry.

They return to the log flume every day, but to Harry, there's no better ride than Space Mountain.

After an initial scuffle with William—leading Mummy to declare that if the boys can't work out who takes the front seat, they'll have to leave the park—Harry yields to his older brother.

William only wants one turn. So does Mummy.

Harry goes around and around and around on the roller coaster more than half a dozen times.

"My policeman had to get off and vomit on the bench!" he cackles.

The Disney security team brags that after handling US presidents and Hollywood celebrities, managing "Lady Di" is "a piece of cake," but this is exactly the sort of "low-key" holiday Diana wanted—accompanying her adrenaline-fueled sons around Disney World, looking like any other tourist in her Bermuda shorts, sunglasses, and T-shirt.

Diana's well aware that their hotel is full of reporters and tourists, all hoping for a glimpse of her and her boys, so she's a *bit* surprised that more photographers haven't found them.

One sharp-eyed Disney visitor successfully identifies the Princess of Wales while waiting in line. "I knew it was her because of her hair. It was perfect. One hundred percent humidity and she still looks good." Another visitor's mind goes blank upon spotting Diana at a performance. "I can't remember one single thing about the show that was on the stage, but I remember her smile."

William and Harry stand transfixed in front of the breakfast buffet at the Grand Floridian.

There's eggs and bacon, fruits and jams, pancakes and sausages, pastries and potatoes. It's a spectacular array. Some of the enticing food is unfamiliar, though.

"What's that bread with holes in it, Mummy?"

Diana flicks her eyes over the table. "It's a waffle with honey."

"Can we have some?" William wheedles. "Papa says honey is good for you."

"Papa," she says firmly, "would go ballistic if he saw this."

He truly would. While Diana revels in giving the princes a taste of normal life, including junk food on occasion, Charles these days is a devoted organic gardener who's turned his beloved Highgrove into an experimental farm.

"Oh, bloody organic!" Prince Philip exclaims when he encounters his son's homegrown produce.

Charles is so enthused that he has published a book called *Highgrove: An Experiment in Organic Gardening and Farming* and is producing a line of organic foods under the name Duchy Originals, which carries a version of his Duke of Cornwall crest on the packaging.

"To get the best results, you must talk to your vegetables," Charles once earnestly told the press. Diana throws the line back at him during marital spats, yelling, "If only I was as important as your garden. Go on, talk to your flowers!"

In truth, Diana also loves flowers and delights in beautiful bouquets like the fragrant arrangements of freesias, calla lilies, and orchids that greet her in the Disney suite.

It's telling that her master-gardener husband never brought her a single bloom.

Chapter 47

December 1993
London

D iana needs a break. It's been almost exactly a year since her official separation from Charles, and after more than a decade as a
working royal, she's never felt more scrutinized.

Still, she's continued her duties on her own—to the point of righteous
frustration. *I'll bloody well show that family. Just watch me. I'm not going to
have anybody say that I have let the side down. Nobody!*

But the constant media intrusion has left her depleted and exhausted.

"Over the next few months I will be seeking a more suitable way
of combining a meaningful public role with, hopefully, a more private
life," she tells a stunned crowd on December 3 at a charity lunch at the
London Hilton on Park Lane. To that end, she says, "I will be reducing
the extent of the public life I've led so far."

This decision, she adds, "has been reached with the full understanding
of the Queen and the Duke of Edinburgh, who have always shown me
kindness and support."

After emphasizing that her first priority remains her children, Diana
says, "I hope you can find it in your hearts to understand and to give me
the time and space that has been lacking in recent years."

Stepping back doesn't mean stepping away, of course.

Sometimes it even means stepping up.

A little less than two weeks later, Diana decides the time has come for William and Harry, eleven and nine, to witness firsthand some of the charity work she supports.

It's important to her that her sons understand their privileged position and the responsibility that comes with it. They may still be children, but they are second and third in line to the throne, and William is destined to one day be king of England. She doesn't want them to be overly sheltered or out of touch.

"I want William and Harry to grow up in the real world outside the 'Big House,'" Diana says, "to experience what most people already know—that they are growing up in a multiracial society in which everyone is not rich, or has four holidays a year, or speaks standard English and drives a Range Rover."

As she tells Wharfe, "I know it's going to be tough, Ken, given who they are, but it is so, so important to me that they grow up not only knowing who they are, but what the world is really like."

Palace insiders are sometimes taken aback at Diana's informality with the princes—at her fondness for ordering takeout for them to eat on trays in front of the TV, for example, or even stepping out for fast food.

"Cancel lunch for the boys," Diana once told royal chef Darren McGrady. "We're going to McDonald's."

"Oh my God, Your Royal Highness," McGrady replied. "I can do that, I can do burgers."

"No," she assured him—the whole point was to get the Happy Meal. They're like any other children: "It's the toy they want."

Not everyone agrees with Diana's desire to raise her sons as "normal boys." Their first nanny, Barbara Barnes, butted heads with Diana and felt "the princes need to be treated differently, because they are different." The nanny Charles hires post-separation, outdoorsy twenty-eight-year-old

Alexandra "Tiggy" Legge-Bourke, also feels she knows best when it comes to the boys. "I give them what they need at this stage: fresh air, a rifle, and a horse," she says. Unlike their mother, Tiggy sniffs, who "gives them a tennis racket and a bucket of popcorn at the movies."

But Diana's focus on the real world goes far beyond fast food and pop culture. She's also determined to show her sons the gritty side of life outside the palace.

Early in the morning of December 14—too early for the paparazzi to be on alert—Diana brings her sons with her for the first time to the Passage Day Centre, the homeless shelter and charity she's been visiting for years.

The young princes assist in passing out clothing and food to the patrons. One man, who comes into the shelter after a night spent outdoors, walks up to William, who's handing out hot beverages. The man knows exactly who William is—and he doesn't care.

"Give me that," he says gruffly. "I'm not interested in you."

It's an eye-opening experience for the prince, one Diana uses to help gently educate him.

"You see, William, this is what happens," she explains to him. "Not everybody likes us."

Yet regardless of a person's attitudes or circumstances, Diana impresses upon her sons, all people are still entitled to be treated with humanity and kindness. A sense of compassion is necessary for her boys to learn how to "lead from the heart."

She leads by example, and together they record their visit by signing the facility's guest book.

Chapter 48

January 1994
Australia

P rince Charles embarks on a twelve-day tour of Australia. On January 26, he takes the stage overlooking the oval in Sydney's Tumbalong Park, where a crowd has gathered for Australia Day ceremonies.

Everyone is listening, but one young man is watching more than most. He rushes the stage, armed with a starter's pistol.

He fires two shots at Charles.

They're blanks.

The man is David Kang, a twenty-three-year-old student protesting the suffering of Cambodian boat people held in detention camps in Australia. He'd written a letter to the prince and gotten an answer from a staff member saying that Charles couldn't get involved.

"I thought it was a stunt for a minute, and then I thought no, this is serious," says a bystander who assisted in taking Kang down. "I came round from the second row and just got a good headlock on him."

After the danger is past, Charles brushes himself off, straightening his cufflinks and smoothing his hair, and continues the ceremony—though he admits to officers that the attack felt like "being charged by an elephant in Kenya."

Charles is on a determined quest to rehabilitate his image after his separation from Diana. It's working.

"Prince Charles was fantastic. He was as cool as a cucumber," the bystander says.

It was his survival instincts kicking in, Charles explains. "A thousand years of breeding have gone into this, you know," he quips to *The Australian*. "I can't worry about whether people are going to be rushing out of the crowd, or something, and bop me on the head because you can't get on with life then."

In a television interview with Nine Network, Charles says, "We are not all like James Bond or Indiana Jones." Making hand gestures indicating karate, he continues, "You don't step to one side and go 'blatt'!"

He soon gets another chance to prove himself.

In February, during a five-day tour of New Zealand, Charles is in the midst of inspecting yachts in Auckland when an older man suddenly approaches.

"I want to remove the stink of royalty!" the man says, holding a metal object up above his head.

The prince's security detail surrounds the antiroyalist and dive-tackles him seconds before he can let loose his weapon: a can of air freshener.

Four months later, in June, Charles is one of eleven passengers aboard the Queen's Flight, en route from Aberdeen to Islay, an island in Scotland.

Charles has a lot on his mind. Today is the day a TV documentary featuring several interviews he gave to journalist Jonathan Dimbleby is set to air. It's a sympathetic portrayal but risky, because he's also chosen to publicly admit his marital infidelity.

When Dimbleby asks Charles whether he tried to be "faithful and honorable" when he married Lady Diana Spencer, in July of 1981, Charles replies, "Yes, absolutely," before clarifying after a moment, "Until it became irretrievably broken down, us both having tried."

He's looking forward to being on the remote island when the program airs this evening.

Eager for distraction, Charles approaches the captain, RAF squadron commander Graham Laurie, and requests that he be the one to land the aircraft.

The Prince of Wales rose to group captain in the Royal Air Force once he earned his wings at RAF College Cranwell, in 1971. But in the twenty-three years since, he hasn't been vigilant about keeping up his training.

Laurie agrees to hand over the controls.

It's a mistake.

Charles lands the aircraft but skids the wheels. He activates the brakes, but it's too late. Laurie tries to take over and compensate for Charles's errors, but he's unable to prevent the aircraft from blowing three tires, then sliding off the runway and sinking into the muddy ground.

"It wasn't quite a crash," Charles says in his own defense, embarrassed. "We went off the end of the runway, unfortunately. It is not something I recommend."

Nor are the next day's headlines: CHARLES, THE PRINCE WHO FELL TO EARTH, the *Daily Mail* reports, but the story about the prince's near crash and the more than $1 million in damage he caused is buried on page 7.

The front-page news is THE THRILLA HE LEFT TO WOO CAMILLA.

Last night, Diana attended a *Vanity Fair* gala just as Charles's tell-all documentary aired, and it's clear where public sympathies lie.

The photos are all of Diana entering the gala in a beautifully fitted black off-the-shoulder dress with a short, asymmetrical hem. Her seven-strand pearl necklace, with the sapphire centerpiece that was a wedding gift from the Queen Mother, is the same one she wore to dance with John Travolta at the White House nearly ten years ago. The dress, designed by Christina Stambolian, has been in her closet for three years, never worn. But on the night that her husband has finally told the truth about his long-term affair, it's the perfect choice. The press names the slinky gown her "revenge dress."

The injury the documentary and Charles's unapologetic confession has caused to the monarchy is incalculable. Polls report that "an astonishing 84 percent of people think that Charles has damaged the image of the Royal Family by confessing his affair with Camilla Parker Bowles," and nearly half of respondents think it foretells the end of the monarchy altogether.

Chapter 49

December 25, 1994
On the road to London

D iana can't wait to get away from Sandringham.

 She's made her appearance. Not spending Christmas with her sons is so, so hard, but being among the rest of the royal family is worse.

Especially Charles.

Diana says her farewells as quickly as she can, then slides into the driver's seat of her blue Mercedes and exhales.

Anything will be better than this. She'd rather be home alone at KP watching the *EastEnders* omnibus.

She follows serenely behind the police escort that accompanies her part of the way. But as they reach the M11, the police car veers away.

There's almost no one else on the road.

This is her chance.

Diana accelerates to sixty miles per hour, then eighty. A hundred. She pushes it even further, all the way to 120 miles per hour.

She throws her head back, and as she laughs in exhilaration, she catches a glimpse in her rearview mirror of a convoy coming up behind her.

The press never quits, even on a holiday.

As she reaches the M25, instead of continuing, Diana waits until nearly the last moment, then unexpectedly pulls over to the side of the road. She gets out of her Mercedes, and as the journalists' cars are forced to pass her by, she offers them all a big smile and wave.

Then she gets back in her car and continues home. She can imagine what they're thinking: "Here's the world's most glamorous woman, who could ring anyone and spend the day with whoever she wants, and she's spending it alone."

Perhaps she'll watch *EastEnders* after all. She really does love it.

Chapter 50

June 1995
London

I t's William's thirteenth birthday, and he's on his way home from school to celebrate at Kensington Palace. He's stunned at what he finds there.

Supermodels Naomi Campbell, Claudia Schiffer, and Christy Turlington, all waiting for him at the top of the palace stairs.

Is this actually happening?

William's face flushes hot. He's "completely and utterly sort of awestruck" at the surprise of finding that not one, not two, but *three* of the most famously beautiful women in the world have come for tea. It's as if the posters on his bedroom wall have spontaneously come to life.

"I think I pretty much fell down the stairs on the way up," William admits. "I went bright red and didn't quite know what to say and sort of fumbled."

Not exactly cool, but the trio of gorgeous supermodels deems it "so sweet."

It's all his mother's doing, of course. As is the cake she's gotten him for his birthday . . . in the shape of an enormous pair of breasts.

"What on earth is this?" is royal chef Darren McGrady's reaction as he stands, baffled, in front of the refrigerator.

McGrady often leaves meals for Diana to heat up over weekends when the boys aren't at home—he laughingly declares the princess an "awful cook" who nearly burned down the royal kitchen on one occasion—and even pens cooking instructions on sticky notes. So he's unprepared when he comes into work that morning to find an X-rated cake.

"I went down to the refrigerator, opened the door, and I was just confronted with the biggest pair of boobs I've ever seen in my life," McGrady exclaims.

It's a special cake, the butler tells him, that Diana personally ordered for Prince William's birthday. McGrady is speechless. Diana hadn't informed him in advance about the racy dessert. "I wish I'd taken a photograph of it!"

When he's presented with the risqué cake and they all sing "Happy Birthday," William can again feel his face coloring as Harry shouts, "Wow! Can I have that cake for *my* birthday?"

Mummy's naughty sense of humor is legendary. William knows better than to open his mail in front of the other boys at school, because Mummy loves to send him "the rudest cards you could imagine" and then write "really nice stuff inside." He's always having to hide the cards and notes that contain dirty jokes. It's massively awkward. But he loves it.

The exquisite embarrassment she's causing him today, though, will be hard for her to ever top.

On September 5, William begins at Eton, an elite boarding school located just across the River Thames from Windsor Castle, the nine-hundred-year-old palace where Granny and Prince Philip usually spend weekends. He is officially enrolled as "Wales, Prince William of," but refuses to allow his schoolmates to address him as "sir." At school he's mainly known as "Wales."

Even though Eton was founded in 1440 by King Henry VI, William is the first heir to the throne to be educated there. But it's a tradition on the

Spencer side of his family, and he's proud to be following in the footsteps of his uncle Charles and grandfather Johnnie.

It's not nepotism, either: his parents are both really pleased with how well William has done on his Common Entrance exams—"My boy's got a good brain, considering how hopeless both his parents were," Diana says—and his new headmaster announces that "Prince William's performance gives us every ground for supposing that he will flourish at Eton."

Like Ludgrove, Eton is a boys-only school, but first-year students have many rules to learn, starting with "school dress," consisting of a white dress shirt and matching white bow tie, striped trousers, and a black waistcoat and morning coat with long tails. And unlike Ludgrove, which shelters its 200 students on private grounds, there are nearly 1,300 students at Eton, not to mention the tourist-filled town itself.

Here, William is much more exposed. "Prince William must be allowed to run, walk, study and play at Eton, free from the fear of prying cameras," the Press Complaints Commission decrees, but even with Scotland Yard's Royalty and Diplomatic Protection Group watching over him, he still has to duck the press everywhere. Worse, without the headmaster curating his access to media, as is still done for Harry at Ludgrove, William now sees newspaper and television coverage of his parents *constantly*. It's relentless.

As much as William would like to sink into anonymity, though, that's not his role in life. On Sunday afternoons, he travels to Windsor Castle—a fifteen-minute walk or six-minute drive—where he has tea at four o'clock with Granny. Grandfather Philip was the one to first suggest it, though he always allows the queen and her grandson space for private conversation. William talks about his school days while Queen Elizabeth in turn counsels him about royal duty, as her father, King George VI, did for her.

The queen imparts serious wisdom to her one-day successor, but William and Granny genuinely enjoy each other's company. There's also Darren McGrady's chocolate biscuit cake. The queen has the dessert "sent into the royal dining room again and again," the chef says. "If there is anything left when she has it at Buckingham Palace, it then goes to Windsor Castle so she can finish it there." William grows very fond of the cake, too, during his weekend visits with Granny.

On November 19, Diana unexpectedly arrives after one of those Sunday teas for an in-person talk with William about an upcoming BBC *Panorama* interview she's taped.

"It's going to air tomorrow night, and I didn't want it to catch you by surprise," she tells him. "Don't worry. Everything will be fine—I promise," she says before heading off.

She couldn't be more wrong.

Thirteen-year-old William is "filled with dread" as he sits down to watch the program the next night in the privacy of his headmaster's study. The interview is so much worse than he could've imagined. His mother publicly discusses her bouts of depression and self-harm. She's openly dismissive of the monarchy, and she admits to infidelity on both her part and his father's.

William is horrified.

Absolutely mortified.

And angry.

Obviously, he feels terrible for Mummy and what she's endured—some of which he's learning about along with the rest of the world—but how can he defend her when she's just exposed the royal family and spilled their private traumas all over television?

Mummy, he feels, has made fools of their entire family. Including him.

Almost a week passes. William avoids his mother's calls. By the time he goes home to KP over the weekend, his conflicting feelings of sympathy and shame, and his sense of royal duty, come to a head, and he and Mummy have the biggest blowup *ever*.

By the next day, they're both able to apologize. But this is an embarrassment that isn't easily shaken off.

Chapter 51

December 1995
London

T he queen has had enough.

After the scandalous *Panorama* interview, the Princess of Wales's presence in the family is no longer deemed suitable.

"Whatever goodwill there might have been at Buckingham Palace towards her as a person," Diana's press secretary, Patrick Jephson, surmises, "the offense she had caused was too great."

One week before Christmas, a letter arrives from the queen addressed to "Dearest Diana" and signed "With love from Mama." There's no hint of glad tidings. In "the best interests of the country," the queen's decided, Charles and Diana are to forgo their planned lengthy separation and instead have an "early divorce."

Diana is cut to the quick, yet jokes half-heartedly to Jephson, "D'you know, Patrick, that's the first letter she's written to me."

Charles quickly follows with a letter of his own, also requesting a divorce. Earlier this year, six months after Charles's own ill-received television interview, Camilla Parker Bowles and her husband likewise announced their intention to divorce—leading the *Sun* to declare Camilla, Charles, and Diana "three tragic souls who face a future alone."

But only Diana, who does not want a divorce, feels forlorn.

In mid-February of 1996, she is summoned to a meeting with her soon-to-be former mother-in-law, Queen Elizabeth, to discover that her own opinion carries no weight. The matter has apparently already been discussed with, and decided by, everyone except her.

"Whatever may transpire in the future, nothing will change the fact that you are the mother of both William and Harry," the queen assures her. Yet the monarch says, "The present situation is not doing anybody any good, either country, family, or children."

That's one thing easily agreed upon.

Diana settles in with her lawyers to hash out the rest.

Eight months later, on August 28, 1996—a little over a month after what was officially their fifteenth wedding anniversary—the divorce is finalized. Diana retains joint custody of the children, will continue to live at KP, and will be allowed use of the royal jets.

She is also awarded a hefty sum of money—some $22.5 million in cash up front, plus around $600,000 a year—and is allowed to maintain possession of her royal jewelry, to be eventually bequeathed to her sons' wives, should they marry.

Sometime earlier, Diana and Prince Philip have a rather tense exchange.

"If you don't behave, my girl," the prince warns her, "we'll take your title away."

Diana, daughter to Earl Spencer, is unruffled. "My title is a lot older than yours, Philip," she coolly replies.

Philip, who's always had a fond relationship with Diana (referring to the queen and himself as "Ma and Pa" in his letters to her), guffaws at her reply.

And it's true: the Spencers have far deeper English roots than the Windsors do.

In the end, she retains the title "Diana, Princess of Wales," but is stripped of her formerly elevated form of address. A notice in the *London Gazette* announces that Diana, as "a former wife ... of the Prince of Wales shall not be entitled to hold and enjoy the style, title or attribute of Royal Highness."

The loss chafes—deeply.

The Palace swears Diana herself suggested dropping the "HRH." The papers report that "Prince Charles was said to be adamant that she give it up." The queen intimates that she wouldn't have prevented Diana from keeping the honorific but says, "Speaking personally, I think that the title 'Diana, Princess of Wales,' would be more appropriate."

Perhaps. But as Diana's press secretary, Patrick Jephson, points out, "You must remember that she didn't join the Royal Family to be Princess. She joined the Royal Family to be Queen."

Whichever of them insisted upon it, losing "Her Royal Highness" is ultimately the most jarring change. Though Diana will remain "regarded as a member of the royal family," the technicality means that she is now officially separated in title from the rest of them, and if the separation is enforced, she would be required to curtsy to those who hold the HRH title—including her own sons.

Diana, more attentive than ever to William's opinion these days, asks her son how he feels about her diminished royal status.

Sensitive to his mother's distress, William tells her, "I don't mind what you're called. You're Mummy." And he reassures her about losing her HRH status. "Don't worry, Mummy, I will give it back to you one day when I am king."

Chapter 52

1996
London

T he divorce has not helped Diana's search for love.

"I so understand why Jackie married Onassis," Diana muses to Richard Kay, a confidant as well as a reporter for the *Daily Mail*, about the former First Lady's controversial second marriage. "She felt alone and in need of protection—I often feel like that."

Diana dates a few men in her social set, some more seriously than others. One American billionaire, Teddy Forstmann, even proposes marriage.

A New York financier twenty years Diana's senior and owner of the private jet company Gulfstream, Forstmann isn't the most handsome of her suitors, but he's well traveled, well connected, and has loads of charisma. Plus *heaps* of money. Forstmann offers a tantalizing vision of the kind of financial security Aristotle Onassis brought to the widowed Jackie Kennedy—and, considering Forstmann's then potential presidential run, Diana deadpans to friends, "How do you follow being married to the Prince of Wales unless your next husband is the President of the United States?"

Teddy Forstmann is "funny, wise, kind, good at listening, and interested in other people," a friend says, but his popping off to a nightclub shortly after bringing up the subject is "a strange way to suggest marriage." Though Diana doesn't take his proposal seriously, the tycoon is besotted enough to continue sending her flowers every week.

For years.

Another American suitor comes calling via Hollywood. Actor-producer-director Kevin Costner approaches Diana with an intriguing offer: a chance to star in a sequel to his 1992 hit film, *The Bodyguard*.

Diana is a massive fan of the film, which details the romantic relationship that develops between a singer, played by pop diva and first-time actress Whitney Houston, and her bodyguard, played by Costner.

The sequel would feature his same character sparking a similar romantic relationship with a princess he's protecting.

"I'll tailor it for you if you're interested," Costner tells Diana of the script.

"I am interested," she replies.

Her son William is over the moon about the idea, which comes with a $10 million offer. "Mummy, *Kevin Costner*. Ten *million* dollars. You have to do it!"

This isn't the right moment, Diana tells Costner, though with considerable encouragement. "Look, my life is maybe going to become my own at some point. Go ahead and do this script and when it's ready I'll be in a really good spot."

She gives a similar answer to singer George Michael, her longtime friend, who calls that year on her birthday. They'd met in 1989 at the World AIDS Day concert in Wembley Stadium and had "clicked in a way that was a little bit intangible" immediately. The megastar considers the princess not only "a special, lovely person" and "the Elvis of compassion" but also "the only person that I knew who made me feel like an ordinary person."

Diana vents to Michael about the divorce details. "It's been pretty grim," she says. "Not a very loving, compassionate family, this one I'm leaving."

"I'd love to see you," the singer says. Diana would also love to share a chin-wag and a bottle of wine but knows how that could look.

"George, can I wait until this has all quietened down? Just lawyers. You know what they're like," she says. But how about him? Is life treating him kindly?

He's well, George Michael tells her. He's in love.

"Oh lucky you, lucky you" is Diana's response.

"Hello, it's William's Mum here," Diana speaks into a tape recorder. "Welcome to the family business. I rather suspect THAT got your attention! Anyway, brace yourself for a one-way chat."

She's lit upon the idea of making tapes for her sons' future wives, sharing some stories and warnings about joining royal life. "You have to be someone truly special. If you weren't, you wouldn't be my William's wife," she teases, but she's serious about her wishes for their happy future. "My fondest dream is for you and William to have a life filled with love and joy," she says. "Cherish your children for me. They carry my heart. Let them know I love them and will always watch over them."

She ends with a kiss and presses Stop on the recording.

Now to make a tape for Harry, too.

After more than fifteen years under the rule of the Palace, Diana finds reinvention an exhilarating prospect.

Assuming that without her HRH title the value of her patronage is too diminished to be of much use, she has dropped her involvement with more than a hundred charity organizations. She's kept only the six closest to her heart: the National AIDS Trust; Centrepoint, a charity benefiting the homeless; the English National Ballet; the Leprosy Mission (dear to her because of her friend Mother Teresa); Great Ormond Street Hospital for Children; and Royal Marsden Hospital.

It's at Royal *Brompton* Hospital where she first encounters Dr. Hasnat Khan, a heart surgeon originally from Pakistan.

"I think I've met my Mr. Wonderful," Diana tells friends. Khan, unlike anyone else she's known, has no interest in celebrity and is initially unmoved by Diana's charm offensive.

"It is doubtful if in her entire adult life Diana, the Princess of Wales, had ever made less of an impression on someone!" remarks the friend who witnessed their first meeting.

The two share a mutual sense of compassion, and that's how they eventually connect.

"I found my peace," Diana confesses to a friend. "He has given me all the things I need." She dreams of the two of them having a wonderful "normal" life together, calling it the most fulfilling relationship she's ever had.

She enjoys doing domestic chores for him, such as ironing his shirts, and when they go to the pub together, she brings out her favorite disguises: a long, dark wig, sunglasses, and jeans. Even venturing to the bar to order her own drinks and chat with the barman is an adventure. Far from being annoyed when they have to queue instead of being whisked into an establishment, Diana is delighted at the opportunity to meet so many other people in line. She tells another friend that she's discovered the joys of prepared dinners, "these very clever little meals that you just put in the microwave, and you put the timer on and press the button and it's done for you!"

Whatever their relationship needs, Diana's willing to do it—including exploring the possibility, since Hasnat is Muslim, of converting to Islam. But to Hasnat, even "a very good relationship with no personal problems" is insufficient to overcoming the obstacle the media presents.

"I did not want that sort of lifestyle," he tells her.

It will simply never work.

Chapter 53

Summer 1996
London

O h God, let's face it, even I have had enough of Diana now—and I *am* Diana," the princess admits to the *Daily Mirror* editor, Piers Morgan, whom she's invited to KP for an off-the-record lunch.

"It's been ridiculous recently, just one thing after another. But I can't stop the press writing about me, can I?" she says knowingly. "I meet a lot of ordinary people, and they are always so kind to me. They shout out things like, 'Eh, Di, I know what you're going through, luv,' and I laugh and think: 'If only you really knew. He's worrying about his allotment or whatever, and I've got things like the future of the monarchy on my mind.'"

The future of the monarchy may well come down to her son William. He's currently home from Eton, so Diana decides to bring him with her to the lunch. William has got to learn to handle the press.

"Would you mind awfully if William joins us?" she asks Morgan, flattering him with the follow-up: "I just thought that given you are a bit younger than most editors, it might be good for both of you to get to know each other."

"Yes, ma'am, I think I can stretch to allowing the future king to join us for lunch," replies the clearly delighted reporter.

Already six feet tall and with a floppy blond hairdo, William is good-looking, even with braces. A lanky teenager now, he's been thriving at Eton as "just one of the lads"—though occasionally distressing his long-time protection officers by slipping off for a bit of independence.

Diana's happy with his success in academics and sports, but to be honest, she's especially pleased at how well he's doing socially. She tells her friends, "There's no messing around at Eton about someone being heir to the throne. If you're not popular, charming, intelligent, or good at games, you're not going to rate, are you?"

William is relaxed and comfortable at the lunch with Morgan. He asks his mother for wine, all the while making her laugh by saying naughty things about Camilla.

"Oh, Mummy, it was hilarious," he says as he recounts a TV program he's seen, which put up "a photo of Mrs. Parker Bowles and a horse's head and asked what the difference was. The answer was that there isn't any!"

As for the queen, in her photo in yesterday's paper, "her hands looked like she'd been in the garden all day; they were all big and dirty!"

Mindful of going too far, Diana puts a stop to that.

"Sorry, Mummy, but it's true: Granny did look really funny."

Morgan jokes with them as well, admitting that the "hottest photo to get" is either Charles and Camilla, Diana and a new man, "and now, of course, William with his first girlfriend," eliciting groans.

"All the girls love a nice prince," Diana says teasingly.

The only moment of tension comes when Morgan asks Diana if she regrets having done the *Panorama* interview. "No, I wanted to do it, to put my side over," she says, then adds resolutely, "But I won't do it again. Once is enough. I have done what I set out to do."

"Did you think it was a good idea, William?" the reporter asks.

The prince flushes. "I'd rather not say."

Even though today's lunch conversation is off the record, William doesn't speak another word.

Chapter 54

January 1997
Angola

D iana arrives in Luanda, Angola, with a BBC documentary crew. She's nervous as she gets off the plane from London. This is her first visit to a war zone—Angola's only recently coming out of a decades-long civil war—and she's here as part of a Red Cross humanitarian effort to draw attention to the victims of land mines. Diana's motto is "If I'm going to talk on behalf of any cause, I want to go see the problem for myself and learn about it." Which brings her here to Africa.

It's not an official royal visit but a four-day working trip, and she's taken care to treat it that way, down to the clothes she's packed. No glamorous ball gowns or power suits, just T-shirts and jeans, chino trousers and sleeveless shirts. Other than two bodyguards, the only staff she's brought with her is her butler, Paul Burrell.

There's no stopping 123 journalists—and eight television crews—from following her. And that's the whole point.

"I've been given the gift to shine a light into the dark corners of the world, and get the media to follow me there, I have to use it," Diana tells friends. "I have all this media interest, so let's take it somewhere where they can be positive." Of the anti–land mine cause, she confides, "I thought it would help if I could be part of the team raising the profile around the world."

It does. "Nobody took a blind bit of interest in land mines until she came along," notes veteran *Daily Telegraph* reporter Lord William Francis Deedes, who goes by Bill. Now the media is following her in droves. "Three or four other planes landed and journalists just poured out—double or maybe triple the numbers we were expecting," comments a stunned aid worker. They've hosted other dignitaries in the past, "but what came off the plane for Diana was just unbelievable."

Her star power is necessary. The scene in Angola is more dire than what she's been prepped to expect, and Diana can't help but be shocked.

"Why are those children playing on that rubbish heap?" she asks, but it's a rhetorical question. It's obvious there's nowhere else for them to go. "I've never seen scenes like it before, I've never been in this environment," she muses as they pass a sea of tin-roofed shanties housing the poor outside the bombed-out capital. The heat—not to mention the smell—is insufferable.

"I'd read the statistics that Angola has the highest percentage of amputees anywhere in the world, that one person in every 333 had lost a limb, most through land mine explosions. But that hadn't prepared me for reality," she admits. "It's very humbling."

Yet Diana's also in her element. She feels the same urge to bring compassion and humanity to the victims here that she does with AIDS patients and the homeless.

Christina Lamb, foreign correspondent for the *Sunday Times*, admits she was originally cynical about Diana's motives. But while many of the "royal hacks" would clearly rather tail the princess to ski resorts or Caribbean islands—they're "not very keen on this new Diana going to difficult places," Lamb scoffs of her London colleagues—Diana herself is undaunted, radiating "a kind of aura that made people want to be with her, and a completely natural, straight-from-the-heart sense of how to bring hope to those who seemed to us to have little to live for."

It's particularly evident when Diana visits a ward full of child victims. She stops to talk gently with a seven-year-old girl who's been horrifically injured after stepping on a land mine, stroking the girl's hand and adjusting the sheet around her.

"The first thing she did was something instinctive. She made the child decent, covered her up. It was the thing a mother would do. She was concerned for the child's dignity," says photographer Arthur Edwards, there covering the expedition for the *Sun*.

After Diana leaves the ward, the little girl asks Lamb, Edwards's rival reporter, "Who was that?"

"She's a princess from England, far away," Lamb replies.

"Is she an angel?"

To the British politicians back home, Diana is not an angel but a "loose cannon," someone who is sticking her nose where she shouldn't.

Daily Telegraph reporter Bill Deedes defends her. "She has this yearning so many of our younger people have today to take a hand in the world's woes, to tie up wounds, to cherish the afflicted. If the mother of our future King," he writes, "feels drawn in that direction, no matter what form it takes, we should stop carping and doubting. We should be glad."

Diana herself pushes back. "I am a humanitarian—always have been, always will be."

It rattles her that the politicians can't see that.

"There's still unexploded bombs everywhere. Don't pick anything up. If you find you've wandered off the path, stand still."

Diana's about to go out onto a live minefield.

She tries to keep her nerves under control as Paul Heslop of the HALO Trust helps adjust her protective gear. The Britain-based Hazardous Areas Life-Support Organization, or HALO, has been working in the area to remove unexploded land mines.

He shows her where they've recently uncovered a mine and how they'll have her detonate it safely. "Just press a button and there will be a bang, and you will have got rid of one of these things."

"One down, 17 million to go," Diana says softly as she pushes the button.

The black smoke in the distance is proof they've been successful, but the whole area is still extremely dangerous.

Heslop feels the pressure as well. "I did not want to be on the front page of the news the next day as the man who'd blown up Princess Diana," he says.

Diana steels herself for the next bit. She walks out solo onto the active minefield for the planned photo op, keeping to the pathway that's been shown to her.

Except. Turns out the photographers weren't ready for Diana to walk the minefield when she did, and the Red Cross has noticed that only the HALO logo and not theirs is visible on her body armor. Could she do it again? they ask in jest.

Diana's well aware of the power these images will have back home. To everyone's amazement, she agrees to turn back around and walk it a second time.

"I never thought I would ever see a princess walk through a real mine-field," says photographer Michael Dunlea of the *Express*. "But when we asked her, she did it twice, for the cameras."

"I think once I made it, I would have left it," admits royal reporter Robert Jobson, "but there we are."

As for Diana, the images from Angola are seared into her memory. "If my visit has contributed in any way at all to highlighting this terrible issue," she writes to the British Red Cross, "then my deepest wish will have been fulfilled."

Chapter 55

May 1997
Eton

A s Parents' Day at Eton approaches, William makes a decree. Neither his mother nor his father is to attend.

Though they both behaved themselves at last year's occasion, this is the first since their official divorce, and, William has decided, they will simply attract too much attention.

"It is some comfort to ordinary mothers," opines the *Express,* "to know that even the world's style icon is an embarrassment to her son at a school's big day." He secretly invites Tiggy Legge-Bourke, his former nanny, instead. "William's liking for the horsey Legge-Bourke can be seen as a youngster's natural attraction for the naughty, fun-aunt type," the paper goes on to say, but with the exception of Camilla, William could hardly have picked a parental stand-in more likely to upset his mother.

Now twenty-nine, Tiggy's been the boys' nanny ever since 1993, when Diana and Charles were first separated, but the young woman quickly got under Diana's skin by referring to the princes as "my babies." Nor does Diana appreciate her less-than-vigilant attitudes to child minding. Just a few weeks back, on April 19, photos from up at Balmoral emerged showing Tiggy accompanying twelve-year-old Harry on a shoot: Harry was driving the Land Rover, without a seat belt, while Tiggy sat in the back smoking cigarettes.

There's jealousy at play here—both over the boys, who adore Tiggy, and over Charles, who has a warm relationship with the young woman. It's no question that the sporty Tiggy is more Charles's "type" than Diana has ever been. A family friend says, "The boys are crazy about her, but they don't want to upset Mummy. It's a bit of a problem."

But though Diana's crushed that William has invited Tiggy in her and Charles's place for Parents' Day, she's the one who declared the nanny uninvited from William's confirmation, back in March. The situation became so fraught that Tiggy quit. Is this her son's revenge? Very possibly.

When an article comes out in the *Sun* saying that Diana called Tiggy "thoughtless, idiotic and foolish" for attending the event at Eton, Diana is forced to issue an official statement refuting it, claiming, "Contrary to the reports appearing in the media this week, the Princess of Wales was more than pleased that Tiggy Legge-Bourke was able to be with Prince William on parents' day" and that Diana "has not uttered a single word either in public or privately about this occasion."

As if anyone will believe that.

Chapter 56

June 1997
New York City

T he very lifestyle that's so off-putting to Dr. Hasnat Khan is what's poised to bring Diana great success in Manhattan on the evening of June 25.

Christie's is auctioning off seventy-nine of Diana's gorgeous couture gowns, and William has masterminded the event.

"Mummy, you're running out of cupboard space and you're not going to wear any of those again," he tells her. "Why don't you have a sale of your dresses for charity? The Americans would go wild for this." Then he cheekily adds, "And I'll take ten percent!"

It's an ingenious idea.

Diana chooses the AIDS Crisis Trust and the cancer research fund at the Royal Marsden Hospital as recipients for proceeds and easily persuades the venerable Christie's auction house to participate. The firm even agrees to waive its commission fee. And William wasn't wrong about the lack of closet space—when Meredith Etherington-Smith, the creative director of Christie's International, arrives at KP to discuss with Diana which dresses to select, she's overwhelmed by the hundreds of gowns to choose from.

"You can see my problem," Diana remarks.

"I certainly can," replies Etherington-Smith.

Together, they cull through four hundred gowns to collect the most distinctive—the best known and most photographed—and settle on seventy-nine to bring to auction.

"It's been quite an event sorting out the frocks—memories flooding back and some excellent ones too," Diana remarks. "Yes, of course it is a wrench to let go of these beautiful dresses," she adds. "However, I am extremely happy that others can now share the joy that I had in wearing them."

The dresses chosen are a snapshot of the designers and fashions Diana's followed since her 1981 marriage. There are forty-nine garments by designer Catherine Walker, ten by Victor Edelstein, five by Bruce Oldfield, three by Murray Arbeid, two by David and Elizabeth Emanuel, two by Jacques Azagury, and eight by other designers—including the famous "revenge dress," by Christina Stambolian.

Comedian Joan Rivers, who attends an advance viewing in Manhattan, drily comments that as much fun as it is to tour the gowns here, "it's going to be even more fun next year to go to all the bar mitzvahs and see" them again. "All sorts of ladies all over Long Island are going to be very happy," she says.

Not only Long Island—auction attendees come from all over the country, particularly Florida, Texas, and California. "We just came to Never-Never Land to get a piece of the fairy tale," one buyer says. That's what people are buying: the celebrity connection. "Ownership counts," admit the auctioneers, just as it did in Jacqueline Kennedy Onassis's Sotheby's estate sale.

While Diana skips the actual auction—it's too gauche to be present in person—she monitors closely from afar. "She wants a fax so that the butler can bring it with the breakfast tray," said Etherington-Smith.

The sale far exceeds expectations, bringing in almost double the estimates. Among the notable sales are two Catherine Walker dresses—the pale-blue chiffon "Grace Kelly" dress with its matching stole, which Diana wore to Cannes, goes for $70,700, and her "Elvis" dress, a beaded white silk crepe sheath with a matching jacket, is bought by the Franklin Mint for $151,000. Christina Stambolian's asymmetric black silk crepe "revenge dress" goes for $74,000.

The most spectacular sale of the night is the "Travolta" dress, Victor Edelstein's midnight-blue velvet off-the-shoulder gown, worn by Diana at the White House in 1985, when she danced with John Travolta. Bidding tops out at an incredible $222,500, "breaking a previous Christie's record of $145,000 for a garment: the costume that Mr. Travolta himself wore in the movie 'Saturday Night Fever,'" reports the *New York Times*.

In all, the auction brings in over $3.25 million, averaging more than $41,000 per dress. It's an excellent result.

What's more, the princess "was quite amazing with dealing with the people who were serving her in any way, and there wasn't a soul at Christie's who didn't love her by the end of that year," says Diana's friend Christopher Balfour, head of Christie's UK.

"Isn't it wonderful? Three million dollars for some old frocks!!" Diana exclaims to William.

He's delighted. "So where's my ten percent?"

"It was stunning the amount made by the auction last week," Diana writes to her friend Liz Tilberis, editor of *Harper's Bazaar,* on July 1, 1997. "How typical of the Americans to be so totally generous. I can always rely on them!"

July 1 also happens to be Diana's thirty-sixth birthday, her first birthday since the divorce.

That evening she attends a charity event at the Tate Gallery, dressed in a black Chantilly-lace Jacques Azagury dress (a surprise gift from the designer that day), which she teams with an emerald choker.

"It's my birthday and I'm going to spend the evening with people I don't know and don't particularly like," she tells her hairdresser. "The only exception is my brother." Charles Spencer is her companion at the

Chanel-sponsored event. Diana loves Chanel designs but won't wear any pieces that display the logo. The linked *C*'s remind her of Charles and Camilla's initials.

She receives ninety bouquets of flowers from friends and admirers—including former beau Teddy Forstmann—but her favorite gift comes from twelve-year-old Harry, who gathers a group of his Ludgrove classmates together to sing "Happy Birthday" over the telephone.

An interview she gave to *Vanity Fair* runs on her birthday under the headline DIANA REBORN, including upbeat quotations from friends stating that she is finally "living her life the way she wants to live it." Italian fashion designer Gianni Versace is quoted as saying that Diana has "found herself—the way she wants to live" and that she exudes "a kind of serenity."

Diana herself says, "Nothing gives me more pleasure now than being able to love and help those in our society who are vulnerable," adding, "If I can contribute a little something, then I am more than content."

Is she lonely? Maybe. But signs point to thirty-six being a fresh new start.

Chapter 57

July 1997
Saint-Tropez, France

I want that room!"

Twelve-year-old Harry is not backing down from his argument with nine-year-old Omar Fayed. Omar's mummy told Harry and William that as their guests, the princes could pick any room they want on the Fayed family's new yacht, the *Jonikal*. But Omar disagrees.

There's no shortage of space aboard the five-star 195-foot yacht, with its crew of sixteen. But both boys want the same bedroom, and neither one is budging. Much door slamming ensues.

Up on deck, Omar's older sisters, eleven-year-old Camilla and fifteen-year-old Jasmine, roll their eyes. William, also just turned fifteen, is ignoring the bickering and reading a book. Mummy is lying on her towel and listening to her Walkman.

They're on the yacht in Saint-Tropez as guests of the Fayed family. Though they're not especially close, they've all known the family for a long time; Mohamed Al Fayed, who owns the Harrods department store, was good friends with Grandpa Johnnie, and he always sends them the coolest presents from "Uncle Mohamed" on their birthdays and at Christmas.

He's invited them out to his luxurious thirty-bedroom villa on the French Riviera, Castle St. Therese, before, but this is the first time Mummy has said yes. Aside from some petty squabbling with the other kids, Harry is having plenty of fun—sailing, swimming, Jet-Skiing, and just splashing about in the water. And he *is* still a bit of a mummy's boy. He enjoys having so much of her undivided attention on holiday, and how she comes and tucks them all in at night.

Harry's also endlessly curious about the yacht itself, not only the public areas but also the galley and the machine room, and he follows the crew about to—politely—inquire whether there's anything he can do to help. "He'd have climbed up a mast and manned the crow's nest, if we had one," an impressed crew member says.

In addition to the kids, Uncle Mohamed's adult son, Dodi, from his first marriage, is also here. He's younger than Papa but older than Mummy and is full of funny stories and generous gifts. Mummy seems to like him.

What none of them likes is the constant paparazzi—*again*. They try to hide by ducking down behind balcony railings or under towels.

"Who told them we were going to be here? Why can't they just leave us alone?" William yells before storming belowdecks to get away from their long-range lenses, and Mummy goes to ask the photographers to leave them in peace.

"William is freaked out!" she complains to the press, including—as usual—James Whitaker and Arthur Edwards. "Do you want the boys to grow up hating the lenses?" For good measure, she also chastises the journalists for being unfair to Mohamed Al Fayed, her "father's best friend." She rants a bit about going to live abroad, which she's been mentioning increasingly often.

The next day, though, William has a change of heart. "We mustn't let them spoil our holiday," he announces. "Let's just give them what they want."

So Harry, William, and Mummy decide to simply ignore the press and continue to enjoy themselves. Even Omar says the princes are "super delightful," and the whole trip has "lovely family vibes." Mummy declares their time in Saint-Tropez to be "very nearly perfect."

The idyll is cut short when Mummy gets a call about her friend Gianni Versace—whom Harry met at KP not too long ago, when his mother hosted a joint lunch for the designer and musician Elton John.

Gianni Versace has been killed.

Chapter 58

July 1997
Saint-Tropez, France

D iana sits on the deck of the *Jonikal,* gazing out to sea.
She can't believe that Versace has been murdered.
"Do you think they'll do that to me?" she asks one of Dodi's
bodyguards.

On July 15, a serial killer who harbored a malicious obsession shot Gianni Versace at point-blank range in front of his home in Miami Beach.

One week later, on July 22, thousands of mourners pack into the Duomo in Milan, Italy, to remember the fashion designer. Through his business acumen, Versace built a billion-dollar brand distinctive for its Medusa logo, but he was best remembered for his creativity, his curiosity, and his kindness.

"Gianni and I were like brothers," says Elton John. He and Sting perform a sorrowful rendition of "The Lord Is My Shepherd" to a tearful audience, including fellow designers Karl Lagerfeld and Giorgio Armani, celebrity clients Trudie Styler and Carolyn Bessette-Kennedy, *Vogue* editor Anna Wintour, and supermodel-muse Naomi Campbell.

Despite the bright colors and sequined fabrics Versace is known for, the whole congregation is wearing black, though the altar is draped in white and decorated with white flowers.

Diana wears pearls with her sheath dress and carries her namesake Versace handbag, the Lady Di. She first came to know the Italian fashion designer in 1991, when she was photographed for the cover of *Harper's Bazaar* in a stunning ice-blue Atelier Versace gown, and she found his bold and figure-conscious pieces just the jolt of sexiness she was looking for in her own wardrobe.

Beneath the ceiling, quarried from pink-white Candoglia marble and soaring to nearly 150 feet, Diana sits beside Elton John.

It's been more than sixteen years since she and the rock star met at Prince Andrew's twenty-first birthday party at Buckingham Palace, and they've been close friends ever since. Or at least they were until earlier this year, when they fell out over a joint project with Versace that Diana had pulled out of at rather the last moment this past February.

The designer had put together a coffee-table book titled *Rock and Royalty,* whose proceeds were earmarked for the Elton John AIDS Foundation, and Diana wrote a glowing foreword saying that "the optimism that shines from the pages of this book" is proof that the designer "loves mankind"—but she later withdrew her endorsement out of fear that some of the edgy photographs in the book might upset her delicate relationship with the queen. It certainly upends her relationship with John.

Yet as soon as Diana hears the tragic news of Versace's murder, she tracks John down at his home in Nice, not far from where she was vacationing in Saint-Tropez.

"I'm so sorry," she tells him. "It was a silly falling out. Let's be friends."

John accepts. The argument has gone on too long already, lingering simply because they've both been "too proud to pick up the phone" until the tragedy of Gianni Versace's death reconnects them.

At the service, Diana and John occasionally grasp hands. When a photographer snaps a photo of her leaning toward him in what appears to be a gesture of support, though, the princess is just looking for a mint.

"The warm words of comfort coming from her lips at that exact moment were actually: 'God, I'd love a Polo,'" Elton John says with a laugh.

It's a much-needed moment of levity during a somber occasion, and their reconciliation sparks a discussion of the ways in which Diana can support John's AIDS foundation and the ways he can support her land-mine charity.

Plans are made to have lunch the next time they're both in London.

Chapter 59

H appy birthday to you," sing five thousand people in unison. The crowd has gathered at the gates of Clarence House in honor of the Queen Mother's ninety-seventh birthday.

In a floral dress, hat, and a triple strand of pearls, the Windsor matriarch cuts a festive yet diminutive figure alongside her great-grandson Prince William, who at age fifteen already stands over six feet tall. Their destination is Hyde Park, where the King's Troop fires off a forty-one-gun birthday salute.

Fourteen royals, including Princes Charles and Harry, Queen Elizabeth, and Princess Margaret, return to Clarence House for a celebration in the Queen Mother's private gardens. Under the trees is a table set with Windsor heirloom china and crystal for a meal of lobster and lamb, with strawberries and cream for dessert. Charles, who has always been particularly close to his grandmother, takes the place of honor at her right.

When the moment arrives, courtesy of the Guild of Professional Toastmasters, to pop a nebuchadnezzar of Champagne—the equivalent of twenty bottles—the family raises a glass.

Diana, who on August 28 will mark the one-year anniversary of her divorce from Charles, is absent.

PART 5
The People's Princess

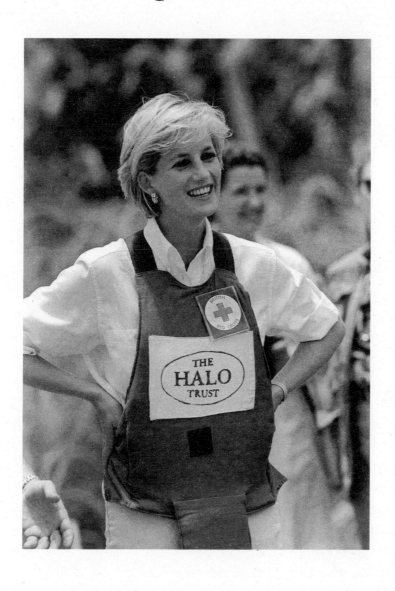

Chapter 60

August 7, 1997
En route from Portsmouth to Scotland

Aboard the royal yacht *Britannia,* the queen's annual summer cruise begins, charting a route toward the Western Isles of Scotland.

William and Harry stand at a guardrail with their cousins Peter and Zara Phillips, Princess Anne's children. This will be the four young Windsors' last chance to play aboard the five-story ship. After traveling more than a million nautical miles—and hosting the honeymoons of four royal couples, including Charles and Diana—the "floating palace" is set to be decommissioned on December 11, 1997.

"*Britannia* is the one place where I can truly relax," the queen says, though breaking news remains a constant.

One name dominates the headlines.

The *Express:* DIANA'S CRUISE WITH PLAYBOY: PRINCESS SPENDS FIVE IDYLLIC DAYS WITH SON OF HARRODS BOSS.

The *Daily Mail:* DIANA: IT'S A REAL ROMANCE.

The *Daily Mirror:* DIANA: I'M SO IN LOVE.

The *Sun:* ROMANTIC MEAL IN NEW LOVE'S LONDON FLAT—THEN FARE-WELL KISS BEFORE BOSNIA.

As the papers engage in frenzied bidding wars for photos of Diana and

Dodi's Saint-Tropez holiday, reporters churn out features and opinion pieces.

"The term 'playboy' may have been invented" for Dodi Fayed, writes *Evening Standard* correspondent Gervase Webb. "If I were the royal family," the columnist continues, "I'd be pulling the remaining hair out by now."

But the more significant headline is from two days ago: DEFIANT DIANA OFF TO BOSNIA. She's on a humanitarian trip to visit land-mine victims in Bosnia and Herzegovina.

Prime Minister Tony Blair likely approves—his recent defeat of Tory PM John Major for the top office came in part because of Major's opposition to a land-mine ban.

"Things can only get better," the Labour leader promised in his spring campaign.

A promise they'd all like to believe. As Diana flies east in a private jet borrowed from financier George Soros, the *Britannia* sails on.

Chapter 61

August 8, 1997
Bosnia and Herzegovina

K en Rutherford—an American who cofounded the Landmine
Survivors Network, based in Washington, DC, after losing his
legs in Somalia in 1993—has invited Diana on a private tour of
Tuzla. The city in northeastern Bosnia and Herzegovina is known for its
deposits of rock salt…and the destruction wrought by cluster bombs
during the three and a half years of the Bosnian War.

Diana's Sarajevo welcoming party includes the British ambassador
plus sixty reporters and photographers there to document her visits with
land-mine victims.

The exact scope of her work is widely debated, but Diana is clear: "If I
must define my role," she's said, "I'd rather use the word 'messenger.'"

In Tuzla, the charred ruins and the conditions endured by people
struggling to survive in war-torn cities are deeply distressing. Diana asks
her driver to stop the convoy of security and press vehicles. "I have seen
lots of poverty but I have never seen such devastation," she says. "I've
never been to a war zone like this before."

The seriousness of her work here doesn't deter the press from probing
further into the details of her romantic life.

"What is the situation with Dodi?" a Reuters reporter asks during a walk through Tuzla.

When Diana pretends not to hear, other journalists repeat the question until it's impossible to ignore. She stares coldly and cuts the tour short.

She visits a tiny village, its distant backdrop the 1984 Winter Olympics stadium, where British skating duo Jayne Torvill and Christopher Dean won a gold medal for ice dancing to Maurice Ravel's *Bolero*. The structure is now scarred with bullet holes sustained during the Siege of Sarajevo, the same conflict that's left behind active land mines. It's only been two years since those Olympics structures were used as battlements during the fighting.

"What's all the hassle?" a child asks his friend.

"Oh," the boy answers, "some Diana is moving in."

Only briefly. The princess works fifteen-hour days, hugging wounded children who've lost their limbs and meeting a paraplegic volleyball team. Despite the grueling schedule and the hassles from the press about her love life, the princess's sly sense of humor never dulls. As he did in Angola, veteran *Telegraph* journalist and anti–land mine activist Bill Deedes accompanies her on the trip. In between meetings with land-mine victims, she invites the deadline-bound reporter to "have a gin and tonic"—only to produce bottled water.

Of their time visiting the Bosnian land-mine victims, Deedes writes, "None of them was quite clear who she was, but all had long and harrowing stories."

"I have a real feeling of closeness with the most humble people," Diana says. "My father always taught me to treat everyone as an equal. I've always done so, and I'm sure that Harry and William will follow in my footsteps."

On August 10, after three days in Bosnia, Diana again boards George Soros's jet for the return flight to London. The plane is stocked with newspapers.

Splashed across the *Mirror* is a blurry full-page long-lens photo of a swimsuited Diana and Dodi embracing on the deck of a yacht. This photograph, instantly dubbed "The Kiss," is said to have earned Italian cameraman Mario Brenna $1 million. Inside, the paper touts, are "10 pages of the most sensational pictures ever."

Throughout the flight, Diana pages through the papers as her butler, Paul Burrell, sits by her side, offering soothing words.

The *Express* reveals a secret trip to Paris. There, on July 26, Diana and Dodi toured the Villa Windsor, a fourteen-room limestone mansion in the Bois de Boulogne. The Duke and Duchess of Windsor had lived there in exile following his 1936 abdication as Britain's King Edward VIII to marry American divorcée Wallis Simpson.

There's fevered speculation that the house, now under fifty-year lease by Dodi's father, Mohamed Al Fayed, could become a marital home for Diana and the Harrods heir should she choose to reside abroad.

Almost no one is discussing the work she's doing in Bosnia. Even the papers that mention it are only using it as an excuse to compare it with her earlier holiday.

"This is the real Diana," the *Express* proclaims the following morning, contrasting details of the bidding war for Diana's Mediterranean vacation photos with images of Diana standing in a cemetery near Sarajevo with a mother who'd lost her son in the Bosnian War.

"Diana consoled her the way only Diana can," says an aide to the princess. "When the woman left the graveyard, she was smiling."

Diana turns the page to see a dismaying spread. Above an article quoting Dodi as saying that his eight-month 1986 marriage to Californian model Suzanne Gregard "put me off the institution for life" is a mocked-up wedding photo of Diana in a white gown and pearls and Dodi in morning dress. The fantasy ceremony takes place on July 1, 1998, with John Travolta and Mother Teresa among the guests. The honeymoon destination: the Ritz Paris.

Chapter 62

August 12, 1997
Aberdeenshire, Scotland

I n the sunshine near the River Dee, the press waits in a state of anticipation. It's been sixteen years since a photo call has been held on
the queen's estate. The last time was in August of 1981, when the
newly wed Prince and Princess of Wales stood near where fifteen-year-
old Prince William now smiles shyly into seventy cameras.

He's not alone on the stony riverbank. Casually dressed in collared shirts
and belted trousers, William and Harry stand beside a kilted Prince Charles.

Photographer Jayne Fincher deems twelve-year-old Harry the more
outgoing of the two brothers. While Harry smiles brightly, a blushing
William keeps his head down. Still, the very act of his stepping forward
impresses tough critics of the royal family.

"This young man is a winner," says a senior American TV producer
looking on as William throws stones into the river and plays with his
Labrador, Widgeon. "He has the good looks of a film star, a young Robert
Redford. He will go down great guns in the USA."

The royal family could use the boost.

A new poll shows a stark drop in public support for the royals:
down from 70 to 50 percent since Charles and Diana's separation and
divorce.

Chapter 63

August 14, 1997
London

D iana denies potential wedding plans with Dodi. "Absolutely not," she tells Richard Kay of the *Daily Mail*. And to the *Express:* "I haven't taken such a long time to get out of one bad marriage to get into another one."

She is not believed.

"The Dodi and Di saga is set to run and run," the *Express* declares. "But what on earth could happen next?"

A week later, Diana ducks down in an old Volvo, her driver, Colin Tebbutt, at the wheel and on the watch for paparazzi. Diana's returned at midday from five days cruising the Greek islands with her friend Rosa Monckton. Now, after a few hours at home in Kensington Palace, she's off again to Battersea Heliport, hidden behind windows covered in coats.

She waits with Tebbutt outside the facility, in southwest London. For twenty minutes, there is no sign of Dodi.

When his Range Rover appears, surrounded by guards on motorbikes, Tebbutt is blamed for running behind. Diana's driver snaps, "You were late. She is Her Royal Highness the Princess of Wales. I will take her away. She'll come with me and you won't have a princess."

The Harrods helicopter flies forty miles to a private airfield, where the Harrods Gulfstream awaits. Diana and Dodi are off on a weeklong holiday, their third together in forty days.

The green-and-gold private plane arrives in Nice just before midnight. Under tight security, Diana and Dodi transfer from a luxury launch to the *Jonikal*. A crew of twelve sets sail for Saint-Tropez, then south for Saint-Jean-Cap-Ferrat, southern Italy, and Sardinia.

Paparazzi helicopters scour the Mediterranean in search of Diana aboard the *Jonikal*. "Shoot them down!" Dodi shouts when they fly overhead.

Back in June, Diana gave a wide-ranging interview to the French newspaper *Le Monde* from Kensington Palace. It comes out on August 27, dubbing her "the big-hearted princess."

Reaction to the piece is swift and intense. Diana is attacked for crossing the line of royal neutrality when she praised the Labour party's anti–land mine stance and condemned the Tory position as "hopeless."

"The press is ferocious," she says in the interview. "It pardons nothing. It looks only for mistakes. Every intention is twisted, every gesture criticized."

As for her future in Britain, "I think in my position any sane person would have left long ago. But I cannot. I have my sons."

And her causes. "I will run to whoever calls me in distress," Diana is quoted as saying. "I work by instinct. That is my best adviser."

From her stateroom, Diana calls Kensington Palace and postpones her homecoming. "I'm not going to come back into a barrage of press. I'll come back Sunday."

She'll wait out the controversy far away. With Dodi.

Chapter 64

August 28, 1997
Sardinia

On a sandy beach in Sardinia, butler René Delorme dons an evening suit and bow tie to serve Champagne and caviar.

Diana and Dodi toast to a significant anniversary. One year ago today, Diana officially became divorced from the Prince of Wales.

———⊗⊗⊗———

"When are you coming home?" Diana's butler, Paul Burrell, asks her on Friday.

"I'm coming home on Sunday, Paul," she confirms. "I'm just bored. I am on this boat, it's freezing cold downstairs, it's boiling hot out. I need to come home."

Diana uses her satellite phone to make more calls.

"You're not doing anything silly," her friend Annabel Goldsmith asks, "like getting married?"

"Don't worry," Diana answers. "I need another marriage like a bad rash on my face."

⟨⟨∞⟩⟩

Diana breakfasts aboard the *Jonikal*. René Delorme senses her excitement at going home. All she can talk of is seeing her boys, who've been on holiday with their father and grandparents at Balmoral for the last few weeks.

She would prefer to go straight to her sons, but she and Dodi will take an overnight in Paris first.

The Harrods Gulfstream takes off from Olbia, Sardinia, and two hours later touches down at Le Bourget airport, northeast of Paris, where Fayed family bodyguards Kieran "Kez" Wingfield and Trevor Rees-Jones usher Dodi and Diana into a waiting Mercedes. A Range Rover driven by Henri Paul, deputy chief of security at the Ritz Paris, follows behind with staff and luggage.

Photographers on motorbikes immediately give chase. Dodi tells the chauffeur, Philippe Dorneau, to speed up and lose them. Diana vehemently disagrees.

She's fearful that the speeding Mercedes feels unsafe. "Slow down!" she screams at the driver.

Finally, they evade their pursuers and Dorneau resumes Dodi's intended itinerary. Instead of the Ritz Paris, in City Center, he brings Diana on a second visit to Villa Windsor.

As soon as the Mercedes stops in front of the fourteen-room mansion, Diana opens the rear passenger door and steps onto the cobblestone driveway.

Then she enters the building alone. Her cheeks are flushed, her features drawn. She looks unhappy. Maybe afraid.

Dodi remains in the car with the chauffeur and bodyguard Rees-Jones. It's clear they're all rattled, perhaps for different reasons.

Rees-Jones has told the villa's security chief, Ben Murrell, that "Dodi always came up with his own plans which basically meant problems for the security people."

Dodi follows her inside. His father maintains much of the house as a

Windsor museum, keeping only the seven rooms on the top floor as a private residence.

The separation is meaningless to Diana. She looks away from the glittering golden mirrors lining the walls. From her point of view, all she sees here is the former home of her ex-husband's great-uncle, the Duke of Windsor, best remembered as the defiant King Edward VIII, who abdicated the throne and was exiled for love.

The rooms are like a mausoleum.

They're full of ghosts.

After twenty-eight minutes, Diana has had enough. She'll never live at Villa Windsor.

Chapter 65

August 30, 1997
Paris

I 've never spoken to a princess before," says Claude Roulet, nervous
assistant to the hotel president.

"Just call me Diana," she says, placing a reassuring hand on his
arm.

Dodi's father owns the Ritz, so they're assured its best accommodation.
The 2,600-square-foot first-floor Imperial Suite has hosted Winston
Churchill, President Richard Nixon, and Madonna.

Immense gold knobs open a fifteen-foot-high front door into rooms
with twenty-foot ceilings painted in trompe-l'oeil and furnished with
Empire pieces in velvet, satin, and gold. The main bedroom replicates
Marie Antoinette's at Château de Versailles.

It's *wonderful*.

Diana strolls through the sunlit rooms, the tall windows overlooking
Place Vendôme. Dodi has matters to attend to, so she makes a late afternoon hair appointment—and a few phone calls.

She reaches the friend she calls Ricardo—*Daily Mail* reporter Richard
Kay—as he's walking through the London shopping district of Knightsbridge. While he's window-shopping, Diana urgently says, "I'm getting
out of all public duties."

It's a decision she's reached—and reversed—at various points, but she simply cannot endure another controversy like the one over this week's *Le Monde* piece.

"I've just had enough of the constant criticism."

She turns the conversation to William and Harry before telling Kay, "Unplug your phone and get a good night's sleep."

She calls Balmoral, catches her sons in the midst of a game with their cousins.

They don't talk long. She'll see them tomorrow.

At seven thirty, Diana and Dodi go shopping on the Champs-Élysées. Harry's thirteenth birthday is two weeks away, and he's asked for a PlayStation.

I worry about my sons. Am I a good mother? I don't see them for months and then I spoil them rotten.

Sometimes I'd like a time machine.

When they return to the Ritz a few minutes before ten, they discover that thirty cameramen have been waiting for hours near the front entrance.

Henri Paul, deputy chief of hotel security, begins negotiating with the paparazzi, trying to clear them off.

He brings a black Mercedes around to the back entrance, where Diana and Dodi are standing, holding hands.

It's 12:17 a.m. when they climb inside the car.

"There were too many photographers after Diana and Dodi," says fellow cameraman Andre Godeaux, who declines to follow the couple.

"I did not see any point in getting involved."

Chapter 66

August 31, 1997
Paris

D r. Frederic Mailliez drives into the tunnel under the Pont de l'Alma on his way home from a friend's party. It's 12:26 a.m.

The tunnel is filling with smoke.

It must be a fire, Mailliez thinks.

Then he sees a smoldering hunk of twisted steel sitting on the opposite roadway. The car's front has been crushed to the point where it's nearly half its original size. The front windshield is demolished, pebbled glass scattered everywhere across the ground. A car horn is blaring.

He pulls over and sticks a flashing blue light onto his car roof, identifying him as an emergency worker with SOS Médecins, a company that provides private 24-7 medical care and emergency medical services around Paris.

As he draws closer, Mailliez quickly assesses the situation.

Four passengers—three men and a woman on her knees on the back floor, trapped between the front and rear seats. The man in the front passenger seat is breathing.

Mailliez runs back to his car to call emergency services.

"There's been an accident on the Pont de l'Alma," he says. "Four people. Two dead, two severely injured. I need two emergency ambulances."

The woman in the back seat is almost unconscious and is having difficulty breathing. She's not saying much, just moaning about how much she hurts. He realizes the woman is speaking English.

"An ambulance will soon be here," Mailliez tells her. He tries to comfort her as best he can. "Everything will be okay."

Flashbulbs are going off behind him. There are ten, maybe as many as fifteen, photographers moving around, taking pictures of him and the car.

Why are there so many journalists?

⸺◦◦◦⸺

At 12:32 a.m., firefighter Sergeant Xavier Gourmelon arrives at the scene with his ten-man team aboard two fire trucks from the nearby Marlar fire and ambulance station.

He approaches the wreckage. The driver appears to be dead, but the passenger next to him is alive and trying to speak despite gruesome facial injuries.

"Where is she?" the man says in English. "Where is she?"

"None of my men speak English," Gourmelon tells him. "It's best for you to keep still and not move. Don't worry, we're looking after everyone."

In the back seat is a woman with blond hair. She's moving a bit, not much, but she's alive. There's no blood on her, but Gourmelon notices she has a slight injury on her right shoulder.

The man splayed across the back seat isn't moving at all.

"My God," the woman says in English. "What's happened?"

Gourmelon holds her hand as a colleague fits her with a cervical collar. Her breathing is normal.

"My God," the woman says again. She moves her head, taking in the devastation surrounding her.

⸺◦◦◦⸺

The first ambulance arrives at 12:40 a.m.

Mailliez introduces himself to Dr. Jean-Marc Martino and gives his assessment of the woman in the back seat of the car.

The young woman, Mailliez believes, *has the best chance of coming out all right.*

Martino conducts an emergency assessment of the casualties, then turns his attention to the blond woman.

His eyes widen in recognition.

It's Lady Di.

The princess is speaking, but she's not making sense.

"Leave me alone," she says. "Leave me alone."

Martino specializes in anesthetics and intensive-care treatment. He sees that Diana has suffered an upper limb fracture—a complication for removing her from the vehicle.

She goes into cardiac arrest as soon as they move her.

Martino intubates her, and Gourmelon administers cardiac massage.

Diana's heart starts beating again.

They transfer her into the ambulance, but her blood pressure is dropping, indicating internal bleeding. When Martino deems it stable, the ambulance heads off to Pitié-Salpêtrière Hospital.

Gourmelon returns to the fire station and calls his wife, despite the late hour. "She was asleep and I told her about the accident and Princess Diana. I said that she had suffered a cardiac arrest but I'd managed to revive her."

En route, Martino orders the ambulance stopped. Diana's blood pressure is dropping again. *Something abnormal is going on.*

Chapter 67

August 31, 1997
Aberdeenshire, Scotland

T he hour is approaching 1:00 a.m. when Sir Michael Jay, Britain's ambassador to France, phones Queen Elizabeth, Prince Philip, and Prince Charles with the news that Diana has been involved in a car crash in Paris.

Adviser Julia Cleverdon helps Charles decipher the early morning tangle of communications between the prince's team at Kensington Palace and the castle's first-floor family quarters. KP is in direct contact with the London papers, which are working their connections with Paris emergency services.

Charles is told at first that Diana has broken her arm.

He must visit her in the hospital.

While the queen roots herself to the telephone, Charles restlessly paces the castle halls.

What to tell his sons? And when?

BBC airwaves

"May the saints welcome you to paradise," a somber male voice intones.

BBC One's late-night broadcast is the French New Wave film *Borsalino*, starring Jean-Paul Belmondo as a Marseilles gangster who steals the affections of his rival's girlfriend, then attends his funeral.

At 1:45 a.m., the on-screen priest finishes his scripted eulogy.

BBC News breaks in with an urgent announcement. "We are getting reports that Diana, Princess of Wales, has been badly injured in a car accident. As yet, the report is unconfirmed."

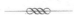

Balmoral

At 3:45 a.m., Robin Jarvin, assistant private secretary to the queen, receives from Sir Michael Jay shattering news he's duty-bound to convey to Charles.

"Sir, I am very sorry to have to tell you, I've just had the ambassador on the phone. The princess died a short time ago."

"Why?" Charles asks. *Why?*

The queen and Charles agree—while William and Harry are sleeping in their beds, the television must be removed from the princes' sitting room.

He wakes them at 5:15 a.m.

Paris

A reporter broadcasts from the street, speaking quickly, intensely. "She had a serious wound to the left ventricle. They tried cardiac massage, but it was no good."

"We could not revive her," anesthesiologist Dr. Bruno Riou of Pitié-Salpêtrière Hospital tells the Associated Press.

—⚮—

Canary Wharf

Former prime minister Margaret Thatcher sends a private message to Charles Moore, editor of the *Daily Telegraph:* "Don't forget, in everything you publish, that her boys will read and remember what you say."

Moore can count on the words of Bill Deedes. The eighty-four-year-old newsman is one of the few to have earned Diana's trust.

He assigns Deedes to make a broadcast for the BBC and then start writing a 2,500-word profile. Five minutes from their headquarters, at Television Centre, Deedes's driver gets a call. "Does Lord Deedes know that Diana is dead?"

—⚮—

France

"This is the most tragic and senseless death," says Elton John from his home in Nice. He just saw Diana in Italy, at the funeral of their mutual friend Gianni Versace. He's also less than fifteen miles from Monte Carlo, where in two weeks it will be the twenty-fifth anniversary of Princess Grace's fatal car crash.

"Her death reminds me of Princess Grace," Pascale Tremblay, a waitress in a Parisian bakery, remarks. Diana "was a truly magnificent woman, a super human being. She was as good as she was beautiful."

—⚮—

Canary Wharf

At the *Telegraph* offices, Bill Deedes's fingers are propelled by memories, flying across the keys of his typewriter. It was only three weeks earlier that he and Diana toured the land-mine sites of Bosnia and Herzegovina; only six months ago, they were together in Angola.

After their trip to Bosnia, Diana had sent him a thoughtful thank-you gift via US diplomatic courier—six of Deedes's favorite Brooks Brothers shirts, perfectly sized.

Today, his shirt cloth is stained with tears.

Diana, Deedes writes, was an adored "injured angel" who to photographers "became the pot of gold at the end of the rainbow."

London

The city wakes to the news that Diana is gone.

"She was a Marilyn Monroe," royal historian David Starkey comments. "She was a James Dean. She died like James Dean."

Chapter 68

August 31, 1997
Aberdeenshire, Scotland

W hat do you say to children?" Charles asks his adviser Julia Cleverdon. "How do you explain this?"

It's plain to Cleverdon that the prince is in agony.

So is she. Two weeks earlier, she faced these same impossible questions when she lost her husband, John Garnett, on holiday in Greece. In an instant, she became a single mother to their daughters, Charity and Victoria.

Now it's Charles's turn to plunge into the unknown.

Crathie Kirk, Aberdeenshire

"If you are a Christian and your mother has been killed," the Queen Mother tells her lady-in-waiting, "it is a comfort going to church."

The matriarch is riding in the first of three royal limousines driving to the eleven thirty Sunday service at nearby Crathie, the Scots-Gothic granite church on a hilltop whose cornerstone was laid by Queen Victoria in 1893.

Three passengers are inside the second car. Charles, dressed in his traditional Rothesay Hunting kilt, sits between William and Harry, wearing dark suits and black neckties.

The queen's told her grandsons, "We are going to pray for your mummy's soul."

Two hundred onlookers watch as the queen and Prince Philip emerge from the third car, dressed in mourning black.

Through their private entrance, off the south transept, the royals enter and take seats in carved wooden pews, the one closest to the front embellished with the imperial monogram of Queen Victoria.

William is hoping to "pray to Mummy."

He's not alone. One hundred local parishioners bow their heads as visiting minister Reverend Adrian Varwell and Robert Sloan, the Queen's Chaplain in Scotland, begin the service.

Though during the hour of worship Diana's name remains unspoken, its three syllables are on everyone's lips and in their hearts.

Near the altar is a stained-glass rendering of Saint Margaret, mother of three kings. Every detail in the church is a reminder.

William, sitting beside Harry, comforts his younger brother as the reverends speak.

"We remember all those who at this time need to know your presence," Reverend Sloan says. "All those whose lives are darkened by tragedy and grief need to know more than human comfort and friendship."

After the service, the queen acknowledges the crowd outside Crathie with a tiny smile and a wave.

Reverend Sloan observes Charles and the boys as being "remarkable, very, very good indeed, despite what must have been going on in their lives and hearts in the last six hours."

His fervent wish for Charles: "That there is hope. Whatever happens in the world, there is still a tomorrow."

The Queen Mother worries for her great-grandsons. "Those poor little boys. I don't think they have taken it on board yet."

Chapter 69

August 31, 1997
Sedgefield

P eople everywhere, not just here in Britain, kept faith with Princess Diana," says Prime Minister Tony Blair.

Dressed in a dark suit and black tie, he's standing in the rain outside St. Mary Magdalene Church, where he's attending Sunday services with his family.

Blair's conversations this morning with the queen and Prince Charles are private. The words he's about to speak belong to the world.

"They liked her, they loved her, they regarded her as one of the people. She was the People's Princess and that is how she will stay, how she will remain in our hearts and memories for ever."

RAF Northolt

RAF squadron commander Graham Laurie is woken at 2:00 a.m. by his son, who's come home from a party with news of the fatal car crash.

Laurie, who's flown Princess Diana hundreds of times aboard the Queen's Flight, reports to RAF Northolt. Prince Charles has scheduled a 10:30 a.m. flight to Paris.

The squadron is prepared. They've recently been trained in responding to a death in the royal family, though the model was the ninety-seven-year-old Queen Mother, not the thirty-six-year-old princess.

The engineers on base don't have much time to retrofit the cargo hold of the royal squadron's BAe 146 with the flat bed and ball bearings needed to transport Diana's coffin.

Calcutta

Mother Teresa shares memories of Diana, who she says was "a very good friend, in love with the poor, a very good wife, a very good mother. She was very concerned for the poor. She was very anxious to do something for them. That is why she was close to me."

Pitié-Salpêtrière Hospital, Gascon Cordier Pavilion

A policeman watches over "Patricia," the code name Diana's been given on her chart, in honor of a patron saint of Naples who died young after sharing her wealth with the poor.

The officer sees "her pale face, her eyes closed," lids seemingly "made up with a night blue."

The head nurse, Beatrice Humbert, tells investigators, "I was waiting for a smile, and then I thought, 'We'll never see this smile again.'"

Butler Paul Burrell retrieves an object from the suitcase he's brought this morning from Kensington Palace.

He shows nurse Jeanne Lecorcher a rosary. "These were a gift to the princess from Mother Teresa," Burrell says, extending the beads.

The nurse eases them into Diana's clasped hands.

Burrell adds a photo of her sons that he's found in her handbag.

Prince Charles arrives, along with Diana's sisters, Lady Jane Fellowes and Lady Sarah McCorquodale. Sir Michael Jay, British ambassador to France, shows them into the room.

Charles, Jane, and Sarah are given a few minutes alone with Diana.

Jane can't stop her tears.

"She was religious in putting on her seat belt. Why didn't she put it on?" Sarah asks, then answers herself. "We'll never know."

An Anglican priest leads a recitation of the Lord's Prayer.

It's time to bring Diana home.

By late afternoon, mourners have amassed in the streets outside the hospital.

"People want to see her and they should," Charles tells the police. "There is no reason to sneak out. We have to leave normally."

In breathless silence, thousands watch as members of France's Republican Guard carry the coffin into a black-and-silver hearse.

The crowd is awed. Shouts of "Diana, we love you!" come through a spontaneous wave of applause. "We'll never forget you!"

En route to RAF Northolt

"It all seems unreal," Charles says to Sir Michael Jay on the drive to the military airport southwest of Paris.

Pilot Graham Laurie calculates the flight time and route of the RAF BAe 146. Aircraft "spotters" are certainly monitoring civil air traffic control frequencies. He opts for secure ultra-high-frequency military radio.

We need to keep it as discreet as we can, he thinks just before takeoff. As always.

Laurie recalls the last time Charles and Diana traveled together on the Queen's Flight—the four-day "togetherness tour" to South Korea, in November of 1992, the month before the royal couple separated.

Then there was gloom.

Today there is sadness.

But there is also precision.

Guided by the air traffic controllers, Laurie lands the plane at 7:00 p.m., exactly the time Prime Minister Tony Blair and eight RAF pall-bearers have been called to the tarmac.

By order of the queen, Diana's coffin is draped in the Royal Standard, the red-blue-and-gold flag representing the sovereign and the United Kingdom.

Charles bears witness, then boards another flight, which will take him to Balmoral and his grieving sons.

Chapter 70

August 31, 1997
Los Angeles

Virgin Atlantic chief Richard Branson is on a return flight to London when the news reaches him.

"I couldn't believe what the captain was saying. I was completely shocked and very upset, as were all the other passengers. My thoughts are now with her family and the Fayeds."

Tom Cruise describes to CNN the through-traffic road, two hundred yards long, that curves deep beneath the Pont de l'Alma.

"I've actually been in that same tunnel being chased by paparazzis," he says of the conditions Diana faced in her final moments. "They run lights, and they chase you and harass you the whole time. It happens all over the world, and it has certainly gotten worse."

Kevin Costner has wrapped filming in the Pacific Northwest for his post-apocalyptic thriller, *The Postman.* He's busy editing the film for Christmas release when he receives a package.

Inside is the script for his next big film: the sequel to *The Bodyguard*, costarring Princess Diana.

Dublin, Lansdowne Road

U2's lead singer, Bono, walks onstage wearing a cape.

Since last night's show, the first of two in Dublin, the world has changed. Waves of emotion swirl through the crowd of forty thousand.

The band plays one long set and eight encores—including "MLK," written in honor of slain civil-rights leader Dr. Martin Luther King Jr. "Sleep tonight and may your dreams be realized," Bono sings as Diana's face appears on the screen behind him.

He then tells the crowd, "I didn't expect the news would have affected me this much."

Everyone feels the same devastation. All around the stadium is the glow of lighters sparked and raised in tribute.

The audience departs to a voice from the past. Earlier today, Bono chose Elton John's 1974 hit about Marilyn Monroe, "Candle in the Wind," to be the exit music playing over the loudspeakers. John's homage to a shining star set too soon perfectly evokes the fresh tragic loss of the newly crowned "People's Princess."

"Like Elton John and Bernie Taupin's Norma Jean (Marilyn Monroe)," writes Jonathan Glancey, cultural critic for the *Guardian*, "Diana, Princess of Wales lived her life like a candle in the wind, never knowing, it seems, who to turn to when the rain set in."

With the identical lyric, the *Express* captions a full-page photo of Diana dressed in summer whites, looking chic and carefree in swept-back hair and dark sunglasses.

Chapter 71

A t St. James's Palace, Charles's London home, thousands of mourners fill four condolence books with their thoughts about Diana, lying at rest in the palace's Chapel Royal.

⸙

The royal family remains in Balmoral, but in Diana's memory, a woman visiting from Dallas puts her tour ticket for Buckingham Palace away.

"It would be too disrespectful to go into the Palace," she decides. "This is like when Kennedy died. No one alive today will ever forget anything about this day. I feel almost intrusive being here as a foreigner but Diana was a Princess for the world, not just Britain."

⸙

In Knightsbridge, London, Harrods lowers its flag to half-mast.

⸙

The queen consults with the Spencer family, who believes that instead of an official state occasion, a "people's" funeral is "right and proper." The queen announces that at 11:00 a.m. on September 6, the ceremony at Westminster Abbey "will be a unique event for a unique person."

The names of two thousand invited guests are largely drawn from Diana's Christmas-card list, including Peter Hubble, manager of a Knightsbridge jewelry store the princess frequented.

Well, she's gone. Nobody knows me now, he keeps thinking—until the moment he receives his invitation by phone, which leaves him "shaking with emotion."

Prince Philip is on a conference call with government relations directors, planning Diana's funeral. Memos from Downing Street are tracking costs, projecting that "something around £5 million will be the final figure—scarcely a deck on the Royal Yacht."

"It's about the boys," Prince Philip says, his voice anguished. "They've lost their mother."

TV cameras will be barred from Diana's burial.

"This part of the day will be entirely private," says the princess's brother, Earl Spencer. "Only immediate members of Diana's family will be in attendance for a very brief ceremony, to be conducted by a priest who is a family friend."

Preparations are under way at the vault in the Spencer Chapel at Church of St. Mary the Virgin, Northamptonshire. It's been the family burial ground for four centuries and twenty generations, from Sir John in 1522 to Diana's father, Johnnie, the eighth Earl Spencer, in 1992.

Diana rests in the airtight lead-lined coffin of a royal, designed to preserve her body as long as one year.

⊸⊸⊸

"He is very patriotic about this country," spokesperson Michael Cole says of Mohamed Al Fayed, who arranges for the burial of his forty-two-year-old son, Dodi, at Brookwood Cemetery, twenty-five miles south of London. In a coffin draped with black fabric, Dodi is buried in a simple, private Islamic ceremony.

⊸⊸⊸

A city policeman is unused to the changed soundscape. "Listen to that," he says. "It's so quiet. I've never heard it like this. Never."

All thoughts are on William and Harry.

The *Times* publishes a heartfelt editorial by Libby Purves. "I propose that the Princes William and Harry should now be a taboo subject for all media until each is 18," she writes. "No insulting platitudes about 'the grieving process,' no opera glasses trained on their faces at the funeral, and in the months to come, no pictures captioned 'Sad Harry learns to smile again.'"

The brothers, sometimes in the company of their nineteen-year-old cousin, Princess Anne's son, Peter Phillips, and their former nanny, Tiggy Legge-Bourke, spend long hours walking the grounds of the Balmoral estate.

Diana's funeral is now three days away, and the princes' role remains unclear.

It's one of Charles's many burdens.

"Cancel all your engagements and give those two boys a cuddle," the *Sun* demands of their sleepless, distressed father, who during his solo walks on the moors, the *Daily Mail* claims, "weeps bitter tears of guilt."

Chapter 72

September 4, 1997
London

B BC Radio 1 is overwhelmed with emails and calls, tens of thousands of identical requests that propel a 1974 song into the Top 40.

William has an idea. Elton John should sing at Westminster Abbey.

While the senior royal advisers and government officials are debating the suitability of a rock star taking a central role in such a solemn occasion, public opinion weighs in.

"There could be no finer funeral tribute to Diana, Princess of Wales," states the *Telegraph*, "than a specially modified 'Candle in the Wind' sung by Elton John."

He's in the United States when the invitation to perform comes from Diana's sister Lady Sarah McCorquodale.

"I'll do anything you want," he says.

John gives an exclusive interview to Barbara Walters outlining his plan. After the service, he says, "I will record a piano-and-voice version of the song," its rewritten lyrics for his dear friend published in every British newspaper. "And I'm going to put it on my new single and give all the money to start Di's charity foundation off."

———∞∞∞———

Fayed family spokesman Michael Cole remains committed to Diana and Dodi's romance, symbolized by a $200,000 diamond ring Dodi presumably intended to give Diana.

"What that ring meant, we shall probably never know," Cole says at a press conference. "If the planet lasts for another thousand years, people will still wonder about its significance."

———∞∞∞———

New York

On NBC's *Today* show on September 5, actor Michael Douglas is talking with host Matt Lauer. "In all due respect to Princess Diana," the Oscar-winning star of *Wall Street* says, "someone like Mother Teresa, when she dies...will we have anywhere near that kind of outpouring for her?"

Hours later, in Calcutta, Mother Teresa suffers a fatal heart attack.

———∞∞∞———

Buckingham Palace

The *Sun* asks, WHERE IS OUR QUEEN? WHERE IS HER FLAG?, while the *Express* begs the monarch to SHOW US YOU CARE.

The Union flag *should* be flown at half-staff over Buckingham Palace "if that is what the people want," William says to his father.

The queen returns from Balmoral to London, but she won't bend on the flag, which by tradition is lowered only on the passing of a sovereign.

Outside the palace gates, she and Prince Philip leave their limousine to walk among Diana's mourners and their bouquets, flags, photographs, stuffed animals, balloons, and personal notes.

The crowd applauds, demonstrating the people's support of the monarchy.

An eleven-year-old girl holds five red roses in her arms.

"Would you like me to place them for you?" the queen asks.

"No, Your Majesty," the girl says. "They are for you."

***

Westminster Abbey

Elton John is at the piano, rehearsing for his momentous performance. For fifty minutes, Earl Spencer listens quietly, along with Tony and Cherie Blair.

A royal protection officer is floored by "the most moving thing I have seen. Elton was emotionally drained."

***

Standing on the grass in front of a sea of mourners' gifts, a woman explains to a camera crew the depth of her feelings for Diana: "People say you never even touched her hand. Well, I never touched God either, but I still love Him."

William, in a double-breasted gray suit and long bangs nearly covering his downcast eyes, and Harry, in a single-breasted blue suit, arrive to find their home surrounded—by flowers.

They salute the tearful crowds who've placed them there.

"It seems like hundreds of thousands of flowers are scattered from the gates of Kensington Palace all the way down to Kensington High Street," Harry says.

Chapter 73

September 5, 1997
London

I n late afternoon, the queen stands next to a window in Buckingham
Palace. Dressed in a black suit, a diamond brooch, and a multistrand
pearl necklace, she's about to do a live broadcast. Visible through
the window are the palace gates, where a steady stream of mourners
leaves flowers for Diana.

Flouting her tradition of addressing the nation only at
Christmastime — broken just once before, during wartime — Queen Elizabeth speaks "from the heart" as "your queen and a grandmother" on the
"devastating loss" of Diana, praising the princess as an "exceptional and
gifted human being."

"I admired and respected her for her energy and commitment to
others," the queen says, "especially for her devotion to her two boys."

William Tallon, page to the Queen Mother, steals into the Chapel Royal for
the second time today. At each end of Diana's coffin, a candle burns.

This early evening, the last before the funeral, he places two bouquets,
one from him and the second from the Queen Mother. As he's resting her
flowers atop the coffin, he notices a change in its height.

"Oh, that's for the boys," the chaplain says of the lower vantage point. "They're waiting next door in the vestry till you've gone. They're going to view her then."

At eight fifteen, under the cover of rainfall and the Queen Mother's bouquet of white lilies, Diana's coffin is brought to her home, Kensington Palace.

Charles, William, and Harry are still undecided as to how they'll participate in tomorrow's funeral procession.

—❧—

"I think it's unfair on them," Charles Spencer says of his nephews. "They're so young."

Prince Philip is taking the long view.

"If you are really going to have a monarchy," he insists, "you have got to have a family, and the family has got to be in the public eye."

Still, it's important to him to comfort his grandsons, as he once comforted John F. Kennedy Jr.

In 1963, Philip traveled to Washington for President John F. Kennedy's funeral.

The day before the ceremony, the president's young son, John Jr—nearly three years old at the time, the same age Prince Andrew was then—was asking "Where's Daddy?" and complaining that he "didn't have anybody to play with."

Imagine Jackie Kennedy's surprise when she opened the door to the White House playroom and found Prince Philip and John Jr. playing games on the floor.

Eighteen months later, Philip also held John Jr.'s hand at the dedication of Britain's Kennedy memorial.

Now Philip turns to William and makes him a solemn promise.

"I'll walk if you walk."

Chapter 74

September 6, 1997
London

T he Queen's Flag Sergeant lowers the Union flag over Buckingham Palace to mark the start of Diana's funeral.

"This is a mark of respect for the princess on the day of her funeral," says a palace spokesperson, indicating a historic change in protocol.

It's a few minutes after nine on a bright, still morning when the gun carriage holding Diana's coffin departs Kensington Palace for the two-and-a-half-mile journey to Westminster Abbey. On the palace gate is tied a ballet slipper with a handwritten message on its pink satin: "You were a Cinderella at the ball, and now you are a Sleeping Beauty."

The Welsh Guards surround the carriage while police patrol the one million mourners who've thronged the streets.

A mile into the procession route, the cortege expands by five.

Prince Philip steps behind the carriage, alongside Prince William, Earl Spencer, Prince Harry, and the Prince of Wales.

Once a minute, the abbey's tenor bell tolls for the lost princess.

——⬥⬥⬥——

Ken Wharfe, Diana's personal protection officer from 1987 to 1993, receives an invitation to the funeral but declines. He's already been tapped to oversee security at the event.

He goes on foot to Westminster Abbey from Buckingham Palace—there is no alternative, since all the roads are closed—overwhelmed by the scent of flowers and the sight of so many mourners. *How on earth can this be happening?* Wharfe thinks, still struggling to adjust to Diana's death. *What a waste; what a terrible, utter waste.*

At ten o'clock, Westminster Abbey begins to fill with nearly two thousand guests, including more than fifty heads of state. The queen, Queen Mother, and Prince Philip are the last to arrive, at ten fifty.

Photographer Tim Graham stands outside the abbey. The only press photographer to receive an invitation, he also turned down being a mere spectator today. As the royals approach, he's poised at the doorway to take one final picture.

Eleven o'clock. The end, he senses, of an era.

Lady Jane Fellowes is the second reader at the service, following Lady Sarah McCorquodale and the hymn "I Vow to Thee My Country," requested by William in remembrance of his parents' wedding.

"Time is too slow for those who wait," Jane begins, reading a poem by Henry van Dyke.

The congregation gasps at the sound of her voice, identical to Diana's.

Royals, family members, and celebrity guests are further gutted by Tony Blair's emotional reading of 1 Corinthians 13. Then Elton John, in a Nehru-jacketed black suit, steps to the grand piano.

This is it, John realizes as he starts playing.

When he sings, "Your candle's burned out long before your legend ever will," nearly thirteen-year-old Harry begins sobbing, face in hands.

Approaching the final verse, John says to himself, *You've got to get through this because she would have got through it, if the roles were reversed.*

In the congregation, Diana's friend George Michael has forgotten his handkerchief and is "bawling his eyes out, really streaming." The singer prays for William and Harry, "that after time, they will feel her presence in everything they do—and know their mother's love will never leave them."

In Hyde Park, the funeral rites are projected to thousands of mourners. They watch in silence until Elton John ends his song for Diana. Their applause is loud enough to be heard inside the abbey, two miles distant.

When the clapping subsides, Earl Spencer steps forward.

"Your greatest gift was your intuition," he addresses his sister, "and it was a gift you used wisely."

He casts the royals—and the media—in opposition to a British girl who "needed no royal title to continue to generate her brand of magic."

His searing tribute earns applause from Princes Charles, William, and Harry, along with the crowds outside the abbey.

The queen and Prince Philip keep silent, eyes forward.

Chapter 75

September 6, 1997
London

Producer George Martin is waiting for Elton John in Townhouse Studios. He's famous for his work with the Beatles, but today his skills will be tested as never before.

Elton John is filled with raw emotion, recording "Candle in the Wind 1997" while still fresh from performing it at Westminster Abbey. In two takes, John nails the piano and vocals, then Martin adds his arrangement of strings and woodwinds.

"It's essential," John says, "that the single come out as soon as possible so that people could have a remembrance of her."

A release date for the double-A-side single, with "Something About the Way You Look Tonight," is set for September 23.

Road to Althorp

As the nation observes a moment of silence for Diana, even the traffic lights glow an extended red—until the limousine carrying her body begins its seventy-five-mile drive toward Althorp accompanied by a swell of applause.

People nearest the moving vehicle start tossing the flowers in their hands.

The stems steadily strike the car windows until the driver has to turn on the windshield wipers to clear his view. Still, so many flowers amass on the roof and hood that the car must be stopped to clear them.

Even in death, the Spencer family fears for Diana's safety. Charles Spencer has changed his mind. He's chosen to make the family estate, not the family crypt, her final resting place.

Police on motorbikes escort the car onto the highway and into Great Brington. The hilltop village's name means "town on the brink," and it's already viewed as a changed place. Locals worry that Diana's grave "will be like Elvis's grave. Everybody will want to come here just to pay their respects."

They certainly do today, all the way to the russet stone wall surrounding Althorp, where they finally fall away as the family proceeds to a spot on the property known as the Oval, an ornamental lake with a central island.

Here Diana will find the privacy she's always craved.

Chapter 76

September 7, 1997
New York City

D iana's hopes and aspirations for William are published in the pages of *The New Yorker.*

At a June lunch at the Four Seasons when she was in New York to promote her charity dress auction, she'd confided in Tina Brown, editor of *The New Yorker,* and Anna Wintour, editor of *Vogue.*

"I try to din into him all the time about the media—the dangers, and how he must understand and handle it," Diana said. "William—I think he has it. I think he understands. I'm hoping he'll grow up to be as smart about it as John Kennedy Jr. I want William to handle things as well as John does."

"Nothing I went through could compare to what they are facing," John F. Kennedy Jr. himself says of Princes William and Harry after Diana's death. "I was able to lead a normal life from about the age of five. I went to boarding school then college."

"All I want to do is get on with my life at Eton," William says.

Four days after his mother's funeral, the prince returns to his place as a third-year student.

According to a classmate's father, the kindest condolence is silence.

Regarding Diana, "It will be your duty never to mention her," the father advises his son. "You must pretend that nothing has happened and just carry on."

That advice is not heeded by everyone. In William's room at school, six hundred letters of condolence await.

The words are far more meaningful than the useless tokens he's already given away—including a high-tech tennis racquet from the United States.

"I've got one racquet, what do I need two for?"

Many celebrities, including Elton John and Steven Spielberg, send mementos, but after Harry opens a package containing a tea towel imprinted with his mother's face, he refuses to open any more.

Kensington Palace

Queen Elizabeth's sister, Princess Margaret, is distressed. It's been almost a week since Diana's funeral, and she can smell bouquets rotting outside her twenty-room residence, apartment 1A at KP.

The Royal Parks service oversees the citywide cleanup, which is projected to last weeks. The accumulation of flowers—sixty million of them—is immense. Crews collect somewhere between ten and fifteen tons of bouquets and assorted gifts. They don't throw them away. In memory of Diana's charity work, teddy bears are brought to needy children. Patients in hospitals and nursing homes receive the freshest of the flowers. Even the dead flowers have a purpose. They'll be mulched for fertilizer in Kensington Gardens.

The significance of the work is clear, even to the youngest volunteers. "I'm going to tell my children when I'm older," a Boy Scout says, "and they probably will be proud of me that I did it."

Ludgrove

In the five days since Harry returned to Ludgrove, the school's rules have tightened. Newspapers are banned, and students are "asked not to mention cars or mothers."

Today is September 15, Harry's thirteenth birthday. It's a Ludgrove tradition that parents visit boys to share a slice of birthday cake.

When a car drives up to the school, Harry runs to greet the passenger with a hug.

Aunt Sarah—Lady Sarah McCorquodale—is holding a gift-wrapped box.

Inside is a PlayStation.

It's from Diana. It's the video-game console she bought for Harry in Paris.

Chapter 77

June 27, 1998
Althorp

T en months after Diana's death, and five days before she would have turned thirty-seven, her brother, Earl Spencer, opens the family's ancestral home to fifteen thousand fans—of pop music and of the late princess.

The Diana, Princess of Wales Tribute Concert is also the public's first chance to see the Althorp estate. Tickets quickly sell out, though many complain that the price—£39.50 ($63)—makes it the most expensive concert in Britain.

The proceeds, her brother says, will go to the Diana, Princess of Wales Memorial Fund, but the Spencer family will keep some undisclosed portion of the £9.50 ($15) ticket fees generated by a second project: a museum dedicated to Diana.

Diana's friends call the whole memorial endeavor "Dianaland" and find it a bit tacky.

Earl Spencer invites Princes Charles, William, and Harry to attend the concert and tour the photographs and memorabilia, exhibited in the Althorp stables. They decline.

So do Phil Collins, Elton John, Paul McCartney, George Michael, and other musicians—some citing scheduling problems and others complaining about the unaffordable concert ticket prices.

Diana's friends and favorites Cliff Richard and Chris de Burgh come through, along with Duran Duran. The band kicks off a tribute set list with its 1982 hit "Save a Prayer."

***

On August 31, 1998, the first anniversary of Diana's death, the royals return to Crathie for a private service on a Monday marked as "a time for personal reflection."

And expansion.

The queen's eighteen-foot-long Rolls-Royce drives toward a narrow lane in Ellesmere Port, Cheshire. The chauffeur struggles to navigate its width and height through the approach, ultimately removing the Royal Standard flying atop the car.

Today marks a first for the seventy-two-year-old monarch—a visit to the restaurant most beloved by William and Harry: McDonald's.

Wearing a suit the same bright shade as the golden arches, she greets workers, asking if they've been busy.

Gwynneth Lewis, a grandmother on staff, says, "I suppose the Queen would like to know what her grandchildren get up to and I'm sure they like to eat hamburgers."

***

"Remembering Diana is important," the bishop of Birmingham reflects about the anniversary. "But so is letting go. It is time to let Diana rest in peace."

Flashes of truth burn brighter than memory.

In that moment and every moment since, Katharine Graham of the *Washington Post* hears her dear friend Diana bare her soul.

"Do you gamble?" she remembers someone asking the princess.

"Not with cards," Diana replies. *"But with life."*

PART 6
The Heir and the Spare

Chapter 78

September 3, 1998
Eton

O ver here, lad!"

Harry, less than two weeks shy of his fourteenth birthday, greets the photographers with a wide smile, a far cry from the toddler who once threw fistfuls of dirt at the cameramen, yelling, "Go away, mens! Go away, mens!"

His reedy frame is swimming in his new Eton uniform—the same tailcoat, vest, and striped trousers all the students wear—but he's too excited to care.

William, now in his fourth year at Eton, stays away from the photo call, but the brothers live in the same dormitory, Manor House, both for security and personal reasons.

The first year since Diana's death has been long and hard for the boys—Harry especially. On August 30, 1997, hours before Diana died, Charles had written her a letter about whether it might be best for Harry, who is young for his grade and not a strong student, to remain at Ludgrove for another year.

"Harry's full of energy but he flips from one thing to another and then loses interest," Diana observed. "William's very sensitive, and Harry's very artistic and sporty and doesn't mind anything." But Diana's main concern regarding Harry's going to Eton was that "if he doesn't go there, everyone will think he's stupid."

After Diana's death, it was a simple decision to keep Harry in safe and familiar surroundings at Ludgrove. The only downside was that the brothers wouldn't have each other to lean on. "I'm very worried about Harry," William had admitted to Prince Charles back in September of 1997. "I don't want to go away from him now."

William wants Harry to join him the following year, so Harry knuckles down to pass his exams so it can happen.

"He used to have quite a laissez-faire attitude to his studies, but he spent his final year working really hard," says one of Harry's close school friends. "His work took his mind off everything else and for once we'd spot Harry in the library."

Harry's determination to earn a spot at Eton and make his mother proud pays off, and the brothers are together once more.

The previous year hasn't been all grieving and studying.

In March of 1998, Charles took both boys with him on a trip to Canada, where CBC's *The National* identifies fifteen-year-old William as the main attraction. "Hundreds of screaming, swooning teenage girls" turn out "to give a pop star's welcome to a shy young prince."

William visibly reddens at being the center of so much attention, heightened by Harry's antics. "Go on, wave at that lot," he teases as the crowd shouts William's name. "Wave at the girls and make them scream."

The teenagers declare Prince William "hot," "the most gorgeous guy in the world," and "boyish cute, but we find it sexy."

As one fourteen-year-old girl says with a sigh, "He is rich and he is gorgeous and he is a prince. What more could you ask for?"

Diana would agree—as William became a good-looking teenager, she nicknamed him "DDG," for "drop-dead gorgeous," and correctly prophesied that "the girls are going to love him."

"Whether Prince William actually likes this treatment is very much in doubt," the CBC correspondent notes, and William says as much in the interview he gives on his sixteenth birthday, that June, under the headline I HATE BEING A PIN-UP PRINCE.

Chapter 79

November 14, 1998
Gloucestershire

Today is Papa's fiftieth birthday.

Tonight marks the sixth of seven parties thrown for Prince Charles. The first one, way back on July 31, had been intended as a surprise but was unfortunately leaked by the media a week before. William and Harry had planned it for their father months in advance, both to divert suspicion . . . and to distract themselves from the first anniversary of their mother's death.

Family, friends, and award-winning writer-actors Emma Thompson, Stephen Fry, and Rowan Atkinson joined the two princes in a performance that opened with a sketch set in the seventeenth century, in which Atkinson's curmudgeonly character, Edmund Blackadder, attempts to appease Fry's King Charles II on the monarch's fiftieth birthday. Prince Charles roars with laughter, extremely touched that his sons went to such trouble on his behalf.

A recording of the sketch airs tonight on ITV, but Charles is too preoccupied to watch television. Last night, the queen and Prince Philip held a huge birthday celebration at Buckingham Palace, but today, his actual birthday, is the main event.

Camilla Parker Bowles is throwing him a private party at Highgrove.

And William and Harry are coming.

Queen Elizabeth and Prince Philip are not.

The queen has flatly refused to acknowledge Camilla—whom she calls "that wicked woman"—saying, "I have absolutely no desire to meet her." The Queen Mother is even more vehement—she won't allow Camilla's name to be spoken in her presence.

William and Harry have been far less dramatic. William takes the lead in arranging a casual encounter shortly before his June birthday. He's heard so much about Camilla over the years—little of it good—but he's ready to find out for himself. Besides, by his calculation, "eighty per cent of the boys at Eton have stepmothers." It's time, he feels, to see what kind of person she actually is.

Camilla is the more nervous of the two, coming out of that first meeting with Prince William "trembling like a leaf" and declaring, "I really need a vodka tonic," as she pours herself a stiff drink. A few weeks later, she also meets with Harry for the first time. It goes smoothly, though she does accuse him of eyeing her "suspiciously."

Both boys are ready to extend an olive branch Camilla's way . . . as long as she doesn't try to move in on Diana's territory.

Royal reporter Richard Kay warns, "Robbed of his mother, William is not ready for a mother figure—nor, incidentally, is Harry." Luckily for them all, Camilla could hardly be more different from Diana in appearance and temperament. Perhaps, theorizes one of Charles's friends, "It's precisely because she is nothing like the mother they loved that Camilla is so nonthreatening in their eyes."

"Whatever makes you happy, Papa," William says to his father.

After a lavish dinner for several hundred guests, Charles and Camilla step out on the dance floor to ABBA hits from their youth. The dancing goes on until the wee hours—when William and Harry re-create the striptease routine from the film *The Full Monty*.

"They danced, swayed and swaggered to Hot Chocolate's song 'You Sexy Thing,' which features in the film," the *Sun* reports. It's clearly not the first time that the brothers, who go as far as removing their shirts and unbuttoning their trousers before bursting into laughter, have performed this bit.

"They know every step of the dance routine," says a school friend, "and it has become their party piece whenever they get together with friends."

Chapter 80

December 20, 1998
Windsor

T he queen decides to invite her grandsons and a dozen or so of their Eton schoolmates to Windsor Castle for a holiday dinner. "It would be a pleasant gesture," she says, so that "William and Harry can entertain their friends."

Her Majesty, says a Palace spokesperson, "is incredibly fond of her grandsons" and "wants them to feel as relaxed and at home at Windsor as she is."

It's not easy to feel cozy in an ancient castle. But like any doting grandparents, the queen and Prince Philip have been to see William perform in a school play, a production of *The Tempest,* and William—now accompanied by Harry—still makes the short trek from Eton for Sunday tea with his grandparents in the paneled Oak Room at Windsor.

The one-on-one time William spends with Granny is invaluable. "She's just very helpful on any sort of difficulties or problems I might be having," he says. "She's been brilliant, she's a real role model." The teenager appreciates how "she won't necessarily force advice on you. She'll let you work it out for yourself. She's always there for a question or two—for whatever it is you might need. But, just as she probably had to, she feels that you have to work it out for yourself, that there are no set rules. You have to make it work. You have to do what you think is right."

The holiday invitation to stay over at Windsor Castle is eagerly accepted by the boys and fourteen of their friends.

After the meal, the queen tells her grandsons that she's "delighted the dinner party went so well" and that she "loved every minute" of it.

The monarch routinely stays up late, often until nearly midnight. When she finally heads off to bed—leaving a pack of teenage boys loose in Windsor Castle after hours—the party turns rather boisterous, in part because of the predinner cocktails and wine pairings served throughout the evening. At around 11:30 p.m., Harry (the only completely sober one of the bunch) has a brilliant idea.

They should all go sledding!

He leads a group of tipsy schoolmates to the pantry, where they load themselves up with silver serving trays, then troop outside in the freezing weather.

The boys take turns using the royal silver to slide down the hills of the castle grounds, shouting and laughing until after midnight.

Throughout his first year at Eton, Harry settles into life under his older brother's wing. "William is very protective toward his brother," family friends tell Richard Kay. "For his part, Harry worships William. There used to be a lot of fighting between the two—rivalry I suppose—but they're over that now."

"Harry is quieter and just watches," Princess Diana said of her younger son in a 1987 interview, when the boys were five and three. "No. 2 skates in quite nicely."

It's been rather bumpy of late, though.

"Prince William has developed into a strong and independent character since the tragic loss of his mother," says a close source who knows them both. "But Prince Harry has not found it so easy to cope. Everyone thought that William was the sensitive one. In fact it is Harry who has found it most difficult to deal with his grief."

"William is deep like his dad and stubborn, and Harry is a hothead like me; he does the first thing that comes into his head. They will look after the heir and I will look after the spare," the princess often said. As it turns out, what gets "the spare" through is his sense of mischief. As Diana would say, "Harry's the naughty one, just like me."

He develops a reputation as the class clown, playing pranks on the teachers. "Harry would be the one snorting with laughter, but he never got caught and no one ever ratted on him as we all liked him too much," remarks a classmate. "The more invincible he realized he was, the more he played up."

And of course, as a schoolmate's parent notes, "the masters cut him some slack, not only because he was a prince—though that was the larger part of the reason—but also because he had lost his mother so tragically. Who could forget that poor little twelve-year-old walking behind his mother's coffin?"

Chapter 81

Autumn 1999
Gloucestershire

There's been a shooting at Highgrove.

Down in London, Prince Charles's press secretary takes a call from the estate's gardener. "I've got a problem," he tells her. "The moorhen's dead."

Even though Charles is currently at Highgrove himself, the gardener is reluctant to break the news in person. "The Prince of Wales is very fond of this bird," he explains.

The gardener refuses to point fingers at who may have shot one of Charles's favorite waterbirds but reluctantly admits that "the boys were seen walking in the vicinity of the pond."

William and Harry. They'd visited earlier, though now they're both back at school in Eton.

The press secretary dials Charles. "I'm so sorry to trouble you, Sir, but I've got some sad news," she tells him. "The moorhen's dead."

"Oh my God, I loved that bird," laments the prince. He's quick to piece together what must've happened. "Those bloody boys!" he exclaims.

He tells the press secretary to get in touch with William and Harry at school and find out which one of them shot the bird. "And I want an apology."

At Eton, the brothers are called into their housemaster's office.

"Your father's very upset," Andrew Gailey says to them, "because someone has shot the moorhen."

"Shot the moorhen?" repeat the boys innocently.

"Which moorhen is that, Dr. Gailey?" William asks, feigning ignorance.

"The one you told me not to shoot!" Harry exclaims.

So much for bluffing their way out of this one. But Harry admits responsibility and confesses to his father, "I'm so sorry Papa, it was me, I shouldn't have done it."

Charles accepts the apology. He's upset about the bird, but the truth is that he's always encouraged the boys in their shooting pursuits, even when they were very young.

Charles sees shooting and hunting as "manly sports," like polo. Even Diana—who had no interest in any of it—puts out a public statement in 1996, when then fourteen-year-old Prince William shoots his first stag up at Balmoral, saying that she "respects that he has interests in every arena and would not question them." And she listens when William begs her not to take on the presidency of the Royal Society for the Prevention of Cruelty to Animals. "Every time I kill anything, they will blame you," he points out.

"I don't know why I'm always portrayed as an 'Anti,'" Diana tells a friend, "because I'm not. After all, I was brought up in the country." She and Charles even met on a hunt, and in October of 1981, when they were newlyweds, Diana made headlines for shooting a stag herself at Balmoral.

"She's become a modern-day Diana the Huntress," one of the other hunters there that day says. "She hit it straight with a remarkably good shot. It was amazing!" Another report claims she'd only injured it, but that is quickly refuted. "The crack-shot princess made a 'clean' one-shot kill," a member of the hunting party says. "Prince Charles would not allow anyone to even handle a gun unless he or she was a good clean shot."

Both reports note that Diana fainted when the animal was

gutted—although what no one realizes then is that the young Princess of Wales may have already been pregnant with William at the time.

Soon after the shoot at Balmoral, Diana decides she's done with hunting.

"I'm just not interested in it anymore," she says, stating that she'd only killed that stag because "they wanted me to."

Some of her distaste comes from her antipathy toward her in-laws, especially after the divorce. The royals "pushed the princes into the traditional 'maleness' of the Royal Family—the foxhunts and polo—away from the emotional, raw, open, honest side of their psyches that Diana was reinforcing," notes Diana's speech coach, Richard Greene. "One of the main reasons she disliked it so much was because," a source comments, "it was yet another thing that was going to further 'Windsorize' them and take away time they could spend with her during the summer." The source added, "She sometimes told friends she hated being apart from them in August when they were 'off killing things.'"

"What is it with this family that they love killing things?" Diana gripes to chef Darren McGrady. It upsets her to think of her boys with "blood on their hands." One time, after the boys come in from shooting rabbits, she scolds them. "You should both be ashamed of yourselves. It's wrong to kill little animals," she says. "I shall now call you both the 'Killer Wales.'"

The boys find this nickname hilarious.

"Don't laugh," their mother snaps. "It's not funny. You've been involved in the murder of some innocent creatures. A little bunny rabbit is not doing harm to anyone."

Diana also stopped wearing fur—even faux fur—after being targeted by antifur activists in the 1980s.

"So that went back into the cupboard, never to be seen again," she declares of a white fur coat she wore to meet Elizabeth Taylor, which set off a maelstrom of criticism even though Diana was quick to reveal it was fake. And on a chilly November evening in 1989, at the Tiffany Ball at Cliveden House, she teases glamorous *Dynasty* star Joan Collins out of wearing her mink by wagging a finger at the actress and declaring, "Naughty, naughty. You mustn't wear fur—mustn't wear fur!"

The table erupts with laughter at the royal decree, and Collins swiftly sends her mink away. But two days later, when Collins takes ill with the flu and a fever of 104 degrees, the actress can't help wondering, *My God, have I died because Princess Diana wouldn't let me wear my fur?*

The antifur activists are delighted to claim Diana as a convert to their cause, listing her name in every campaign.

So much of it, as Diana understood and tried to explain to her sons, is about public perception.

"Remember, there's always someone in a high-rise flat who doesn't want to see you shoot a Bambi," she warns them.

William gets a taste of this backlash in November of 1999, when he makes his public debut foxhunting with the Duke of Beaufort's Hunt and is blasted both in the press and by Parliament for being so "insensitive and arrogant" as to "publicly endorse hunting."

Even more dangerous are reports from Scotland Yard that William and his father, Prince Charles, have been targeted by an animal rights organization known for violence. William has also received death threats from extremists who are upset about his foxhunting.

Yet the princes—all three of them, father and sons—love hunting.

And in Diana's absence, a friend notes, "William and Harry belong to the Windsors now."

Chapter 82

Spring 2000
Eton

William is set to graduate from Eton soon, covered in glory—and funky waistcoats.

He has performed solidly in his exams, received the Sword of Honour in the Combined Cadet Force, and was elected into Pop, the prestigious Eton society for elite prefects.

"It's true," says someone in the know. "Poppers rule the school."

As a Pop, William is allowed to wear checked trousers and flashy waistcoats: he has a collection of these vests, some with polka dots and bold colors and one from a tailor he shares with Paul McCartney and Elton John that features a Union Jack motif and the words GROOVY BABY.

He isn't too worried about looking cool, though. He'll walk around with braids in his long, floppy bangs, which his friends have styled as a joke, or "wearing someone else's pullover. He usually looked a bit of a mess," says a classmate with a laugh.

As a prefect, William is allowed a certain amount of authority over other students, but he doesn't abuse the position.

"He wasn't always trying to show people who's boss or anything like that," a friend notes. "He was just very enthusiastic, very committed to everything he did. If someone was having a rotten time of it, he would encourage them. Or he'd kid with them—but never mean, always in fun. Will got on with everybody. I don't think I can say that about anyone else at Eton."

"William was pretty cool and he wouldn't hand out detentions and punishments even though he could," another schoolmate says. "He was very easygoing and very humble; he didn't go around using his title to get him anywhere, if anything he downplayed it. If people made a deal about who he was he would color up and move the conversation away from him. He just wanted to be William and like everyone else."

What he *doesn't* want, William makes clear, is to be called His Royal Highness.

Technically, that's allowed once he turns eighteen, but the very idea upsets him. He makes a special request of his father and the queen: he'd like to postpone using the title for another five years, until he's twenty-three and has graduated from university.

Sometimes William fantasizes about stepping away from everything, telling his father, "I shall go backpacking in Nepal and never come back."

Harry is ready to step in. "I shall be King Harry. I shall do the work. I'd love it!"

His mother rather agreed. While her nickname for William may have been DDG, for "drop-dead gorgeous," her nickname for Harry was "GKH," for "good King Harry."

"She thought he'd probably be better equipped for the role in the future than William," remarks royal correspondent Robert Jobson.

"William is waiting patiently for the monarchy to be abolished," Diana joked. "It would make things so much easier for him!"

But though she stopped short of advocating for the line of succession to skip over Charles, Diana did go on record with her concerns about whether her then-husband "could adapt" to the "top job."

"Being Prince of Wales produces more freedom now, and being king would be a little bit more suffocating," she'd once remarked. And as for Prince William? She sidesteps with a question of her own.

"William's very young at the moment, so do you want a burden like that to be put on his shoulders at such an age?"

Chapter 83

Autumn 2000
South America

I t's not fair," storms William. "Everyone else is allowed to go backpacking, why can't I?"

"Prince Charles said he would love Prince William to travel before knuckling down to his studies," says a close source—but it must be "vocational, educational and safe."

Once tempers cool, a compromise is reached. William begins his gap year before entering university by doing survival training in Belize with 150 Welsh Guards, part of the British Army infantry.

"Exhilarating," he says of the experience, which includes tromping through jungles and sleeping in hammocks.

Next up is three weeks of scuba diving off an island in the Indian Ocean near Mauritius, under the guidance of the Royal Geographical Society.

In October, William joins Raleigh International in Patagonia for nearly three months of manual labor.

Like all members of the expedition, including middle-class kids and at-risk youth from several nations, William is tasked with raising money before setting out. He successfully meets his goal several times over by participating in a charity water polo match—though when asked if his father has chipped in, William concedes that "he might have helped slightly."

"I chip in all the bloody time!" Charles cracks.

In the tiny mountain village of Tortel, all the young volunteers, male and female, sleep in the same room and share a single toilet—which they also take turns cleaning. "The living conditions here aren't exactly what I'm used to. You share everything with everyone. I found it very difficult... because I am a very private person. But I learned to deal with it," the prince says.

"William coped very well, and what struck me about him was how normal he was," one of his fellow volunteers recalls. "He said he wanted to be treated like everyone else, and he was. When you saw him cleaning the toilets, it wasn't for the cameras, he really did clean the lavatories."

"I don't like being treated any different at all, I don't like special treatment at all," William says.

The expedition leaders do their best to ensure he isn't getting any. "To be honest, no one knew there was a prince of England in their midst until he arrived, but word got out very quickly—we couldn't keep that secret for sure," says Malcolm Sutherland, one of the leaders.

Not that it changes anyone's attitude.

"William's like one of the lads," says fellow volunteer Paul Coward. "You can just have a laugh with him." Volunteer Kevin Mullen agrees: "Wills is good fun. He's a joker and popular with everyone."

And he doesn't scoff at doing his share of the hard work—tutoring children at the local school, carpentry, wood chopping, house painting, cooking (not his strong suit), cleaning, and even taking a turn as the DJ on the local radio station.

"Hello all you groove jets out there," William rumbles as he fiddles with the controls. "For any of you people who are in a bit of a mood for looove, this song is for you," he says. "This is 'Tortel Love' and we are in the mood for some real grooving here..."

"He'd still be there if we'd given him the chance, he just loved it," says expedition leader Sutherland. "It was probably the last time he could go for a long period away from the public eye; I wonder if he knew that then."

Chapter 84

August 3, 2001
Gloucestershire

S illy old father, get on with it!" William shouts.

It's the usual stuff.

The boys are egging Charles on in today's game, a charity match at Cirencester Park Polo Club. They're up 2–1 in the second period of play, and all three princes are fiercely competitive.

I really want to win.

It's been more than eleven years since Diana told Charles he was too old to keep playing polo, yet here he is at fifty-two, still astride a polo pony, holding his own in a match alongside his strapping sixteen- and nineteen-year-old sons.

"We work really well as a team because we all sort of think really alike," William says of playing with his father and brother. "But when someone does wrong you get two very stern faces looking at you and you get the bollocking afterwards."

The boys now dwarf their five-foot-ten father: William is six foot two, and Harry is catching up rapidly. "This is just to show how quickly I'm shrinking," Charles jokes. He lovingly refers to William and Harry as his "ideal sons."

It is great fun being able to play with them.

They're both strong players who showed an early interest in polo—much to their father's and grandfather's delight—even though, according to Richard Kay, the naturally left-handed William has had to train especially hard to "literally become right-handed" while playing the game.

Charles is also trying hard—perhaps too hard. He turns his pony quickly...and they both go down, horse and rider.

Harry comes trotting over to the spot where his father is lying on the ground. "Oh, Papa's just snoring!"

But it's worse than that.

The Prince of Wales has been knocked unconscious. "The pony came down sideways and I must have landed absolutely smack on my head. Completely felled me."

It's his second recent fall—he broke his shoulder earlier this year, tumbling from his horse during a fox hunt.

The ambulance comes to take him to Cirencester Memorial Hospital. "We don't think there's been any broken bones but we are waiting for reports from the hospital," a spokesperson reports.

"I finally woke up," Charles recalls, "seemed a long time afterwards." He chastises his sons in mock distress for not showing appropriate concern. "There I was, busily swallowing my tongue, quietly dying. Can you imagine, they tried to kill me so they could walk off with my ponies!"

Harry gives him a grin: "And the rest!"

Charles finally decides enough is enough. This will be the last time he plays in a match. "It's awful having to give it up," he says. "I love it—played for almost forty years and broken various parts of my anatomy."

But the important part, as William points out: "We won the game so it was okay."

Chapter 85

September 24, 2001
St. Andrews, Scotland

Applications to the University of St. Andrews, in Scotland, have been up significantly ever since the Palace announced in August of 2000 that Prince William would be joining the incoming "freshers" class in September of 2001. "The university," notes the director of admissions, "is delighted with the rise." It's a 44.4 percent increase over the past twelve months.

Specifically, an increase in applications from young American women.

There's basis for optimism when it comes to dreaming of a royal romance—St. Andrews has a reputation as the top matchmaking university in Britain: 10 percent of its alumni marry fellow students.

In addition to being the home of Scotland's oldest university, St. Andrews is best known as the spot where golf originated and as a mecca for players from all over the world. Yet the town has always been something of a best-kept secret...until the most eligible bachelor in the world moves in.

"I wish the lad well but if he took up golf it would be a nightmare. We'd be run over with wee lassies, camera crews and paparazzi," warns one golfer.

"We could really do without competition from William," complains a first-year male student. "There are some gorgeous students up here but he's a major babe magnet and none of us could really hope to compete."

Since leaving Patagonia in December, William has rounded out his gap year by spending January and February working on a dairy farm, then devoting more than three months to studying game preservation in Africa. That experience was spectacular, "but the best bit was in England. I loved working on a farm," he claims. "I got my hands dirty, did all the chores and had to get up at 4am. I enjoyed the fact that I was put in as a hand and was just another guy on the farm."

William's had a little bit of a rough reentry. "I loved my gap year and wish I could have another one," he says. Now, facing the barrage of cameras awaiting him on his first day of university leaves the nineteen-year-old rather shell-shocked.

William Wales, as he asks to be called, moves into the residential dorm St. Salvator's Hall, a.k.a. St. Sally's, with other freshers in a normal fifteen-by-fifteen room just like every other student's—except that his 160 dorm mates have all been personally vetted, and he's got royal protection officers in the rooms surrounding his.

Some students question why he needs the security, though it's naive to imagine that the heir to the throne isn't a target. The PPOs try to keep their distance, and William's MO is to laugh them off.

"I don't know what their game is, but they are constantly following me around," he jokes. More seriously, though, as Richard Kay comments, "William likes to do his own things without people knowing, which is frightfully difficult when you are second in line to the throne."

But the teenager has a point when he tells a friend, "Now I understand why my mother gave up her detectives. No one can stand being watched *all* the time. It's...suffocating."

St. Andrews is the hardest adjustment he's had to make so far, especially after his globe-trotting year. It takes a while for him to warm up to life in the isolated northern university town. He plays football on Wednesdays and joins the water polo team but still holds himself a little apart—instead of using the university gym, for example, he gets a membership to the private gym at the St. Andrews Bay Hotel, requiring a drive out of town. "I want a bit of space," he says.

"I think he was really nervous when he arrived," recalls Charles's press secretary. "He was very unsteady for a little while after that. He'd had a fantastic gap year, going anywhere on the globe that he'd wanted, and suddenly he was stuck here in this corner of Scotland, not knowing anybody, just one or two guys from Eton whom he didn't know that well, and he was very much alone."

By Christmas break, he's starting to "wobble" and thinks perhaps he won't go back for his second term.

"William was a long way from home, and he wasn't happy," notes the Lord Rector of the university. "He got 'the blues'—which happens."

"I don't think I was homesick," William admits. "I was more daunted."

Prince Philip is having none of it.

"William needs to knuckle down and not wimp out," his grandfather barks.

The PR would be disastrous not only for St. Andrews but also for William personally, the press team points out. He would be "seen as a quitter," and leaving the school "would be taken as a snub by the Scottish people."

The prince has a heart-to-heart with his father. Charles is "very understanding about it," William says. "We chatted a lot and in the end we both realized—I definitely realized—that I had to come back."

He starts his second term in January of 2002 and quickly recognizes that there's fun to be had when he throws himself into university life and strikes up friendships with several other students. There's a reason the school is nicknamed "St. Randies," after all—it's notorious for its thriving social scene.

"It's just fine, very good fun. I'm enjoying it a lot," William says upon his return. "I just hope I can meet people I get on with. I don't care about their backgrounds."

One of the people in his group of friends is a fellow first-year student also living in St. Sally's, a cute, sporty brunette named Catherine Middleton.

That March, William accompanies several other students to a charity fashion show that students are putting on at the St. Andrews Bay Hotel to raise funds for victims of 9/11.

He's got a good seat in the front row.

Kate's one of the models walking the runway. She's not usually a flashy or sexy dresser, so William is stunned to see her come out wearing a see-through black strapless dress (actually a skirt that she's pulled up over a bikini with a bandeau top).

She's a knockout!

"She was in a very daring dress, in a sheer, stocking-like dress," William's friend Ben Duncan remembers. "He was sitting front row and his eyes were like stalks."

The smitten prince turns to another pal, Fergus Boyd, and whispers, "Wow, Fergus, Kate's hot!"

Life at university has just gotten a lot more interesting.

Chapter 86

April 2002
London

The bells of Westminster Abbey toll 101 times.

Her Majesty Queen Elizabeth the Queen Mother has passed away, at age 101. More than a million mourners come out to toss flowers on the road in front of her hearse as it progresses from Westminster Abbey—where seventy-nine years ago she married Prince Albert, Duke of York (the future King George VI); where sixty-six years ago she was crowned Queen Consort; and where fifty years ago she attended the king's funeral—to Windsor Castle, where she will be interred beside her late husband.

King George VI was never meant to be king at all. It was only when his elder brother, King Edward VIII, abdicated in 1936 to marry the American divorcée Wallis Simpson that Edward's younger brother Bertie ascended the throne and took the name George VI. His early death, at age fifty-six, after serving as king for just over fifteen years, is the reason his daughter Elizabeth became queen in 1952, when she was only twenty-five.

"Put the country first, whatever happens" has long been the motto of the Queen Mother, whose patriotism was legendary during World War II, but Prince Charles also calls her "quite simply the most magical grandmother that you could possibly have, and I was utterly devoted to her."

"Gran-Gran" also liked "a good giggle," recollect her great-grandsons.

"She loved to hear about all my friends and all they got up to and relate it to her own youth," William says. "And she loved to hear about how much trouble I got into at school."

When William starts at St. Andrews, she advises, "Any good parties, invite me down!"

"I said yes, but there was no way," remarks the prince. "I knew full well that if I invited her down, she would dance me under the table."

Despite her close relationship with her great-grandsons, the Queen Mother leaves her entire estate—reportedly worth more than £70 million, or $100 million—to her daughter Queen Elizabeth II. Although there are oft-published rumors that the Queen Mother left the two young men well over £10 million, with the lion's share going to Harry, in truth no one other than the queen receives anything.

But Prince Charles *is* planning to move into his grandmother's house.

And he's eyeing her jewels—one ring in particular.

Charles has long been the Queen Mother's particular favorite. Some say he reminds her of his grandfather, her late husband, Bertie: "unsure, lacking in confidence, needed to be built up."

Things hadn't worked out as well between Charles and Diana as the Queen Mother and Lady Fermoy had hoped when they were matchmaking their grandchildren, but for that she doesn't blame Charles—except on one point. She and her daughter the queen both feel that "the Prince of Wales has put his own gratification and interests before duty by pursuing his relationship with Camilla," relates a Palace courtier, "and she can never forgive that."

So while Charles has been adamant that he intends a future with Camilla Parker Bowles—and the queen has reluctantly come around to the idea—a remarriage could *never* happen as long as the Queen Mother was alive.

But now the way is clear.

Shortly after the funeral, Charles launches his plans to move the Prince of Wales's office and official residence in London from St. James's Palace to Clarence House, his grandmother's home of fifty years, once renovations are complete.

And his redesign plans include an en suite set of rooms for Camilla.

Chapter 87

June 2003
Eton

Prince Harry punches the air in glee as he carries the last of his belongings out of Manor House in a black plastic trash bag. He's eighteen and eager to leave school behind after his final exams.

"I didn't enjoy school at all," he readily admits. "I wanted to be the bad boy."

The papers have already labeled him "the bad boy of Buckingham Palace" and "Hedonist Harry" after the press got wind of some poor choices he'd made in the summer of 2001, running with a crowd of wealthy, upper-class young people nicknamed "the Glossy Posse." Stories about Harry's underage drinking and various intoxicated exploits are not untrue, but they are misleading.

He's put that behind him for now.

The exams have been a real trial for him, a total "nightmare."

"Every now and then a test would come up and I'd be absolutely useless—and I've been like that from stage one of my youth," he admits.

"To this day, there are all sorts of stories doing the rounds," says an Old Etonian, "of how the school had to alter its academic requirements so that Harry could pass tests. And even then, he'd fail them, to the despair of his masters."

But the school provost puts forth a wider definition of success. An appropriate motto for Eton, he says, would be "Excellence without arrogance." And while "academic standards are pretty high, we don't really aspire to be top of the league." The school's aims, he says, are broader: "We believe in academic ability, intelligence, skill at games and a wider contribution to cultural life."

Harry does excel at sports in his later years at the school—"He turned up at Eton a slightly scrawny boy of about five feet and he left having shot up to about six feet with a lot more muscle," says one of his teammates—and by his final year he is named House Captain of Games (allowing him to wear a wing collar and a white bow tie).

"You had to be prepared for a beating especially when you were playing against Harry," went the word. "He was totally fearless and very aggressive when he played. It earned him a lot of respect at Eton because he was able to show he could look after himself."

That was out of necessity, Harry argues. "People would see me on the rugby field as an opportunity to smash me up," he says. "There were people in my own school during interhouse rugby competitions that would put in bigger tackles because it was me."

Besides sports, Harry's abilities shine best in the CCF, the Combined Cadet Force, where he is promoted to lance corporal in October of 2002 and leads a detachment of forty-eight cadets in Eton's respected Tattoo as parade commander. The one area where Harry truly thrives is military life. Although he doesn't receive the Sword of Honour, as William did, Harry has a natural aptitude and an innate ability to connect with his fellow cadets.

"Harry knew what he was talking about and he didn't take any rubbish," says a fellow CCF cadet. "He was very good about motivating us and he cared about his men and wanted us to do well in drill test."

University studies are off the table, though Harry is eager to attend Sandhurst, the prestigious military academy, as long as he can squeak by on at least two academic exams.

But first, like William, he'll take a gap year... or two.

Harry crisscrosses the globe during his gap year—which technically lasts from June of 2003 until May of 2005—though Harry's chosen activities (playing polo in Argentina and working on a cattle ranch in Australia as a jackaroo, a kind of outback cowboy) are less widely lauded.

The exception is the work Harry does in Lesotho, a country in southern Africa that he visits in the summer of 2004. It's not his first trip to Africa—he loves the continent and has visited several times, often on safari adventures arranged by his beloved former nanny Tiggy. (He once remarked, "You know, if I could have it another way, I think I'd be a safari guide in Africa.") But unlike those trips, the eight weeks that Harry spends in Lesotho are truly about helping a suffering population.

It's exactly the kind of work Diana would do.

Lesotho, he learns, has the second-highest HIV infection rate in the world. In 2000, the numbers were so high that King Letsie III was forced to declare HIV/AIDS a natural disaster. Thirty percent of the population was infected. And the ones most affected are the orphans left behind.

Nineteen-year-old Harry quickly bonds with thirty-eight-year-old Prince Seeiso, the king's younger brother. Despite the age gap, they "got on like a house on fire." A member of the prince's household staff notes that "Seeiso had just lost his mother, Queen Mamohato, who was rather like Diana. She too had been very engaged in charity work, particularly with community-based organizations working with children."

"I met so many children," recalls Harry, "whose lives had been shattered following the deaths of their parents—they were so vulnerable and in need of care and attention." He arranges with Tom Bradby of ITV News for a documentary crew to come out so that he can draw attention to their plight. "This is a country that needs our help," Harry says.

The documentary raises $2 million—and viewers see for themselves that Harry is kind and helpful and earnest, not just the loutish "Playboy Prince" the newspapers call him. "I've always been like this," he explains gently. "This is my side that no one gets to see." Speaking of his desire to continue his mother's work, he says, "All I'm out here doing is what I want to do, what she'd want me to do."

"I'm not going to be some person in the Royal Family who just finds a lame excuse to go abroad and do all sorts of sunny holidays and whatever," he says. "I mean, I'll do the best I can."

Harry recalls of Diana, "She had such warmth, she wanted to make people feel special. She realized she was in a unique position and could make people smile and feel better about themselves."

"She got close to people," he says of his mother, "and went for the sort of charities and organizations that everybody was scared to go near, such as land mines in the third world, she got involved in things that nobody had done before, such as AIDS. She had more guts than anybody else."

"I want to carry on the things that she didn't quite finish. I have always wanted to, but was too young."

He and Prince Seeiso start a charity named after Diana's favorite flower. "We came up with the name Sentebale, which means 'forget-me-not' in Sesotho, the language of Lesotho," Harry explains. "This charity is a way in which Prince Seeiso and I can remember our mothers who both worked with vulnerable children and people affected by AIDS. I really feel that by doing this I can follow in my mother's footsteps and keep her legacy alive."

Chapter 88

April 2005
Windsor

T he three princes are all in love.

Prince Harry visits South Africa during his gap year and falls hard for law student Chelsy Davy, whom he'd earlier met through mutual friends in England. By the autumn of 2004, the press catches on to the besotted couple—she calls him "Haz," and he calls her "Chedda"—though Harry keeps most details close to his chest. "I would love to tell everyone how amazing she is," the gallant prince tells reporters. "But once I start talking about that, I have left myself open."

Royal correspondent Robert Lacey calls Chelsy "a bright and bouncy white Zimbabwean," and journalist Tina Brown describes her as "a hand grenade of a girl. She's a great young man's girlfriend. I don't think anyone is expecting them to marry."

Prince William, meanwhile, has been quietly dating Kate Middleton since their first year at St. Andrews. They manage to keep their relationship a secret for a remarkable length of time, especially given that they move in together, but they're outed to the press when they're spotted kissing on the slopes of Klosters while on a ski trip in 2004. The next day's headline in the *Sun* is: FINALLY . . . WILLS GETS A GIRL.

William goes on the attack when bombarded with questions about his potential marriage plans. "Look, I'm only twenty-two, for God's sake!" he explodes. "I'm too young to marry at my age. I don't want to get married until I'm at least twenty-eight or maybe thirty."

Prince Charles, on the other hand, is more than ready to get married again, and on February 10, 2005, he and Camilla Parker Bowles formally announce their plans to wed. Charles proposes to Camilla with a platinum art deco ring from the late Queen Mother's collection. The ring features a five-carat emerald-cut diamond at its center and additional baguettes on the sides.

William and Harry put out a statement, saying, "We are both very happy for our father and Camilla and wish them all the luck in the future." Harry adds that Camilla has "made our father very, very happy, which is the most important thing. William and I love her to bits." William is more reserved. "Very happy, very pleased. It will be a good day," he says, adding of his role during the ceremony, "As long as I don't lose the rings it'll be all right. But with the responsibility I'm bound to do something wrong."

The queen is lukewarm, but she and Prince Philip put out a supportive message as well, saying, "The Duke of Edinburgh and I are very happy that the Prince of Wales and Mrs. Parker Bowles are to marry."

After a brief civil service on April 9, 2005, at Windsor Guildhall—attended by only twenty-eight people, including Camilla's son and daughter and Charles's boys but not the queen—the newlyweds move to St. George's Chapel in Windsor Castle to receive an official marriage blessing from the archbishop of Canterbury, which Queen Elizabeth and Prince Philip *do* attend.

Despite a few last-minute alterations to their original plans—a different Windsor Castle location was scrapped because it would have opened the venue to other couples for the next three years, and their original date of Friday, April 8, had to be moved so Charles could attend Pope John Paul II's funeral—the wedding is a success.

At long last, they are husband and wife.

PART 7
Cadets Wales

Chapter 89

September 2005
Sandhurst

H arry is clear and certain.

"I want to fight for my country," he says.

It's been this way since the younger prince was a small boy, dressed in his little fatigues and requesting assignments from Diana's PPO Ken Wharfe. "I remember saying to his mother, 'You'll have trouble getting this boy out of the army one day,'" Wharfe recalls. "It was always where he wanted to be."

Diana recognized it herself. "She was explaining to me Harry's always loved the military," journalist Ingrid Seward says, remembering one of her last conversations with Diana. "That's what he wanted to do from the age of five."

Becoming a commissioned officer requires passing the Regular Commissions Board (RCB) selection examinations, then completing forty-four weeks of coursework at the Royal Military Academy Sandhurst.

The first five weeks after his arrival, in May, were the most extreme. "Serve to lead," the school motto declares. It's a goal accomplished by near total deprivation from the comforts of civilian life: visitors, electronic communications, and alcohol are all banned, and the physically and psychologically demanding training causes 15 percent of the two hundred or so cadets in each class to drop out.

"Nobody's really supposed to love it," Harry says. "It's Sandhurst. The infamous first five weeks, it's a bit of a struggle but I got through it. Obviously you've got a platoon of thirty guys so everyone's going through the same thing and the best thing about that is being able to fit in as just a normal person."

For Harry, that means celebrating his twenty-first birthday, on September 15, dressed in green coveralls that make him look "half like an inmate and half like a gardener" and "running down a ditch full of mud, firing bullets." Harry's survived military hazing from fellow recruits who called him "Sick Note" when he battled a summer bug and blistered feet. Tonight, he'll raise a beer with them.

Sandhurst is in Surrey, thirty miles southwest of London and a world away from royal life. In stark contrast to William's twenty-first—an *Out of Africa*–themed fancy-dress celebration for three hundred guests at Windsor Castle—Harry decides, "I'm not having a party. I'll probably be in a ditch in the middle of Wales. I might let off a party popper."

There's only one place Harry wants to go: the front line.

Since October of 2001, Great Britain has been part of the coalition forces in the US-led War on Terror.

In an interview published on his birthday, Harry declares the depths of his determination. "There's no way I'm going to put myself through Sandhurst and then sit on my arse back home while my boys are out fighting for their country."

William, as the future king and eventual head of Britain's armed forces, also has military aspirations. Like Harry, he's set on joining the British Army, not the Royal Navy, where their father and grandfather served.

"I am absolutely delighted to have got over the first hurdle," William says in October, upon receiving his own marks from the RCB. The recent university graduate scores seven points out of ten on the "raw intelligence test" (besting his brother's results by three points) and impresses senior officers as "athletic, well co-ordinated and quite bright" with "good leadership skills."

"But I am only too well aware," he says, "having spoken so much to Harry, that this is just the beginning. I am really looking forward to taking my place alongside all the other cadets at Sandhurst."

Soon, two men on the academy roster will answer to "Officer Cadet Wales."

Chapter 90

O nly one person answers to "my adorable Kate."

On January 3, she surprises her prince with a party. Five days later, on the eve of her twenty-fourth birthday, William reports to Sandhurst.

He toasts his girlfriend as being "always in his thoughts."

Over the New Year's holiday, the pair skied the fastest, sheerest Alpine "black runs"—and kept the press guessing about their next move. The day before their return to London, cameras caught up to them on Casanna Alp, near Klosters, where the couple exchanged a public kiss.

The headlines cheer KISS ME KATE, but it will be five long weeks before the young couple will have another chance. William packs two photos to keep by his dorm-room bed: one of the queen and one of Kate. He also packs an ironing board, a requirement for every cadet.

It's raining heavily on January 8 when two royal Range Rovers arrive at Sandhurst. The Surrey campus is twelve miles from Thorpe Park, the amusement park where Diana, William, and Harry enjoyed their favorite thrill rides—Loggers Leap, Thunder River, and Depth Charge.

Today, Charles accompanies William to the steps of Old College, where they're greeted by the Sandhurst commandant, Major General Andrew

Ritchie; the academy adjutant, Major George Waters; and Sergeant Major Vince Gaunt.

"No doubt Prince Harry has given his brother a few tips," Major General Ritchie says, "but they'll be training separately."

As a third-term student, Harry isn't even due to report until tomorrow at 6:30 a.m.

Inside, William is issued a name tag that reads WALES.

"Bye, Pa," he says to Charles.

Then officer training begins.

"The last thing I want to be is mollycoddled," William says. "I want to go where my men go and I would want to do what they do."

But first comes the regulation "grade 3 haircut."

The military hairstyle Major General Ritchie describes as "short" remains an uncomfortable fit. On a Sunday visit to a military cemetery, the prince is seen continually touching the top of his head, where his hair is thinning.

William readily takes to the tactics and weapons training—learning first-aid and hand-grenade techniques as well as how to use firearms, including a Browning 9mm pistol and an SA80 5.56mm assault rifle. He keeps his single room inspection-ready and learns field survival skills.

On February 17, William is one of 269 cadets participating in the Long Reach, a forty-mile march through the Brecon Beacons, in the Black Mountains of southern Wales. The wintry conditions expose the platoon to sleet, snow, wind, and bitterly cold temperatures.

Twenty-four hours spent entirely outdoors with limited sleep and rations is a dual test in individual strength and team building. William carries a pack nearly equal to his body weight and attempts to boost his flagging energy with bites of chocolate as he urges others on. Yet all around him, men succumb to the relentless conditions, and nearly a third of the class drops out. William digs deep, mustering the will to check in at all nine waypoints and complete the march.

———∞∞∞———

Wearing a Russian-style fur hat and a beige herringbone coat, Kate steps into the royal box at the Cheltenham Gold Cup steeplechase race. She's there as a guest of Charles and Camilla, who presents the trophy to the winning racehorse, War of Attrition.

Kate charms the crowd of bettors eager to wager that she and William will be engaged before the 2007 festival.

Though an engagement is a requirement to ensure that Kate will be protected by the Metropolitan Police Service's SO14 Royalty Protection Group, Charles worries for Kate's safety. A study is needed—at his expense, he insists—into any "credible threats" to her well-being.

Before long, the *Express* reports that "Kate will receive her own 24-hour security detail, fueling speculation that an engagement is to be announced."

Chapter 91

Spring 2006
London

F ootball is a game I love playing and watching," William says.

At Clarence House, the twenty-three-year-old prince accepts a new role from the chairman of the Football Association, the sport's governing body.

As president-designate of the FA, William harbors a deep-seated enthusiasm for the game, though he jokes that his new position is good for "loads of free tickets" and Prince Charles ribs him, saying that "they must've been desperate" to fill the post given William's poor skills on the pitch.

During his school days, he "got into football big time," Prince William says, playing house matches and declaring his lasting allegiance to the Premier League team Aston Villa, based in Birmingham. Harry supports London-based Arsenal, but William enjoys throwing in with a team that can "give me more emotional rollercoaster moments."

"It was the first team I went and watched play in an FA Cup," he recalls. "I must have been about 12 or 11 and I went with a load of mates.

"It was fantastic, I sat with all the fans with my red beanie on, and I was sat with all the Brummie fans and had a great time. It was the atmosphere, the camaraderie and I really felt that there was something I could connect with," the prince says.

"I liked the idea that Villa had a real history, winning European Cups and stuff like that. I felt a real connection with the club," he states. "Villa felt like a really proud Midlands club and it felt very special."

He doesn't mention where his other sporting passion lies.

Motorbikes.

Whenever he can, William dons his Arai full-face helmet with a black visor and Alpinestars boots and gloves and starts up the four-cylinder high-performance Triumph Daytona 600 motorbike that he gifted himself for his twenty-first birthday.

He'd been wanting a motorcycle for years and even took an elective course in motorcycle maintenance during his last year at Eton in hopeful anticipation that he'd get the 125cc Kawasaki he asked for on his seventeenth birthday. He had to wait a bit longer: after passing his driver's test in 1999, he instead settled for a white Volkswagen Golf with the personalized license plate WILLS 1.

Riding a motorbike "is a risk," William concedes to his concerned father and grandmother, but by his calculation, "as long as you've had sufficient and thorough training you should be OK. You've just got to be aware of what you're doing."

"I just enjoy everything about motorbikes," he says, though there is a certain aspect of riding that helps ease the stress of being the most high-profile officer candidate at Sandhurst. When William slips into his motorbike leathers and helmet and accelerates his new Honda CBR 1100XX Super Blackbird—which tops out at 175 miles per hour, faster than some Ferraris and Porsches—"it does help being anonymous with my motorcycle helmet on because it does enable me to relax."

Royal correspondent James Whitaker, who witnessed Diana "constantly fleeing from the paparazzi" pursuing her on motorbikes, is surprised to see "her son using a motorbike for the same sort of reasons."

The Super Blackbird is the latest in a progression of increasingly powerful bikes William owns—faster than those ridden by the team of four experts from the SO14 Royalty Protection Group, which Charles assigns to tail the prince on the open roads.

"My father is concerned that I'm into motorbikes," William admits, "but he doesn't want to keep me all wrapped up in cotton wool."

Chapter 92

April 2006
Sandhurst

I t's been fifteen years since the last time Queen Elizabeth attended the "passing out" ceremonies at Sandhurst, which confer officer status on a class of cadets.

In the bright sunshine on April 12, as the queen inspects the 218 rising cornets—second lieutenants—she stops in front of her twenty-one-year-old grandson Harry. Her broad smile broadcasts the depths of her pride in his achievements as a soldier and a leader.

Prince Harry's cheeks color at the intense attention, and he can barely contain his nervous laughter.

It's an emotional moment.

Yet Harry can't rest until he settles a score between brothers. For months, the princes have kept a running joke over Harry's superior rank.

"He's determined not to have to salute me," Harry says of William. "But it's the army, isn't it?"

The younger prince's higher rank is fleeting, since as a university graduate William will gain immediate seniority in December, upon completing his officer training.

As Harry is commissioned into the Household Cavalry's prestigious Blues and Royals regiment, William offers him a one-time salute—"a moment which I really, really enjoyed," Harry says.

When the queen and Prince Philip depart Old College, the brothers stand together to salute their grandparents. William and Harry are both wearing a gift from their grandmother—a Golden Jubilee Medal, to commemorate her fifty-year reign.

The evening party offers elaborate entertainments, from roller coasters to casino tables to the dance floor, where Harry dances with his girl-friend, Chelsy Davy. At midnight, celebratory fireworks erupt along with cheers as the graduates embark on a Sandhurst ritual—ripping away the velvet stripes covering the officers' stars on their uniforms.

Harry's military future looks so bright that bookies get in on the action. Odds are thirty-three to one that his retirement rank will be general.

"The boy has come of age," the *Daily Star* pronounces.

⁂

Cornet Harry Wales is at the Bovington Tank Range aboard a Scimitar—the same light reconnaissance vehicle he climbed on during a trip he and his mother made to a military base in Germany in May of 1993, when he was eight years old and obsessed with "all things military." He's dressed as he was on that childhood day, in a khaki helmet and headphones—plus today he's equipped with the fully wired headset he needs to coordinate with his crew as he operates the aluminum-hulled machine.

The Armour Centre in Dorset, in southwestern England, is where Harry will undergo the requisite five-month training in order to realize his dream of serving on the front line as an armored reconnaissance troop leader in command of eleven soldiers and four tanks.

⁂

On December 15, 2006, Queen Elizabeth returns to Sandhurst for her second Sovereign's Parade within the year. Prince William carries a rifle and escorts his platoon's banner, his six-foot-three frame clearly visible to Charles, Camilla, and Kate in the audience. When 233 cadets stand for review, the queen greets William with a soft "Hello."

The newest member of the Household Cavalry's Blues and Royals regiment wins praise for acting as one with the troops. "On a riot-training exercise," a junior under officer says, "he was grabbing potatoes and lobbing them at the force protection people just like the rest of us."

It's Kate who stands out. She is the last guest to be seated—in the front row—wearing a coat the same deep red color as William's ceremonial sash.

Chapter 93

January 2007
London

K ate works three days a week as an accessories buyer at the head office of Jigsaw, the upscale fashion chain founded by Belle and John Robinson.

In exchange for a donation to a local hospital, the Robinsons had lent William and Kate their beachfront vacation home on Mustique, a private island in the Grenadines. During their May 2006 holiday at Villa Hibiscus, a five-bedroom home with a gazebo and an infinity pool, Kate enjoyed piña coladas while William's "poison" was vodka cranberry. Neither enjoyed the paparazzi who followed them everywhere, from exclusive island cocktail bars to a billionaire's yacht. Swimsuit photographs taken of the couple sell to the tabloids for £80,000.

Back in London, while William continues his military training, interest in Kate escalates—and the photographers know exactly where to find her. Jigsaw operates out of a converted Edwardian house where two chefs prepare daily staff lunches.

Kate cheerfully joins in the kitchen chat, grateful for Belle Robinson's understanding that her high-profile romance requires a flexible work schedule—and sometimes an escape hatch.

"Listen, do you want to go out the back way?" asks Robinson.

The front drive is filled with TV crews and cameras.

"To be honest," Kate answers, "they're going to hound us until they've got the picture. So why don't I just go, get the picture done, and then they'll leave us alone."

She's wrong.

Fifty paparazzi plus camera and video crews from the Associated Press, ITV, Channel 4, and the Press Association cluster around the entrance of Kate's Chelsea flat on her twenty-fifth birthday.

The £40 Topshop dress she's photographed wearing sells out instantly, but the intense admiration is frightening.

"More than anything," William insists in a formal statement, he wants Kate "left alone."

Though he doesn't compare Kate's experience to the media pressures his late mother faced, Ken Wharfe does. "History appears to be repeating itself despite claims that lessons have been learned after the loss of Diana," the retired royal protection officer says. "As far as I can see, the warnings have not been heeded."

It's reminiscent of what Charles wrote in a 1983 letter about the press hounding Diana during their trip to Australia. "There is no twitch she can make without these ghastly, and I'm quite convinced mindless, people photographing it... What has got into them all? Can't they see further than the end of their noses and to what it is doing to her? How can anyone, let alone a 21-year-old, be expected to come out of all this obsessed and crazed attention unscathed?"

The damage may have already occurred.

In mid-March, William follows Harry's path to Bovington Tank Range for five months of training to become a reconnaissance commander, then on to attachments with the navy and RAF so that he'll have a working familiarity with every branch of the British military he'll one day command.

And in April, a different undercover operation takes place. He and Kate break up.

"How are things going with William?" a friend asks Kate at a London dinner party on April 12.

"It's finally over between us," she answers, without a trace of emotion despite the end of a six-year romance.

Her friends listen to Kate describe a breakup by mutual consent, and then they're off to Kitts, a nightclub on Sloane Square named after the vacation destination in the Lesser Antilles, known for its Caribbean rum.

Chapter 94

April 2007
Windsor

A rmy chiefs are in crisis talks. "If they can get a bomb inside the Iraqi parliament then who's to say they can't get one inside the Blues and Royals officers' mess!"

The subject of urgent debate is the status of Harry's imminent deployment to Iraq as a Scimitar tank commander.

A leader of last week's extremist attack has put a price of £250,000 on the twenty-two-year-old prince's head, threatening, "We planted our people inside British bases and they are our constant source of information. They have orders to track Prince Harry's movements. Once we have that information we will make appropriate plans to capture him."

The Blues and Royals circle around Harry. "His troop will not just protect him, but all the guys. They are all there to do their bit." But it falls to the head of the British Army, General Sir Richard Dannatt, Chief of the General Staff, to assess conditions in the wake of the menacing claims.

The general makes a secret visit to Iraq. Credible intelligence reports reveal that Harry is the target of sniper and smuggling plots, including a plan to transport him from Iraq to Iran, where rescue would be unlikely.

As a headline in the *Telegraph* reports on May 16: IRAQ IS TOO

DANGEROUS FOR HARRY, SAYS ARMY, quoting General Dannatt's determination that "these threats expose not only him but also those around him to a degree of risk that I now deem unacceptable."

The Ministry of Defence criticizes the army's position as extreme, saying, "The threat level changes all the time. There is nothing to say Harry couldn't serve in Afghanistan or still go to Iraq at a later date. He could go out there in six or seven weeks time."

Yet his regiment is due to deploy in three days.

At Combermere Barracks, Harry contemplates quitting the army. "If I'm going to cause this much chaos to a lot of people then maybe I should just, well, bow out," he says, "not just for my own sake, for everyone else's sake."

In command of the Household Cavalry Regiment is Lieutenant Colonel Edward Smyth-Osbourne. He knows that regular officers are feeding off the unrest surrounding the prince's deployment status: "We have always known he wouldn't go," one of them tells the *Express*. "He's a posh boy and there was no chance of him fighting in the first place." So Smyth-Osbourne must act quickly.

"You're coming to Afghanistan with me," the lieutenant colonel tells Harry. "I know you haven't been able to go to Iraq but I'm going to make damn sure you get to Afghanistan, so hang in there."

Chapter 95

H ello, Wembley!" Harry greets the 63,300 fans who've turned out at the glass-and-steel stadium for the July 1 Concert for Diana, in addition to the five hundred million people in 140 countries potentially watching on live television.

"If it goes wrong," he's told the BBC, "it'll be very nerve-racking."

A standing ovation shakes the preshow jitters off the "ginger Bob Geldof," as William calls his brother, after the organizer of the July 1985 Live Aid concert.

That show was held at the old Wembley Stadium, where their mother talked and laughed backstage with George Michael and Elton John—who's tonight's opening act. The Concert for Diana is held in the new Wembley Stadium, built on the site of the original, which Prince William officially opened a few months earlier in his role as Football Association president.

William says of today's show, "This event is about all that our mother loved in life, her music, her dancing, her charities and her family and friends."

The crowd cheers, ensuring that the next six hours of music by Diana's favorites, from Rod Stewart to Duran Duran, will fulfill the princes' wish to give her "the best birthday present she ever had."

Today, she would have been forty-six.

A luminous portrait of Diana by Mario Testino is projected onto a jumbo screen rising from the stage. It's almost as if she can hear her friend Elton John singing the lyrics to "Your Song." *My gift is my song, and this one's for you.*

Between the pop performances, the English National Ballet dances a scene from *Swan Lake,* and Josh Groban leads a medley of Andrew Lloyd Webber show tunes.

Wearing a white three-piece suit with a black tie and backed by a full choir dressed in black, Sean "Diddy" Combs opens his performance with remembrances of Diana. "So beautiful. So graceful. So compassionate. So royal. An incredible mother."

Between verses of "I'll Be Missing You," with its samples of "Every Breath You Take" by the Police, he pauses to address the boxed seats where the princes are sitting.

"Prince William, Prince Harry. We love you. We respect you."

The brothers clap and dance, cheering along with the audience as Combs says what everyone is feeling. "We miss you. Our princess."

Harry has his girlfriend, Chelsy Davy, on one side, and his brother, William, on the other. Kate Middleton is also there, two rows back. She and William quietly reconciled around a month ago but are keeping it from the media. Or trying to, at least—the *Sun* photographer Arthur Edwards, sitting in the royal box with his wife as a guest of the princes, spots William and Kate tucked away in a corner, deep in conversation. "Looks like it's on again," his wife says of the couple's romance.

As the twenty-four performances draw to a close, William is called back onstage.

"Thank you to all of you who have come here tonight to celebrate our mother's life," he tells the audience. "For us this has been the most perfect way to remember her, and this is how she would want to be remembered."

Harry has a personal message for his fellow soldiers serving in Iraq. "I wish I was there with you. I'm sorry I can't be. But to all those on operations at the moment, we'd both like to say: stay safe."

Five days before the tenth-anniversary memorial service for Diana, Camilla makes an announcement. "On reflection I believe my attendance could divert attention from the intended purpose of the occasion."

William and Harry had invited their stepmother to the ceremony—to be held at the Guards' Chapel, which serves their regiment, the Household Cavalry—but public sentiment backs her decision not to attend. Just trying to organize seating in the chapel for the Spencer and Windsor sides of the family is headache enough. Arrangements become so complicated that William throws up his hands.

Harry, meanwhile, picks up the phone. "I want to speak to my father, put him through."

"William gets quite buttoned up inside and angry about things and often it's his brother who makes it happen," a family friend says. "William's quite complicated and Harry's not at all complicated. He's one of the most straightforward people I've ever met. Everyone adores him."

Harry gets right to the heart of the issue when Charles comes on the line at Highgrove.

"Right Dad, you're sitting here, someone else is sitting there," Harry tells him, explaining that he and William will sit on opposite sides of the altar. Harry will be with the Spencers, William with Queen Elizabeth and the senior royals.

"All right? Are you happy?"

"Oh yes, I suppose so," Charles says.

The bishop of London presides over the noontime service. Charles, William, and Harry, dressed in mourning black and regimental ties, followed closely by the queen, in vivid purple, lead the procession of nearly five hundred guests into the chapel, in Wellington Barracks, near Buckingham Palace.

William and Harry have chosen every detail, working together via iPod and text messaging. They've chosen the words that will be spoken and the musical selections that will be performed—by choirs from the Guards' Chapel, Eton, and the Chapel Royal singing together to commemorate their mother's outreach "to the excluded and forgotten."

As they did on the day of Diana's funeral, people carrying flowers crowd the streets so they can see and hear the broadcast on outdoor screens. They listen in reverent silence as William, who bites his lip to quell the emotion of the day, reads from St. Paul's letter to the Ephesians. Its message of inner strength and spirituality is echoed by the bishop, who speaks of first meeting Diana when she was preparing for her wedding and praises her gift for finding "the right word or the right gesture to bring cheer and comfort."

It's Harry's speech that brings the congregation to tears.

"William and I can separate life into two parts," he says. "There were those years when we were blessed with the physical presence beside us of both our mother and father.

"And then there are the ten years since our mother's death. When she was alive we completely took for granted her unrivaled love of life, laughter, fun and folly. She was our guardian, friend and protector."

The brothers wrote the words together, but Harry's delivery is deeply personal.

"She will always be remembered for her amazing public work. But behind the media glare, to us, just two loving children, she was quite simply the best mother in the world.

"We would say that, wouldn't we? But we miss her. Put simply, she made us and so many other people happy. May this be the way that she is remembered."

As Harry bares his heart to those who loved his mother best, he also keeps a secret the queen shared during this eventful memorial summer.

"She actually told me," Harry later reveals to the press. "She told me I'm off to Afghanistan, so that's the way it was supposed to be."

The jumble of feelings he describes as "a bit of excitement, a bit of 'phew,'" is building toward the achievement of an elusive goal, to "finally get the chance to actually do the soldiering that I wanted to do ever since I joined, really."

Chapter 96

Autumn 2007
London

A t the Royal Courts of Justice, Lord Justice Scott Baker addresses the inquest panel of five men and six women. It's been 3,865 days since the fatal crash in a Paris tunnel, and the questions continue, even after French and British police investigations—in the form of the three-year, $7 million Operation Paget—determine that it was "a tragic accident."

"Mohamed al-Fayed has maintained throughout that the crash was not an accident but murder," the judge notes, "in the furtherance of a conspiracy by the Establishment."

Opening evidence is Ritz Paris security footage never seen by the public. As Diana's familiar face flashes on the courtroom screen, jurors watch the wrenching images of her last hours alive.

Dressed in a camouflage jacket accessorized with pearl-drop earrings, Kate lies in heather growing on the queen's Balmoral estate. She's holding a rifle aimed at a deer-shaped metal target.

Kate is new to the hunting activities deeply ingrained in the royal family, so Charles teaches her how to use the telescopic sight to line up a shot as far as a mile away.

She shoots, more successful in scaring birds than in hitting the target.

Animal-rights activists swiftly take issue, connecting the mid-October shooting lessons with the fur hat Kate wore to last year's Cheltenham Gold Cup race.

"Some have compared Kate to Diana," a PETA spokesperson says, "but Diana never wore fur and she also turned against blood sports."

Eleven days before Christmas, Harry is at RAF Brize Norton, where a C-17 Globemaster aircraft is loading troops and equipment bound for Forward Operating Base Dwyer, in Afghanistan. Cornet Wales carries his Bergen rucksack, filled to capacity with the protective gear he'll need, from Osprey body armor and goggles to a Kevlar helmet and sunscreen.

On Christmas Day at the queen's Sandringham estate, the royal family gathers around the mahogany table in the Queen Mary–style formal dining room. As they toast to Harry's safety and success, hoping the British media blackout as to his whereabouts will hold, he's in Helmand Province inside a bullet-scarred Islamic school.

Nepalese British Army soldiers—known as Gurkhas—roast chickens they've just killed using long kukris, or knives. To Harry, the meal the comrades share around the fire is the "best Christmas of his life."

On New Year's Eve, he begins serving as a forward air controller. Under his radio call sign, Widow Six Seven, the prince guides two US F-15 fighter jets as they release five-hundred-pound bombs onto their targets: a grid of Taliban bunkers.

Coordinates lock. Explosions detonate.

Chapter 97

January 2008
Afghanistan

T he streets of the once bustling economic district of Garmsir, outside Forward Operating Base Delhi, in southern Helmand Province, are nearly deserted, their structures damaged by heavy bombing exchanged by Taliban and coalition forces as each has relinquished and regained control. Harry is here on a weeklong patrol.

"Just walking around, some of the locals or the ANP [Afghan National Police] they haven't got a clue who I am, they wouldn't know," Harry says.

Still, he's careful, "wary about the fact that I do need to keep my face slightly covered. Just on the off chance that I do get recognized, which will put other guys in danger."

The six men in a secret service unit—SAS—serve as Harry's "guardian angels." He admires the "great soldiers" who treat him "as though I was just another officer."

He isn't.

"It's bizarre," Harry says. "I'm out here now, haven't really had a shower for four days, haven't washed my clothes for a week and everything seems completely normal. I think this is about as normal as I am going to get."

On January 7, the prince's anonymity is compromised. The Australian women's magazine *New Idea* breaks the international embargo by reporting where Harry is—and why—in a web post. The post isn't widely read—Harry isn't briefed on it—yet the Ministry of Defence institutes further precautions. Harry's SAS squad tightens around him, a shadow nearly as close as the Scotland Yard personal protection he's known all his life.

Harry's comrades nicknamed him "Bullet Magnet" when he was denied deployment to Iraq over safety concerns. Suddenly the military humor is more grounded in truth than the MoD would like.

Harry moves to Forward Operating Base Edinburgh, where he joins the coalition mission to capture Taliban stronghold Karis de Baba. The rigor of performing high-stakes reconnaissance work in the extreme desert climate wears on Harry. So does the isolation. His morale is at a low point when he receives kind words from home that bring back memories of his mother.

"William sent me a letter saying how proud he reckons she would be," Harry says. "Hopefully she would be proud. She would be looking down having a giggle about the stupid things that I've been doing, like going left when I should have been going right."

On January 17, after less than two weeks with 1 Squadron of 1 Elementary Flying Training School, William takes his first solo flight, lifting off in the Tutor, a propeller-driven Grob 115E, from RAF Cranwell, 107 miles north of London.

"It was an amazing feeling," William says after landing the light aircraft earlier than scheduled because of winter weather conditions. "If you had a list of the top 50 things to do before you die, flying solo would be in there."

The February 28 headline in the news aggregator *Drudge Report* reads: PRINCE HARRY FIGHTS ON FRONT LINES IN AFGHANISTAN. Its source: *New*

Idea magazine. The media blackout is destroyed, and so is Harry's deployment. London's *Evening Standard* is the first to announce in Britain that HARRY FIGHTS THE TALIBAN, even as Air Chief Marshal Sir Graham "Jock" Stirrup takes decisive action "to withdraw Prince Harry from Afghanistan immediately."

"There's always someone out there who is willing to ruin the party," Harry says. "Well, job's done."

At Kandahar, he boards a TriStar long-range transport from the 216 Squadron alongside 170 injured comrades, some of them unconscious, bound for treatment at Selly Oak Hospital, in Birmingham.

"Those are the heroes," Harry says. "The bravery of the guys out there was humbling. I wouldn't say I'm a hero. I'm no more a hero than anyone else."

Seven hours later—at 11:29 a.m. on March 1—the TriStar lands. Harry exits the aircraft dressed in desert combat fatigues. His downcast eyes can't hide his disappointment that his deployment has ended.

His proud father and brother are waiting on the tarmac.

"Welcome back," William says, and as a fellow military man, he cuts straight to the point. "How was it?"

Charles addresses the assembled press. "As you can imagine, it's obviously a great relief to see him home in one piece."

Questions turn to the sensitive topic of a member of the royal family engaging in mortal combat. "It's war, it's hell," Harry says, but "you do what you have to do, what's necessary to save your own guys."

William decides to cut the interview short. Looking toward Miguel Head, the chief press officer at the Ministry of Defence, the prince makes a definitive sign, moving his hand across his throat.

"Thank you, the interview's over," Head says.

William and Harry load his gear into a waiting Audi Avant. Harry will be stationed at the Royal Artillery Barracks at Woolwich, in London, but his homecoming happens at Highgrove.

On April 1, Harry is promoted in rank. He's a full lieutenant, battle-tested.

Chapter 98

April 2008
Berkshire

A helicopter is hovering over the heads of Kate Middleton and her parents, readying for its descent.

Having met in the airline industry, where he was a pilot and she was a flight attendant, Michael and Carole Middleton are more familiar with aircraft landings than most. But the sight of a twin-rotor forty-eight-seat RAF Chinook lowering into the paddock adjoining their Bucklebury home is extraordinary.

William, who is eight days from earning his RAF wings, is at the controls of the fully crewed £10 million helicopter, which costs £15,000 per hour to operate. The Chinook is on the ground for twenty seconds, and no one disembarks before the helicopter reascends to continue its one-hundred-mile training run, ending at RAF Odiham, in Hampshire, sixteen miles from the Middleton estate.

When the *Express* headline reports an OUTCRY AS WILLIAM POPS OVER TO KATE'S IN HIS RAF COPTER, one Ministry of Defence spokesperson responds that "battlefield helicopter crews routinely practice landing in fields and confined spaces away from their airfields as a vital part of their training for operations." An anonymous military source explains the extraordinary access to one of forty-eight Chinooks in the British fleet: "In theory any pilot could do this but it's basically because he's the prince."

———❧———

On April 7, after six months and testimony from 278 witnesses, a jury votes nine to two that Diana's death was an "unlawful killing" that was "caused, or contributed to, by the speed and manner of the Mercedes and the speed and manner of the following vehicles." This verdict departs from the findings of the 2006 Operation Paget investigation.

William and Harry issue a joint statement, saying of the jurors, "We agree with their verdicts." They can't change the past, but they can honor it. "The two of us would like to express our most profound gratitude to all those who fought so desperately to save our mother's life on that tragic night."

———❧———

Prince Charles, in his RAF uniform, stands opposite his son. William is graduating today, April 11, from Royal Air Force College at RAF Cranwell. Charles presents him with a pair of ceremonial pilot's wings like the ones he earned in 1971, continuing the tradition of royal pilots.

Two days earlier, Charles and Camilla celebrated their third wedding anniversary. William arranged a special gift—a Chinook flyby of Birkhall, the home on the Balmoral estate that Charles inherited from the Queen Mother.

Though the couple was not at home to see the airborne tribute, an eyewitness spotted it. "This helicopter came out of the blue and in seconds was over the rooftops of Birkhall. Everyone knew it was William," the witness notes, especially given that state aircraft aren't allowed to descend lower than two thousand feet within a four-mile radius of royal residences. "The RAF have the best pilots in the world but I doubt they would get the go-ahead to fly over Birkhall at under 250 feet."

After graduation, William takes to the skies again. In what's cleared as a training mission, he flies a Chinook to Woolwich Barracks, where he picks up a passenger: Harry. Their cousin Peter Phillips is having his bachelor party weekend in an island location reachable only by plane, ferry—and helicopter.

"Whether it can be considered a reasonable training evolution or not," a military insider says, "the average Joe is going to view it as an expensive taxi."

"I'm working on my license," William says a few weeks later, in response to an eighty-two-year-old woman who prematurely congratulates him on having earned it. "I'm trying to do as much flying as I can. But I've been accused of wasting money—joyriding."

"He said he'd got in a bit of trouble for flying," the woman tells the *Express,* "but he was very nice about it."

Chapter 99

Spring 2008
Surrey

H i, I'm the guy who was on the plane with you," Harry says to twenty-one-year-old Royal Marine Ben McBean on April 21. McBean, who's lost his left arm and right leg, was on the same transport as Harry when they were both coming home from Afghanistan in February. "I was staring at you for half an hour. I'm Harry. A real honor to finally meet you properly."

Harry and William are visiting wounded soldiers at Headley Court, a medical rehabilitation center. McBean demonstrates the use of his artificial limbs. "I'm over the moon, because I'm free again," he says. "Next year, I'm going to run the London Marathon to raise money for Help for Heroes."

Dressed in suits and regimental ties, the princes exude the warmth and compassion they inherited from their mother and have made their own.

"Harry knows the ins and outs," says Lance Sergeant Adam Bell, who's also recovering from the loss of a leg. "It's more like talking to an officer than talking to a royal."

On May 5, 160 soldiers—all of whom have battled on the front lines against a resurgent Taliban force—parade along the streets of Windsor, headquarters of the Household Cavalry Regiment. Harry leads the way in the center of the front row. William sits inside a hangar at Combermere Barracks, one of six hundred people gathered to view a ceremony led by Prince Charles's sister, Princess Anne. Harry waits his turn to receive a silver disk, the Operational Service Medal. Aunt and nephew exchange a smile as she pins the medallion to his chest.

William embarks on the next phase of his military career, joining the Royal Navy on May 9. The two-month training course at Britannia Royal Naval College, in Dartmouth, will build on his service in the army and the RAF, making him the first contemporary royal active in all three branches.

At Kensington Palace, Harry meets with General Sir Richard Dannatt to discuss when and how he can make his second deployment.

"Why not think about flying?" Dannatt asks. "You're pretty anonymous in a helicopter. We've got attack helicopters, communications helicopters—Apache, Lynx—you can fly either of those."

When Dannatt details the training timeline—three phases, nearly two years—Harry is quick to answer, "That's far too long."

"Yup," Dannatt says in agreement, "but it's actually a really good skill to have; I think you'd enjoy it and there's a very high probability that we'll still be in Afghanistan and you can get back there."

On June 16, Kate stands on the Galilee Porch at St. George's Chapel dressed in a dark suit with white polka dots and a black-and-white headpiece. The seven thousand spectators outside Windsor Castle are cheering as much for her as they are for William.

He's on parade, joining the ranks of the senior royals by becoming the one thousandth Knight of the Garter. The chivalric line dates to

1348—which explains the costumes they're all wearing. The order's regalia includes blue velvet robes and heron-plumed hats, and William looks visibly ill at ease.

During the solemn investiture ceremony, he dips his head and looks at the chapel floor in a gesture that recalls Diana's famous "Shy Di" mannerism. William perfected the bashful look in his teenage years in a futile attempt to dissuade photographers and girls, though at nearly twenty-six he no longer has his "big blonde fringe" to gaze up through.

Suddenly, Kate can't suppress her nervous laughter.

"Oh my God!" she exclaims to Harry, who's sitting next to her. The pair dissolves into giggles.

With the resolve of his namesake and founder of Windsor Castle, William the Conqueror, William holds his composure.

"The time I spent with the RAF earlier this year made me realize how much I love flying," says Flying Officer William Wales, who's transferring his service to the RAF from the army, where he currently serves as a lieutenant in the Blues and Royals regiment.

"I now want to build on the experience and training I have received to serve operationally—especially because, for good reasons, I was not able to deploy to Afghanistan this year with D Squadron of the Household Cavalry Regiment."

William has signed on to the RAF's Search and Rescue Force. Soon he will begin an eighteen-month training course in which he will learn to fly Sea King helicopters.

Five weeks following William's September 15 announcement, Harry announces his own plans to train with an Army Air Corps regiment. Lieutenant Henry Wales has "already proved his worth as a trooper in Afghanistan," a military insider says. "By the time they're finished, he will be a deadly helicopter killer."

Chapter 100

June 2009
Shrewsbury

W e're both here just doing our bit, trying to become helicopter pilots," Harry says the year after he announced his transfer to the Army Air Corps, emphasizing his deployment goals. "To get out to Afghanistan again would be fantastic and my best chance is to do it from a helicopter. I hope to be better than the best."

"If Harry can do it then I can do it," William says. It's June 18, 2009, three days before his twenty-seventh birthday, and the brothers are standing on an airfield tarmac at Defence Helicopter Flying School, giving a rare joint interview. As the future king, William's frontline aspirations remain "in my mind, of course. If you talk to everyone else it's impossible. I still remain hopeful there's a chance."

Since January, when the brothers established a household separate from Charles, they've shared a cottage off the RAF Shawbury base. "First time, last time we'll live together," Harry jokes, with William riffing that he does all the cooking while "Harry does do washing up but then he leaves most of it in the sink and then I come back in the morning and I have to wash it up."

"Oh the lies, all lies," retorts Harry.

When the refrigerator's empty, they drive their £85,000 Range Rover Vogue to the Tesco in nearby Shrewsbury. Their mission: groceries. They fill a cart with bottles of alcohol, sweets, and William's favorite cheese, President Brie, then stop at their beloved McDonald's, where their mother took them for special treats.

⸙

With the six-figure bequest Diana left them earmarked for charitable work, in October the princes establish the Foundation of Prince William and Prince Harry. Charles's longtime adviser Julia Cleverdon senses their innate understanding of "the immense entrepreneurial energy" surrounding effective philanthropy but counsels them to choose only those patronages that correspond to their passions. "They have to feel it strongly or it is tokenism," says their private secretary, Jamie Lowther-Pinkerton.

William's first patronage, Centrepoint, is one he "inherited" from his mother, who was patron there from 1992 until her death in 1997.

The organization works with homeless people, especially the young. On Centrepoint's fortieth anniversary, in November of 2008, William recalled visiting the center with Diana when he was a young teenager and how the "example of selfless service that Centrepoint represents has stayed with me, and that is why it was the first charity I wanted to be associated with."

Centrepoint's CEO, Seyi Obakin, is the first to challenge the prince to take action, and in December of 2009, William accepts.

Suiting up in cold-weather gear, he and Obakin spend a night in sleeping bags arranged over cardboard boxes and behind garbage bins in an alleyway near Blackfriars Bridge, in London's West End. Three days before Christmas, temperatures are below freezing, and there is "no shielding," Obakin says, "from the bitter cold or the hard concrete."

At 6:00 a.m., the pair rises and returns to the Centrepoint shelters to serve breakfast to the hungry and homeless.

"I cannot, after one night, even begin to imagine what it must be like to sleep rough on London's streets night after night," William says. "I hope that by deepening my understanding of the issue, I can help do my bit to help the most vulnerable on our streets."

Chapter 101

An oil painting commemorating William, Harry, and their military service has just been put on exhibition at London's National Portrait Gallery. It is the first double portrait of the princes, who posed at Clarence House wearing their Blues and Royals dress uniforms and service medals. The artist, Nicky Philipps, says she wanted to give viewers "a behind-the-scenes glance at the human element of royal responsibility and to emphasize their brotherly relationship."

Harry assesses the painting. "I'm a little bit more ginger in here than I am in real life, I think," he says, adding—with a wink of sibling rivalry—"and he got given more hair so, apart from that, it is what it is, but it's nice. It could have been worse."

What's best for Harry is a second deployment. Helicopters, he's convinced, are "my easiest way of getting back to the front line." He studies textbooks after hours, working through the requisite technical and other requirements with a little help from recent graduate William. Though the tandem-cockpit Apache attack craft interests every fledgling pilot, Harry likes the intricacies of flying the larger troop and supply carrier, saying he's become "a bit of a Lynx lover."

Ultimately Harry scores high enough, in the top 2 percent of Army Air

Corps trainees, to qualify for the Apache—but he's assigned to the Lynx for safety reasons.

"That's all I wanted to hear—that I was capable of doing Apache," Harry says, "but I've got to go to Lynx."

In early May, a week before graduation, Chief Flying Officer David Meyer appeals on Harry's behalf up the chain of command. "If this was anybody else we'd be sending him straight to Apache."

Harry has his own appeals to make. "Listen," he tells Meyer, "I need to speak to my father; I need to speak to the queen; I really want to speak to my brother."

He comes back to Meyer. "I want to go sit in a cockpit."

On May 7, Charles presents Harry with his provisional pilot's wings, just as he'd done with William in January.

Chelsy Davy, dressed in a cream miniskirt suit, beams from the audience. Her and Harry's off-and-on romance feels decidedly *on*.

Harry is already looking ahead, past today's honor. "There is still a huge mountain for me to climb if I am to pass the Apache training course," he says. "I think it will be one of the biggest challenges in my life so far."

Meanwhile, William is training to fly Sea King helicopters—and waging a campaign with the Ministry of Defence. "My brother did it, now it's my turn," he insists, adding, "I still remain hopeful there's a chance" to deploy to Afghanistan. "I think as future leader of the armed forces it's really important that you at least get the opportunity to be credible and to do the job I signed up for, as best I can. That's all I want to do."

Chapter 102

T wenty-eight-year-old William charters a helicopter to fly him and Kate 11,500 feet above sea level to reach Kenya's remote Lake Alice, five miles from the equator.

William's familiar with the area, nicknamed the "Balmoral of Africa" because of its royal connections. Lake Alice itself is named after Queen Elizabeth's aunt Princess Alice, who visited in the 1930s. And it was at the nearby Treetops safari lodge in 1952 that a twenty-five-year-old Elizabeth "went up a tree a princess and came down a queen" upon receiving the news that her father, George VI, had died in his sleep.

For three weeks now, William has been carrying a precious object in his backpack: an eighteen-carat white gold ring, in the center of which is a twelve-carat oval sapphire surrounded by fourteen diamonds.

"It was my mother's engagement ring," he says as he proposes to Kate on October 20, "so I thought it was quite nice because obviously she's not going to be around to share the fun and excitement of it all—this was my way of keeping her close to it all."

"It's beautiful," Kate says. "I just hope I look after it. It's very, very special."

William swaps with Harry to get the ring. After Diana's death, both boys chose mementos from their mother's jewelry. William picked Diana's gold Cartier Tank watch, which her father, Earl Spencer, had given her, while Harry asked for her engagement ring. "I remember when I held Mummy's hand when I was a small boy and that ring always hurt me because it was so big," he recalls.

It's Harry's idea, though, that William use the ring to propose to Kate. "Wouldn't it be fitting if she had Mummy's ring?" he suggests. "Then one day that ring will be sat on the throne of England."

After the proposal, the newly engaged couple—who introduce themselves to staff as Willy and Kate—stay overnight in a cabin three miles from the lake, so remote that guests must bring their own groceries.

"I had a wonderful 24 hours," Kate writes in the visitors' book on October 21. "I love the warm fires and candle lights—so romantic!"

William is too far away from his family to share the happy news in person, so he keeps that Kate has accepted his proposal a secret, even from the queen.

Channel 4 ignores a written plea from Sir Jock Stirrup, the head of Britain's military, and airs a program called *The Taking of Prince Harry*. Actor Sebastian Reid plays a prince grappling with the repercussions of a potential kidnapping from the front lines.

The broadcaster maintains, "The potential risk to Harry, should he be redeployed to Afghanistan, is real and a legitimate subject for documentary."

William and Kate are still reveling in their secret engagement even after they return to England. To mark Remembrance Day, William flies to Camp Bastion, in Helmand Province, to attend a service honoring the British soldiers who've given their lives in Afghanistan. "Even after death," the RAF flight lieutenant writes in a tribute published on November 14 in the *Sunday Telegraph*, "those who have paid the supreme sacrifice still serve us all by uniting us in a common realization that, through their example, an overriding sense of duty and a willingness to defend freedom at any cost are the values which really count, the finer traits of humanity to which we should all aspire."

The next day, William flies home. He has three important phone calls to make.

Chapter 103

November 16, 2010
London

T he Prince of Wales is delighted to announce the engagement of
Prince William to Miss Catherine Middleton, Clarence House
tweets, in one of its earliest posts.

The eighty-four-year-old queen also tweets her congratulations, and
Harry chimes in from flight training: "I'm delighted that my brother has
popped the question! It means I get a sister, which I've always wanted."

"It's the most brilliant news. I'm just so happy for both of them,"
Camilla tells a reporter, while Charles's remark is loving but wry: "They've
been practicing long enough."

Kate's "got a naughty sense of humor," William says, "which really
helps me because I've got a really dry sense of humor."

The couple is at Clarence House, where they're giving an exclusive
interview to Tom Bradby of ITV News, the same reporter who visited
Harry in Lesotho.

Bradby, better known as a political reporter than a royal interviewer,
feels the pressure of the celebratory moment. He jokes with William
before the interview: "My main aim is not to f*** up your happy day."

"That would be really helpful, Tom, thank you. Do try not to," William
shoots back.

Kate, like Diana, dresses in sapphire blue for her engagement interview—in Kate's case a wrap dress from the label Issa—to match the ring. Kate turns earnest when describing the moment William proposed. "It was very romantic. There's a true romantic in there. I really didn't expect it. It was a total shock...and very exciting."

After speaking with Bradby for fifteen minutes, the couple moves to a state room at St. James's Palace for a wider interview with royal reporters. Though Kate is understandably nervous, William is for once relaxed and welcoming of photographers, calling out to veteran photographer Arthur Edwards and others by name.

"The timing is right," William says. "We are both very, very happy. When I first met Kate I knew there was something special about her."

She's a twenty-eight-year-old woman who's facing what she calls a "daunting prospect"—joining the royal family. "Hopefully I'll take that in my stride," she says.

Questions turn to the person on everyone's mind: Diana.

"Obviously, I would have loved to have met her and she's obviously an inspirational woman to look up to," Kate says.

"There's no pressure, though," William says. "Like Kate said, it's about carving your own future. No one's trying to fill my mother's shoes. What she did was fantastic. It's about making your own future and your own destiny and Kate will do a very good job of that. We are hugely excited and we are looking forward to spending the rest of our lives together and seeing what the future holds."

Chapter 104

November 2010
London

On November 23, a press briefing at St. James's Palace quells fevered speculation by announcing that William and Kate's "classic royal wedding" will be held at Westminster Abbey on April 29, 2011.

The queen's private secretary presents the couple with a guest list of 777 names entirely unfamiliar to either bride or groom. William appeals to his grandmother. "Listen, I've got this list, not one person I know—what do I do?"

"Get rid of it," the queen says. "Start from your friends and then we'll add those we need to in due course. It's your day."

As the invitations go out, sixty artisans from the Royal School of Needlework stitch the appliqué for Kate's dress. Though the wedding is not a state occasion, the dress design is guarded as tightly as a state secret.

The skilled lace workers follow strict protocol, washing their hands every half hour and replacing their needles every three hours to keep the tools "sharp and clean."

The wedding preparations intensify, and so do William's quests for adrenaline-fueled adventures.

Inspired by Harry's "Prince of Wheels" appearance at the July 2009

British Motorcycle Grand Prix—where he and professional rider Randy Mamola, on a two-seater 1000cc Ducati X2 superbike, famously popped a wheelie—William acquires an even faster Ducati for £20,000. He revs the black 1198SP's engine from zero to sixty in 2.5 seconds, then tops it out at 180 miles per hour, outpacing his personal protection officers.

Charles is worried as ever about William's and Harry's fearlessness on their high-performance motorbikes. It's not the princes' driving skills, their father says. "It's about other cars not being able to see you."

The Army Air Corps is more concerned about continuing to keep Harry out of enemy sight lines. At Wattisham Airfield, Suffolk, Harry joins 662 Squadron of 3 Regiment, where he'll become battle-ready on the Apache.

Harry excels in flight exercises and is rewarded by Chief Flying Officer David Meyer with a prize role: that of copilot gunner, the person who sits at the very head of the aircraft, one seat ahead of the pilot.

He'll also stand beside William as best man on his and Kate's wedding day.

It's 2:00 a.m. on April 27 when several companies of the Royal Navy, the British Army, and the Royal Air Force begin assembling in full dress uniform. In three hours, they'll process along the royal wedding route, from Westminster's Wellington Barracks past the Houses of Parliament and on to Westminster Abbey. Military band members march in formation, carrying but not playing their instruments.

An RAF officer instructs them in crowd control: "On the day, you'll have your heels on the white line."

The night before Diana's wedding, she rode a bicycle belonging to the Queen Mother's page around the kitchen of Clarence House, ringing the bell and singing, "I'm going to marry the Prince of Wales tomorrow!"

Now that William's the groom, he takes to the road, his helmet's visor down as he rides his Ducati through the streets. Though people are already gathering in anticipation of the wedding festivities, William can "look right at them," he says, "and they can't see my face!"

Tomorrow the prince's famous features will top the red tunic of the Irish Guards. Colonel William's first choice is the Guards' black frock coat, but the queen disapproves.

"We had a couple of discussions over this matter," William says, "but as I learned from growing up you don't mess with your grandmother and what she says goes."

Though William's army uniform "disappoints" a few of his search-and-rescue RAF colleagues, Harry understands the numerous reasons why his brother agrees to become the first groom since Mark Phillips, Princess Anne's ex-husband, to wear military red at his wedding.

"Once you're in the military," Harry says of Queen Elizabeth, "she means a lot more to you than just a grandmother. She is the queen. And then you suddenly, it's like start realizing, you know, wow, this is quite a big deal. And then you get goose bumps and then the rest of it."

Chapter 105

April 29, 2011
London

At precisely 10:10 on the morning of April 29, the brothers make the five-minute journey from Clarence House to Westminster Abbey.

Harry can't contain himself when he catches a glimpse of William's bride. "Christ! She looks stunning!" he tells his brother, out of earshot of the 1,900 guests congregated in the abbey.

Sparkling atop Kate's head are nine hundred diamonds in the Cartier Halo tiara the queen has lent her for the day.

When Queen Elizabeth enters the abbey, resplendent in a daffodil-colored suit, it's time for the bishop of London to convene the service.

On the arm of her father, Kate walks the hundred meters down the abbey's nave to the high altar, her train carried by Pippa Middleton, her sister and maid of honor. Pippa's cowl-neck cap-sleeve white dress has been designed by Sarah Burton of Alexander McQueen, but it's Burton's bridal creation—Kate's fitted white-and-ivory satin gown with hand-worked lace overlay and an eight-foot train—that's been eagerly awaited by two billion viewers worldwide.

Husband and wife, the bishop says, should "make one another their work of art."

Although William briefly struggles to place the ring on Kate's finger after they recite their traditional Anglican vows, the couple is officially married, and Kate is now Princess William of Wales. Earlier today, the queen has also titled the couple the Duke and Duchess of Cambridge and bestowed on them additional honorifics that tie them to England, Northern Ireland, and Scotland.

"It's amazing," the queen says at the close of the ceremony.

The abbey's Company of Ringers sounds five thousand peals of the church bells, and—just as Charles and Diana did on their wedding day—William and Kate ride in the 1902 State Landau coach from Westminster Abbey to Buckingham Palace.

"Oh, wow!" Kate gasps at the sight of two million people crowded outside the palace gates.

As the royal family assembles on the balcony, an expectant hush falls over the crowd.

"Is it going to be ok to do it now?" William asks his new wife.

He kisses her quickly, then more deeply, asking her, "Do another kiss. Do another kiss. Come on, one more."

The crowd cheers with heartfelt emotion.

"The kiss was magical," one spectator says. "I am in tears."

"Princess Diana would have loved this," says another, "but she'll be watching over them."

⬡⬡⬡

Now that the heir to the throne is married, reporters spot the next potential royal romance: one between William's best man and Kate's maid of honor. Former England cricket captain Michael Vaughan tweets: Let's all pray for Harry...pray that he gets lucky tonight with Pippa...Go on Harry.

"Pippa? Ha!" Harry says of his brother's new sister-in-law. "No, I am not seeing anyone at the moment. I'm one hundred percent single."

And he is. While his ex-girlfriend Chelsy Davy does attend William and Kate's wedding, she and Harry split up back in 2009, when Chelsy realized definitively that the public demands of a royal life were not for her. "She valued her privacy and guarded it so carefully," a friend says. They remain close, and Chelsy even helps Harry write his best-man speech. But the royal wedding only solidifies for her that she made the right choice. "I still have feelings for Harry," she says. "Of course I do. But I can't live the rest of my life like that. It's just too much."

Midafternoon, William and Kate drive from Buckingham Palace to their new home at Clarence House. The license plate of their 1970 Aston Martin convertible, which Charles has reconfigured to run on wine-based biofuel and which is decorated today with balloons and ribbons, reads JU5T WED.

Kate changes into a floor-length ivory satin evening gown, also designed by Sarah Burton of Alexander McQueen, and it's on to the evening reception.

"Now to the bit I like," Harry says. "Let's go inside." To the party.

There's a traditional fruitcake as the wedding cake, beautifully decorated with a soft white icing and a British floral theme. It stands three feet tall, with eight tiers, and weighs 220 pounds.

And in a nod to the Sunday teas William and Queen Elizabeth shared, their mutual favorite chocolate biscuit cake—this one standing three tiers tall and containing thirty-five pounds of chocolate and 1,700 McVitie's Rich Tea biscuits—is served as a groom's cake.

"I still remember Princess Diana bringing William down to the kitchens," says royal chef Darren McGrady, for "a glass of orange juice and a piece of chocolate cake." The young prince was such a fan of the chocolate biscuit cake, McGrady recalls, that "we even had to share the recipe with the Prince of Wales's chefs at Highgrove, so they could make it for him there, too."

When Harry takes the mike for the best-man speech, he gets the three hundred dinner guests laughing by saying, "William didn't have a romantic bone in his body before he met Kate."

After a few more words, he turns to his older brother, his voice filled with emotion.

"Our Mother would be so proud of you," Harry says.

PART 8
Officers and Gentlemen

Chapter 106

October 2011
El Centro, California

D ressed in a camouflage uniform and carrying his gear, 564673 Captain Harry Wales descends the stairs of an Army Air Corps plane.

Harry's at US Naval Air Facility El Centro, 110 miles east of San Diego—world famous as the setting for the classic military movie *Top Gun*.

He's one of twenty British pilots arriving for Exercise Crimson Eagle: eight weeks of advanced Apache training. "I count myself very, very lucky to have the chance to fly helicopters and even luckier to have the chance to fly the Apache," he says. "It's a fantastic piece of kit, it's like flying a robot."

Despite the twenty-seven-year-old being considered one of the world's most eligible bachelors in the wake of his brother's wedding, Harry's proud to identify himself as "an Ugly," the call sign for the £45 million Apaches—and the pilots who fly them.

"I've always wanted to be an Ugly," he says. Like the rest of his unit—662 Squadron, 3 Regiment Army Air Corps—Harry wears a GO UGLY EARLY patch and comments that the helicopter "is a pretty ugly beast and I think it's very cool."

"It's a joy for me because I'm one of those people who loves playing PlayStation and Xbox, so with my thumbs I like to think I'm quite useful," he adds with charming self-deprecation.

"Harry can't pass an exam in his life but my God he can fly a helicopter," says a close friend. "You don't get to be an Apache pilot unless you're in the top ten per cent." While William is "a steady bloke, unemotional and unflappable," Harry is "a romantic."

The local women—and those in nearby San Diego—certainly hope so. The flurry of excitement online over a potential romance with the prince evokes one of the attack helicopter's slogans: "Always outnumbered, never outgunned."

"Everyone is hoping they'll be the next princess diary stories," says one woman at the El Centro bar Burgers & Beer.

But notoriously single since his breakup with Chelsy Davy, Harry always answers the same way whenever he is asked the question "When are you going to get married?"

"Not for a long time."

For the moment, his focus is on his tactical training. Harry puts the Apache through day and night maneuvers and is in charge of its fearsome weaponry, including Hellfire missiles and rockets. The desolate terrain of the California military ranges here replicates desert conditions in Afghanistan—including the heat, with temperatures topping one hundred degrees.

Harry and the other Exercise Crimson Eagle participants are granted a single forty-eight-hour leave, and the class chooses Las Vegas as its recreation destination. During Thanksgiving week and under tight security detail, Harry visits XS, a nightclub at the Wynn Hotel, where he's photographed wearing a blue plaid collared shirt and whispering into the ear of a brunette waitress.

Colonel Barry Jenkins of the British Army Royal Artillery would approve—at least of what Harry's wearing. A detailed memo from the colonel has been circulating, taking other junior officers to task for their poor choice in civilian clothes. "It is not just the quality but the untidy, scruffy manner in which it is worn," Jenkins laments, comparing poor choices in suits and ties to those seen on "semi finalists from TV programme *The Apprentice*." Instead, he advises, "If in doubt, follow Princes William and Harry for civilian clothing direction."

Harry and William certainly look elegant the following month, in black tie for a December event at London's Imperial War Museum.

"I am a young Army officer, a serving soldier," Harry says at the Millies, an awards ceremony honoring the "bravest of the brave among Britain's soldiers, sailors and airmen."

"Like my brother," he continues, "I share many of the same hopes, the same aspirations to go on operations, and the same fears, as all who serve our Queen and country."

What's not the same for Harry is his level of fame and what that means for his life as a soldier. In February, Hornby, a British toy company specializing in trains, debuts under its Airfix line a soldier doll modeled on a 2008 photograph of Harry on patrol in Helmand Province. The three-inch plastic figure is sold complete with replica weapons and military equipment—though the prince's famous face is obscured.

Harry's celebrity also means he is specifically targeted. No one awaits his return to Afghanistan with the 16 Air Assault Brigade more than the Taliban, who constantly monitor the prince's movements. That same February, Taliban spokesman Zabiullah Mujahid announces: "We will continue to defend against all the invaders, but we will use all our power to kill or capture the Prince."

Harry's unfazed. There will be no media blackout or extra security next time.

"The thinking is that being an Apache pilot is quite an anonymous job and the Apache is already a target," royal sources say. "They can't be more of a target than they already are."

Chapter 107

May 2012
London

ays ahead of Queen Elizabeth's Diamond Jubilee, the sixtieth anniversary of her coronation, ABC News airs a special titled "The Jubilee Queen with Katie Couric," including interviews with William and Harry as well as their cousins Princesses Beatrice and Eugenie.

Twenty-nine-year-old William, who celebrated his first wedding anniversary last month, tours Clarence House with Couric. As they walk the gardens, helicopters fly noisily overhead.

"Seriously, can't you do something about that?" Couric jokes.

William laughs and replies, "Yeah, let me ring someone up!"

He's open and at ease with the popular American reporter. He brings her to Buckingham Palace, where she curtsies to the queen at a royal garden party, and their interview veers into William's relationship with his grandmother—and his mother.

William reveals he's most saddened that Diana is "never going to get a chance to meet Kate." Their wedding, he says, was "the one time since she's died where I've thought to myself it would be fantastic if she was here, and just how really sad for her, more than anything, not to be able to see it." Harry's take on it is "I think she had the best seat in the house probably."

The newlywed prince is at something of a crossroads. For example, he is considering leaving the military next year. Not because he wants to—"I really enjoy my time in the Air Force," he says, "and I'd love to continue it"—but because "the pressures of my other life are building. And fighting them off, or balancing the two of them, has proven quite difficult."

Also on the near horizon is the inheritance his mother left him, which William will collect when he turns thirty, next month. William is due to receive his half of the approximately £20 million total on June 21, and Harry, now twenty-seven, will receive the remaining share upon his own thirtieth birthday, in September of 2014.

There's been some speculation in the press about what an increased net worth of around £10 million will do for William's lifestyle choices—specifically, whether he and Kate might buy property outside of Kensington Palace. "What they do about a home will all depend on what he chooses to do about work," a friend comments.

When in doubt, William always looks to his grandmother for guidance. No one has more "selflessness and duty" than the queen, "my incredible role model," William says. Theirs is a particularly special bond. "The future of the monarchy really rests on William's shoulders, and the Queen knows that," remarks one of Prince Charles's former staff members. "She invested a great deal of time grooming him to be king—more time than she ever spent with her own son."

At the same time, William tells Couric, "I still think she's just my grandmother, really," adding, "I'm probably a bit of a cheeky grandson, like my brother as well."

Harry agrees. "In a small room with close members of the family, then she is just a normal grandmother," he tells Couric when the journalist catches up with the younger prince in Brazil, where he's acting as an official representative of the queen on a Diamond Jubilee tour. "It's only really sort of been over the last sort of five, eight to ten years that I've actually really learned to sort of understand and accept the huge deal that she is around the world, especially within the U.K."

This trip to Brazil is the second one that Harry's taken on behalf of the queen—following the success of his first one, to the Caribbean, Central America, and South America, earlier this year—and the new responsibility he's taking on is viewed by many as a sign that the Playboy Prince is putting his partying ways behind him. "I will help out my grandmother whenever she needs me," Harry says. He's also recently moved next door to Kate and William's place at Kensington Palace.

"Prince Harry and Prince William are a double act for the rest of their lives," a source close to the senior royals remarks. "They are very loyal and trust each other. Loyalty is key. Harry is very respectful towards William."

Diana brought her sons up that way. Even though she wanted them treated equally, "she was very conscious that both had a role to play," her good friend Rosa Monckton says. "She was grooming Prince Harry to be of support to his brother."

What Harry's looking for now is someone to support *him*.

"I've longed for kids since I was very, very young," he tells Couric. "I'm waiting to find the right person, someone who's willing to take on the job."

This is exciting news for the posse of "Harry Hunters" on the London social scene, all looking for a romantic connection with the prince. What Harry doesn't mention is the woman he's been dating since his cousin Princess Eugenie introduced them earlier this year: Cressida Bonas, a twenty-three-year-old actor and model who studied dance at the University of Leeds and is descended from British nobility. Whether she'll be interested in taking on that job is still to be determined.

"I don't think you can ever be urged to settle down," Harry later elaborates. "If you find the right person and everything feels right, then it takes time, especially for myself and my brother. You ain't never going to find someone who's going to jump into the position that it would hold. Simple as that."

Less surprising but equally exciting to royalists is the admission that William is also ready to be a father. "I'd rather like to have children," he says. "So that's the key thing really."

Chapter 108

Summer 2012
London

Queen Elizabeth's Diamond Jubilee celebration kicks off on June 2, 2012, with Derby Day at Surrey's Epsom Downs racecourse. Unfortunately, neither Prince William nor Prince Harry is in attendance—a royal aide reports that William is "taking flying exams toward his captaincy" and Harry is "involved in pre-deployment training."

But by the next day, they're both by her side aboard the barge *Gloriana* for a sail down the Thames. Named after a character in Edmund Spenser's *The Faerie Queene*—the Faerie Queen herself, whom Spenser modeled after Queen Elizabeth I—and constructed especially for the jubilee, the 210-foot barge is festooned with flowers from the royal gardens and leads 670 smaller boats on a celebratory voyage down the river to a soundtrack of Beatles songs. An ensemble called Rhythm on the River performs the band's hits for the royal family. The following day, on June 4, at the Victoria Memorial, in front of Buckingham Palace, Sir Paul McCartney serenades the queen at the sold-out Diamond Jubilee Concert with a solo performance of a Beatles medley, including "Magical Mystery Tour," "All My Loving," and "Let It Be."

Princess Anne sings along.

As McCartney launches into "Live and Let Die," his Wings-era theme song to the 1973 James Bond film of the same name, fireworks explode overhead, illuminating the palace.

McCartney jokes that the queen "will be forced to unleash the corgis" on any crowd members who fail to depart the concert "in an orderly fashion."

But once the sing-along to "Ob-La-Di, Ob-La-Da"—performed by all concert participants, including Dame Shirley Bassey, Sir Tom Jones, Kylie Minogue, and Sir Cliff Richard—dies away, Charles takes the stage.

After first thanking "Your Majesty—Mummy," and "all the wonderful people that made tonight possible," he shares distressing news.

"The only sad thing about this evening," he tells the audience watching live and on the BBC broadcast, "is that my father couldn't be with us because, unfortunately, he was taken ill but if we shout loud enough he might hear us in hospital."

When Prince Philip turned ninety last year, he announced that he was "winding down" from official royal duties, saying, "I reckon I've done my bit." He is released from the hospital just in time for his ninety-first birthday, on June 10. And he's fully recovered in time to be by the queen's side the following month, at the opening of the 2012 Summer Olympics, in London.

But first there's also another legendary figure by her side: Agent 007, James Bond, Britain's most famous fictional MI6 intelligence operative.

Queen Elizabeth gamely stars with the reigning Bond actor, Daniel Craig, and a cast of stunt doubles in a short movie by Oscar-winning director Danny Boyle that parodies the 007 series. "Good evening, Mr. Bond," the queen says before the pair leaves Buckingham Palace by helicopter. They then seemingly parachute into London Stadium, at Queen Elizabeth Olympic Park.

Cameras cut to a live shot of the monarch entering the stadium's VIP seats.

"Never can Her Majesty have been introduced to her public in a manner like that," marvel the live television announcers. "And the crowd have loved it."

"Both of us were slightly surprised with our grandmother's secret hobby that she had of parachuting," Prince Harry deadpans. "You don't expect the Queen to do something like that. What she does in her spare time is, you know, that's her spare time. But I think unbelievably good sport for her to do that."

"To be honest we were kept completely in the dark about it, that's how big the secret was," Prince William admits, adding, "In fact she did such a good performance that she has now been asked to star in the next Bond film, so I'm thrilled for her."

At the closing ceremonies, on August 12, the queen doesn't take a speaking role. Harry—whom the press now calls "statesmanlike and regal"—represents her at the VIP event, where royal cousin and equestrian Zara Phillips is honored for earning a silver medal for Britain.

It's the most significant and high-profile royal role twenty-seven-year-old Harry has ever played, and he's widely praised for how well he handles it. He's "cemented his image in the public eye as a prince of the people, a down-to-earth ambassador," the *Daily Mail* gushes, labeling him "the Royal Family's secret weapon."

"People used to say to me, 'You really must find something for Harry to do,'" says Jamie Lowther-Pinkerton, the princes' secretary. "Now they say, 'God, you've got to find something where the country can really capitalize on Harry,' which is great."

"Harry has learned some hard lessons along the way that he needs to be careful about what he says and does," former BBC royal correspondent Jennie Bond remarks. "Harry's grown up but he hasn't become stuffy."

A week later, opinions are a bit different.

Days after the closing ceremony, Harry heads to Las Vegas for a "boys' trip" with friends. Ever since his early teens, the younger prince has been known to enjoy a raucous good time. Last year, while visiting Hvar, Croatia's party island, a "drink-fueled" Harry splashed fully dressed into a nightclub's decorative fountain—though fellow revelers dismiss it as a well-mannered prince simply enjoying a night out.

Editor Tina Brown is sure Diana would have put a stop to that particular behavior. "Diana had a sense of the media, a strong sense of how the royals could get their image right. You never saw pictures of her coming out of nightclubs with her skirt up. She never looked a mess, or inappropriate. And she was very strict with her children when it came to manners."

On this trip to Vegas, Harry does manage to avoid any outrageous public behavior. What goes on during a private event, though, soon becomes widely publicized.

While staying at the Wynn, on the Sin City strip, Harry attends a party in a hotel suite. Photos leaked to the celebrity gossip website *TMZ* show Harry ending a game of "strip billiards" entirely naked, save for a necklace and an event wristband, in the company of an equally nude female. On August 22, the day after the photographs go public, Harry flies back to London, staying "in the upstairs cabin" of a 747 jet, prepping himself for return to what a former faculty member at the Royal Military Academy Sandhurst calls "an interview without coffee."

"If he'd just come back from active service and was letting off steam it might be different," the Sandhurst instructor says, but superior officers demand to know why Captain Wales broke Army Air Corps rules by engaging in such "social misbehavior."

The elder royals aren't happy, either.

"My father's always trying to remind me about who I am," Harry says, "but it's very easy to forget in the Army."

His misadventures in Las Vegas, Harry admits, are "a classic example of being too much Army and not enough Prince." Still, he points out, "At the end of the day I was in a private area and there should have been a certain amount of privacy that one should expect."

The London mayor, Boris Johnson, counters, "The scandal would be if you went all the way to Las Vegas and you didn't misbehave in some trivial way."

Chapter 109

September 2012
Afghanistan

P rince Harry—or Captain Wales, as he's known in the army—is full of "pride and anticipation" to be heading back to Afghanistan after qualifying as an Apache pilot this past February following eighteen months of training.

And while his brother and fellow helicopter pilot, RAF Flight Lieutenant William Wales, is "incredibly proud" of Harry, it doesn't stop them from debating the merits of their respective flying machines. According to a royal source, "Prince Harry tells Prince William he is flying a washing machine, because the Sea King is such an old, reliable workhorse, and William tells Harry he is flying a computer game because the Apache is so sleek, fast and advanced."

No matter which helicopter comes out on top, the brothers share a significant achievement. In the history of Britain's modern armed forces, they are the first two members of the royal family simultaneously on operational service.

At RAF Brize Norton, northwest of London, Harry boards a troop carrier that lands under cover of early September darkness at Camp Bastion. The base, which houses more than twenty thousand British and American soldiers, is in a remote desert location in Helmand Province.

Harry's regiment is part of the Joint Aviation Group, providing support to the NATO-led International Security Assistance Force (ISAF). For the next four months, he'll serve his long-awaited second deployment as part of 662 Squadron, the Army Air Corps unit credited with dispatching two Taliban per week, the highest "kill rate" in Afghanistan.

"Killing insurgents is what the machine Harry flies is there for," says a Ministry of Defence spokesperson. "You cannot put it any other way."

Taliban leaders retaliate by threatening to use "all their power to kill or capture" Captain Harry Wales as he speeds at over two hundred miles per hour across desert skies in his Apache, which can identify up to 250 enemy targets in seconds. If his copter goes down, Harry's been trained in resisting—and surviving—enemy capture.

On September 14, the day before Harry's twenty-eighth birthday, Camp Bastion is attacked by insurgents. Two US Marines are killed.

"After swift action by ISAF forces, which included UK personnel, the incident was contained," the Ministry of Defence in London states.

"No-one can say whether Harry is still in the base," a military source reports, "but it's unlikely to be by coincidence that he arrived a week ago—and a large-scale attack began hours before his birthday."

Harry later refutes media claims that the attack "was all about me" but admits it was a "bit of a reality check."

"The prince was seen in naked pictures in England," Taliban spokesperson Zabiullah Mujahid says. "To cover this shame, maybe he can atone by showing he is fighting beside their soldiers in Afghanistan."

More chilling is the warning posted on Shumukh al-Islam, a terrorist website: "Insha'Allah (God willing), his aircraft will be destroyed and he will return to the old queen in a black coffin."

Chapter 110

September 2012
France

The *Daily Star* sounds the alarm on September 15: KATE'S BEING HUNTED 'LIKE PRINCESS DI.'

The Duke and Duchess of Cambridge, as William and Kate are known, are vacationing in the South of France at a château on loan from Prince Charles's cousin Viscount David Linley, son of Princess Margaret and the Earl of Snowdon.

The private property can just be seen through the trees from a hilltop vantage point on a public road half a mile away. That's where French paparazzi, equipped with sophisticated long lenses, stake out their territory and—in an incident that recalls pregnant Diana's red bikini babymoon photos and Harry's recent nude Vegas pictures—invade the couple's reasonable expectations of privacy, capturing photographs of Kate sunning topless by the pool.

The photos are purchased by the French edition of the magazine *Closer* and published a week later under the headline OH MY GOD!

The royal couple is on a diplomatic trip to Malaysia when the news breaks.

William is *furious*.

"It was the angriest I've ever seen him," says a member of their team.

"It was the angriest I've ever seen any human being, actually. It brought back home to him everything his mother had had to put up with."

The Palace is quick to condemn the invasion of privacy. "The incident is reminiscent of the worst excesses of the press and paparazzi during the life of Diana, Princess of Wales, and all the more upsetting to the Duke and Duchess for being so," the statement reads. "It is unthinkable that anyone should take such photographs, let alone publish them."

"My wife and I thought that we could go to France for a few days in a secluded villa owned by a member of my family, and thus enjoy our privacy," William says. "The clandestine way in which these photographs were taken was particularly shocking to us," highlighting "painful" memories of the harassment his mother faced and the manner of her death in France fifteen years earlier.

William and Kate immediately take their complaint to a nearby courthouse, citing "a breach of private life," then calmly continue with their planned Far East Diamond Jubilee tour of Malaysia, Singapore, and the Solomon Islands.

Duty—and dignity—before all. William has learned that lesson well.

"I want the Queen to be watching this at home and thinking, 'Well done; shoulders back, chest out, get on with it,'" the Duke of Cambridge says.

When commentator Piers Morgan unleashes a Twitter scold—There's a reason The Queen's never been photographed topless or playing naked billiards. It's called, ironically, 'common sense'—supporters of the young royals shout him down. And although still seething with anger over the intrusion, William is able to make light of it in public.

In Borneo, the couple is fitted with harnesses so they can view the jungle canopy from atop a 138-foot-tall *Parashorea tomentella* tree. While awaiting the ascent, William turns to the assembled press accompanying them. "I don't suppose any journalists would like to go up ahead of us?" He cracks a smile as they all guffaw, commenting within earshot of official photographer Ken Goff, "Girls don't have the same wardrobe malfunctions as men do. I hope I don't have any wardrobe malfunctions."

A little more than two months after the photo scandal, Kate's playing field hockey in high-heeled boots during a visit to her prep school, St. Andrew's. The former field hockey captain has returned to open a new Astroturf field and spend the weekend with her family. Photographers are invited, but their access is restricted, and they aren't allowed any close shots of Kate.

That Sunday, the weekend is cut short when the duchess is taken ill, rushed by car from Berkshire to London's King Edward VII's Hospital.

William races to stay ahead of the inevitable speculation. He places hurried calls to the queen as well as his father and brother with the news that Kate is around eight weeks pregnant but suffering from hyperemesis gravidarum, acute morning sickness, and in danger of dehydration.

With the press camped outside the hospital, an official announcement goes out from St. James's Palace on Monday, December 3. The world reacts with joy. I am delighted by the news that the Duke & Duchess of Cambridge are expecting a baby, Prime Minister David Cameron tweets. They will make wonderful parents.

The press is delighted by this new topic to cover, monitoring Kate's every movement and smile just as they did during Princess Diana's first pregnancy, thirty years earlier. "The whole world is watching my stomach," Diana had groused. "Diana, funny enough," notes journalist Ingrid Seward, "had terrible morning sickness and she said the Royal Family never heard it," since the princess did her best to maintain her event schedule. "She was doing her duty and feeling absolutely ghastly so once again Diana is there, paving the way for Kate."

In late 1981, the *Sun* ran the headline I'M FEELING DI-ABOLICAL with a story about her struggles.

"I'm fed up with this morning sickness," Diana confided to another young woman while at a royal engagement that November, when she was around twelve weeks along with William. "Some days I feel terrible. Nobody told me about morning sickness."

"It's much better after the first three months," the other woman reassured her.

"No one told me that either," exclaimed the twenty-year-old mother-to-be. "Now I can't wait until the first three months are over."

Interviewed from Afghanistan, Harry jokes about the baby news. "It's about time. I can't wait to be an uncle."

Even as he congratulates the couple, though, it's clear that Harry's mind is on recent events.

"I just hope that she and him—but mainly Catherine—hopefully that she gets the necessary protection to allow her as a mother-to-be to enjoy the privacy that comes with. I seriously hope that's going to be able to happen."

Chapter 111

January 2013
Afghanistan

C aptain Wales is returning home from his second tour in Afghanistan after four and a half months on active duty.

Like any other soldier who's been deployed, Harry says, "I
really am longing to catch up with people." But to the journalists inquir-
ing, he stipulates that it'll be "behind closed doors—you guys aren't
invited."

Harry's animosity toward the press has been growing, and although
his combat details aren't leaked this time around, he's uneasy with the
on-base interviews—the last of which is cut short by an urgent call to
duty. Harry, still on film, is seen tearing off his microphone and racing to
join his troops when the call comes.

For the twenty-eight-year-old prince, initiating action in combat requires zero emotion. He's very matter-of-fact about its being part of the
job. "You get asked to do things that you would expect to do wearing
this uniform—that's as simple as that, really." He confirms that everyone
in his Apache squadron has "fired a certain amount" in daytime and
nighttime missions over Helmand Province, where dangerous conditions
require him to keep a pistol inside the helicopter, which he regards as "a
very small office."

"Take a life to save a life" is his moral calculus. "That's what we revolve around. If there's people trying to do bad stuff to our guys then we'll take them out of the game."

Prince William, who pivoted to becoming a search-and-rescue helicopter pilot in 2010 when it became clear that frontline combat was unlikely to be in the cards for him, is in the midst of a three-year tour at the remote base RAF Valley, in Anglesey, Wales, until at least the autumn of 2013. Eight times a month, he's on twenty-four-hour shifts, living on base near the giant yellow Sea King rescue helicopters.

"It's a fantastic job," William says. "It's a job but it's emotional, it's physical and it's very demanding."

But Harry still envisions a potential combat role for his brother, flying medical casualty pickups in Chinook helicopters. "I don't see why he couldn't," Harry says. "No one knows who's in the cockpit. Yes, you could get shot at. But if the guys who are doing the same job as us are being shot at on the ground, I don't think there's anything wrong with us being shot at as well. People back home will have issues with that, but we're not special. The guys out there are."

In May, Harry travels to America for a weeklong military-themed tour that begins in the nation's capital. He surprises military families invited to a party at the White House, dines at the British embassy, appears on Capitol Hill, and visits soldiers recovering from combat wounds at Walter Reed National Military Medical Center.

To an army veteran who survived a bomb blast in Afghanistan as a double amputee, Harry enthuses over a high-tech lab designed to help soldiers relearn to walk using video tools and prostheses. "We've got nothing like this back in the UK," he says. "You guys, as Americans, are used to the technology. We are always behind."

Harry is even more eager to participate in an event for wounded veterans and active service members: the Warrior Games, held at the US

Air Force Academy, where more than two hundred personnel compete in Paralympics-style events.

He opens the games on Saturday, May 10, alongside Olympic swimmer Missy Franklin and US Navy lieutenant Bradley Snyder, a Warrior Games swimmer who lost his sight when struck by an IED in Afghanistan. The evening before, at a prelaunch reception in Denver, Harry thrilled the crowd by joining them in singing "Happy Birthday" to Franklin, who was turning eighteen.

"I didn't know you had Pimm's in America," Harry teased the swimmer over cocktails made with the British liqueur, then quizzed her about her medal count from last year's Summer Olympics in London—one bronze and four golds.

"So you went straight from bronze to gold? What about silver?" he joked. "You skipped that one."

"I love the royal family," Franklin, who grew up in Colorado, says. "All my friends can't believe how lucky I am to be here. I think everyone just has so much respect for Prince Harry. My London gold is now my favorite medal because he touched it."

On Saturday, Harry joins the British seated volleyball team for an exhibition game, wearing a team Union Jack jersey and reaching so far forward to make a hit that he falls onto his face. His efforts impress Olympian and volleyball star Misty May-Treanor, who tweets: Thank you Prince Harry for changing people's lives & making a difference. A true honor to have met u.

A British colonel and military liaison based in Colorado praises Harry for "giving a focus to the Warrior Games that only a veteran can. Harry knows how to talk to soldiers and they love him for it."

"He knows what it's like out there," says volleyball team member Dave Henson, an army captain. "He's been on the ground and in the air."

This isn't Harry's first trip to Colorado. He visited twice as a boy, when his mother brought him to Aspen for skiing and white-water rafting. In her honor, Harry's recently become a patron of one of her dearest causes, HALO Trust, the British charity that for twenty-five years has promoted land-mine clearance. In August, he'll go to Angola, as she did, to follow up on the work HALO continues to do there.

In addition to keeping Diana's dream alive, Harry has one all his own—bringing the Warrior Games to Britain. "I don't see how it wouldn't be possible to fill a stadium with 80,000 people," he tells the crowd in Colorado Springs, "not to watch the Olympics, not to watch the Paralympics but to watch wounded servicemen fight it out amongst each other."

Harry returns home to news of an extremist's arrest for an assassination plot against him and continuing death threats from the Taliban. "He is a target for many reasons," remarks a royal source. "Harry's security team cannot be complacent."

His onetime personal protection officer Ken Wharfe agrees and makes a personal appeal to the prince, who "as a young boy was never out of his soldier uniforms" and whose "current high-profile military role has made him very much a target."

Wharfe says, "Harry will think, 'I can handle this.' But he has to be very careful. This threat should not be played down. This is a warning."

Chapter 112

July 2013
London

D o you want Kate's baby to be a boy or a girl?" ten-year-old Fay Batey asks the queen on July 17. The monarch is on a walka-bout outside Buckingham Palace, where just over a month earlier the Duchess of Cambridge, in a pink coat with pearl buttons and pearl-drop earrings, appeared on the palace balcony for the Trooping the Colour parade—Kate's last royal event before her due date.

"I don't think I mind," Queen Elizabeth tells the schoolgirl, then adds, "I would very much like it to arrive because I'm going on holiday soon...I wish it would hurry up. No sign of it yet!"

The "Kate Wait" is already under way outside the private Lindo Wing at St. Mary's Hospital—the same ward where Diana gave birth to William some thirty-one years earlier. Photographers put up ladders to stake out their positions and remain at their posts for weeks. Finally, on Monday, July 22, the Palace alerts the press via email: "Her Royal Highness The Duchess of Cambridge was safely delivered of a son at 4:24 p.m. The baby weighs 8lbs. 6oz. The Duke of Cambridge was present for the birth. The Queen, The Duke of Edinburgh, The Prince of Wales, The Duchess of Cornwall, Prince Harry and members of both families have been informed and are delighted with the news. Her Royal Highness and her child are both doing well and will remain in hospital overnight."

Before the traditional announcement can be posted on the palace gates, three cheers erupt from the crowd gathered there to await the arrival of the infant prince, who's now bumped his uncle Harry down a spot in the line of succession.

"Morning, Granddad," Charles is greeted when he and Camilla visit East Yorkshire on July 23. Charles is beaming. "I am enormously proud and happy to be a grandfather for the first time," he says.

At 7:14 p.m., William and Kate are both dressed in blue when they emerge from the Lindo Wing for the traditional presentation of the royal newborn. Kate's hair is perfectly styled, and her Jenny Packham–designed crepe de chine polka-dot dress is an homage to the one Diana wore when she first showed baby William to the cameras.

"It's the first time we have seen him, really," William says of his new-born son, "so we are having a proper chance to catch up."

"It's very emotional. It's such a special time," adds Kate. "I think any parent will know what this feeling feels like."

"The first born is very special," Queen Elizabeth remarks upon the arrival of her first great-grandson (and third great-grandchild, after Princess Anne's two granddaughters).

William turns to his wife. "He's got her looks, thankfully." Making light of his own rapidly receding hairline, he jokes of the baby's hair, "He's got way more than me, thank God."

Asked what the baby will be called, William says, "We are still working on a name so we will have that as soon as we can."

The baby's full name—George Alexander Louis, or His Royal Highness Prince George of Cambridge—is announced two days later. Charles and Diana had waited a week to share William's official name, and the future Queen Elizabeth and Prince Philip took an entire month before revealing the names they'd chosen for Charles.

As an uncle, Harry says he'll be sure the baby "has a good upbringing, keep him out of harm's way—and make sure he has fun."

He puts William on notice: "I only hope my brother knows how expensive my babysitting charges are."

Chapter 113

Winter 2013
London

I still do not know what came over me," Prince William says.

One minute, he's sitting in the audience of a gala event to benefit Centrepoint, and the next, he's up on stage belting out the backing vocals to Bon Jovi's "Livin' on a Prayer" alongside pop star Taylor Swift.

How did he get here?

On November 27, William is hosting a fundraising gala at Kensington Palace for Centrepoint, one of the charities closest to Diana's heart. William picked up the mantle as patron for the charitable organization, which supports young people in need of housing, in 2005. He'd visited several times with his mother when he was a child, and in 2009 he even spent a night "sleeping rough" out on the cold city streets to experience the difficulties for himself.

Tonight's experience is a shock of a different nature.

Things start off normally enough—a lot of glad-handing and small talk of the sort William has done his whole life. "I try and be charming and interactive," he says, knowing how much it means to people.

As he waits to watch Jon Bon Jovi take the stage, though, he's already switching to private mode. *My job is done. I'll get a dinner in a minute, and I might be able to have a chat to some people,* he thinks. *I'm off-duty a little bit now.*

But when Bon Jovi begins performing, Taylor Swift, who's seated to William's left, turns to the prince. "She puts her hand on my arm," he recounts, "looks me in the eye, and says, 'Come on, William. Let's go and sing.'"

William follows her, trancelike, to the stage. "I got up like a puppy and went, 'Yeah, okay, that seems like a great idea. I'll follow you.'"

Halfway through the song, he exchanges a high five with Swift, even as he's desperately trying to recall the lyrics and sweating through his tuxedo. While he's perfectly comfortable delivering speeches onstage, singing is another matter entirely. *Am I standing on the stage singing "Livin' on a Prayer" when I don't even know the words?*

But with the crowd cheering him on, he makes a decision. *Well, if they're enjoying it, then the night is for them. So sod it. I can't be the doofus who's going to ruin it for everyone.*

"At times, when you're taken out of your comfort zone, you've got to roll with it," William says. "There's so many pressures, but I think making a fool of yourself is okay. It's okay to not take yourself too seriously and have those moments where you let go, and you just go, 'Do you know what? I'm okay with this.'"

Even further out of his usual comfort zone a few weeks later is William's brother, Harry.

On December 13, 2013, Prince Harry and a team of disabled veterans reach the South Pole as part of a charity trek through Antarctica organized by Walking With The Wounded, one of Harry's own long-supported causes.

"A half-day on Friday and we get to the South Pole on Friday 13th," Harry announces. "Unlucky for some, lucky for us."

His teammates have nothing but praise for the prince. "He knows what he's doing. He's got his military training...so he's a good extra pair of hands," says Major Kate Philp, who lost a leg in active duty. There's no special treatment because of his status, either. "We wouldn't let it be any other way and he wouldn't want it to be any other way."

It's Harry's second big trek with the organization: in 2011, he also trained to go on a fundraising excursion to the North Pole. "Prince Harry was never, ever shy of helping," says Private Jaco van Gass, who lost an arm to an RPG in Afghanistan. "There's not a lazy hair on his body."

Although Harry was only able to accompany the group on the first portion of that North Pole trek—needing to return early for William and Kate's wedding—he made sure to keep spirits raised during his time with his teammates by surprising them with a special treat: a huge ice cream cake he'd hidden in his sled. "Every night," Van Gass says, "he would come around and give us a slice of cake for dessert."

This time, for the South Pole excursion, Harry jokes that new dad William is "just quite jealous that I managed to get away from a screaming child." But while the trip could be considered "slightly mad," Harry puts the spotlight squarely on the charity he's backing. "So what to minus 50, so what to 90 mile-per-hour winds," he says. "Occasionally you've got to put yourself through that for a good cause."

It's not all about hardships and deprivation, however. Even before they reach their destination and toast their success—including drinking Champagne kept chilled in one of double-amputee teammate Duncan Slater's prosthetic legs ("We decided to use my legs as a primitive ice bucket," Slater admits. "I don't know why we did it, but we did!")—Harry's already keeping morale up. Like his brother, he's adept at connecting with others. "Harry was a real team player," Slater remarks. "There was always something to do and he was always instigating it. There were so many wind ups. He probably spread himself quite thin. He would spend time with each team every day. He was always making sure he mixed, bringing everyone to the fore. It was very nice as he was as tired as everybody else."

"I am so proud to be patron of Walking With The Wounded," Harry proclaims. The charity aims to "raise awareness of the debt this country owes to those it sends off to fight—only for them to return wounded and scarred, physically and emotionally." But the goal is also "to demonstrate to those who have suffered lifechanging injuries that anything is still possible" and that veterans "simply want to be treated the same way as before they were injured. With respect."

Chapter 114

April 2014
Australia

T he Duke and Duchess of Cambridge—and their adorable baby boy, Prince George—are on a three-week tour of Australia and New Zealand, where locals "can't seem to get enough" of the young family. "Polls show the popularity of the monarchy is up," the *Mirror* states, "and even staunch republicans are singing their praises as a celebrity couple."

At nine months old, Prince George is the same age that William was when he traveled to Australia with his parents in March and April of 1983, on the Prince and Princess of Wales's visit to the two British Commonwealth countries.

At a play date with other babies in Wellington, New Zealand, one parent quickly spots George's command over the toys in the room and observes that "no-one was going to stand in his way" of taking "the one that he wanted"—behaviors reminiscent of those that inspired his father's schoolboy nicknames Basher Wills and Billy the Basher.

Photographers' cameras click madly when on April 22 Kate and William re-create Charles and Diana's iconic pose against the backdrop of Uluru, the iconic sandstone rock formation in central Australia. After the photo call, the Aboriginal dancers who perform for the couple don't ask them to join in, but the hip-hop DJs they meet at a youth project outside Adelaide are more insistent.

"It's all yours," William tells Kate as the Duke and Duchess of Cambridge stand before a turntable.

"William's got lots more experience than I have," demurs Kate, elegant in a pale Alexander McQueen suit, the label that also created her wedding dress. Yet when each takes a turn scratching a record to the DJ's beat, Kate—who as a child studied piano, flute, and voice—reveals she's got rhythm.

William shares his musical tastes with the young performers he and Kate meet. "I like my house music," he says. "I like a bit of rock 'n' roll, a bit of R&B. I'm not a big heavy metal fan."

Nor is he enthusiastic about taking part in a break-dancing demonstration.

Next time, William promises, he'll "do some 'popping.'"

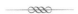

Harry, who turns thirty years old on September 15—and will inherit his share of his mother's estate, currently valued at $16 million—is in the process of pivoting his military career.

"I don't know what normal is anymore and I never really have done," he remarks to a reporter after returning from Afghanistan. "There are three parts of me; one wearing a uniform, one being Prince Harry, and the other one which is the private-behind-closed-doors stuff."

Harry's once again a swinging bachelor, his relationship with actor-model Cressida Bonas having crumbled given her skittishness over the kind of attention that being with a prince garners. She's the second serious girlfriend now that Harry's lost, at least in part, because of too much media pressure.

Even Diana hadn't foreseen the level of press intrusion her younger son would endure, assuming the media would focus on William, not Harry. Back in 1995, she'd advised the young daughter of a friend to "look at all the press. William will be king, and this is what it will be like." Instead, Diana playfully suggested that the girl consider her younger son. "Harry will end up getting all the girls."

He certainly has no trouble attracting them. Keeping them seems to be another matter.

"It's challenging, you can't deny it," says Cressida's half brother, Jacobi Anstruther-Gough-Calthorpe. "It's not something that is easy for anyone dating a royal or marrying into the family or anyone in the royal family themselves. I think on some level it is different to any other type of fame."

In January, Harry left the Army Air Corps and joined the Ministry of Defence. Instead of flying Apache helicopters, he's now working on behalf of veterans—and in March, he announces his vision for a version of the Warrior Games he'd seen in Colorado: the Invictus Games.

Harry envisions the Invictus Games as a four-day athletic competition for wounded soldiers in nine international team sports. His inspiration for the name comes from William Ernest Henley's 1875 poem "Invictus," composed while Henley, who suffered from tubercular arthritis, was recovering from a second leg amputation.

Planning the games gives Harry "nerves about everything"—including "whether it was going to come together, whether people are going to turn up, whether we were going to fill seats."

On September 11, 2014, he stands at a podium addressing an audience of five thousand in London's Queen Elizabeth Olympic Park. The unusual positioning of the lectern, oddly placed in the center of the crowd, only adds to his tension.

"Whoever's idea to put me here was...yeah," Harry grumbles, under the watch of his father, brother, and all the athletes who've assembled from thirteen countries to compete in the inaugural Invictus Games. When the warrior athletes start chanting as Harry faces them from beneath an enormous screen labeled HRH PRINCE HENRY OF WALES in golden yellow letters, he's visibly rattled. "I was so nervous, I was shaking," he admits. Yet he doesn't allow his confidence to falter, saying, "I have no doubt that lives will be changed this weekend."

"Harry has been involved every day," the games' chairman, Sir Keith Mills, says. "He has pulled his sleeves up and has got stuck in. He's passionate about helping."

For Harry, the highlight of the games comes in two gold-medal moments, when the UK team defeats the American team in both wheelchair rugby and wheelchair basketball.

"We were underdogs in the final but we beat the US at their own game," says Team GB's wheelchair basketball captain, Adam Nixon, who lost a leg in Iraq to an IED explosion.

"You are a legend," Prince Harry exclaims of the basketball win, coming up to shake Nixon's hand and pose for photos with the family.

On September 14, the Foo Fighters front man, Dave Grohl, waits off-stage to perform during the closing ceremonies as Harry reads the athletes a personal message from Queen Elizabeth and Prince Philip, followed by his own tribute. When the Foo Fighters take the stage at Olympic Park for an eleven-song greatest-hits set, Grohl says the band's hit "My Hero" "goes out to all the heroes tonight." Before blowing the crowd a kiss and playing their last song, he tells the athletes, "Thank you very much for making this one of the most special occasions of our lives."

There's one person not having a good time, however.

Harry spots five-year-old Isabelle Nixon crying because she's too small to see the band.

Recognizing her as Adam Nixon's daughter, the prince doesn't hesitate to hoist the delighted little girl up on his shoulders so she can get a good look at the stage.

"She just danced along to the Foo Fighters with him and hasn't stopped smiling since," Nixon says. His wife, Taryn, adds, "Isabelle now says she's a princess and tells all her friends she danced with 'Uncle Harry.' He was the perfect gentleman and made everyone's day."

"I was completely over the moon. I was chuffed to bits," says Isabelle.

Chapter 115

Spring 2015
Australia

R ED HEADS RULE!
 The sign, carried by twelve-year-old redhead Ethan Toscan, catches Harry's eye. He admires the schoolboy's sign and shakes his hand, telling him, "Being a red head is the No 1 thing a person can ever be."

A year after William and Kate's successful tour of Australia and New Zealand, Prince Harry is in Canberra to lay a wreath at the Tomb of the Unknown Australian Soldier, where thousands of enthusiastic locals cheer at the sight of Harry wearing the white-jacketed tropical dress uniform of the Blues and Royals—popularly known as the *An Officer and a Gentleman* uniform. The following day, he will report for duty with the Australian Defence Force, where he'll serve for the month of April.

It's his last big military assignment. Come June, Captain Harry Wales will officially leave the army. "After a decade of service, moving on from the Army has been a really tough decision," Harry says when he reveals his intentions, in March. "The experiences I have had over the last 10 years will stay with me for the rest of my life. Inevitably most good things come to an end and I am at a crossroads in my military career."

The news comes as a surprise to many who felt that Harry was destined for a lifelong career in the military, but William understands the situation better than most. He left the military himself in November of 2013, a few months after Prince George's birth, and no longer flies search-and-rescue missions with the RAF—though in July, he will pivot to flying air ambulances (and donating his full salary), at least in part over concerns that he hadn't put in his full time with the RAF. William's departure broke the expectation that helicopter pilots repay their £800,000 training costs by serving for six years, though a Kensington Palace spokesman quickly replies that "William has spent eight years in the military, three in the RAF, racked up 1,300 hours, went on more than 150 search-and-rescue missions, helping to rescue 150 people, often in precarious flying conditions. We believe he has done more than his fair share."

The Duke and Duchess of Cambridge, who celebrate their fourth wedding anniversary on April 29, are also about to expand their family again. At 6:00 a.m. on May 2, nine days past her due date, Kate is admitted to the Lindo Wing of St. Mary's Hospital in labor with her and William's second child.

Reporters have been amassed outside the hospital for weeks, but they don't have long to wait for the news from Kensington Palace that at 8:34 a.m. a healthy baby girl weighing eight pounds and three ounces was born. The royal couple kept the baby's gender a surprise even to themselves, but baby watchers have clearly been hoping for a princess. Bookies in London give the name Alice as a front-runner for a little girl, setting the odds at five to four; Charlotte and Elizabeth are tied for second, with odds at six to one.

Charles, who's been wishing for a granddaughter, says that he and Camilla are "absolutely delighted." William brings George to meet his baby sister, and by 6:00 p.m., the world gets its first glimpse of the little princess. As Kate emerges looking perfectly polished in a yellow Jenny Packham dress printed with buttercups, carrying her newborn daughter swaddled in a white knitted shawl and cap, one journalist exclaims of the duchess, "I cannot believe she has had a baby today!"

The princess's name is announced on May 4: Charlotte Elizabeth

Diana, names honoring both her paternal grandparents, Charles and Diana, and her great-grandmother Queen Elizabeth. With her deep-set blue eyes, broad smile, and light brown hair, Charlotte's appearance resembles the Windsors more than the Spencer clan—she even draws comparisons specifically to the queen—but the Princess of Cambridge shares a first and middle name with her great-uncle Charles Spencer's youngest daughter.

Perfect names, the ninth Earl Spencer tweets when he learns the news. My 2-year-old Charlotte Diana will be thrilled at the cousinly name-sharing.

Only one of them will likely inherit the magnificent Spencer Tiara. The Palace is negotiating with Diana's brother to secure it for Charlotte, the only daughter of William, the future king.

Her uncle Harry travels back to the UK to meet his niece for the first time in late May.

"She's beautiful," he declares.

She's also the first female born under Britain's new rules of succession, whereby both the daughters and sons of the Prince of Wales are eligible for the throne.

"The reason I am now fifth," Harry says of his place in the line of succession, "is because of my nephew and niece, and I could never wish them away. They are the most amazing things ever."

He's playful with the children. "I think the key to that is to grow up, but also to be able to stay in touch with your childhood side," he speculates, also giving weight to the wisdom he's found through military service. With the end of his service fast approaching, Harry reflects on the "epic" life lessons he's learned. "I dread to think where I'd be without the Army," he admits. "Without a doubt, it does keep you out of trouble." He doesn't hesitate to suggest that his nephew and niece one day consider entering military service as well. "It's done no harm, just good, for me, and I know it's the same for William."

"Since I was a kid I enjoyed wearing the combats, I enjoyed running around with a rifle, jumping in a ditch and living in the rain, and stuff,"

Harry says. "But then, when I grew up, it became more than that, it became an opportunity to escape the limelight."

Of course, he's never completely able to escape it. In mid-July, Tom Cruise has an American casting agent put "the offer out to his team to hit up Buckingham Palace and get Prince Harry" to join the cast of *Top Gun 2,* a story of how military drone technology affects the culture of fighter pilots. Cruise, who made a career-defining star turn as the ace flier Pete "Maverick" Mitchell in the original 1986 blockbuster, "doesn't just want Harry as gimmick casting but someone who offers real experience and knowledge of flying in combat."

"Not only is Harry qualified but his involvement would be a huge PR coup for the movie," says the agent.

Cruise's plan to entice Harry recalls Kevin Costner's 1997 appeal to Diana to star in *The Bodyguard* sequel as a woman who falls in love with her protector.

When Diana and Costner spoke by phone about the role, the princess asked sweetly, "Are we going to have, like, a kissing scene?"

"Yeah, there's going to be a bit of that," Costner replied, "but we can make that OK, too."

Harry doesn't need his love life to be scripted. Though it's been more than a year since his breakup with Cressida Bonas, whose fashion career has since risen to new heights as the face of luxury brand Mulberry, Harry says he's "very happy not having a girlfriend." Despite being open about his desire for children, he scoffs at comparisons to lovelorn fictional characters. "I'm no Bridget Jones," he insists.

"I don't think you can force these things," he says. "It would be great to have someone else next to me to share the pressure, but you know the time will come and whatever happens, happens."

Chapter 116

Spring 2016
London

W hat's your secret?" Harry asks his grandmother, who turns
ninety on April 21, 2016.

Queen Elizabeth is the first British monarch to reach that
age. She's proven that a devotion to duty sustains her, and knows the
power of appearances. She's not keen on the ginger beard Harry's sporting these days, and she taps his thirty-three-year-old brother on the
shoulder, telling him to "Stand up, William," when he bends over to talk
to his two-year-old son as they're all on the balcony of Buckingham Palace during the Trooping the Colour Parade.

After sixty-four years on the throne, she's also bringing other royals
deeper into the fold. Charles had joined her trusted advisory body, the
Privy Council, in 1977, and she now invites Camilla and William to
attend their first Privy Council meeting at the palace. From the ranks
of that group come the members of the Accession Council, which bears
responsibility for the succession of the monarchy.

For William, that's in the distant future.

Since July 2015, he has been serving the public as a helicopter copilot
with the East Anglian Air Ambulance.

"There were a lot of raised eyebrows in the Palace when he wanted to do that," a source close to William reveals. "While the Queen and his father backed him, some senior courtiers questioned whether it was becoming of a future king to be doing a middle-class role, hanging out with ordinary people."

But William is "determined that other people's expectations in the media or the system shouldn't get in the way of his own values." And another former Palace courtier echoes the sentiment, saying that the prince "knows what he wants" and is "assertive but cool at the same time. It is already very clear that he will have a purpose in life that relates to the real world as well as his birthright of the throne."

William's first call with the medics is to the scene of a suicide. That same week, a middle-aged man suffers chest pains and collapses in a village in Suffolk. Onlookers vie to capture pictures of William, in uniform and wearing sunglasses, inside the cockpit of the bright yellow H145 helicopter that flies the patient to Norfolk and Norwich University Hospital at speeds up to 167 miles per hour.

In October of 2015, William and his crew are called to the site of a fatal car crash. The driver's seventeen-year-old nephew has sustained a fractured pelvis and several broken ribs and falls into a coma, unaware of the role of his royal rescuer until he wakes up in the hospital, weeks later.

"We were first on the scene," William says, "and in such circumstances we all had to pitch in to fight to save the young man's life. It is days like this, when you know you have made a difference, that give you the determination to keep going."

The second in line to the throne defends his choice to put his young family first despite being called "Workshy William" and "Will-not" for taking on fewer duties than the ninety-year-old queen. He recognizes that "at some point, there's probably going to be a lot more pressure and re-sponsibility from my other side of my life. At the moment, I'm juggling the two of them"—his royal responsibilities and his ambulance work—"and a young family, and I'm enjoying it and I enjoy the challenge."

The Cambridges have two homes, both gifted to them by the queen as wedding presents: Kensington Palace apartment 1A, the longtime residence of her beloved sister, Princess Margaret, and Anmer Hall, a newly renovated eighteenth-century house on the Sandringham estate.

William finds family life at Anmer Hall "very peaceful," but becoming a father of two has taken some getting used to. "There's wonderful highs and wonderful lows," he says. "It's been quite a change for me personally. I'm very lucky in the support I have from Catherine, she's an amazing mother and a fantastic wife." Even so, he admits, "I've struggled at times. The alteration from single, independent man to going into marriage and then having children is life-changing."

Princess Charlotte is "a little joy from heaven," while Prince George, nearly three, can be "a right little rascal sometimes. He keeps me on my toes, but he's a sweet boy."

"As far as we're concerned, within our family unit we are a normal family," he says. "There'll be a time and a place to bring George up and understand how he fits in the world. But right now, it's just a case of keeping a secure stable environment around him and showing him as much love as I can as a father."

May of 2016 marks Princess Charlotte's first birthday—and the second year of the Invictus Games, set to take place at the ESPN Wide World of Sports Complex, in Florida's Walt Disney World, from May 8 to 12. There had been no games in 2015, allowing extra time for planning and fundraising. The third games have already been set for September of 2017, seventeen months away, in Toronto.

The Canadian prime minister, Justin Trudeau, is in on an all-star promotion for the upcoming 2016 games. A video is tweeted to Harry's phone. It's from the White House.

"Hey, Prince Harry, remember when you told us to 'bring it' at the Invictus Games?" First Lady Michelle Obama asks, as the president joins in with "Careful what you wish for!" Three military officers behind them then pull faces, adding a "Boom" and a "mic drop" gesture.

Harry and Queen Elizabeth team up to respond in kind, the queen smirking as she delivers the line, "Oh, really? Please," evoking the same sly sense of humor that was on display in her James Bond parody video, from the 2012 London Olympics opening ceremonies.

"If you've got the ability to be able to ask the Queen to up one on the Americans, then why not," says Harry of teaming up with his grandmother. "I certainly enjoyed it, and I know she did as well."

Trudeau's video shows him doing a push-up near the members of the Canadian Invictus team, who are among five hundred athletes from fifteen countries competing in ten events, from archery to wheelchair tennis (a new event for these games), over the next several days. There's even a lighthearted swimming competition between service dogs.

"I've been hugely honored to hand out gold, silver, and bronze medals over the course of this competition, but what meant the most to me, was handing out your Invictus Foundation medallions this evening," Harry says at the closing ceremonies. "Those medallions are the real prizes, for the years of intense rehabilitation you've put yourselves through to be here."

"Never stop fighting and do all you can to lift up everyone around you," he proclaims. "I'll see you in Toronto."

Before leaving Orlando, Harry manages a late-night trip to Disney World, his first since visiting with Diana in August of 1993.

"It's one of my very, very happy memories, of going to Disney World with my mum," Harry recalls. "I went on 'Space Mountain' 14 times. I was like, 'This is absolutely fantastic. This is the best thing ever.'" Of course, it's a little different at age thirty-one versus at age eight. "When you are that age you are invincible. And you slowly become uninvincible as you start breaking things!"

It's bittersweet to be back. "It's a huge shame that she's not here," he says, while trusting his mother would appreciate what he's working toward with Invictus. "I hope she'd be incredibly proud of what we've managed to achieve."

For an hour, Harry revisits the rides of his childhood: Splash Mountain, Space Mountain, and several others.

It's a magical evening in the Magic Kingdom.

Chapter 117

May 2016
London

N ever complain. Never explain" is the unofficial motto of the Windsors.

But William and Harry are their mother's sons, and like her, they're not afraid to raise awareness of an issue others may consider taboo: mental health. "We realized no one was talking about it, no one wanted to talk about it," William says.

Diana, one of the first royals to ever speak openly about her own struggles, had already blazed a trail for them. "What my mother believed in is if you are in a position of privilege or a position of responsibility and if you can put your name to something that you genuinely believe in," Harry says, "then you can smash any stigma you want."

"We need to normalize the conversation about mental health," William asserts, adding, "be upfront and matter-of-fact about it, and not ashamed or hide it in the dark where it festers."

"There may be a time and a place for the 'stiff upper lip,'" he acknowledges, "but not at the expense of your health."

In 2016, William, Kate, and Harry start the charitable initiative Heads Together. "Heads Together wants to help everyone feel much more confident with their everyday mental health," Kate says. Their May 16 launch event, at London's Queen Elizabeth Olympic Park, is a boxing demonstration focused on ways to release stress through exercise.

It's a tactic Harry has been using for years and one he feels can benefit anyone.

"Everyone can suffer from mental health issues," he says, "whether you're a member of the royal family, whether you're a soldier, whether you're a sports star."

"I can safely say that losing my mum at the age of 12, and therefore shutting down all of my emotions," the prince reveals, "has had a quite serious effect on not only my personal life but my work as well." Instead of confronting his grief, Harry says, "my way of dealing with it was sticking my head in the sand, refusing to ever think about my mum, because why would that help? It's only going to make you sad, it's not going to bring her back," he recalls. "So from an emotional side, I was like, 'Right, don't ever let your emotions be part of anything.'"

"I really regret not talking about it. For the first 28 years of my life, I never talked about it."

Silence only makes the memories grow stronger.

William also suffers from the sudden loss of his mother, but it's the emotional toll of his job as part of the East Anglian Air Ambulance that's made him take notice.

"You have a reluctance to talk about it," William says of the traumatic cases he's worked. "You don't want to, you know, burden other people. You also don't want to think, 'Oh, is it just me? Am I the only one who's really affected by that?'

"My personal life and everything was absolutely fine. I was happy at home and happy at work, but I kept looking at myself, going, 'Why am I feeling like this? Why do I feel so sad?' And I started to realize that, actually, 'You're taking home people's trauma, people's sadness, and it's affecting you.'"

"From what I hear, Prince William is quite a wounded man," journalist Tina Brown commented years earlier. "He masks it well with Windsor self-control and training but he is wounded. One of the reasons Kate Middleton was enduring was because he needed someone he could depend upon.

"I wouldn't be surprised if there were a lot of buried hurt within him that will maybe surface later."

Yet William is the person Harry credits with first pushing him to try therapy.

"My brother—God bless him—has been an enormous support," Harry says.

"This is not right, it's not normal, you need to talk about this stuff, it's okay," William had told his brother.

As the nineteenth anniversary of Diana's death approaches, William visits a hospice. There he talks with Ben Hines, a fourteen-year-old boy who recently lost his mother to cancer.

"I miss her so much," Hines says.

William places a reassuring hand on the boy's arm. "I know how you feel. I still miss my mother every day," the prince tells him. "The important thing is to talk about it as a family. It's OK to feel sad. It's OK to miss her."

For William, the raw emotion of visits with Hines and others suffering similar losses, combined with the sights and stresses of air-ambulance rescues, is mounting. When the next day he and Kate go to London's YoungMinds mental health charity to listen to real-time calls of youth in distress, William requests "an easy one."

"I'm carrying a lot of things at the moment," he explains to volunteers. "I'll be in floods of tears at the end otherwise. I've had too many sad families with the air ambulance, so I can't have any more stuff."

Journalist Bryony Gordon interviews Prince Harry about Heads Together and is amazed at how openly he discusses his struggles.

"In Britain, we don't talk about our feelings," she says. "It has always been a sign of strength and dignity to keep it all inside, and our Royal family have always been the embodiment of that, God bless them. But Prince Harry just redefined strength and dignity for a new generation.

"He has shown the world that talking about your problems is nothing to be ashamed of—that actually, it is something to be positively encouraged. And I can think of no more fitting tribute to his mother than that."

PART 9
The Cambridges and the Sussexes

Chapter 118

Autumn 2016
London

On November 2, *Time* magazine asks: IS PRINCE HARRY DATING ACTRESS MEGHAN MARKLE? HERE'S WHAT WE KNOW.

Royal reporter Camilla Tominey broke the "world exclusive" story three days earlier under the dueling headlines HARRY'S SECRET ROMANCE WITH TV STAR (*Sunday Express*) and PRINCE HARRY'S SECRET US TV LOVER (*Daily Star Sunday*). Following Tominey's lead, journalists assemble a mystery-solving timeline of what is revealed to be a months-long relationship.

Details converge: Thirty-five-year-old Meghan Markle—three years older than thirty-two-year-old Harry—stars on the popular TV legal drama, *Suits,* as paralegal Rachel Zane. The two connect through mutual friends when Harry's in Toronto, where the show films, for an Invictus Games reception. They start dating in June, the *Telegraph* reports, after Harry gets Meghan's number and asks her for a date via text message.

Meghan and Harry hit it off quickly. "Almost immediately they were almost obsessed with each other," a friend of the couple says. Harry's romantic intensity, William tells Charles, is "like something I have never seen...it feels like I have lost my best friend."

Photos from Wimbledon show Meghan sitting in the royal box on

June 28 and July 4, and other snaps show Meghan and Harry wearing matching blue-beaded bracelets. There are clues of a transatlantic romance: Meghan's July 5 Instagram post from Buckingham Palace captioned that she is "gutted" to depart; she and Harry spotted at a Toronto Halloween party.

On November 1, *People* magazine reports that the relationship is so serious that Harry has already introduced Meghan to his father. Harry cancels his next booking on British Airways flight BA93 from London to Toronto and brings Meghan back to London instead. She stays overnight at Kensington Palace, where Harry lives in the "Nott Cott," or Nottingham Cottage, a Sir Christopher Wren–designed two-bedroom dwelling. William and Kate had lived there as newlyweds while their KP apartment, 1A, was undergoing renovation, and now they return to the familiar space specifically to meet Meghan.

There's no royal welcome from the press. Meghan's lifestyle blog, *The Tig*, named after her favorite red wine, Tignanello, is parsed for her romantic expectations. "There's something so incredibly romantic and beautiful" about "a guy writing a girl a letter," she'd once posted, though "I can't think of anything less becoming than a man who talks about people behind their backs."

The coverage of Meghan's past—including her divorce from a film producer and her "African-American mum and a dad with Dutch and Irish heritage"—couldn't be more public. While Harry's never lacked for dates and has often been paired with eligible women, as royal biographer Katie Nicholl points out, "the fact that Meghan was an actress, American, biracial, and a divorcee made her far more interesting and somewhat more controversial than most of Harry's exes."

Royal expert Ingrid Seward explains the culture gap: "Americans are different. So for somebody from a flat in LA to be with the Royal Family it would be like being in outer space."

The cuts quickly go far deeper. On November 3, Meghan's dismissed as a "Brit dunce" for not knowing "that a dragon is the symbol of Wales" when she's interviewed about *Suits* on the UKTV comedy channel

Dave. The speculation that "Prince Harry could marry into gangster royalty—his new love is from a crime-ridden Los Angeles neighbourhood" is particularly petty.

Barely a week after the news first breaks, Kensington Palace takes the unusual step of verifying the relationship. "The past week has seen a line crossed," reads a statement from Harry's communications secretary. "His girlfriend, Meghan Markle, has been subject to a wave of abuse and harassment. Some of this has been very public—the smear on the front page of a national newspaper; the racial undertones of comment pieces; the outright sexism and racism of social media trolls and web article comments." The release continues, "Prince Harry is worried about Ms. Markle's safety and is deeply disappointed that he has not been able to protect her."

William, whose "heart to heart" conversation with his brother informed Harry's emotional public plea, has Kensington Palace underscore that "the Duke of Cambridge absolutely understands the situation concerning privacy and supports the need for Harry to support those closest to him."

Harry quickly takes action, looking to Scotland Yard's elite officers in the Royalty and Diplomatic Protection Group to safeguard Meghan—at his own expense.

The news about Harry's new girlfriend is warmly received in the Caribbean, where the prince is on a fifteen-day tour of seven nations, a diplomatic trip to shore up support for the queen.

"I believe we are expecting a new princess soon," Antigua's prime minister, Gaston Browne, enthusiastically tells Harry in front of three hundred guests at a charity gala. "I want you to know that you are very welcome to come on your honeymoon here."

Harry deflects the invitation, instead recalling happy memories of visiting Antigua with his mother during the final months of her life. The prince is traveling between St. Vincent and Grenada when he breaks the news that Meghan's met the queen—and her infamously temperamental corgis.

"I've spent the last 33 years being barked at—this one walks in, absolutely nothing," Harry tells the *Telegraph*.

Meghan, the owner of two dogs, one of whom she's already moved to London, says that the corgis were "just laying on my feet during tea" with the queen. "It was very sweet."

Christmas tree merchant Zaqia Crawford says the same of Harry and Meghan. In mid-December, the couple arrives on foot to premium retailer Pines and Needles, in South London's Battersea Park. "It was totally clear they were a couple. It wasn't overly affectionate or anything like that—they were just doing cute, coupley stuff, like making each other laugh and being excited. They were really cool."

And decisive. They reject a twelve-foot £186 tree in favor of a six-foot Nordmann fir for £65. "I thought he'd go for the biggest one around," one shopper says of Harry, "but he just wanted a little six-footer."

"It's fun to be good and it's boring to be bad, but you can be naughty as well," jokes Harry in the ITV documentary *Prince Harry in Africa*, which premieres on December 19, 2016, and in which he discusses his work with Sentebale, the HIV/AIDS charity he cofounded in 2006 with Prince Seeiso of Lesotho. On a serious note, he explains, "I want to do something really constructive with my life. I want to do something that makes my mother proud. My mother stood for something. There's a lot of unfinished business and a lot of work that my mother never completed."

A week earlier, Meghan published an essay in the UK edition of *Elle* titled "Meghan Markle: I'm More Than an 'Other.'" "Being 'ethnically ambiguous,' as I was pegged in the industry," she writes, "meant I could audition for virtually any role."

As Harry tells ITV broadcaster Tom Bradby, he's decided to go for a new role of his own. "I was fighting the system going, 'I don't want to be this person. My mother died when I was very young and I don't want to be in this position.' But now I'm just so fired up and energized and lucky enough to be in a position to make a difference."

It's been ten years since Harry and Prince Seeiso set up Sentebale in memory of their activist mothers, who both died young. Meghan, too, is drawn to the continent: earlier in 2016, she visited Rwanda in support of World Vision's clean-water project.

Botswana also holds a special place for the couple. Shortly after they met, Harry persuaded Meghan to join him in Botswana for their third date, where they "camped out with each other under the stars," he says, "effectively on holiday together in the middle of nowhere"—a make-or-break trip that helped forge their bond.

"I have this love of Africa that will never disappear," Harry says in the documentary, "and I hope it carries on with my children as well."

Chapter 119

Summer 2017
London

On July 27, 2017, William pilots his last air-ambulance helicopter flight.

He's stepping down to spend more time on his growing royal duties—and his growing family. Less than two months later, on September 4, comes the announcement that the Duchess of Cambridge is pregnant with their third child. As with George and Charlotte, her hyperemesis gravidarum—acute morning sickness—means that the news is released earlier than it might otherwise have been.

Her illness also means that on September 7, William tends to their four-year-old son solo on George's very first day of school. Like any hands-on father, William drives George to school in the family car, unbuckles him from his car seat, then leads him by the hand into his classroom, toting his son's school backpack. Father and son pose together on the steps in an image decidedly evocative of the Princess of Wales with William and Harry.

Unlike the crowds of photographers that confronted William and Harry on their first days, the scrum of press here has been kept deliberately small.

Instead of the all-boys Wetherby, which both William and Harry attended, William and Kate have chosen Thomas's Battersea Prep School, a private school that the press describes as "a coed school in a middle-class area of London." Here Prince George will forgo his royal title and go by the name George Cambridge.

"It went well," William tells reporters of George's first day. "There was one other parent who had more of an issue with their children—so I was quite pleased I wasn't the one."

The other parents may be the ones with first-day jitters. "We are all excited but also worried. What if one of our kids bites George, and what if the school fees rocket?" one concerned mother wonders.

On November 27, 2017, just over a year after news broke that they were dating, Harry and Meghan are all smiles as they pose for a photo shoot officially announcing their engagement.

The location is one of Diana's favorite spots, the Sunken Garden at Kensington Palace. The garden is classically designed, with floral displays that change with the seasons. Diana visited often, talking with the gardeners about the blooms and reflecting on their beauty. The garden was entirely replanted with white flowers earlier this year in tribute to Princess Diana, and the couple has chosen to have their photos taken here at the White Garden specifically for the connection to Harry's mother, so that, as Meghan says, "Diana is part of this with us."

After the official announcement and photos, the newly engaged couple sits shoulder to shoulder on a comfortable sofa at Nottingham Cottage for an exclusive interview with the BBC.

"Tell us about your ring," broadcaster Mishal Husain says.

Harry takes the lead, since he designed Meghan's ring himself. On a band of yellow gold—"her favorite"—are three diamonds. "The main stone itself I sourced from Botswana and the little diamonds either side are from my mother's jewelry collection," he says, explaining his intent to include Diana in order "to make sure that she's with us on this crazy journey together."

"It's beautiful," Meghan says of the ring. "It's incredible."

"What do you think your mother would have thought of Meghan?" Husain asks.

"Oh they'd be thick as thieves, without question," Harry answers confidently. "I think she would be over the moon, jumping up and down, you know, so excited for me, but then, as I said, would have probably been best friends with Meghan.

"Days like today," he continues, "I really miss having her around and miss being able to share the happy news. But you know with the ring and with everything else that's going on I'm sure she's..."

"She's with us," Meghan says.

"I'm sure she's with us," Harry adds, "jumping up and down somewhere else."

"Hip hip hooray! Hip hip hooray! It's a boy, born on St. George's Day!"

The cry goes up from the crowd on April 23, 2018, upon hearing the news that at 11:01 a.m., the Duchess of Cambridge has given birth to an eight-pound, seven-ounce baby boy.

Once again, reporters have spent weeks assembled in anticipation outside the private Lindo Wing of St. Mary's Hospital. The royal baby misses sharing a birthday with his great-grandmother Queen Elizabeth by only two days—although arriving on St. George's Day, which celebrates the patron saint of England, is an awfully good omen for the newest prince of the realm.

"My mom is just, like, Diana-obsessed," says a Dutch tourist celebrating the news. "I just FaceTimed her and she started crying."

"Thrice the worry now," William says, holding up three fingers to symbolize his children: four-year-old Prince George; Princess Charlotte, who'll turn three in nine days, on May 2; and the infant prince, whose name is revealed on April 27 to be Louis Arthur Charles. The name Louis—which is a middle name for both his father and older brother—is chosen in tribute to Lord Louis Mountbatten, Prince Philip's uncle and Prince Charles's beloved mentor.

Royal superfan Terry Hutt, so well known in his British flag–emblazoned suit that the queen herself has nicknamed him "Union Jack Man," keeps vigil outside the hospital for weeks before Prince Louis's birth—as he previously did in anticipation of Princess Charlotte and Prince George—despite being days away from turning eighty-three. Hutt's royal baby vigils date back to 1948, when he waited outside Buckingham Palace for news of Prince Charles's birth.

"It's fantastic to have another newborn baby," Hutt says when the news of the latest prince is announced.

"Now it's Harry's turn," he adds.

Comedians joke of the third-time uncle, "Harry just got demoted again" to sixth in line for the throne. Yet he's received from the queen a high military honor, succeeding his grandfather as Captain General Royal Marines, a coveted title the Duke of Edinburgh held from 1953 until he retired from royal duties, in 2017.

Prince Louis arrives a week before his parents' seventh anniversary and less than a month before Harry and Meghan's highly anticipated May 19 wedding.

Since Harry served as his brother's best man, the assumption is that William will do the same. "He hasn't asked me yet," William says wryly as the wedding date approaches. "So," he adds with a laugh, "it may be a sensitive issue."

Finally, on April 26, Kensington Palace tweets, Prince Harry has asked his brother The Duke of Cambridge to be his Best Man at his wedding to Ms. Meghan Markle.

The close proximity of Louis's birth to Harry and Meghan's wedding makes a busy spring for the Palace. The term *whirlwind* is frequently used about the couple's wedding plans—at least by anyone who has forgotten the speed with which Charles and Diana courted—but unlike the Prince of Wales and his bride-to-be, these two are very clearly besotted with each other.

"Harry has made no secret of wanting to settle down and have a wife and family of his own," notes royal biographer Katie Nicholl. "When Harry met Meghan it really was love at first sight. He knew very quickly that she was the one."

The timing of the wedding is important for another reason. Harry, who is "incredibly close to his grandfather," says Nicholl, wants to be certain that Prince Philip, the ninety-six-year-old Duke of Edinburgh, can be there, "fit and healthy."

As it happens, that's quite a close call. On April 13, just over a month before the May 19 nuptials, Prince Philip is released from the hospital following hip surgery and has since been working with a physical therapist. He's determined to move through the nave of St. George's Chapel at Windsor Castle without a walking stick.

"The Duke has amazing willpower," a royal aide says. "When he sets his mind to something he gets on and does it. He has been walking up and down stairs several times in succession."

Chapter 120

May 2018
London

O n the morning of Saturday, May 19, Prince Harry steps into his private garden at Kensington Palace. Sprigs from a myrtle tree planted by Queen Victoria in 1845 and another that provided myrtle for Queen Elizabeth's 1947 wedding are woven through Meghan Markle's bouquet. What's missing is his mother's touch. Harry carefully picks the most beautiful spring blossoms, including his mother's favorite forget-me-nots, a heartfelt addition to the arrangement his bride will carry down the aisle.

The wedding will take place in a few hours at St. George's Chapel, a location chosen for both sentimental and practical reasons. The fifteenth-century Gothic chapel is "a very special place" for the couple, Harry's communications secretary notes, and it's where Harry's christening was held, in 1984. In addition, its location on the grounds of Windsor Castle makes it especially convenient for Prince Philip.

It's also—relatively speaking—a more intimate space than Westminster Abbey (where William and Kate were wed in front of 1,900 people) or St. Paul's Cathedral (the site of Charles and Diana's wedding, which held 3,500 invited guests). The guest list for Harry and Meghan's wedding numbers only 600, though another 1,200 members of the public have been invited to the grounds.

Those invited to the ceremony receive a seven-page document crafted with military precision. The *Telegraph* summarizes it as HARRY AND MEGHAN'S WEDDING RULES: NO PHONES, NO GIFTS, NO SWORDS—and especially no cameras. "All guests will be asked to surrender mobile telephones," the instructions specify, "and any devices used for image capture."

The only person permitted to photograph the wedding day is Alexi Lubomirski. The cameraman, himself a Polish prince, trained in Paris with Mario Testino, who famously photographed Diana and took William and Kate's engagement portrait.

Among royalty, family members, and dignitaries are familiar celebrity faces, including Meghan's longtime friend, tennis superstar Serena Williams and her husband, Reddit cofounder Alexis Ohanian; human rights lawyer Amal Clooney and her movie star husband, George Clooney; Meghan's former fellow cast members from *Suits*; footballer David Beckham and his wife, designer Victoria Beckham, a onetime member of British pop group the Spice Girls; and American media giant Oprah Winfrey.

Harry has also invited his former girlfriends Chelsy Davy and Cressida Bonas. Both are attending—though neither one has an invitation to the exclusive two-hundred-person evening reception.

A cry pierces the hush inside St. George's Chapel. One of the ten bridesmaids and page boys—including Prince George and Princess Charlotte—is overcome with excitement.

The ninety-two-year-old queen is about to enter. She's wearing a floral print silk dress in lime green, gray, and purple, designed by Stewart Parvin and accented by a matching hat. At 11:52 a.m., Queen Elizabeth II takes her place among the royal family, who are seated closest to the altar. The "Iron Duke," as Philip's doctors dub him, honors Harry by attending the ceremony despite the pain of a recently cracked rib.

Prince Philip, Prince William, Earl Spencer, Prince Harry, and the Prince of Wales walk in Diana's funeral procession. Breaking from traditional mourning black, Charles wears a navy-blue Savile Row suit that was a particular favorite of Diana's. (*Jeff J. Mitchell/AFP via Getty Images*)

Teenage girls treat fifteen-year-old Prince William like a pop star, much to thirteen-year-old Prince Harry's amusement. (*Frank Gunn/ AFP via Getty Images*)

The royal family gathers for the 101st birthday of the Queen Mother, Prince Charles's grandmother and William and Harry's great-grandmother. (*Sion Touhig/ Getty Images*)

Prince William thrives at Eton, where generations of Spencers have been educated. (*Anwar Hussein/WireImage*)

William spends his gap year traveling and doing volunteer work on multiple continents. (*Tim Graham Photo Library via Getty Images*)

In 2001, William enrolls at University of St. Andrews in Scotland. (*Anwar Hussein/Getty Images*)

Harry follows his brother to Eton, where he finds his greatest successes on the sports fields and in cadet training. (*Kirsty Wigglesworth-Pool/Getty Images*)

At age eighteen, Prince Harry is happy have his final exams behind him. (*Stefan Rousseau/PA Images via Getty Images*)

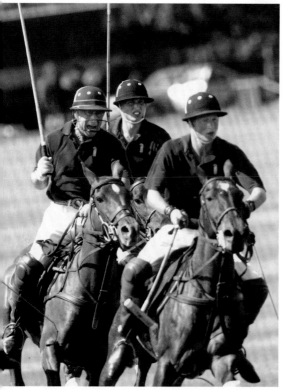

The Prince of Wales is joined by both of his sons on the polo field. (*Carl De Souza/Getty Images*)

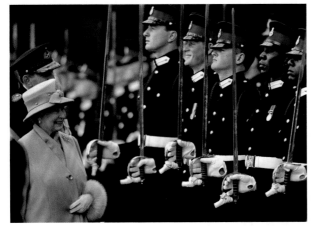

In April 2006, Queen Elizabeth smiles at Prince Harry as he and his class at the Royal Military Academy at Sandhurst become officers. *(Dylan Martinez/ Alamy Stock Photo)*

After he graduates from St. Andrews, Prince William follows Harry into the military academy. Both brothers are referred to as "Cadet Wales." *(Anwar Hussein/ Alamy Stock Photo)*

The queen returns to Sandhurst in December 2006 to honor Prince William's rise into the ranks of military officers. *(Dylan Martinez/ Alamy Stock Photo)*

William and Harry greet the 63,300 fans who pack Wembley Stadium on July 1, 2007. Their Concert for Diana is held on what would have been her forty-sixth birthday. *(Stephen Hird/Alamy Stock Photo)*

Elton John performs against a backdrop of his late friend, Diana, Princess of Wales. *(John Stillwell/PA Images via Getty Images)*

Prince Harry returns from active duty in Afghanistan. *(Max Mumby/Indigo/Getty Images)*

On April 29, 2011, Prince William marries Kate Middleton and Queen Elizabeth grants them the titles of Duke and Duchess of Cambridge. (*Anwar Hussein/ Getty Images*)

Prince Harry honors wounded veterans by creating the Invictus Games in 2014. (*Max Mumby/Indigo/Getty Images*)

Inspired by Diana's humanitarian work, William, Kate, and Harry start Heads Together, a charity dedicated to mental health initiatives. (*Samir Hussein/WireImage*)

Prince Harry and his grandfather, Prince Philip, share a laugh. *(Phil Walter/Getty Images)*

Harry and his fiancée, American actress Meghan Markle, walk with William and Kate on Christmas 2017. *(Geoffrey Robinson/ Alamy Stock Photo)*

On May 19, 2018, Prince Harry marries Meghan Markle, and Queen Elizabeth grants them the titles of Duke and Duchess of Sussex. *(Ben Stansall/AFP via Getty Images)*

William and Kate, the Duke and
Duchess of Cambridge, attend a
theatrical performance with their
three children (*left to right*): Prince
Louis, Princess Charlotte, and Prince
George. (*Aaron Chown/WPA Pool/
Getty Images*)

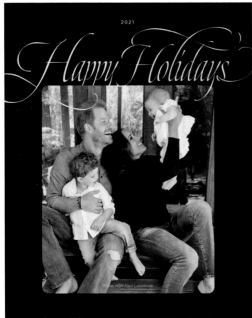

Harry and Meghan, the Duke and
Duchess of Sussex, share a holiday card
featuring their two children: Archie
and Lilibet Mountbatten-Windsor.
(*Alexi Lubomirski/Handout/The Duke
and Duchess of Sussex via Getty Images*)

William and Harry unveil
a statue of Diana, Princess
of Wales, at Kensington
Palace on what would have
been her sixtieth birthday.
(*Dominic Lipinski/Alamy
Stock Photo*)

Poised at the top of the aisle, Meghan is serene. Her white silk bateau-neck gown, by British designer Clare Waight Keller for Givenchy, and her Queen Mary Bandeau Tiara, with its ten-diamond centerpiece—on loan from the queen—are illuminated by the seventy-nine panels of light in the West Window, made of Tudor-era glass. A scrap of the blue dress Meghan wore on her first date with Harry is sewn inside her wedding gown as her "something blue." Her sixteen-and-a-half-foot-long silk tulle veil, which is hand-embroidered along the hem with flowers from each of the Commonwealth's fifty-three countries, she saw for the first time only this morning.

The elegant bride walks alone until she reaches the choir, the area of the church where the royal family is seated. Prince Charles steps forward, and thirty-six-year-old Meghan takes the arm of her sixty-nine-year-old soon-to-be father-in-law.

"You look lovely," Charles says.

"Thank you, Pa," Harry says when Charles and Meghan reach the altar.

He's standing beside his best man, William, both wearing dark blue doeskin frock coats, the dress uniform of the Blues and Royals regiment, where they've both served. Since Harry's resigned from the armed forces, he required the queen's permission to wed in uniform—and to keep his beard, which goes against military rules and the queen's preferences. Harry's captain's uniform displays his pilot's wings along with ribbons signifying his four most important military honors: his status as a Knight Commander of the Royal Victorian Order, his Operational Service Medal for Afghanistan, and the queen's Golden and Diamond Jubilee Medals. William wears the queen's ciphers, EIIR, at his shoulder and carries a precious gift from their grandmother—a Cleave & Company gold wedding band for Meghan, made from royal Welsh gold.

"There's power, power in love," Most Reverend Michael Curry says. The top bishop in the American Episcopal Church, speaking at Meghan's invitation, ends his sermon with an impassioned "We gotta get y'all married!"

Once they exchange vows and rings before the archbishop of Canterbury, Justin Welby, the newlyweds emerge into the bright May sunshine.

"Do we kiss now?" Meghan asks Harry as they stand together on the chapel steps.

"Yes," he answers his bride.

At the lunchtime reception, hosted by the queen for the newly titled Duke and Duchess of Sussex at St. George's Hall, the Prince of Wales gives a touching speech.

"My darling old Harry, I'm so happy for you," Charles concludes, which leaves his younger son quite emotional, though Harry recovers enough to later ask an important question of the assembled guests. "Does anyone here know how to play the piano?"

It's a bit of a setup. None of the six hundred guests knows that Harry's invited Elton John to perform a far happier reprise of his moving tribute to Diana at her funeral. Today she's remembered with "Circle of Life," "Your Song," and "I'm Still Standing."

A night of celebration lies ahead, but as John sings the lyrics to "Tiny Dancer"—"Looking on / She sings the songs"—all present pause to imagine Diana among them.

Before they head to the evening reception for two hundred at nearby Frogmore House, Meghan changes into a sleeveless white silk crepe Stella McCartney halter dress, and Harry swaps his military uniform for a sleek tuxedo. Harry also gifts his new wife a family treasure—a £75,000 ring featuring an emerald-cut aquamarine bordered by solitaire diamonds and set in twenty-four-carat yellow gold. Kate may wear Diana's famed engagement ring, but what Harry presents to his bride is one his mother chose for herself—one she'd commissioned to replace it. Luxury jeweler Asprey created the art deco–style ring for Diana, who first wore it at the preview of her June 1997 dress sale at Christie's in New York.

"I would like you to allocate all my jewellery to the share held by my sons," Diana wrote in a letter, "so that their wives may, in due course, have it or use it."

The ring sparkles on Meghan's right hand as she waves from the passenger seat of the blue E-Type Concept Zero Jaguar convertible Harry's driving, its license plate encoded with their May 19 wedding date: E190518.

"It's not often that you see a prince get married," exclaims a visitor from the Dominican Republic swept up in the glamour of the day, marveling of the new royal bride, "She was just a normal girl."

Chapter 121

O n October 15, there's a new #royalbaby hashtag trending on Twitter: Meghan is pregnant this is not a drill we are going to have POC's (Princes and Princesses of Colour) what a time to be ALIVE #royalbaby.

Kensington Palace announces the news while the Duke and Duchess of Sussex are on their first royal tour to Australia, New Zealand, and the Pacific islands Fiji and Tonga, where the locals, gripped by "Meg Mania," are dazzled by Meghan's bright smile and £120,000 designer touring wardrobe.

At the Sydney Invictus Games in October of 2018, Harry tells the crowd, "We have been so happy to be able to celebrate the personal joy of our newest addition with you all," and Meghan addresses the competitors and fans, saying, "On a very personal note, I just wanted to thank all of you for welcoming me into the Invictus family." The Australian press returns her affections, embracing Meghan as the "Queen of Hearts."

Back in London, headlines run in the opposite direction: DUCHESS DIFFICULT? asks the *Express.* A sleepless Meghan takes to soothing her distress with 4:30 a.m. yoga sessions in Nottingham Cottage—until the queen grants them a household outside Kensington Palace: Frogmore Cottage, in Windsor Home Park.

Family concerns are piling up. In mid-January of 2019, ninety-seven-year-old Prince Philip is the focus when he rolls his Land Rover on a rural road near Sandringham, colliding with another car and injuring two passengers. Two days later he's back on the road, driving without a seat belt. Almighty God, the bishop of York tweets in prayer, We humbly beseech thee to bless Philip Duke of Edinburgh. He'd given up his pilot's license at age seventy-six, but it takes a police warning and intense family pressure to persuade Philip in mid-February to surrender his driver's license.

In mid-March, William and Harry, who share their grandfather's love of speed, bring their relationship to a screeching halt.

"After a lifetime of being the nation's favorite royal double act," the brothers are dismantling their joint charitable organization, the Royal Foundation of the Duke and Duchess of Cambridge and the Duke and Duchess of Sussex.

The pressure has been building for some time, and when the "Fab Four"—as William, Kate, Harry, and Meghan are dubbed—appeared on a panel together, they awkwardly fielded questions from the moderator.

"All the work that you do together is great, but working together as family do you ever have disagreements about things?"

"Oh yes!" William said with emphasis.

"Healthy disagreements," Harry added, quick to joke that while the arguments come "thick and fast," it was nothing unusual. "Working as family does have its challenges, of course it does," he said, "but we are stuck together for the rest of our lives."

As William's told the BBC, "There are disagreements, obviously, as all families have, and when there are, they are big disagreements."

—⊸⊸⊸—

"Their Royal Highnesses have taken a personal decision to keep the plans around the arrival of their baby private," Buckingham Palace announces during the final weeks of Meghan's pregnancy. "The Duke and Duchess look forward to sharing the exciting news with everyone once they have had an opportunity to celebrate privately as a new family."

That won't stop Union Jack Man, Terry Hutt, from heading to Windsor on April 30—his own eighty-fourth birthday—in the hope that the new royal baby will be born that day. "When any of them have babies," Hutt observes of the royals, "they seem to have it when my birthday comes along—they just keep on missing."

Meghan misses the chance as well. By the night of Sunday, May 5, her labor is overdue. With her pregnancy potentially in distress and no time to inform senior royals, Harry and the couple's Scotland Yard protection team make the decision to rush Meghan for treatment at a medical facility later confirmed to be the upscale Portland Hospital.

At 5:26 Monday morning, May 6, she safely delivers a seven-pound, three-ounce baby boy.

A beaming Harry gives an impromptu press conference at Windsor Castle, telling reporters, "I'm very excited to announce that Meghan and myself have had a baby boy early this morning, a very healthy boy," and expressing admiration for his wife. "It's been the most amazing experience I could ever have possibly imagined," he says with a laugh. "This little thing is absolutely to die for, so I'm over the moon."

When asked what the baby is called, Harry answers, "Still thinking about names," but he's ready two days later when the press returns to St. George's Hall, at Windsor Castle, to be officially introduced to Archie Harrison Mountbatten-Windsor.

Prince Charles has long envisioned a "slimmed-down monarchy" of seven, including the queen and Prince Philip, himself and Camilla, William and Kate, and Harry. Based on a ruling made by King George V more than a century ago, Archie's relationship to the sovereign is too distant to qualify him as an HRH while his great-grandmother is still on the throne—though he could potentially inherit the title of Prince Archie once his grandfather Charles ascends.

For the photo call, Harry cradles the baby as he and Meghan smile at each other and at their son.

"He has the sweetest temperament," Meghan says of Archie.

"Give us a peek at him. We can't quite see his face," a reporter says.

"He's already got a bit of facial hair as well, wonderful," Harry banters before carrying the baby to meet "two special people, the Queen and the Duke."

The Royal Collection Trust, the charitable organization that oversees the queen's art collection and public tours of her homes, generated millions in revenue by selling wedding merchandise featuring Meghan and Harry. It comes as a surprise to royal fans who bought limited-edition mohair teddy bears (silk paws imprinted with a golden crown), velvet royal-baby cushions, and a range of china to commemorate the births of the Cambridge babies that they will have nothing with which to memorialize Archie's birth.

A spokesperson for the trust says simply, "We have no new ranges to announce."

On December 18, 2019, Queen Elizabeth hosts Christmas lunch at Buckingham Palace.

In a palace kitchen, she's cooking with Princes Charles, William, and George. They're making plum puddings, a traditional dried-fruit dessert for the festive season. George's antics as he thrusts a wooden spoon into the pudding keep Charles laughing—and occupy a videographer who's recording footage to be broadcast during the queen's annual Christmas message.

In the Throne Room, veteran royal photographer Ranald Mackechnie is finalizing weeks of preparation for his second official photograph of these four royals.

Dressed in shades of blue and white, the queen, Charles, William, and six-year-old George embody four generations standing in alliance as a new year and a new decade begin. The gold-and-crimson color scheme of the Throne Room makes a dramatic backdrop. The embroidered thrones the queen used during her 1953 coronation will someday belong to her three heirs. In a moment of stillness, Mackechnie captures their confident, forward-looking smiles.

Mackechnie's first portrait of the queen and the three future kings was taken in April of 2016, in honor of Queen Elizabeth's ninetieth birthday. In a slightly less formal tableau, the four are assembled in the palace's White Drawing Room: the queen and Charles seated together, William seated slightly apart, and a grinning two-year-old George standing upon a stack of foam blocks. The photograph was transformed into a commemorative postage stamp.

Harry was out of the frame in the 2016 photo. Today he's out of the country.

On November 13—having already missed summering with the queen at her beloved Balmoral when Meghan was busy in London, guest-editing the September 2019 issue of British *Vogue*—Harry and Meghan had announced their plans: "Having spent the last two Christmases at Sandringham, Their Royal Highnesses will spend the holiday this year, as a new family, with the Duchess' mother."

"The feeling is that Harry and Meghan have rather alienated themselves from the rest of the family," a royal source had said, adding, "If they do come for Christmas it might be a particularly frosty one."

As it turns out, they'll be traveling to North America, where it's rumored that they're searching for a second home.

At Sandringham on December 20, Philip takes ill. He walks into the hospital under his own power but stays for precautionary observation until Christmas Eve. As the royal family gathers around their increasingly fragile patriarch, the queen prepares her Christmas message to the nation. On her desk she places photographs that signify the monarchy's past, present, and future: her father, King George VI; Prince

Philip; Charles and Camilla; and the Cambridges' family Christmas portrait.

"Two hundred years on from the birth of my great, great grandmother, Queen Victoria," the queen says, "Prince Philip and I have been delighted to welcome our eighth great grandchild into our family."

But it's noted that the child, Archie, is not pictured in the queen's photo display. Nor are his parents.

The queen summarizes the year, which also saw the seventy-fifth anniversary of the Allied D-Day invasion at Normandy and the fiftieth anniversary of the Apollo 11 moon walk: "The path, of course, is not always smooth, and may at times this year have felt quite bumpy, but small steps can make a world of difference."

The fleeting nod to family unrest prompts instant and intense speculation. The calendar has yet to turn when on December 29 the *Sunday Express* asks the looming question: WILL 2020 BE A MAKE OR BREAK YEAR FOR ROYALS?

Chapter 122

2020

London

I couldn't see anyone's face," William says.

He's talking with the BBC about his lifelong anxiety over public speaking.

"You definitely get a bit of anxiety thinking, 'This has got to go right, I can't mess this up' and there were a lot of people watching."

William's navigating the pressures of being a working royal. But he's discovered an unexpected cure: aging. If he doesn't wear contact lenses, he can see his speech notes but not the faces of the people looking up at him from around a room.

Harry's feeling even more strain. "Every time I put a suit and tie on and having to go do the role," he says, "to go 'Right, game face' look in the mirror, right let's go," he reddens with anxiety and feels "two or three degrees warmer than everybody else."

Yet the audience on the internet is faceless. And there seems to be an overwhelming backlash against his wife, Meghan.

Speaking in an ITV documentary, the duchess says, "When I first met my now-husband my friends were really happy because I was so happy. But my British friends told me, 'I'm sure he's great but you shouldn't do it because the British tabloids will destroy your life.'"

"Meghan does seem to be an inadequate vessel for the rage that has been rained on her," notes sociologist Gary Younge. The outsize and polarizing reactions to the Duchess of Sussex speak to something larger.

"I've put it down to a clash of cultures," *Telegraph* reporter Camilla Tominey tells *The New Yorker.* "The royal world is very different—it's much slower-paced, and hugely hierarchical," she says, adding, "It's a bit like 'Downton Abbey.'"

The intrusion and negative press strongly affect the Duke of Sussex. Harry's had enough.

"My deepest fear is history repeating itself," he says. "I've seen what happens when someone I love is commoditized to the point that they are no longer treated or seen as a real person. I lost my mother and now I watch my wife falling victim to the same powerful forces."

He decides to do something about it.

On January 8, the day after Harry and Meghan return from a six-week trip to Canada, they post an unexpected message to @SussexRoyal on Instagram and to their new website, SussexRoyal.com: "We intend to step back as 'senior' members of the Royal Family and work to become financially independent, while continuing to support Her Majesty The Queen," the announcement reads, stating their wish to "carve out a progressive new role within this institution."

Reaction to the "War of the Windsors" is swift and divided.

Where royalists see "a young man in distress caught between love for his family and love for his wife," others are quick to criticize the couple for wanting "more red carpets, not fewer."

"What is so shocking," a BBC correspondent observes, "is how unhappy they both seem. The sun-drenched wedding of the year before seems like a dream; here are two people visibly struggling with their lives and positions."

The royal family is scrambling to stay informed. The queen, Charles, and Philip had received Harry and Meghan's announcement only ten minutes before it hit the internet, a move that 78 percent of Britons tell OnePoll "insulted" the ninety-three-year-old monarch.

Reports are that the queen is "hurt" and "deeply disappointed" that her grandson Harry didn't confide in her, but there's no time to dwell on bruised feelings. Determined to reach a family resolution in "days, not weeks," she calls Charles, William, and Harry to lunch at Sandringham on January 13. It's a tactic she used when counseling Charles and Diana against separating, but Meghan won't be present. She's already returned to Canada.

Ahead of the meeting, William tells a friend, "All we can do, and all I can do, is try and support them and hope that the time comes when we're all singing from the same page. I want everyone to play on the team."

The family talks for hours. Meghan calls in by phone.

The news comes that the rift can't be mended—ONLY WAY'S MEGXIT, according to the *Daily Star*—and that Harry and Meghan will make two departures, one from their roles as working royals and another from the country entirely.

The next day, the postcard display at the public café at Sandringham has two empty rows. All images of the Sussexes have been removed.

William takes on the role of peacemaker.

"It's sometimes trying to get people to understand that it's OK to have these challenges," he says. A crowd of one thousand has gathered on January 15 outside Bradford City Hall to hear William speak about community building, but the message goes out to Harry. "We just need to deal with them and we need to move forward rather than just be stuck in paralysis and pretend they don't happen."

The queen never pretends. As she famously told the *Daily Mail* in 1989, "Like all the best families, we have our share of eccentricities, of impetuous and wayward youngsters and of family disagreements." After five days of intense negotiations, Harry and Meghan are freed from their royal duties. Their wish to continue "to support Her Majesty the Queen" is firmly denied.

They'll have until the end of March before formally stepping down. That will also mean an imminent end to Harry's honorary military roles—Captain General Royal Marines; Commodore-in-Chief, Small Ships and Diving, Royal Naval Command; and Honorary Air Commandant, RAF Honington—and along with it, the termination of his right to wear a British Armed Forces uniform, though he's allowed to continue displaying his service medals.

On March 6, Harry puts on his best Marine uniform for the last time to attend the annual Mountbatten Festival of Music. When he wore the same uniform at the 2019 event, the look inspired tweets like Duke of Hotness and I ♥ a man in uniform. He looks like a prince from a fairy tale.

Fast-forward one year, and the mood has shifted.

"Signs of real, wistful sadness" are observed in Harry's expression as he enters Royal Albert Hall alongside a Royal Marine contingent, hand in hand with his wife, but the couple is all smiles as they receive a standing ovation of several minutes before being escorted to the royal box. Meghan's £1,295 red Safiyaa capelet gown and red Stuart Weitzman heels complement Harry's uniform, the black lapels of his red dress coat adorned with his Afghanistan service medals.

Three days later is March 9, Commonwealth Day, the annual celebration of the countries symbolically headed by the queen. The service is held at Westminster Abbey, site of William and Kate's wedding—and Diana's funeral. When making the 1997 arrangements, Diana's private secretary, Patrick Jephson, reasoned, "If you get hold of a guest list for the Princess' Christmas drinks in 1995, invite everybody on that guest list and you won't have missed out on anybody important."

Today, importance is pointedly measured solely by order of succession. The senior royals file into the abbey, the queen leading Charles and Camilla, followed by William and Kate, and finally Harry and Meghan. Each sits in a red velvet chair according to royal rank; Meghan is seated next to Prince Edward, eleventh in line to the throne.

William, Harry, and their wives exchange terse hellos.

Meghan shines in a brilliant emerald-green Emilia Wickstead dress with a coordinating fascinator. A South London church official notes, "Did you see how she looked since she has been away? *Radiant.*"

There's symbolism in the matching green lining of Harry's blue suit jacket. His alliance, he's indicating, is to his wife.

As part of their split from the royal family—again bringing to mind Diana's similar demotion after divorcing Charles—Harry and Meghan will no longer be called HRH or Royal Highness, but they can keep their Duke and Duchess of Sussex titles.

Prince Harry is only the second-ever Duke of Sussex. His predecessor was Queen Victoria's favorite uncle: Prince Augustus Frederick, a son of King George III. Augustus similarly asked for clemency from the monarchy when attempting to push against princely limitations for the sake of himself and his wife—and, like Harry, he was denied.

"Royal firstborns may get all the glory," Diana once said, but younger siblings "enjoy more freedom. Only when Harry is a lot older will he realize how lucky he is not to have been the eldest." Which certainly holds some truth—but so does the proclamation given to the thwarted Prince Augustus: "Wherever you go, or wherever you reside, you can never divest yourself of the character of a British Prince."

"They're still royals even if they're not here," the church official comments about Harry and Meghan, noting that the duchess's joining the royal family is seen as "opening up a place for the less in society."

And then comes a royal goodbye to Harry's millions of caring fans.

"I was born into this life," he says in a speech about his future, "and it is a great honour to serve my country and the Queen. When I lost my mum 23 years ago, you took me under your wing. You've looked out for me for so long."

"We are taking a leap of faith. Thank you for giving me the courage to take this next step."

To California, where his mother fantasized about living with her sons.

Days before her death, Diana's frustration with the constant media intrusion had her also considering a move abroad.

"William's told me I should leave England and go and live somewhere else," Diana told *Sun* photographer Arthur Edwards, and she shared with her butler, Paul Burrell, that she was considering starting a "new life" in Malibu.

"Won't it be great?" she enthused. "Think of the lifestyle for the boys. Nobody's judgmental in America, you don't have the class system, you don't have the establishment," she told him.

Now it's her younger son who'll test Diana's California dreams.

From a distance of five thousand miles, across an ocean and a continent, memories of "two-year-old Harry in his mini Paras fatigues and maroon beret or standing to attention as a boy when they changed the guard at Buckingham Palace" hold fast.

So does Harry's attachment to military life. According to his friends, "he is really missing the Army as well as his military appointments. He misses the camaraderie of being in the forces"—and "he can't believe his life has been turned upside down."

Every Remembrance Sunday since he turned twenty-five, in 2009, Harry has laid a wreath for fallen members of the armed forces at the Cenotaph, in Whitehall. In November, he requests that a tribute be made on his behalf.

The Palace again denies him.

On November 8, 2020, Harry stands between past and future and begins a new tradition. "Even when we can't all be together," he tells the military podcast *Declassified*, "we always remember together."

Chapter 123

Spring 2021
London

T he Queen says she is delighted," the *Telegraph* reports on Valentine's
Day 1984, when the Prince and Princess of Wales announce
Diana's second pregnancy with the baby they would name Harry.

Precisely thirty-seven years later, at 7:29 p.m. on February 14, 2021,
Harry and Meghan share the news that "Archie is going to be a big
brother" to a Mountbatten-Windsor sibling.

At 8:56 p.m. comes the reply from Buckingham Palace: "Her Majesty,
Duke of Edinburgh, Prince of Wales and the entire family are delighted
and wish them well."

The news comes a day after the Palace received word that the Sussexes
are planning an "intimate" and "wide-ranging" interview with their wedding guest and California neighbor Oprah Winfrey. The Palace has since
been mulling over whether to end the couple's royal patronages.

Ahead of the "Sandringham Summit" last year, the queen had protected
her husband of seventy-two years from the anguish of his beloved grandson's challenge to royal duty by asking a houseguest to take Prince Philip
out for a drive.

On February 16, 2021, ninety-nine-year-old Philip is a passenger in
a different car with an urgent destination—London's King Edward VII's

Hospital, where he's admitted for observation. On that same day, the Palace announces that it will be impossible for Harry and Meghan "to continue with the responsibilities that come with a life of public service."

"Do what your heart tells you to do," Diana always told her sons. Harry's interpretation of his mother's advice comes at a cost. Today's toll is Meghan stepping down as patron of the National Theatre and Harry cutting royal ties to three sporting organizations.

"Time heals all things, hopefully," Harry tells Oprah Winfrey in the two-hour interview, broadcast on March 7.

Not between brothers.

"No, I haven't spoken to him yet, but I will do," William says days later, reacting to Harry's revelations that as the future king William is "trapped" in his royal role and that the royal family is racist.

William confides in his friends. According to them, "once he got over the anger of how things happened, he was left with the absence of his brother. They shared everything about their lives—an office, a foundation, meetings together most days and there was a lot of fun along the way. He'll miss it forever."

Harry and William's mutual loss is compounded on April 9 by the death of Prince Philip, at Windsor Castle, two months shy of his one hundredth birthday. As gun salutes resound across the country in honor of the Duke of Edinburgh, two princes thousands of miles apart craft their separate and distinct remembrances.

"I will miss my Grandpa," William posts on the Kensington Palace website on April 11 at 2:00 p.m., "but I know he would want us to get on with the job."

Thirty minutes later, Harry's own tribute makes no mention of duty, only joy. "My grandpa: master of the barbecue, legend of banter and cheeky right 'til the end."

At a July 2015 RAF event commemorating the seventy-fifth anniversary of the Battle of Britain, when a photographer took too long framing a royal portrait, Philip had roared, "Just take the f—king picture!" leading Prince William to dissolve into nervous giggles. Diana had warned her sons as children of their grandfather's legendary temper, saying, "Never, never shout at anyone the way Prince Philip does."

The athletic military man with a passion for preserving the planet also had a reflective bent, gauging his eldest son's perception of him. Of Charles, Philip observed, "He is a romantic, I am a pragmatist. And because I don't see things as a romantic would, I'm unfeeling."

Just as he did the day before Diana's funeral, a tearful Charles tours the voluminous floral tributes left for Philip outside Buckingham Palace and Windsor Castle, where the funeral service Philip designed himself is to be held on April 17 at St. George's Chapel.

One admirer has crafted a model Land Rover with THE DUKE R.I.P. lettered across the roof. The miniature is a nod to the dark bronze green military Land Rover Defender TD5 130 that Philip began custom-modifying at age eighty-two, in 2003, specifically for this occasion. Its open top is fitted for carrying his handmade English oak coffin.

The detailed plans unfold entirely on the grounds of Windsor Castle and, like the rest of the senior royals' funeral plans, are code-named after a British bridge: "Operation London Bridge" for Queen Elizabeth; "Operation Menai Bridge" in Wales for Prince Charles; and "Operation Tay Bridge" in Scotland for the Queen Mother—but used for Diana, whose hastily made arrangements were modeled on the plan already in place for Charles's grandmother. Prince Philip's is "Operation Forth Bridge," after the 1890 cantilevered railway structure and UNESCO heritage site in Edinburgh.

According to Philip's wishes, his coffin is hand-carried by Queen's Company, 1st Battalion Grenadier Guards, from the castle's state entrance down a hill to St. George's Chapel. Determined to prevent the simmering tension between the Wales brothers from disrupting Philip's farewell, the queen sets a dress code. No royal men will be in uniform. They must wear morning coats and black ties, though they may add their military medals. Women are to dress in simple black garments.

She then devises a formation to walk behind Philip's coffin. Charles leads a royal contingent that includes her and Philip's four children and three of their grandchildren—with Princess Anne's son, Peter Phillips, positioned between William and Harry.

While the family walks, the queen is driven in a Bentley created for her Golden Jubilee, in 2002. She enters the chapel.

At 3:00 p.m., a hush falls over the streets of London and across the nation, beginning a minute of silence that marks the transition from procession to service.

"She is the Queen. She will behave with the extraordinary dignity and extraordinary courage that she always does," Justin Welby, the archbishop of Canterbury, told the BBC in reflecting on what would surely be "an anguished moment" for the monarch. "At the same time, she is saying farewell to someone to whom she was married for 73 years.

"I think that must be a very, very profound thing in anybody's life."

The archbishop's role today is to bless Philip at his funeral, in the same chapel where he married Harry and Meghan. In stark contrast to the six hundred guests who witnessed the 2018 union, because of COVID-19 restrictions, only thirty family members are present today. Meghan, six months pregnant, is not among them. She remains in California with Archie, her doctors having advised against travel. The *Daily Mail* poses the question upon Harry's solo return to England, in mourning: IF YOU WERE WILLIAM, COULD YOU FORGIVE HARRY?

In the St. George's choir, the queen sits, masked and alone. She wipes away a single tear.

In four days, she'll mark her ninety-fifth birthday—her first as a widow.

On April 21, the queen, who's officially in mourning, has a private lunch with all her children except Charles, who is in Wales. There will be no gun salute from Hyde Park and the Tower of London. There will be no birthday portrait.

A double portrait of William and Kate debuts on April 29. Photographer Chris Floyd captures the couple, both dressed in blue, smiling in front of Kensington Palace in celebration of their "tin" wedding anniversary. The *Express* pronounces, 10 YEARS ON, THE MONARCHY IS SAFE IN KATE AND WILLIAM'S HANDS.

Not yet.

The queen, William says, will "want to hand over knowing she's done everything she possibly could to help, and that she's got no regrets and no unfinished business; that she's done everything she can for the country and that she's not let anyone down—she minds an awful lot about that."

Chapter 124

Summer 2021
London

T he queen's eleventh great-grandchild is born on June 4 in Santa Barbara, California. Harry and Meghan name their daughter Lilibet "Lili" Diana Mountbatten-Windsor. The baby's first name is Queen Elizabeth's childhood nickname. Her middle name is Harry's mother's name. The birth announcement comes less than a month before what would have been Diana's sixtieth birthday.

"Every day, we wish she were still with us," William and Harry say in a joint statement.

The brothers were last seen exchanging a few words following Philip's funeral in April. Harry returns to England to mark their mother's birthday, on July 1, and stands with William and their Spencer relatives gathered for a private ceremony among four thousand blooming flowers in the Sunken Garden at Kensington Palace. There's a new statue of Diana to be unveiled today.

"Ready?" William asks Harry.

Each pulls a cord and removes the green cloth cover to a round of applause.

The ceremony to unveil the sculptor Ian Rank-Broadley's bronze statue—depicting a short-haired Diana with her arms around three children of different races—lasts only thirty minutes. Her admirers have spent far longer bringing candles and flowers to the palace, where the tributes amass, just as they did immediately after the Princess of Wales's death.

⸙

Charles and the queen share a favorite cocktail. Mother and son both enjoy a martini in the evening. But the queen is giving hers up. She's been using a cane to steady her gait, and doctors advise in mid-October that abstaining from alcohol is the best way to maintain her strength ahead of her June 2022 Platinum Jubilee, in celebration of her seventy years on the throne.

On October 20, the queen stays overnight in the hospital "for some preliminary investigations," then cancels a trip to Northern Ireland. In mid-November, she sprains her back and misses the Remembrance Sunday service at the Cenotaph war memorial.

But the queen remains "stoical and mentally strong," say Palace insiders, noting that "her main concern will be to get back to be in fighting form to start the Jubilee celebrations. She's of the generation where you 'suck it up.' It is duty first."

The queen never fails to lead by example. Instead of a large gathering, for the second consecutive year she cancels her traditional Christmas lunch at Sandringham for the good of her family and the country.

It's an especially sentimental season, the queen's first since Philip's death.

"Bringing the family together at Christmas time," William says, "it's always lovely because we're quite spread out doing our things. So we get very little time together." In a perfect world, he says, "we'd bring everyone together, have a big party, and there would definitely be no Covid."

While the queen is writing her annual Christmas message, Kate is "really, really upset," she tells a friend, over her and William's distance from Harry and Meghan.

There might be something she can do to lift everyone's spirits. For weeks, Kate rehearses secretly in the Chapter House at Westminster Abbey. "We've been through such a bleak time," she says in a promotional video for ITV's Christmas Eve broadcast, *Royal Carols: Together at Christmas.* "But I suppose through separation we've also realized how much we need each other—and how acts of kindness and love can really bring us comfort and relief in times of distress."

Dressed in a scarlet Catherine Walker coatdress tied at the neck with an oversize bow, Kate steps to a grand piano. "She picked it up so well," says Scottish singer-songwriter Tom Walker. Kate accompanies him as he sings his new song, "For Those Who Can't Be Here."

"It's really not easy," Walker says, praising Kate, "to go from not playing with other musicians for 10 years to jumping straight in with like a whole band you've never met and camera crews doing live takes that's being filmed in Westminster Abbey"—where Elton John played piano at Diana's funeral. The duchess, Walker says, is a "very talented musician."

"Happy holidays" is the greeting on a December 23 photo card from Harry, Meghan, two-year-old redheaded Archie, and six-month-old Lilibet. Meghan's lifting her baby girl and looking into her eyes—her pose mirroring a 1983 mother-son photo of Diana and William. Harry is wearing a beaded bracelet he chose on a trip to Africa shortly after his mother died. He's rarely removed the keepsake since.

On Christmas Day, a nineteen-year-old man breaches the grounds of Windsor Castle, where the queen is in residence. He's carrying an "offensive weapon."

The intruder is under arrest by the time the broadcast of the queen's Christmas message is complete.

"None of us can slow the passage of time," she says. Her red wool dress by Angela Kelly displays a sapphire chrysanthemum brooch, a memento from her 1947 honeymoon, at Broadlands manor house. The photo on her desk in the castle's White Drawing Room shows her and Philip celebrating their sixtieth anniversary by returning to Broadlands, the queen wearing her honeymoon sapphire.

"Although it's a time of great happiness and good cheer for many, Christmas can be hard for those who have lost loved ones," she says. "This year, especially, I understand why."

Privately, she also takes the step of cautioning Prince William against continuing one of his common practices: piloting himself, Kate, and their three children in a single helicopter.

"She knows William is a capable pilot but does not think it is worth the risk for all five of them to carry on flying together," a royal insider says. "The Queen has told William she is worried that, however good he is as a pilot, bad weather and accidents can strike at any time."

The thought of a potential crash "keeps the Queen awake at night" with worry. "She thinks the future is bright with them at the helm after Charles but if something happened to him and the family it doesn't bear thinking about."

As of March 2022, the queen of England no longer lives at Buckingham Palace.

The royal standard indicating her residence now flies only over the home where Prince Philip spent his final days, the ninety-five-year-old queen having made her move to Windsor Castle permanent and departed Buckingham Palace "for good."

The royal couple first moved into Buckingham Palace after Queen Elizabeth's coronation in 1953—the same decade the palace's plumbing and electrical systems were last updated. Some boilers still predate World War II. The 775-room palace has been the official home of every monarch since Queen Victoria—though Prince Albert complained even then that the place was "a disgrace to the Sovereign and the Nation" and added more imposing architectural details, including the public-facing balcony. Despite its impressive gilt facades, internal repairs are long over-due, and a ten-year £369 million renovation is under way to address an embarrassing overabundance of asbestos, leaks, and even mice.

Prince Charles is on board with his mother's decision to leave Bucking-ham Palace, feeling that its "upkeep, both from a cost and environmental perspective, is not sustainable." Even when he's the sovereign, a friend says, Charles's plan for royal accommodation "will be a much more modest flat-above-the-shop situation."

Rumor has it that William and Kate and their children may join the queen in Windsor Home Park—possibly taking up residence at Fort Belvedere, where King Edward VIII lived in 1936 when he signed his abdication papers—though their best choice may be the sprawling, nineteenth-century Adelaide Cottage, a ten-minute walk to Windsor Castle. It's also quite near to where Kate's parents live, in Berkshire.

Unlike Princess Diana, "neither William or Kate have ever been London people and have never enjoyed the chaos of the city," says royal commentator Katie Nicholl. But "Windsor seems like the ideal situation," because the location is close to the capital and the Cambridges "can easily return for public engagements and events."

It's the Duke and Duchess of Sussex who are unable to easily return these days.

Handing over one of the royal residences in England to Prince Harry is "no longer on the cards," say insiders, and it's a long way from the palace to California, where Meghan and Harry buy Chateau of Riven Rock, a $14 million, eighteen-thousand-square-foot home in the ritzy enclave of Montecito.

In Hollywood, the Sussexes quickly ink deals worth over $100 mil-lion with media giants Spotify and Netflix to "feature stories of hope and compassion from inspirational guests." By 2022, they have yet to produce much content, and Netflix cancels an animated series Meghan and David Furnish, Elton John's husband, intended to co-produce.

Diana also "planned to leverage her celebrity for the causes she cared about," says royal biographer Tina Brown, who recalls the princess sharing her vision for a series of humanitarian documentaries during their last lunch together in June 1997.

"Diana was always ahead of the curve," Brown observes. "Her plan sounds very like what Meghan and Harry are attempting with their entertainment deals today, but with one central difference: It was better thought out."

As the 2022 Platinum Jubilee to commemorate Queen Elizabeth's seventy-year reign approaches, Prince Harry says on February 18 that he "does not feel safe" bringing his wife and children to the UK without being allowed police protection. The announcement dampens hopes that the royal family will meet his nearly one-year-old daughter, Lilibet—whose birthday falls on the anniversary of her great-grandmother's coronation at Westminster Abbey—or see his son, Archie, who was less than a year old when the family moved away.

The timing of their move—just as COVID-related travel restrictions began to appear in the spring of 2020—has added to the family's sense of separation over the last two years. Despite the distance, Harry maintains close contact with the queen. "My grandmother and I have a really good relationship and understanding, and I have deep respect for her," he says, noting that they've been in touch more than ever since he's left England.

On April 14, while en route to the 2022 Invictus Games in The Hague, Netherlands, Harry and Meghan manage a quiet stopover in England for a "lowkey visit" to Windsor with Prince Charles and the queen, who'll turn ninety-six on April 21.

"Meghan and I had tea with her so it was really nice to catch up," he tells reporter Hoda Kotb of the *Today* show. "She's on great form. She's always got a great sense of humor with me." While his remarks about making sure his grandmother is "protected" and "has got the right people around her" leave the Palace bristling, Harry is more focused on "trying to make it possible that I can get my kids to meet her."

He loves "every part" of fatherhood—and senses the support of "Grandma Diana" constantly. "More so now than ever," he notes, it seems that "she's very much helping me."

"I feel her presence in almost everything I do now," he says, "definitely more so in the last two years than ever before, without question."

"She's watching over us."

"I'm sure she's proud of you," says Kotb.

"I'm sure she is," Harry agrees.

William walks along a familiar path bordered by Norfolk pines.

Today his companion is Sam Sanchez, host of the Apple Fitness+ series *Time to Walk*. Their path takes them toward Anmer Hall. When in Norfolk, the prince lives here with Kate, George, Charlotte, and Louis. As William opens the gate, childhood memories come flooding in.

He's transported to the late 1980s, riding in the car with his mother at the wheel.

"My mother, she'd be driving along, singing at the top of her voice," William says.

"And one of the songs I massively remember and has stuck with me all this time, and I still, to this day, still quite enjoy secretly, is Tina Turner's 'The Best.'"

Backstage at the June 1986 Prince's Trust concert at Wembley Arena, Diana met Tina Turner after the spandex-clad superstar singer finished a three-song set, including duets with Eric Clapton and Paul McCartney. It's Turner's 1989 hit that William loves most.

"You'll want to play it again just to keep that family moment going. When I listen to it now, it takes me back to those car rides, and brings back lots of memories of my mother."

Epilogue

1988–1998
London

C harles invites a special guest to Kensington Palace.

The prince sits down to have a one-on-one discussion about *Henry V* with Kenneth Branagh, who played the title role with the Royal Shakespeare Company and who is also writing a film adaptation he plans to direct and star in.

Branagh, a twentysomething actor whose working-class Northern Irish upbringing has taught him little about the life of a royal, can't believe his luck. *How many directors can count a future king as an unofficial adviser on their first feature film?*

"For someone in my position," the current Prince of Wales tells Branagh regarding the historical Henry, "it's someone closer, perhaps, than other characters in Shakespeare."

Charles is speaking quietly, and Branagh makes note of it.

People in authority often do, he observes. *They don't need to raise their voices.*

The two men share a passion for Shakespeare's "incredible insight into the human psyche," and talk turns to a pivotal moment in act 4, scene 1. It's in the midst of the Hundred Years' War, on the eve of the Battle of Agincourt—the cornerstone of Henry's 1415 campaign to reclaim the Aquitaine region, in southwest France, for England.

Vastly outnumbered by French forces, the young king fears his men's morale will plummet, and so he disguises himself in a borrowed cloak to walk among them.

Charles tells Branagh a story from his student days at the University of Cambridge, when the prince similarly tried to get to know his fellow students and townspeople—with frustrating results. When his disguise was too effective, Charles went unrecognized and was unable to engage; but when he was discovered, observers were reluctant to speak freely to him, leaving him to struggle with deep feelings of isolation and solitude.

"It was invaluable for me to see the melancholy that exists in him," Branagh says of Prince Charles. "Also the sense of responsibility, the feeling of having to set an example. Even when the eyes smile there's a sort of gravitas."

For all the first-class life that they lead, he realizes of the royals, *they know it's an accident of birth and one that they need to meet by a commitment to serving others.* And in Charles, he sees "a genuine expression of that."

On October 5, 1989, the Prince of Wales is an honored guest at London's iconic Odeon Leicester Square cinema for the royal world charity premiere of *Henry V,* while Princess Diana visits the London Lighthouse, a center for AIDS patients. Branagh goes on to win two Oscar nominations—for best director and best actor—for his work on the film, and its success boosts the popularity of Shakespeare worldwide.

Charles hopes schoolboys William and Harry will be swept up in the enthusiasm.

He's counting on Harry's excitement at hearing his name spoken aloud in act 3, scene 1, when King Henry famously urges his weary troops, "Once more unto the breach"—a speech that ends with "Cry 'God for Harry, England, and Saint George!'"

Charles inserts a videocassette and presses Play. The opening credits for *Henry V* roll.

The boys are riveted—to the battlefield action sequences.

"They were only keen to replay the gory bits," Charles says later.

He perseveres and in 1993 organizes two father-son Shakespeare-themed outings. He takes Harry to see *A Midsummer Night's Dream* and William to see the Royal Shakespeare Company perform *The Tempest*.

Harry "enjoyed it as much as William did," Charles says. "I was thrilled."

In February of 1998, less than six months after his mother's death, William plays a small role in *The Tempest* at Eton (Harry later does the same in a production of *Much Ado About Nothing*). His grandparents Queen Elizabeth and Prince Philip attend the performance in a show of support.

Later that same year, a caretaker discovers a book in the trash outside the former home of one of Diana's childhood schoolmates. It's a copy of *The Tempest*.

The book contains Diana's signature, circa age fifteen, as well as her handwritten notes in the margins, authenticated by experts at Sotheby's and *Antiques Roadshow*. Across two blank pages at the back of the book, she writes, "This play is summing up a lifetime."

"Shakespeare," Charles believes, "confronts us so often with such eternal truths."

Teenage Diana spots one in act 4, scene 1 of *The Tempest,* in a line of dialogue from the spirit Ariel, and underlines words that forever define her extraordinary life.

> *Shortly shall all my labours end, and thou*
> *Shalt have the air at freedom.*

Notes

Prologue

4   *I'm going to give*: Adapted from Beth Whitehouse, "The Lives of 'the Heir and the Spare,' with and Without Diana," *Los Angeles Times*, August 22, 2001.

5   *William survived*: Adapted from *Diana, Our Mother: Her Life and Legacy*, ITV, 2017, https://www.hbo.com/documentaries/diana-our-mother-her-life-and-legacy.

PART 1: LADY DIANA

Chapter 1

10   *Oh, I would love to live at KP*: Lady Colin Campbell, *Diana in Private: The Princess Nobody Knows* (New York: St. Martin's, 1992), 72.

10   "a potential match": Fay Watson, "Sarah Spencer: Why Did Princess Diana's Sister and Prince Charles Break Up?," *Express*, November 25, 2020.

10   "You're the wicked": James Whitaker, "The People's Princess I Knew," *Mirror*, August 31, 2012.

10   "desperately sorry": Tina Brown, *The Diana Chronicles* (New York: Anchor Books, 2008), 60.

10   *We have known*: Sarah Bradford, *Diana* (New York: Viking, 2006), 42.

Chapter 2

11   "to be with people": Vanessa Thorpe, "Diana Tapes Reveal Queen's Reply to Sobbing Plea over Loveless Marriage," *The Guardian*, July 30, 2017.

12   "But now you have": Tina Brown, *The Diana Chronicles* (New York: Anchor Books, 2008), 114.

Chapter 3

13   "the big house": Roya Nikkah, "Prince Charles 'Won't Live at Buckingham Palace,' Say Royal Insiders," *Sunday Times* (London), September 17, 2017.

13   "The Playboy Prince" and "Action Man": Stuart Emmrich, "In *The Crown*, Josh O'Connor Is Reminding Us That Prince Charles Was Once Hot," *Vogue*, November 18, 2020.

13   "I believe in living life" through "the most popular man": Roy Reed, "Charles, a Dashing Prince, Is Likely to Charm U.S. on Visit," *New York Times*, October 15, 1977.

13   "excellent dancer": Emmrich, "In *The Crown*, Josh O'Connor."

13   "They were trying": Charles, Prince of Wales, "Prince Charles & Tricia Nixon: The Match That Almost Was," interview by Max Foster, CNN, March 11, 2015.

13–14   "A man should sow" and "But for a wife": Sarah Bradford, *Diana* (New York: Viking, 2006), 48.

14   "a much more important" through "That is what marriage": Reed, "Charles, a Dashing Prince."

14   "I personally feel": Sarah Kettler, "Inside Prince Charles' Long Hunt for a Bride," *Biography,* November 11, 2020.

14   "You'd better get on": Kitty Kelley, *The Royals* (New York: Grand Central, 2010), 240.

14   *I've fallen in love*: Reed, "Charles, a Dashing Prince."

Chapter 4

15   "I hated going": Becky Pemberton, "Where Did Princess Diana Go to School?" *U.S. Sun,* June 22, 2021.

15   "at a loose end": Lady Colin Campbell, *The Real Diana* (New York: St. Martin's, 1998), 34.

15   "academically interested": Vanessa Thorpe, "Diana Tapes Reveal Queen's Reply to Sobbing Plea over Loveless Marriage," *The Guardian,* July 30, 2017.

15   "girl who notices": Frank Whelan, "Lady Diana Was a Bride with a History but Not a Past," *Morning Call,* September 9, 1997.

15–16   *I've always loved cleaning* through *I might become a famous dancer*: Campbell, *The Real Diana,* 34.

16   "very shy": Tina Brown, *The Diana Chronicles* (New York: Anchor Books, 2008), 60.

16   "I'm not at all intimidated": Andrew Morton, "How Diana Secretly Recorded Hours of Tapes Pouring out Her Despair over Her Imploding Marriage to Charles," *Daily Mail,* June 10, 2017.

17   "a romantic" and "wouldn't marry": Carole Cuttner, "The Man Who Will Be King," *Time,* May 15, 1978.

17   "There's no question": Sally Bedell Smith, *Prince Charles: The Passions and Paradoxes of an Improbable Life* (New York: Random House, 2017), 115.

Chapter 5

18   "You'd be amazed": Rebecca Cope, "The Spencer Set," *Tatler,* April 1, 2021.

18   "could do blindfolded": Lady Colin Campbell, *The Real Diana* (New York: St. Martin's, 1998), 37.

19   "I sat there": Annabelle Spranklen, "The Real Story of How Prince Charles Fell for Lady Diana Spencer," *Tatler,* May 6, 2021.

19   "No more puppy fat": Kitty Kelley, *The Royals* (New York: Grand Central, 2010), 247.

19   *He knows where* and "The thrill when": Spranklen, "The Real Story."

19   "We'll help you": Kelley, *The Royals,* 254.

19   "It would be nice": Lady Colin Campbell, *Diana in Private: The Princess Nobody Knows* (New York: St. Martin's, 1992), 77.

Chapter 6

20   "We must not be photographed": Harry Arnold, "The Princess and the Press," interview by *Frontline,* PBS, November 16, 1997.

20   "Oh, excuse me": Rosalind Coward, *Diana: The Portrait* (Kansas City, MO: Andrews McMeel, 2007), 24.

20   *I know it's just a job*: William Borders, "Prince Charles to Wed 19-Year-Old Family Friend," *New York Times,* February 25, 1981.

21   "anything imminent" and "fresh, friendly": Mel Laytner, "Prince Charles, Heir to the British Throne, Celebrated His . . . ," UPI, November 14, 1980.

21   "I know you were expecting": Leonard Downie Jr., "Birthday Presence," *Washington Post,* November 18, 1980.

21   "the country home": Sally Bedell Smith, *Diana in Search of Herself: Portrait of a Troubled Princess* (New York: Times Books, 1999), 92.

21   "I dare not say": Tina Brown, *The Diana Chronicles* (New York: Anchor Books, 2008), 135.

21–22   "rubbish" through "I had some supper": Daniela Elser, "Charles, Di and the Love Train," *New Zealand Herald,* November 14, 2020.

22   *The trouble is*: Smith, *Diana in Search of Herself,* 93.

Notes

Chapter 7

23   "You've got to be": Adapted from Harry Arnold, "The Princess and the Press," interview by *Frontline*, PBS, November 16, 1997.

24   *She is exquisitely pretty*: Alessandra Scotto Di Santolo, "What Prince Charles Said to His Friends About Princess Diana Just Hours Before the Wedding," *Express*, July 29, 2019.

24   "You mustn't rush me": Tim Clayton and Phil Craig, *Diana: Story of a Princess* (New York: Atria, 2003), 50.

24   "pleasing his family": "Why Prince Philip Wrote to Prince Charles After First Meeting with Princess Diana," *Geo News*, April 15, 2021.

24   "lasting damage": Sally Bedell Smith, *Diana in Search of Herself: Portrait of a Troubled Princess* (New York: Times Books, 1999), 95.

24   "To have withdrawn": Elena Nicolaou, "The Definitive Timeline of Prince Charles and Princess Diana's Relationship," *Oprah Daily*, November 13, 2020.

Chapter 8

25   "kindred spirit": Alice Vincent, "Diana, Elton and Candle in the Wind: How One Song Captured a Nation's Grief," *Telegraph*, August 31, 2017.

26   "With Prince Charles beside me": John Ezard and Alan Rusbridger, "Charles 'Amazed' by Lady Di's Yes," *The Guardian*, February 25, 1981.

26   "with greatest pleasure": Monique Jessen, "Revisit Prince Charles and Princess Diana's Engagement 40 Years Ago," *People*, February 24, 2021.

26   "God bless that pretty": William Borders, "Prince Charles to Wed 19-Year-Old Family Friend," *New York Times*, February 25, 1981.

26   "I think Diana": Ezard and Rusbridger, "Charles 'Amazed' by Lady Di's Yes."

26   "I can't get used": Glenne Currie, "Di's Itchy Nose," UPI, July 17, 1981.

27   "A splendid brooch" and "A large sapphire": Andrea Blazquez, "Queen Victoria's £1m 'Splendid' Jewel Inspired Kate and Diana's Engagement Ring," *Express*, September 21, 2021.

27   "Prince Charles had always" and "thought it was perfect": Hilary Weaver, "Actually, Prince Charles Picked Out Diana's Engagement Ring," *Elle*, December 18, 2020.

27   "elegant and simple": Paul Burrell, *A Royal Duty* (New York: Putnam, 2003), 54.

27   "My God": Lady Colin Campbell, *The Real Diana* (New York: St. Martin's, 1998), 78.

27   "Oh, a bit chubby": Karen Mizoguchi, "Princess Diana Recorded Her Bulimia Anguish After Prince Charles Called Her 'a Bit Chubby,'" *People*, June 9, 2017.

27   *I'm not walking* and "I might not lose": Campbell, *The Real Diana*, 79.

27   *It gives you a feeling*: Michael S. Rosenwald, "Fact-Checking 'The Crown': Did Princess Diana's Battle with Bulimia Ruin Her Marriage?," *Washington Post*, November 15, 2020.

27   *I can't believe*: Campbell, *The Real Diana*, 79.

Chapter 9

28   "six of everything" and "one long dress": Andrew Morton, *Diana: Her True Story—In Her Own Words*, 25th anniversary ed. (New York: Simon & Schuster Paperbacks, 2017), 74.

28   "real grown-up dress": Morton, *Diana*, 57.

28   "never again wear": Lady Colin Campbell, *Diana in Private: The Princess Nobody Knows* (New York: St. Martin's, 1992), 155.

28–29   "a sanctuary" and "always open and spirited": Alice Newbold, "The Fabulously Frou Frou Dress That Changed Princess Diana's Style Forever," *Vogue* France, September 13, 2020.

29   "It sounds a bit over-the-top": Sarah Rainey, "Diana's Dress of the Century," *Daily Mail*, July 27, 2021.

29   "The British press were rooting": Natalie Finn, "The Epic Story of Princess Diana's Wedding Dress," *E!*, July 29, 2021.

29   "It was a big adventure": Chanel Vargas, "Every Detail About Princess Diana's Iconic Wedding Dress," *Town & Country*, November 12, 2020.

Chapter 10

30 "Are you enjoying": Marie Brenner, "The Wedding of the Century," *New York,* August 3, 1981.

30 "There can be nothing": Lady Colin Campbell, *Diana in Private: The Princess Nobody Knows* (New York: St. Martin's, 1992), 107.

31 "What on earth": Shan Lancaster, "Lady Di's Jet Hit by Lightning," *The Sun,* May 4, 1981.

31 "look after Lady Diana": Stephen Barry, "Lady Diana Finds New House Rules Restrict Her Freedom," *Chicago Tribune,* August 19, 1985.

31 "This is the last": Lady Colin Campbell, *The Real Diana* (New York: St. Martin's, 1998), 76.

31 "It's all right": Barry, "Lady Diana Finds New House Rules."

31 "This is the life": Campbell, *The Real Diana,* 44.

31 "For God's sake": Andrew Morton, *Diana: Her True Story—In Her Own Words,* 25th anniversary ed. (New York: Simon & Schuster Paperbacks, 2017), 189.

31 "The noise you just heard": Lancaster, "Lady Di's Jet Hit by Lightning."

Chapter 11

32–33 "fill the aisle" through "Will I be able to see": Rosalind Coward, *Diana: The Portrait* (Kansas City, MO: Andrews McMeel, 2007), 25, 80, 25.

Chapter 12

34 "someone as special": Sally Bedell Smith, *Prince Charles: The Passions and Paradoxes of an Improbable Life* (New York: Random House, 2017), 143.

34 "I feel positively delighted": John Ezard and Alan Rusbridger, "Charles 'Amazed' by Lady Di's Yes," *The Guardian,* February 25, 1981.

34–35 "Delighted and happy" and "Of course!": Erica Gonzales, "What Prince Charles and Princess Diana's Engagement Interview Looked Like in Real Life," *Harper's Bazaar,* November 15, 2020.

35 "I want to do": Meilan Solly, "14 Fun Facts About Princess Diana's Wedding," *Smithsonian,* November 13, 2020.

35 "Is it possible": Rebecca Flood, "Crown and Out," *The Sun,* October 3, 2018.

Chapter 13

37 "Gosh, it's a lot": Rosalind Coward, *Diana: The Portrait* (Kansas City, MO: Andrews McMeel, 2007), 26.

37 "Ah, somebody I can": Liz Jones, "Make-up Guru Barbara Daly: 'I've Worked with the World's Most Perfect Faces, and I Tell You, There Is No Such Thing,'" *Daily Mail,* March 30, 2009.

38 "I've just put" and "Do you think": Coward, *Diana,* 27.

38 *I am so proud*: Kate Nicholson, "Royal History Rewritten," *Express,* May 23, 2020.

38 "creating a fairy dust": Alice Newbold, "Princess Diana's 'Fairy Dust' Wedding Veil Was Embellished over Long Nights by a Single, Secret Embroiderer," *Vogue* Britain, May 16, 2021.

Chapter 14

40 "Here is the stuff": Meilan Solly, "14 Fun Facts About Princess Diana's Wedding," *Smithsonian,* November 13, 2020.

Chapter 15

41   "Kiss! Kiss!": Robert A. Erlandson, "Wedding Thrust Her to Center of World Stage Fairy Tale Images Will Remain Indelible," *Baltimore Sun,* September 1, 1997.

41   "I am not going to": "The Wedding of the Century," *Life* special issue, *Diana: A Princess Remembered,* reissued June 2020, 61.

42   "Did you bump": Eun Kyung Kim, "Princess Diana's Youngest Bridesmaid Shares Memories from THAT Royal Wedding," *Today,* April 19, 2018.

PART 2: CHARLES AND DI

Chapter 16

45   "Mr. and Mrs. Hardy": Linda Rodgers, "See Princess Diana and Prince Charles During Their Hands-On Caribbean Vacation," *First for Women,* June 26, 2017.

45   *His skin is kissable*: Lady Colin Campbell, *The Real Diana* (New York: St. Martin's, 1998), 45.

45   "Ships, I see no ships!": "Bahama Mama," *The Sun,* February 18, 1982.

46   "a glamorous concoction": R. W. Apple Jr., "Delighted Diana Expects Baby in June," *New York Times,* November 6, 1981.

46   "You simply have": Catherine Armecin, "Queen Elizabeth 'Horrified', 'Annoyed' with Princess Diana's Pregnant-in-Bikini Photos," *International Business Times,* May 20, 2019.

46   "Oh pass me the Kleenex": Arthur Edwards, "The Sun and the Reign," *The Sun,* November 19, 2019.

46   "sick as a parrot": Katie Nicholl, *The Making of a Royal Romance: William, Kate, and Harry—A Look Behind the Palace Walls* (New York: Weinstein Books, 2010), 8.

47   "Is your son": "Princess Diana Gives Birth to Prince William in 1982," *Daily News* (New York), June 22, 1982.

47   *I am so thankful*: Sam Dangremond, "Looking Back at Royal Births Throughout History," *Town & Country,* September 20, 2021.

47   "The baby is lucky": "The Wedding of the Century," *Life* special issue, *Diana: A Princess Remembered,* reissued June 2020, 82.

Chapter 17

48   "two sizes too small": Hilary Weaver, "Princess Diana Detailed Her Memorable Meetings with Grace Kelly and Elizabeth Taylor," *Vanity Fair,* June 15, 2017.

49   "Don't worry, dear": Abbie Llewelyn, "Prince Charles' Brutal Response to Diana's Grace Kelly Request Exposed," *Express,* June 26, 2020.

49   *How wonderful and serene*: Andrew Morton, *Diana: Her True Story—In Her Own Words,* 25th anniversary ed. (New York: Simon & Schuster Paperbacks, 2017), 57.

49   "Even in Hollywood": Rachel Chang, "Grace Kelly and Prince Rainier III Were Introduced for a Magazine Article—and Then Fell in Love," *Biography,* May 27, 2020.

49   "We'll have to ask": Morton, *Diana,* 74.

49   "If you want to": Weaver, "Princess Diana Detailed Her Memorable Meetings."

49   "psychically connected": John Burfitt, "Princess Diana and Princess Grace's Bizarre Bond," *New Idea,* November 17, 2020.

49   "was an outsider": Weaver, "Princess Diana Detailed Her Memorable Meetings."

50   "I suppose I think": Rachel Chang, "The Mystery Surrounding Grace Kelly's Death," *Biography,* May 29, 2020.

50   "Will Charles be there": Sarah Bradford, *Diana* (New York: Viking, 2006), 116.

51   "They say you did brilliantly": Tina Brown, *The Diana Chronicles* (New York: Anchor Books, 2008), 218.

51   "the Establishment": Fred Barbash, "Princess Di Admits to an Affair," *Washington Post,* November 21, 1995.

51   "It's quite amazing": Paul Burrell, *A Royal Duty* (New York: Putnam, 2003), 94.

Chapter 18

52   *She'll never be queen*: Sally Bedell Smith, *Diana in Search of Herself: Portrait of a Troubled Princess* (New York: Times Books, 1999), 106.

52   "Are you sure?": Christopher Andersen, *Diana's Boys: William and Harry and the Mother They Loved* (New York: William Morrow, 2001), 48.

53   "men in gray suits": Lady Colin Campbell, *The Real Diana* (New York: St. Martin's, 1998), 181.

Chapter 19

54   "Look, Mummy!": Christopher Andersen, *Diana's Boys: William and Harry and the Mother They Loved* (New York: William Morrow, 2001), 81.

54   "Whirlwind Will" through "He's quite a handful": Richard Kay, "Who Was More of a Tiny Terror than Prince George?," *Scottish Daily Mail,* July 18, 2015.

55   "Gary!": Jenny Proudfoot, "Prince William Used to Have the Most Hilarious Nickname for the Queen," *Marie Claire,* July 22, 2021.

55   "Who's Gary?": Liam Doyle, "Queen Nicknames," *Express,* August 21, 2020.

55   *I hate it*: Lady Colin Campbell, *Diana in Private: The Princess Nobody Knows* (New York: St. Martin's, 1992), 76.

Chapter 20

56   "the minute you": Hadley Hall Meares, "A Brief History of Queen Elizabeth's Beloved Balmoral," *Vanity Fair,* August 5, 2021.

56   "the most wonderful": Lady Colin Campbell, *Diana in Private: The Princess Nobody Knows* (New York: St. Martin's, 1992), 206.

56   "You'd think the Prince": Piers Brendon, *Eminent Elizabethans: Rupert Murdoch, Prince Charles, Margaret Thatcher & Mick Jagger* (New York: Random House, 2012), 107.

57   "having a child is a miracle": Campbell, *Diana in Private,* 206.

57   "I don't understand": Sarah Bradford, *Diana* (New York: Viking, 2006), 238.

Chapter 21

58   "I have to get" through "I am trying to support": Paul Burrell, *A Royal Duty* (New York: Putnam, 2003), 94.

58–59   "delight" through "the royal couple": Ashley Walton, "Smile That Says It All," *Express,* February 14, 1984.

59   "I fell in love" and "What am I supposed": Lady Colin Campbell, *Diana in Private: The Princess Nobody Knows* (New York: St. Martin's, 1992), 98, 174.

60   "What is it now": Sally Bedell Smith, *Prince Charles: The Passions and Paradoxes of an Improbable Life* (New York: Random House, 2017), 146.

60   "deranged and paranoid": Cortney Drakeford, "Why Princess Diana Was Considered 'Deranged and Paranoid' During Prince Charles Marriage," *International Business Times,* June 24, 2019.

60   "Do not move anything": Campbell, *Diana in Private,* 177.

Chapter 22

61   *Charles and I are the closest*: Andrew Morton, *Diana: Her True Story—In Her Own Words,* 25th anniversary ed. (New York: Simon & Schuster Paperbacks, 2017), 80.

62   "I'm having a boy": Paul Burrell, *A Royal Duty* (New York: Putnam, 2003), 95.

62   "Did you expect" through "a sort of indeterminate color": "The Birth of 'Lovely' Baby Prince Harry in 1984," *Belfast Telegraph,* May 6, 2019.

62   "It's important that the first": Christopher Andersen, *Diana's Boys: William and Harry and the Mother They Loved* (New York: William Morrow, 2001), 63.

62 "How different a character": Sally Bedell Smith, *Prince Charles: The Passions and Paradoxes of an Improbable Life* (New York: Random House, 2017), 177.

62 "It will be lovely" and "I'm sure Harry": Gioia Diliberto, "Hello, Harry!," *People*, October 1, 1984.

63 "just plain Harry": "The Newest Prince: Plain Harry at Home," UPI, September 17, 1984.

Chapter 23

64 "not on speaking terms": Martina Bet, "Princess Anne's 'Displeasure' with Charles Grew into 'Full-Scale Family Row,'" *Express*, August 2, 2021.

64 "We were so disappointed": Lauren Cahn, "The Comment Prince Charles Made After Harry's Birth That Broke Princess Diana's Heart," *Reader's Digest*, June 7, 2021.

64 "The reaction to" and "William has totally": Sarah Bradford, *Diana* (New York: Viking, 2006), 126.

65 "knows he is different" and "Any child": Richard Kay, "Who Was More of a Tiny Terror than Prince George?," *Scottish Daily Mail*, July 18, 2015.

65 "I tell *you* what to do": Christopher Andersen, *Diana's Boys: William and Harry and the Mother They Loved* (New York: William Morrow, 2001), 66.

65 "Barry, how do I look?" through *I'm only happy*: Tina Brown, *The Diana Chronicles* (New York: Anchor Books, 2008), 255–56.

Chapter 24

66 "because it's opening up" through "He just adores": Charles, Prince of Wales, and Diana, Princess of Wales, "The Prince and Princess of Wales...Talking Personally with Alastair Burnet," interview by Alastair Burnet, ABC, November 7, 1985.

66 "a happy start": Jo Thomas, "The Early Education of a Future King," *New York Times*, April 3, 1986.

67 "Don't you mean Granny?": Anna Kretschmer, "The HEARTBREAKING way Prince William found out he'd be king REVEALED," *Express*, May 16, 2019.

67 "Basher Wills" and "Billy the Basher": Becky Pemberton, "Cheeky Royal: Prince William's Unruly Behaviour at School Earned Him a VERY Un-Royal Nickname," *US Sun*, October 22, 2021.

67 "When I'm king": Christopher Andersen, *Diana's Boys: William and Harry and the Mother They Loved* (New York: William Morrow, 2001), 73.

67 "My daddy's a real prince": Katie Nicholl, *The Making of a Royal Romance: William, Kate, and Harry—A Look Behind the Palace Walls* (New York: Weinstein Books, 2010), 28.

67 "You have to look": Andersen, *Diana's Boys*, 94.

67 "He's a typical" and "He's not at all": Charles and Diana, "The Prince and Princess of Wales."

67 "William, Prince of Wails": "Here and There," *Daily News* (New York), February 13, 1984.

Chapter 25

68 "Princess!": Betty Cuniberti, "Charles Hails Welcome Fit for a Princess," *Los Angeles Times*, November 11, 1985.

69 "As a teenager": Howard Chua-Eoan, "In Living Memory," *Time*, June 24, 2001.

69 "Is it proper": Billy Higgins, "Dancing with Princess Diana Was the Scariest Thing I've Ever Done, Admits Legendary Singer Neil Diamond," *Sunday Post*, January 21, 2017.

69 "Would you care to dance": Annie Goldsmith, "John Travolta Reminisces on His Famous Dance with Princess Diana," *Town & Country*, August 9, 2021.

69 "Absolutely": "Princess Diana," *People*, December 23, 1985.

69 "We're good": "The Wedding of the Century," *Life* special issue, *Diana: A Princess Remembered*, reissued June 2020, 94.

69–70 "Maybe some day" and "That would be great": Giles Sheldrick, "Sold for £240,000...the Dress That Princess Diana Dazzled in with John Travolta," *Express*, March 19, 2013.

70 "You gonna have more": Thomas Ferraro, "Here They Come," UPI, November 8, 1985.

Chapter 26

71 "I want it to be": "Prince Charles Restores William's Beloved Childhood Tree House for Prince George," *Hello!*, July 29, 2015.

72 "Ken, do you want" and "They're not being": Ken Wharfe, *Diana: Closely Guarded Secret* (London: John Blake Publishing, 2016), 27.

72 "ended William's tantrums": David Brown, "Wills and Harry's Heartbreak at Death of Nanny," *Free Library*, May 18, 2003.

72 "red carpet fever": Tina Brown, *The Diana Chronicles* (New York: Anchor Books, 2008), 256.

72 "Barry Mannakee died": Sarah Bradford, *Diana* (New York: Viking, 2006), 147.

73 "the unfortunate thing": Vincent Canby, "In Cannes Limelight: Gish and Davis," *New York Times*, May 16, 1987.

Chapter 27

74 *I've got two very healthy*: Charles, Prince of Wales, and Diana, Princess of Wales, "The Prince and Princess of Wales . . . Talking Personally with Alastair Burnet," interview by Alastair Burnet, ABC, November 7, 1985.

74 "Now listen, William" and "I don't like 'tographers": Rob Wallace, "'Rebel Royal Mum': Diana's Legacy as Parent," ABC News, May 23, 2013.

74–75 "You're going to go": Rosalind Coward, *Diana: The Portrait* (Kansas City, MO: Andrews McMeel, 2007), 60.

75 "He is well enough" and "I wouldn't let": "Prince Harry Undergoes Hernia Operation," AP News, May 10, 1988.

Chapter 28

76 "incredible mother": Guy Birchall, "Mayfair Lady," *The Sun*, July 10, 2019.

76 *Go for the hell of it*: Belinda Robinson, "REVEALED: Princess Diana Describes Furious Row with Camilla Blasting 'I WANT MY HUSBAND,'" *Express*, June 19, 2017.

77 "I am not going": Ken Wharfe, *Diana: Closely Guarded Secret* (London: John Blake Publishing, 2016), 138.

77 "I enjoy it": Ingrid Seward, *William & Harry* (New York: Arcade, 2003), 115.

77 "Diana, don't go down": Amber Hicks, "Night Princess Diana Confronted Camilla over Charles and 'All Hell Broke Loose,'" *Mirror*, February 29, 2020.

77 "Please don't go, Ken": Wharfe, *Diana*, 139.

77 "Camilla, I'd like to": Robinson, "REVEALED."

77 "Camilla, would you like" and "I know about": Hicks, "Night Princess Diana Confronted Camilla."

77 "Don't think it's my fault": Seward, *William & Harry*, 149.

78 "I'm sorry I'm in the way": McKenzie Jean-Philippe, "Princess Diana and Camilla Parker Bowles' Awkward Lunch from *The Crown* Happened," *Oprah Daily*, November 18, 2020.

78 "You've got everything" and "I want my husband": Andrew Morton, "The Night I Took On Camilla," *Daily Mail*, June 16, 2017.

78 *There comes a time*: Wharfe, *Diana*, 141.

78 *If I could write*: Chloe Kerr, "The Greatest Fellow," *The Sun*, July 29, 2017.

78 *The first time I experienced*: Lady Colin Campbell, *The Real Diana* (New York: St. Martin's, 1998), 106.

78 "lovey time" and "But come home": Christopher Andersen, *Diana's Boys: William and Harry and the Mother They Loved* (New York: William Morrow, 2001), 90.

PART 3: MUMMY

Chapter 29

81 "When I grow up" and "Oh no you can't": Lucy Devine, "Mummy's Hero," *The Sun,* October 5, 2018.

81 "I don't really want" and "If you don't want": Anna Kretschmer, "Princess Diana's Heartbreaking Worries About Prince William Exposed," *Express,* May 6, 2020.

81 *"You'll* be king" and "Where the hell": Robert Lacey, *Battle of Brothers: William and Harry—The Inside Story of a Family in Tumult* (New York: Harper, 2021), 103.

82 "sleep rough": Rosalind Coward, *Diana: The Portrait* (Kansas City, MO: Andrews McMeel, 2007), 191.

82 "They are human beings" through "Shopping, isn't it": Tina Brown, *The Diana Chronicles* (New York: Anchor Books, 2008), 288, 300.

83 "Your Royal Highness": Coward, *Diana,* 99.

83 "It's all right" through "This is the work": Ken Wharfe, *Diana: Closely Guarded Secret* (London: John Blake Publishing, 2016), 131, 132.

Chapter 30

84 "incredibly confident" and "a bit like talking": "Prince William Turning a Maturer 7," *Los Angeles Times,* June 19, 1989.

Chapter 31

86 *They're always out:* Katie Nicholl, *The Making of a Royal Romance: William, Kate, and Harry—A Look Behind the Palace Walls* (New York: Weinstein Books, 2010), 49.

86 "the Germans": Ken Wharfe, "How Princess Diana and James Hewitt's Affair Unfolded," *New Zealand Herald,* December 20, 2016.

87 "You know my only": Ken Wharfe, *Diana: Closely Guarded Secret* (London: John Blake Publishing, 2016), 57.

87 "After Harry was born": Wharfe, "How Princess Diana and James Hewitt's Affair."

87 "You give me strength": Tina Brown, *The Diana Chronicles* (New York: Anchor Books, 2008), 272.

88 "And so, darling": Daniela Elser, "The Risqué Phone Call No One Was Meant to Hear," *New Zealand Herald,* August 10, 2019.

88 "I was very bad" through "It's not hatred": Brown, *Diana Chronicles,* 309–11, 313.

88 "You don't mind" through "You are the nicest": Anthony Holden, "Diana's Revenge," *Vanity Fair,* February 1993.

88 *Just some salad:* Elser, "The Risqué Phone Call."

Chapter 32

89 "If you look out": Rhiannon Mills, "Princess Diana 'Saved' the Royal Family, Sir Richard Branson Says," *Sky News,* August 28, 2017.

89 "some peace and quiet": Carola Long, "Necker Island—Inside Richard Branson's Caribbean Lair," *Financial Times,* August 3, 2021.

90–91 "But can you guarantee" through "You said that if I did": Ken Wharfe, *Diana: Closely Guarded Secret* (London: John Blake Publishing, 2016), 156–57, 154–55, 152, 163.

91 "He hates the press" and "He sees them as the enemy": "The Man Who Would Not Be King," Johann Hari, *New Zealand Herald,* May 9, 2003.

92 "when the photographers": Wharfe, *Diana,* 164.

92 "We can go to the top": Chris Stone, "Robert Jobson's Royal Podcast: When Prince William Played a Prank on the Press," *Evening Standard,* May 25, 2018.

92 "chief loader" and "a wonderful assault": "Princess Diana's Secret Life," NBC News, September 6, 2002.

Chapter 33

93 "Accident prone" and "in a fair tizz": Laurie Johnston and Robert Mcg. Thomas Jr., "Yet Another Tumble for the 'Accident Prone' Prince," *New York Times,* April 27, 1981.

93 "terrifying matter of seconds" through "Please, Your Majesty": Associated Press, "Prince Flies Home with Body of Slide Victim," *Register-Guard* (Eugene, OR), March 12, 1988.

93 "For heaven's sake": Ken Wharfe, *Diana: Closely Guarded Secret* (London: John Blake Publishing, 2016), 53.

94 "as long as I bounce": "Prince Charles Breaks Arm in Fall from Horse," AP News, June 28, 1990.

94 *Quite the glamour girl*: Wharfe, *Diana,* 52.

94 "It looked for a moment" and "A silly thing to do": "Charles Breaks Arm in Polo Match," *Los Angeles Times,* June 29, 1990.

Chapter 34

96 "My darling Wombat": "Butler 'Stole Diana's Belongings,'" BBC News, October 14, 2002.

97 "I hate you, Papa": Katie Nicholl, *The Making of a Royal Romance: William, Kate, and Harry—A Look Behind the Palace Walls* (New York: Weinstein Books, 2010), 35.

97 "I hate to see you sad": Christopher Andersen, "The Divided Prince," *Vanity Fair,* September 1, 2003.

97 "Papa never embarrasses": Nicholl, *The Making of a Royal Romance,* 40.

97 "Mummies and daddies": Andersen, "The Divided Prince."

97 "You can be as naughty": Matt Roper, "Princess Diana's Hilarious Pranks on Her Sons That Left William 'Bright Red,'" *Mirror,* July 1, 2021.

Chapter 35

98 "Who is it" and "We were told": Adapted from Sarah Vine, "From Shy Di Feather Cut to Sunkissed and Sleek, the Hairdo That Was Diana's Crowning Glory," *Daily Mail,* August 13, 2017.

98 "I've no idea" through "As I normally": Vienna Vernose, "Revealing Princess Diana's Ultimate Beauty Secret," *CR Fashion Book,* December 3, 2020.

98–99 "I hear it is" through "He's incredibly flirtatious": "From the Archive: Vogue's Anna Harvey on Dressing Princess Diana," *Vogue,* November 16, 2020.

99 "Don't think about it" through "solid as a plastic dummy": Lucy Davies, "David Bailey on Diana's 'Terrible Hair,' the Queen's 'Beautiful Skin,' and Living with Dementia," *Telegraph,* March 14, 2022.

99 "Blue eyes should never" and "I think beiges": Lucy Abbersteen, "Why Princess Diana Stopped Wearing Blue Eyeliner in the 90s," *Woman & Home,* November 23, 2020.

99 "Oh, those velvet headbands": Diane Clehane, "This Is What Princess Diana Secretly Called Her Haters," *BestLife,* January 18, 2019.

100 "if anybody can come up": "Prince Charles Bans Aerosols from Household," AP News, February 23, 1988.

100 "One-fourth of an inch": Steven Stolman, "Princess Diana's Personal Hairdresser Shares His Memories of the Late Royal," *Town & Country,* June 11, 2018.

100 "I'll show this family": Vine, "From Shy Di Feather Cut."

100 "Could you come sit": Sam McKnight, "Sam McKnight: A Career Retrospective," interview by Alexandra Venison, posted by *Vogue* Arabia, July 10, 2020, https://www.youtube.com /watch?v=FeQIWT2-A7E.

100 "Sam, what would you do" and "I'd cut it all off": Emily Dixon, "Princess Diana's Hairstylist Shared the Surprising Reason She Cut Her Hair Short," *Marie Claire,* April 7, 2021.

101 "Do it then": Elizabeth Paton, "Why Are We Still Obsessed with Princess Diana's Style?" *New York Times,* February 22, 2017.

Chapter 36

102 "just the thing": Christopher Andersen, "The Divided Prince," *Vanity Fair,* September 1, 2003.

103 "contingency plans": "Prince William Injured in Accident at School," UPI, June 3, 1991.

103 "No one was being nasty": Catherine Armecin, "Princess Diana Comforted Prince William, Harry Visited Brother After This Shocking Accident," *International Business Times,* October 18, 2019.

103 "chirpy and chatting away": "Prince Charles' Son Is Hit with Golf Club," AP News, June 3, 1991.

103 "My heart went cold": Tim Clayton and Phil Craig, *Diana: Story of a Princess* (New York: Atria, 2003), 208.

103 "depressed fracture": Katie Nicholl, *The Making of a Royal Romance: William, Kate, and Harry—A Look Behind the Palace Walls* (New York: Weinstein Books, 2010), 41.

103 *The longest seventy minutes:* Clayton and Craig, *Diana,* 209.

104 "What kind of dad": "Prince William Leaves Hospital After Injury," AP News, June 5, 1991.

Chapter 37

105 "shame bicycle": Simon MacMichael, "'Shame Bicycle' Owned by Princess Diana Sells for £9,200 at Auction," *road.cc,* February 18, 2018.

106 "Diana only married me": Jon Hilkevitch, "On Art's Cutting Edge," *Chicago Tribune,* January 10, 1991.

106 "Ken, you'll have to": Ken Wharfe, *Diana: Closely Guarded Secret* (London: John Blake Publishing, 2016), 58.

Chapter 38

107 "Cabbage" and "Sausage": Abigail O'Leary, "Prince Philip Called the Queen 'Cabbage' Among Series of Cheeky Royal Nicknames," *Mirror,* April 13, 2021.

108 "inappropriate": Anthony Holden, "Diana's Revenge," *Vanity Fair,* February 1993.

108 "Why don't you": Kate Nicholson, "Royal Rage: How Diana Fumed When Queen Tried to Stop Her Inspirational Work with AIDS," *Express,* March 15, 2020.

108 "It's all about touching": Tina Brown, *The Diana Chronicles* (New York: Anchor Books, 2008), 282.

108 "What do you say" and "Well, there is not": Larry King, *The People's Princess: Cherished Memories of Diana, Princess of Wales, from Those Who Knew Her Best* (New York: Crown, 2007), 141–42.

108 "HIV does not make" through "an enormous hug": Emma Dibdin, "The True Story of Princess Diana's Groundbreaking AIDS Advocacy," *Elle,* December 6, 2020.

109 "two tours in one": Kevin Newman, "1991: Prince Charles and Princess Diana, William and Harry Visit Canada," CBC Archives, October 23, 1991, https://www.cbc.ca/archives/entry/1991-prince-charles-and-princess-diana-william-and-harry-visit-canada.

Chapter 39

110 "I believe you sing" and "But they go": Phillip Silverstone, "Sir Cliff Richard: Night Diana and I serenaded Princes William and Harry," *Express,* September 29, 2013.

111 "Do you know": "Cliff Richard Shares Funny Memories with Prince Harry and Princess Diana," *Hello!,* October 25, 2020.

111 "Extraordinary": Abbie Llewelyn, "Princess Diana Heartbreak: How Charles and Diana 'Nearly Reconciled' Before Tragedy Struck," *Express,* April 9, 2020.

111 "when Mummy decided": Associated Press, "Frances Shand Kydd, Mother of Princess Diana, Dead at 68," *South Florida Sun-Sentinel,* June 3, 2004.

111 "bolted": Ken Wharfe, *Diana: Closely Guarded Secret* (London: John Blake Publishing, 2016), 123.

111 "I come from a divorced": Matt Wilkinson, "The Bitter End," *U.S. Sun,* February 12, 2021.

111 "in a day or two": Charles Spencer, "Father's Day Portrait That I Made to 'Di's Dad' 25 Years Ago," *Daily Mail,* June 18, 2016.

112 "Oh my God": Wharfe, *Diana,* 237.

Chapter 40

114   "How is it going" through "You never told me": Larry King, *The People's Princess: Cherished Memories of Diana, Princess of Wales, from Those Who Knew Her Best* (New York: Crown, 2007), 216.

Chapter 41

115   "The boys are well": Lindsay Lowe, "Prince Harry Was 'Constantly in Trouble' at School, Princess Diana Confided in a 1992 Letter," *Parade,* January 13, 2017.

115–16   "He's too young" and "Oh shut up": Ken Wharfe, "An Insight into the Royals," *New Zealand Herald,* August 6, 2016.

116   "walkabout": "Princess Diana, Prince William and Prince Harry Visit Niagara Falls, 1991," posted by CBC, October 22, 2019, https://www.youtube.com/watch?v=t51vowf1edc.

Chapter 42

117   "It's time to spread": Matt Wilkinson, "The Bitter End," *U.S. Sun,* February 12, 2021.

118   "Hugging has no harmful" through "If the immediate family": Anthony Holden, "Diana's Revenge," *Vanity Fair,* February 1993.

Chapter 43

119   "if there's a divorce": Eugene Robinson, "Prince Charles, Diana Will Separate," *Washington Post,* December 10, 1992.

119   "to last a lifetime": Susan Goodman, "Royal Wedding Gifts: Extraordinary and Ordinary," *New York Times,* July 27, 1981.

120   "fuddy-duddy": Lady Colin Campbell, *Diana in Private: The Princess Nobody Knows* (New York: St. Martin's, 1992), 172.

120   "It is announced": Anthony Holden, "Diana's Revenge," *Vanity Fair,* February 1993.

120   "If something has gone wrong": Sally Bedell Smith, *Prince Charles: The Passions and Paradoxes of an Improbable Life* (New York: Random House, 2017), 269.

120   "Oh well": Ken Wharfe, *Diana: Closely Guarded Secret* (London: John Blake Publishing, 2016), 287.

121   "Well, I'd love to": Tim Clayton and Phil Craig, *Diana: Story of a Princess* (New York: Atria, 2003), 245.

121   "MPs Say Charles": Trevor Kavanagh and Simon Walters, "Throne Alone," *The Sun,* December 10, 1992.

PART 4: PRINCESS OF WALES

Chapter 44

125   "Ken, I want" through "Go away!": Ken Wharfe, *Diana: Closely Guarded Secret* (London: John Blake Publishing, 2016), 331, 332.

125–26   "They're only eight" through "She will ski much faster": "The Princess and the Paparazzi: Our Princess Diana News Article for 5 February 2016," *Princess Diana News Blog,* February 5, 2016.

126–27   "Ma'am, it's about" through "No, ma'am, I really don't": Wharfe, *Diana,* 335, 336.

Chapter 45

128–29   "I express the wish": Warren Hoge, "Diana's Two Sons Share the Bulk of Her $21.45 Million Estate," *New York Times,* March 3, 1998.

129   "Super Gran": Natalie Finn, "Princess Diana's 'Little Spencer,'" *E!,* May 14, 2019.

129   "face is on the tea towels": Clive Hammond, "Princess Diana's Heartbreaking Wedding Confession Exposed," *Express,* June 25, 2020.

129   "Diana's face will wash": Marie Brenner, "The Wedding of the Century," *New York,* August 3, 1981.

129   "Meet you on" and "I'll be wearing": Kyle Farrell, "Princess Diana's Pal Recalls Tactics She Used to Escape Palace and Watch Secret Films," *Express,* June 26, 2021.

130   "The Garden House" and "I see your clear need": Caroline Davies, "Letters Reveal Brother Rejected Diana's Plea for a Home," *Telegraph,* October 22, 2002.

130   "There are times I wish": "The 8th Earl Spencer Dies," *Washington Post,* March 30, 1992.

130–31   "Dearest Duch" through "Knowing the state": Davies, "Letters Reveal Brother Rejected Diana's Plea."

131   *Perhaps he has a point:* Ken Wharfe, *Diana: Closely Guarded Secret* (London: John Blake Publishing, 2016), 326.

Chapter 46

133   "My policeman": Simon Perry, "Prince Harry Shares His Hilarious Memory of Riding Space Mountain as a Kid," *People,* May 5, 2016.

133   "Lady Di" and "a piece of cake": Ken Wharfe, *Diana: Closely Guarded Secret* (London: John Blake Publishing, 2016), 352.

133   "low-key" and "I knew it": Craig Dezern, "Disney Gives Diana and Sons Royal Welcome—by Side Door," *Orlando Sentinel,* August 25, 1993.

133   "I can't remember": Suzannah Otis, "Diana, Princess of Wales in Disney: A Real Princess in a Magic Kingdom," *Zannaland!,* August 31, 2009.

133–34   "What's that bread" through "would go ballistic": Ken Wharfe, *Guarding Diana: Protecting the Princess Around the World* (London: John Blake Publishing, 2017), 240.

134   "Oh, bloody organic!": Shayne Rodriguez Thompson, "18 Odd Details We Learned About the Royal Family's Eating Habits," *cafemom,* September 21, 2020.

134   "To get the best": Kim Severson, "Farmer, Cookie Maker, Ecologist and, Yes, the Future King," *New York Times,* April 25, 2007.

134   "If only I was": Wharfe, *Diana,* 52–53.

Chapter 47

135   *I'll bloody well show:* Ken Wharfe, *Diana: Closely Guarded Secret* (London: John Blake Publishing, 2016), 285, 287.

135   "Over the next few" through "I hope you can find": Diana, Princess of Wales, "Time and Space" (speech), December 3, 1993, Headway Club, London, https://www.settelen.com /diana_time_and_space.htm.

136   "I want William and Harry": Christopher Andersen, *Diana's Boys: William and Harry and the Mother They Loved* (New York: William Morrow, 2001), 155.

136   "to experience what": "Prince William," *Royal Report,* September 1999, reprinted in *Britain Express.*

136   "I know it's going": Wharfe, *Diana,* 41.

136   "Cancel lunch" through "It's the toy": Mehera Bonner, "18 Things You Never Knew About the Royal Family's *Insane* Eating Habits," *Marie Claire,* October 3, 2017.

136   "the princes need": Wharfe, *Diana,* 29.

137   "I give them what" and "gives them a tennis": Richard Kay, "Why Harry's Still So Close to Tiggy Legge-Bourke, the Sloaney Nanny Who Drove Diana Half-Mad with Jealousy," *Daily Mail,* January 26, 2018.

137   "Give me that" through "Not everybody likes us": Charlie Smith, "Prince William's Confrontation with Homeless Man as Royal Told 'I'm Not Interested in You,'" *Express,* August 4, 2021.

137   "lead from the heart": Lori Bonne, "The Boys Left Behind," *Chicago Tribune,* September 9, 1997.

Chapter 48

138–39   "I thought it was a stunt" through "Prince Charles was fantastic": "Student Fires 2 Blanks at Prince Charles," *Los Angeles Times,* January 27, 1994.

139   "A thousand years" through "I want to remove": Associated Press, "New Zealot in New Zealand Tries to Freshen British Heir," *Deseret News,* February 7, 1994.

139   "faithful and honorable" through "Until it became": John Darnton, "Prince Charles, in TV Documentary, Admits to Infidelity," *New York Times,* June 30, 1994.

140   "It wasn't quite" and "We went off": Mark Duell, "Moment Prince Charles Crashed Queen's Flight Jet in £1m Smash That Made Heir to the Throne Give Up Flying as Pilot Admits He Should Have Told Him to Pull Up and Try to Land Again," *Daily Mail,* September 17, 2019.

141   "an astonishing 84 percent": Roxanne Roberts and Brooke A. Masters, "Now the Ball's in His Court," *Washington Post,* January 11, 1995.

Chapter 49

143   "Here's the world's most": "You Could See That She'd Been Crying Her Eyes Out," *Daily Mail,* July 4, 2019.

Chapter 50

144   "completely and utterly" through "so sweet": Holly Fleet, "Princess Diana 'Embarrassed' Prince William in Front of Supermodels on His Birthday," *Express,* April 23, 2020.

144   "What on earth": Ainhoa Barcelona, "You'll Never Guess What Saucy Present Princess Diana Gave Prince William on His 13th Birthday," *Hello!,* June 21, 2018.

145   "awful cook": Shayne Rodriguez Thompson, "18 Odd Details We Learned About the Royal Family's Eating Habits," *cafemom,* September 21, 2020.

145   "I went down" and "I wish I'd taken": Barcelona, "You'll Never Guess What Saucy Present."

145   "Wow! Can I": Alexandra Whittaker, "Princess Diana Gave Prince William a Boob Cake for His 13th Birthday," *InStyle,* May 18, 2018.

145   "the rudest cards" and "really nice stuff": Mandi Kerr, "The 'Naughty' Thing Princess Diana Used to Send to School with Prince William," *Showbiz Cheat Sheet,* July 3, 2019.

145   "Wales, Prince William of": Robert Hardman, "Place at Eton for Prince William," *Telegraph,* June 15, 1995.

146   "My boy's got a good": "Prince William," *Royal Report,* September 1999, reprinted in *Britain Express.*

146   "Prince William's performance": Hardman, "Place at Eton."

146   "school dress": Taylor Nicole Rogers, "Inside Eton College, the Exclusive Boarding School That's Been Called 'the Nursery of England's Gentlemen' and That Counts Boris Johnson, Prince William and Eddie Redmayne Among Its Graduates," *Business Insider,* July 24, 2019.

146   "Prince William must be allowed": Robert Jobson, "Prince William, the Press and a Matter of Privacy," *Express,* August 24, 1995.

147   "sent into the royal": Darren McGrady, "Queen Elizabeth II's Favorite Cake: Chocolate Biscuit Cake," *Today,* April 4, 2017.

147   "It's going to air" and "filled with dread": Christopher Andersen, *Diana's Boys: William and Harry and the Mother They Loved* (New York: William Morrow, 2001), 171.

Chapter 51

148   "Whatever goodwill" through "With love from Mama": Sarah Bradford, *Diana* (New York: Viking, 2006), 297, 299.

148   "the best interests" through "D'you know": Christopher Andersen, *Diana's Boys: William and Harry and the Mother They Loved* (New York: William Morrow, 2001), 179, 180.

Notes

148 "three tragic souls": Roxanne Roberts and Brooke A. Masters, "Now the Ball's in His Court," *Washington Post,* January 11, 1995.
149 "Whatever may transpire" and "The present situation": Bradford, *Diana,* 303.
149 "If you don't behave" and "My title is": Tina Brown, "Princess Diana's Legacy Is More Urgent than Ever," *Maclean's,* July 31, 2017.
149 "Ma and Pa" and "a former wife": Bradford, *Diana,* 237, 306–7.
150 "Prince Charles was said": Sarah Lyall, "Charles and Diana Agree on Divorce Terms," *New York Times,* July 13, 1996.
150 "Speaking personally": Bradford, *Diana,* 304.
150 "You must remember": Perry Carpenter, "Princess Diana 'Joined the Royal Family to Be Queen' Not Just a Princess Claims Her Private Secretary," *Showbiz Cheat Sheet,* May 12, 2020.
150 "regarded as a member": Lyall, "Charles and Diana Agree."
150 "I don't mind": Anna Kretschmer, "Revealed: How William and Harry Really Reacted to Diana and Charles' Separation," *Express,* June 21, 2019.
150 "Don't worry, Mummy": Britt Stephens, "The Heartbreaking Thing Prince William Told Diana After She Lost Her Title in the Divorce," *Popsugar,* May 10, 2017.

Chapter 52

151 "I so understand" and "She felt alone": Sally Bedell Smith, *Diana in Search of Herself: Portrait of a Troubled Princess* (New York: Times Books, 1999), 346.
151 "How do you follow": Richard Kay and Geoffrey Levy, "Charles Knew of Diana's Affair…and Didn't Care," *Daily Mail,* July 28, 2017.
151 "funny, wise, kind": Catherine Ostler, "The Billionaire Who Beguiled Diana…and Could Have Saved Her Life," *Daily Mail,* November 22, 2011.
152 "a strange way to suggest": Kay and Levy, "Charles Knew of Diana's Affair."
152 "I'll tailor it" and "I am interested": Rosa Prince, "Princess Diana Wanted to Star in Sequel to The Bodyguard, Says Kevin Costner," *Telegraph,* April 11, 2012.
152 "Mummy, *Kevin Costner*" through "Look, my life": Christopher Andersen, *Diana's Boys: William and Harry and the Mother They Loved* (New York: William Morrow, 2001), 201–2, 201.
152 "clicked in a way": Caroline Howe, "'Things Happened That Made It Clear—She Was Attracted to Me,'" *Daily Mail,* January 4, 2018.
152–53 "a special, lovely person" through "Oh lucky you": Joel Day, "George Michael Heartbreak: 'Only Princess Diana Understood Me,'" *Express,* December 23, 2020.
153 "Hello, it's William's Mum": OK! Staff, "Revealed: The Secret Tapes Diana Made for Prince William's Future Bride," *OK!,* March 23, 2022.
154 "I think I've met" through "He has given me": Sarah Ellison, "Diana's Impossible Dream," *Vanity Fair,* September 2013.
154 "these very clever": Andersen, *Diana's Boys,* 197.
154 "a very good relationship" and "I did not want": Richard Palmer, "Diana Told Me That It Was All Over," *Express,* March 4, 2008.

Chapter 53

155 "Oh God, let's face" through "Yes, ma'am, I think": Larry King, *The People's Princess: Cherished Memories of Diana, Princess of Wales, from Those Who Knew Her Best* (New York: Crown, 2007), 148, 146.
156 "just one of the lads": William Hickey, "Etonian Wills Gives Bodyguards the Slip," *Express,* April 25, 1996.
156 "There's no messing around": Sarah Bradford, *Diana* (New York: Viking, 2006), 234.
156 "Oh, Mummy, it was hilarious" through "All the girls love": King, *The People's Princess,* 149, 145–57, 156.
156 "No, I wanted to do it" through "I'd rather not say": Piers Morgan, "PIERS MORGAN: William Is Right, the BBC Needs to Come Clean and If Its Alleged Lies, Deceit and Fraud over Diana's

Panorama Interview Are Proven—Then All Those Responsible Have Her Blood on Their Hands and Must Be Held to Account," *Daily Mail*, November 19, 2020.

Chapter 54

157   "If I'm going to talk": Marissa DeSantis, "How Princess Diana's Post-Royal Life After Prince Charles Divorce Could Provide Clues to Harry and Meghan's Future Plans," *Evening Standard*, April 3, 2020.

157   "I've been given the gift": Larry King, *The People's Princess: Cherished Memories of Diana, Princess of Wales, from Those Who Knew Her Best* (New York: Crown, 2007), 192.

157   "I have all this media interest": "How Princess Diana Crippled the Case for Land Mines," *Newsweek*, October 24, 2015.

157   "I thought it would help": Robert Jobson and Michael Dunlea, "A Woman of Many Parts," *Express*, August 31, 1998.

158   "Nobody took a blind bit": Sarah Bradford, *Diana* (New York: Viking, 2006), 342.

158   "Three or four other planes" and "but what came off": Luke Mintz, "'I Was Worried I Would Go Down in History as the Man Who Blew Up Princess Diana,'" *Telegraph*, September 27, 2019.

158   "Why are those children": Tim Clayton and Phil Craig, *Diana: Story of a Princess* (New York: Atria, 2003), 312.

158   "I've never seen scenes": "*Heart of the Matter* Special: Diary of a Princess," BBC One, February 11, 1997.

158   "I'd read the statistics": "How Princess Diana Crippled the Case."

158   "It's very humbling": "*Heart of the Matter* Special."

158   "not very keen": Clayton and Craig, *Diana*, 311.

158   "a kind of aura": Christina Lamb, "Yes, I Was a Cynic Until I Met Her," *Sunday Times* (London), September 7, 1997.

159   "The first thing she did" through "Is she an angel?": Tina Brown, "Diana's Final Heartbreak," *Vanity Fair*, July 2007.

159   "loose cannon": Paul Burrell, *A Royal Duty* (New York: Putnam, 2003), 266.

159   "She has this yearning": W. F. Deedes, "Princess Diana: An Injured Angel," *Telegraph*, August 25, 2007.

159   "I am a humanitarian": Burrell, *A Royal Duty*, 266.

159   "There's still unexploded": Mintz, "'I Was Worried I Would Go Down in History.'"

159–60   "Just press a button" through "I did not want": "The Day Princess Diana Stepped into an Active Minefield," *The World*, January 13, 2017.

160   "I never thought": Jobson and Dunlea, "A Woman of Many Parts."

160   "I think once": Darren Hunt, "How Photographers Forced Princess Diana to Walk Through Minefield Twice After Blunder," *Express*, June 12, 2019.

160   "If my visit has contributed": Suyin Haynes, "Prince Harry Is Honoring His Mother's Work in Angola," *Time*, September 27, 2019.

Chapter 55

161   "It is some comfort" through "William's liking for the horsey": Dorothy-Grace Elder, "The Day Wills Came of Age," *Express*, May 30, 1997.

161   "my babies": Richard Kay, "Why Harry's Still So Close to Tiggy Legge-Bourke, the Sloaney Nanny Who Drove Diana Half-Mad with Jealousy," *Daily Mail*, January 26, 2018.

162   "The boys are crazy": James Whitaker, "Give Tiggy the Big E Now!," *Mirror*, May 30, 1997.

162   "thoughtless, idiotic and foolish" through "has not uttered": "Diana Reprimands Aide for Report That She Is Angry with Sons' Ex-Nanny," AP News, May 30, 1997.

Chapter 56

163 "Mummy, you're running out": Sarah Bradford, *Diana* (New York: Viking, 2006), 339.

163 "Why don't you have a sale": Christopher Andersen, *Diana's Boys: William and Harry and the Mother They Loved* (New York: William Morrow, 2001), 200.

163–64 "You can see" and "I certainly can": Elisabeth Bumiller, "Diana Cleans Out Her Closet, and Charities Just Clean Up," *New York Times,* June 26, 1997.

164 "It's been quite an event": Marissa DeSantis, "Princess Diana Praises 'Generous' Americans in Letters Set for Auction," *Evening Standard,* February 18, 2020.

164 "Yes, of course": Cathy Horyn, "Diana Reborn," *Vanity Fair,* July 1, 1997.

164–65 "it's going to be" through "breaking a previous": Bumiller, "Diana Cleans Out Her Closet."

165 "was quite amazing": Rosalind Coward, *Diana: The Portrait* (Kansas City, MO: Andrews McMeel, 2007), 147.

165 "Isn't it wonderful?" through "So where's my ten percent?": Andersen, *Diana's Boys,* 209.

165 "It was stunning" and "How typical": DeSantis, "Princess Diana Praises 'Generous' Americans."

165 "It's my birthday": Sally Bedell Smith, *Diana in Search of Herself: Portrait of a Troubled Princess* (New York: Times Books, 1999), 325.

166 "living her life": Horyn, "Diana Reborn."

166 "found herself" and "a kind of serenity": Michelle Kapusta, "The Heartbreaking Thing Gianni Versace Revealed About Princess Diana Just Before Their Tragic Deaths," *Showbiz Cheat Sheet,* June 28, 2019.

166 "Nothing gives me more": Horyn, "Diana Reborn."

Chapter 57

167 "I want that room!": Katie Nicholl, *The Making of a Royal Romance: William, Kate, and Harry—A Look Behind the Palace Walls* (New York: Weinstein Books, 2010), 67.

168 "He'd have climbed" and "Who told them": Christopher Andersen, *Diana's Boys: William and Harry and the Mother They Loved* (New York: William Morrow, 2001), 216, 212.

168 "William is freaked out!": Sally Bedell Smith, "Diana and the Press," *Vanity Fair,* September 1998.

168 "Do you want the boys": Richard Kay, "Diana's Last Phone Call," *Daily Mail,* August 30, 2017.

168 "father's best friend": Evan Thomas and Christopher Dickey, "The Last Chapter," *Newsweek,* September 15, 1997.

168 "We mustn't let" and "Let's just give": Andersen, *Diana's Boys,* 214.

168 "super delightful" and "lovely family vibes": Danielle Lawler, "All Fayed Up," *Tatler,* January 2022.

168 "very nearly perfect": Andersen, *Diana's Boys,* 217.

Chapter 58

169 "Do you think": Padraic Flanagan, "Diana: Philip Hates Me," *Express,* June 9, 2007.

169 "Gianni and I were like brothers": Amy M. Spindler, "Gianni Versace, 50, the Designer Who Infused Fashion with Life and Art," *New York Times,* July 16, 1997.

170 "the optimism" and "loves mankind": Sally Bedell Smith, *Diana in Search of Herself: Portrait of a Troubled Princess* (New York: Times Books, 1999), 325.

170 "I'm so sorry": Kate Nicholson, "Elton John and Princess Diana's Devastating Fall-Out Revealed," *Express,* November 29, 2019.

170 "too proud": "Elton John: His Life and Career in Pictures," *Telegraph,* January 24, 2018.

171 "The warm words": Elton John, *Me: Elton John* (New York: Henry Holt, 2019), 276.

Chapter 59

172 "Happy birthday to you": Robert Jobson, "Yes Gran, William Is Your Royal Highness," *Express,* August 5, 1997.

Notes

PART 5: THE PEOPLE'S PRINCESS
Chapter 60

175 "floating palace" and *Britannia* is the one place": Melissa Wiley, "Aboard the Royal Britannia Yacht, the British Queen's 'Floating Palace,'" *Business Insider,* April 25, 2021.

176 "The term 'playboy'": "Diana Takes Anti-Land Mine Crusade to Bosnia," CNN, August 8, 1997.

176 "Things can only get better": Tom Gallagher, "Tony Blair," *Encyclopaedia Britannica.*

Chapter 61

177 "If I must define": Annick Cojean, "Final Views Princess Diana's Last Substantive Interview, with Journalist Annick Cojean, Was Published Aug. 27 by the French Newspaper Le Monde. She began by focusing on a photograph," *Baltimore Sun,* September 7, 1997.

177–78 "I have seen lots" through "What is the situation": "Diana's Mission," *Express,* August 9, 1997.

178 "What's all the hassle?": Robert Jobson, "Diana Shows Her Tender Touch," *Express,* August 11, 1997.

178 "have a gin and tonic" and "None of them": W. F. Deedes, "Princess Diana: An Injured Angel," *Telegraph,* August 25, 2007.

178 "I have a real feeling": Cojean, "Final Views Princess Diana's Last Substantive Interview."

179 "10 pages of the most": Steve Myall, "Inside Princess Diana's Last Summer of Love, Heartbreak and Murder," *Mirror,* August 31, 2019.

179 "This is the real Diana" through "When the woman": Robert Jobson, "This Is the Real Diana," *Express,* August 11, 1997.

179 "put me off": Margaret Hussey, "Di's Passport to a Vile Life of Lavish Spending," *Express,* August 11, 1997.

Chapter 62

180 "This young man" and "He has the good looks": Robert Jobson, "Is Brave William the Last Hope for Royals?," *Express,* August 13, 1997.

Chapter 63

181 "Absolutely not": "Diana's Journalist Friend Reveals Secrets of Final Phone Call to Inquest," *Hello!,* December 21, 2007.

181 "I haven't taken": Harry Cooke and Sean Rayment, "Diana Says No to Marriage After Visiting Psychic," *Express,* August 14, 1997.

181 "The Dodi and Di saga": Susan Crosland, Alain de Botton, and Philippa Gregory, "When Truth Becomes Stranger than Fiction," *Express,* August 19, 1997.

181–82 "You were late" through "Shoot them down!": Mike Ridley, "Diana's Last Days," *The Sun,* August 26, 2017.

182 "the big-hearted princess": Maggie Morgan, "Diana Attacks Tories," *Express,* August 27, 1997.

182 "hopeless": Maggie Morgan and Alex Hendry, "When Talking to a Journalist Isn't an Interview," *Express,* August 28, 1997.

182 "The press is ferocious": Annick Cojean, "Final Views Princess Diana's Last Substantive Interview, with Journalist Annick Cojean, Was Published Aug. 27 by the French Newspaper Le Monde. She began by focusing on a photograph," *Baltimore Sun,* September 7, 1997.

182 "I think in my position" through "I work by instinct": Morgan, "Diana Attacks Tories."

182 "I'm not going to": Ridley, "Diana's Last Days."

Chapter 64

183   "When are you coming" through "I need to come home": Claire Anderson, "Princess Diana: The Heartbreaking Reason Diana Was in Paris Before She Died Revealed," *Express,* August 30, 2019.

183   "You're not doing" through "I need another marriage": Sally Bedell Smith, *Diana in Search of Herself: Portrait of a Troubled Princess* (New York: Times Books, 1999), 358.

184   "Slow down!": Sarah Bradford, *Diana* (New York: Viking, 2006), 368.

184   "Dodi always came up": "Al Fayed 'Told Us to Intervene,'" *Shropshire Star,* January 18, 2008.

185   *The rooms are like*: Paul Burrell, *A Royal Duty* (New York: Putnam, 2003), 283.

Chapter 65

186   "I've never spoken": "The Minute-by-Minute Account of Diana's Death," *New Zealand Herald,* August 19, 2017.

186–87   "I'm getting out" and "I've just had enough": Richard Kay, "Diana's Last Phone Call," *Daily Mail,* August 30, 2017.

187   "Unplug your phone": Jonathan Mayo, "Minute-by-Minute Series of the Week Diana Died," *ExpressDigest,* n.d.

187   *I worry about*: Petronella Wyatt, "Princess Diana Once Revealed Decent Men Are Put Off by Me Because of All the Baggage," *U.S. Sun,* June 17, 2021.

187   "There were too many": Jack Gee and John Coles, "Dinner for Two," *Express,* September 1, 1997.

Chapter 66

188   *It must be a fire*: Christopher Andersen, *The Day Diana Died* (New York: William Morrow, 1998), 201.

188   "There's been an accident": "France: Doctor Speaks of His Attempts to Save Princess Diana," posted by AP Archive, July 21, 2015, https://www.youtube.com/watch?v=BCQYu-P3oRI.

189   "An ambulance will soon" and "Everything will be okay": "Doctor at Crash Says Last Words of Diana Were Cries of Pain," *New York Times,* November 23, 1997.

189   *Why are there*: Catherine Gaschka, "First Doctor on Scene Recounts Diana's Fatal Crash in Paris," AP News, August 29, 2017.

189   "Where is she?" through "Don't worry": Nick Pisa, "Di Hero's First Interview," *The Sun,* August 31, 2017.

189   "My God": British Metropolitan Police, "The Operation Paget Inquiry Report into the Allegation of Conspiracy to Murder Diana, Princess of Wales, and Emad El-Din Mohamed Abdel Moneim Fayed," CBS News, 2006, 513, https://www.cbsnews.com/htdocs/pdf/Diana_Study.pdf.

190   *The young woman*: Andersen, *The Day Diana Died,* 206.

190   *It's Lady Di*: British Metropolitan Police, "The Operation Paget Inquiry Report," 513.

190   "Leave me alone": John-Thor Dahlburg, "Final Moments of Princess Reported," *Los Angeles Times,* September 11, 1997.

190   "She was asleep": Pisa, "Di Hero's First Interview."

190   *Something abnormal*: British Metropolitan Police, "The Operation Paget Inquiry Report," 514–15.

Chapter 67

191   *He must visit her*: "Diana's Death Sparked Fallout Between Charles and the Queen over Her 'Monarch Not Mummy' Attitude," *New Zealand Herald,* June 27, 2017.

191   *What to tell*: Robert Jobson, "Silent Suffering of Boy Princes," *Express,* September 1, 1997.

192   "May the saints welcome": "Princess Diana Crash—First BBC News Report (Interrupting 'Borsalino') 1997," posted by elbuccanero, June 8, 2014, https://www.youtube.com/watch?v=FPhCuz8qvWo.

192   "We are getting reports": "Princess Diana's final hours: Aug 30–31 1997," *Telegraph*, October 4, 2007.

192   "Sir, I am very sorry" and "Why?": Ingrid Seward, *William & Harry* (New York: Arcade, 2003), 211, 212.

192   "She had a serious wound": Allison Pearson, "'Diana's Death Forced the Monarchy to Confront How Out of Touch It Had Become,'" *Telegraph*, August 26, 2017.

192   "We could not revive": Christopher Burns, "AP Was There: Princess Diana Dies in Paris Car Crash," AP News, August 26, 2017.

193   "Don't forget": Charles Moore, "What Really Happened in Newsrooms the Day Princess Diana Died," *Telegraph*, August 27, 2017.

193   "Does Lord Deedes know": W. F. Deedes, "Princess Diana: An Injured Angel," *Telegraph*, August 25, 2007.

193   "This is the most tragic": Alice Vincent, "Diana, Elton and Candle in the Wind: How One Song Captured a Nation's Grief," *Telegraph*, August 31, 2017.

193   "Her death reminds me": Burns, "AP Was There."

194   "injured angel" and "became the pot of gold": Deedes, "Princess Diana."

194   "She was a Marilyn": Vincent, "Diana, Elton and Candle in the Wind."

Chapter 68

195   "What do you say": Sally Bedell Smith, *Prince Charles: The Passions and Paradoxes of an Improbable Life* (New York: Random House, 2017), 318.

195   "If you are a Christian": Simon Heffer, "The Queen Handled the Death of Diana Far Better than She Was Given Credit For," *Telegraph*, August 26, 2017.

196   "We are going to pray" and "pray to Mummy": Ingrid Seward, *William & Harry* (New York: Arcade, 2003), 213.

196   "We remember all those" through "Whatever happens": "Courage of Princes at Crathie Services Hours After Mother's Death William and Harry Join Royal Worshippers," *The Herald*, August 31, 1997.

196   "Those poor little boys": Smith, *Prince Charles*, 319.

Chapter 69

197   "People everywhere" and "They liked her": Tony Blair, "Blair Pays Tribute to Diana," BBC, August 31, 1997.

198   "a very good friend": Amanda Prahl, "The Connection Between Princess Diana and Mother Teresa Will Break Your Heart," *Popsugar*, August 13, 2019.

198   "her pale face" and "made up with a night blue": Henry Samuel, "'Amateurish' Security Led to Death of Princess Diana, Says French Policeman Who Watched over Her in Final Moments," *Telegraph*, August 28, 2014.

198   "I was waiting": Graham Johnson, "Diana Lay There . . . I Was Waiting for a Smile and Then I Thought, We Will Never See This Smile Again," *Sunday Mirror*, August 30, 1998.

198   "These were a gift": Christopher Andersen, *The Day Diana Died* (New York: William Morrow, 1998), 23.

199   "She was religious": Libby Purves, "What Breaks You Up Is the Way the Boys Still Feel They Should Have Saved Her," *Daily Mail*, August 22, 2017.

199   "People want to see her" through "We'll never forget": Andersen, *The Day Diana Died*, 23, 30.

199   "It all seems unreal": Sally Bedell Smith, *Prince Charles: The Passions and Paradoxes of an Improbable Life* (New York: Random House, 2017), 318.

199   *We need to keep*: Hannah Furness, "Pilot Who Returned Diana's Body from Paris Reveals How Long They Scrambled to Stop People Listening In," *Telegraph*, August 26, 2017.

199   "togetherness tour": Kayleigh Roberts, "Princess Diana and Prince Charles Showed 'Hatred That Radiated' During Their Trip to South Korea," *Marie Claire*, February 14, 2021.

Chapter 70

201   "I couldn't believe": "So Very Warm, So Very Caring," *Express*, September 1, 1997.

201   "I've actually been": Richard Preston, "News Flashes That Alerted the World," *Telegraph*, August 31, 2002.

202   "Sleep tonight" and "I didn't expect": "August 31, 1997—Dublin, Ireland—Lansdowne Road," U2 ZOO Station Radio, August 31, 1997.

202   "Like Elton John": Alice Vincent, "Diana, Elton and Candle in the Wind: How One Song Captured a Nation's Grief," *Telegraph*, August 31, 2017.

Chapter 71

203   "It would be too disrespectful": Anna Pukas and Ian Gallagher, "A Nation Weeps for Its Queen of Hearts," *Express*, September 1, 1997.

204   "people's" through "will be a unique": Robert Jobson and Roland Watson, "Unique Event for a Unique Person," *Express*, September 2, 1997.

204   *Well, she's gone* and "shaking with emotion": William D. Montalbano, "A Royal Farewell to Diana, Tradition," *Los Angeles Times*, September 5, 1997.

204   "something around £5 million": Andrew Sparrow, "Secret Papers Recall Diana's Final Hours," *Telegraph*, March 16, 2005.

204   "It's about the boys": Lindsay Lowe, "Why Prince Philip Walked with William and Harry at Princess Diana's Funeral," *Today*, April 11, 2021.

204   "This part of the day" and "Only immediate members": Jobson and Watson, "Unique Event for a Unique Person."

205   "He is very patriotic": "Body of Dodi Fayed Arrives at London Mosque for Funeral," AP News, September 1, 1997.

205   "Listen to that": Eugene Robinson, "An Eerie Hush of Sorrow," *Washington Post*, September 3, 1997.

205   "I propose that the Princes" through "Cancel all your engagements": Roxanne Roberts, "Nation Worries About Princes' Future," *Washington Post*, September 3, 1997.

205   "weeps bitter tears": Charles Moore, "What Really Happened in Newsrooms the Day Princess Diana Died," *Telegraph*, August 27, 2017.

Chapter 72

206   "There could be no finer" through "And I'm going": Alice Vincent, "Diana, Elton and Candle in the Wind: How One Song Captured a Nation's Grief," *Telegraph*, August 31, 2017.

207   "What that ring meant": Anne Swardson, "Ritz Hotel Tape Shows Diana Before Crash," *Washington Post*, September 6, 1997.

207   "In all due respect": "Perspectives," *Newsweek*, September 15, 1997.

207   "if that is what the people want": Christopher Andersen, *The Day Diana Died* (New York: William Morrow, 1998), 257.

208   "Would you like me to": Ingrid Seward, "'Diana in a Crash? They Must Have Greased the Brakes,'" *Daily Mail*, August 14, 2015.

208   "the most moving thing": Vincent, "Diana, Elton and Candle in the Wind."

208   "People say you never": Jenny McCartney, "A Prayer for the Princess Who Will Not Be Forgotten," *Telegraph*, September 1, 2002.

208   "It seems like hundreds of thousands": Hannah Furness, "Kensington Palace Braced for New Deluge of Diana Floral Tributes as 20th Anniversary Nears," *Telegraph*, August 25, 2017.

Chapter 73

209   "from the heart" through "exceptional and gifted human being": Dan Balz, "In Rare Address, Queen Laments Britain's Loss," *Washington Post*, September 5, 1997.

209   "I admired and respected her": Christopher Andersen, *The Day Diana Died* (New York: William Morrow, 1998), 260.

210   "Oh, that's for the boys": Tina Brown, *The Diana Chronicles* (New York: Anchor Books, 2008), 476.

210   "I think it's unfair" through "you have got to have": Ingrid Seward, *William & Harry* (New York: Arcade, 2003), 215, 213.

210   "Where's Daddy?" and "didn't have anybody": Scott Stump, "The Tender Story of How Prince Philip Comforted JFK Jr. After Father's Assassination," *Today*, April 12, 2021.

210   "I'll walk if you walk": Ben Hill, "'It's About the Boys': Prince Philip's Comforting Words to Help Wills and Harry Cope with Diana's Funeral, Telling Them 'I'll Walk If You Walk,'" *The Sun*, April 11, 2021.

Chapter 74

211   "This is a mark of respect": Dan Balz, "Queen Orders Flag at Half-Staff at Palace," *Washington Post*, September 5, 1997.

211   "You were a Cinderella": Christopher Andersen, *The Day Diana Died* (New York: William Morrow, 1998), 266.

212   *How on earth*: Ken Wharfe, *Diana: Closely Guarded Secret* (London: John Blake Publishing, 2016), 2.

212   "Time is too slow": "Everything You Need to Know About Princess Diana's Funeral," *Daily Mail*, August 27, 2021.

212   *This is it* and "Your candle's burned": Alice Vincent, "Diana, Elton and Candle in the Wind: How One Song Captured a Nation's Grief," *Telegraph*, August 31, 2017.

212   *You've got to get through*: "Sir Elton John: From Football Clubs and Drug Addiction to Princess Diana's Funeral," *Daily Mail*, May 21, 2010.

212   "bawling his eyes out": Nicole Moschella, "Princess Diana's Death: How Elton John, Richard Branson, George Michael Reacted," *Journal-News* (Butler County, OH), August 31, 2017.

212–13 "that after time": "Lady Diana, Princess of Wales," George Michael: The Box of Fame, http://george.michael.szm.com/Special/Tribute/Tdiana.html.

213   "Your greatest gift" and "needed no royal title": "Everything You Need to Know About Princess Diana's Funeral."

Chapter 75

214   "It's essential": Frank Mastropolo, "When Elton John Remade 'Candle in the Wind' for Princess Diana," *Ultimate Classic Rock*, September 6, 2017.

215   "will be like Elvis's grave": "Diana Returns Home," BBC, https://www.bbc.co.uk/news/special/politics97/diana/althorp.html.

Chapter 76

216   "I try to din into him": Tina Brown, "A Woman in Earnest," *The New Yorker*, September 15, 1997.

216   "Nothing I went through": Kirsten Danis, "Di Saw John as Role Model for Royals," *New York Post*, July 18, 1999.

216   "All I want to do": Ingrid Seward, *William & Harry* (New York: Arcade, 2003), 225.

217   "It will be your duty": Jerry Adler and Donna Foote, "Growing Up Without Her," *Newsweek*, September 15, 1997.

217   "I've got one racquet": Seward, *William & Harry*, 223.

217   "I'm going to tell my children": "London Begins Cleanup of Floral Tributes to Diana," CNN, September 11, 1997.

218   "asked not to mention cars": Seward, *William & Harry*, 226.

Chapter 77

219   "Dianaland": Suzy Menkes, "Remembering Diana, but Moving On," *New York Times,* August 31, 1998.

220   "a time for personal reflection": Menkes, "Remembering Diana."

220   "I suppose the Queen": Paul Gallagher, "The Burger Queen," in Phil Dampier (@phildampier), "From 1998. The Queen's Roller Gets Stuck in a Drive-Through McDonalds," Twitter, August 23, 2020, https://twitter.com/phildampier/status/1297562520224436224.

220   "Remembering Diana": Menkes, "Remembering Diana."

220   "Do you gamble?": Katharine Graham, "A Friend's Last Goodbye," *Newsweek,* September 15, 1997.

PART 6: THE HEIR AND THE SPARE

Chapter 78

223   "Over here": Christopher Andersen, *Diana's Boys: William and Harry and the Mother They Loved* (New York: William Morrow, 2001), 257.

223   "Go away, mens!" through "William's very sensitive": "William's Deep Like His Dad, Harry's a Hothead Like Me," *Daily Mail,* June 30, 2019.

224   "if he doesn't go": Robert Lacey, *Battle of Brothers: William and Harry—The Inside Story of a Family in Tumult,* rev. ed. (New York: Harper, 2021), 170.

224   "I'm very worried" and "I don't want to go": Andersen, *Diana's Boys,* 231.

224   "He used to have quite" and "His work took his mind": Katie Nicholl, *The Making of a Royal Romance: William, Kate, and Harry—A Look Behind the Palace Walls* (New York: Weinstein Books, 2010), 79.

224   "Hundreds of screaming": "'What About Harry?' When 2 Teenage Princes and Their Dad Visited Canada," CBC, March 8, 2021.

224   "Go on, wave at that lot": Andersen, *Diana's Boys,* 243.

224   "Wave at the girls and make them scream": Judy Wade, "Prince William at 30—from the Woman Who's Been There Every Step of the Way," *Mirror,* June 17, 2012.

224   "hot" through "boyish cute": "'What About Harry?'"

224   "He is rich": Andersen, *Diana's Boys,* 245.

225   "DDG" and "the girls are going to love him": Wade, "Prince William at 30."

225   "Whether Prince William actually likes": "'What About Harry?'"

Chapter 79

227   "that wicked woman": Kayla Keegan, "Prince Charles and Camilla's Wedding Involved Way More Drama than Most People Realize," *Good Housekeeping,* November 15, 2019.

227   "I have absolutely no desire": Christopher Andersen, *Diana's Boys: William and Harry and the Mother They Loved* (New York: William Morrow, 2001), 275.

227   "eighty per cent of the boys": Robert Lacey, *Battle of Brothers: William and Harry—The Inside Story of a Family in Tumult,* rev. ed. (New York: Harper, 2021), 192.

227   "trembling like a leaf" and "I really need a vodka tonic": Andersen, *Diana's Boys,* 248.

227   "suspiciously": Lacey, *Battle of Brothers,* 194.

227   "Robbed of his mother" through "Whatever makes you happy": Andersen, *Diana's Boys,* 280, 249.

227   "They danced, swayed and swaggered": "Princes Do Not-Quite-Full Monty," Reuters, November 1998.

228   "They know every step": Andersen, *Diana's Boys,* 260.

Chapter 80

229   "It would be a pleasant" through "wants them to feel": Christopher Andersen, *Diana's Boys: William and Harry and the Mother They Loved* (New York: William Morrow, 2001), 262.

229 "She's just very helpful" through "she won't necessarily force": Robert Lacey, *Battle of Brothers: William and Harry—The Inside Story of a Family in Tumult,* rev. ed. (New York: Harper, 2021), 17, 168.

230 "delighted the dinner party" and "loved every minute": Andersen, *Diana's Boys,* 262.

230 "William is very protective": Andersen, *Diana's Boys,* 284.

230 "Harry is quieter": Lacey, *Battle of Brothers,* 17, 101.

230 "Prince William has developed": Robert Jobson, "Lord Snowdon Takes Prince's Official Photos After Fiasco of Deal over William," *Express,* September 15, 2000.

231 "William is deep": "'William's Deep Like His Dad, Harry's a Hothead Like Me,'" *Daily Mail,* June 30, 2019.

231 "Harry's the naughty one" through "The more invincible": Katie Nicholl, *The Making of a Royal Romance: William, Kate, and Harry—A Look Behind the Palace Walls* (New York: Weinstein Books, 2010), 84.

231 "the masters cut him some slack": Lady Colin Campbell, *Meghan and Harry: The Real Story* (New York: Pegasus Books, 2020), 55.

Chapter 81

232–33 "I've got a problem" through "I'm so sorry Papa": Adapted from Penny Junor, *Prince William: The Man Who Will Be King,* repr. ed. (New York: Pegasus Books, 2013), 151–52.

233 "manly sports": Christopher Andersen, *Diana's Boys: William and Harry and the Mother They Loved* (New York: William Morrow, 2001), 285.

233 "respects that he has interests": Rachel Borrill, "Princess Denies Rift with Son over Hunting," *Irish Times,* December 2, 1996.

233 "Every time I kill": Christopher Andersen, *William and Kate: A Royal Love Story* (New York: Gallery, 2011), 78.

233 "I don't know why": Robert Lacey, *Battle of Brothers: William and Harry—The Inside Story of a Family in Tumult,* rev. ed. (New York: Harper, 2021), 185.

233 "She's become a modern-day Diana": Rose Grady, "Kill-for-Kicks Hunt Stirs a Royal Uproar," *Weekly World News,* November 29, 1981.

233 "The crack-shot princess" and "Prince Charles would not allow": Gregory Jensen, "Princess Diana Under Fire for Deer Shooting," UPI Archives, October 19, 1981.

234 "I'm just not interested": Abbie Llewelyn, "Princess Diana's Brutal Assessment of Beloved Royal Activity," *Express,* August 10, 2020.

234 "they wanted me to": "Animal Lover Meghan Joins Royals for Boxing Day 'Shooting Feast,'" *New Zealand Herald,* December 26, 2018.

234 "pushed the princes": Andersen, *Diana's Boys,* 254.

234 "One of the main reasons": Diane Clehane, "The One Royal Tradition Diana Didn't Want Her Sons to Follow, Sources Say," *BestLife,* September 1, 2021.

234 "What is it with this family": "Animal Lover Meghan Joins Royals."

234 "blood on their hands" through "It's not funny": Lacey, *Battle of Brothers,* 185, 186.

234 "So that went back": Julia Mullaney, "The 1 Outfit Choice That Permanently Damaged Princess Diana's Reputation," *Showbiz Cheat Sheet,* January 6, 2021.

235 "Naughty, naughty" and *My God, have I died*: Larry King, *The People's Princess: Cherished Memories of Diana, Princess of Wales, from Those Who Knew Her Best* (New York: Crown, 2007), 50.

235 "Remember, there's always": "William's Deep Like His Dad, Harry's a Hothead Like Me," *Daily Mail,* June 30, 2019.

235 "insensitive and arrogant" through "William and Harry belong": Andersen, *Diana's Boys,* 285.

Chapter 82

236 "It's true" and "Poppers rule the school": "Pass Notes," *The Guardian,* June 28, 1999.

236 "wearing someone else's pullover": Katie Nicholl, *The Making of a Royal Romance: William, Kate, and Harry—A Look Behind the Palace Walls* (New York: Weinstein Books, 2010), 83.

236–37 "He wasn't always trying": Christopher Andersen, *Diana's Boys: William and Harry and the Mother They Loved* (New York: William Morrow, 2001), 206.

237 "William was pretty cool": Nicholl, *The Making of a Royal Romance,* 94.

237 "I shall go backpacking" and "I shall be King Harry": Andersen, *Diana's Boys,* 184, 185.

237 "GKH" through "She thought he'd probably": Christine-Marie Liwag Dixon, "Strange Facts About Prince Harry," *The List,* February 17, 2021.

237 "William is waiting patiently": Andersen, *Diana's Boys,* 184.

237 "could adapt" through "William's very young": Frederica Miller, "Princess Diana Shock: Diana's Secret Nickname for Prince Harry Revealed Her True Thoughts," *Express,* September 9, 2019.

Chapter 83

238 "It's not fair": Catherine Armecin, "Prince William Argued with Dad Prince Charles over Backpacking During Gap Year," *International Business Times,* February 3, 2019.

238 "Prince Charles said he would love": Richard Reeves, "William Goes for Gaucho Gap Year," *The Guardian,* September 26, 1999.

238 "vocational, educational and safe": Armecin, "Prince William Argued with Dad."

238–39 "Exhilarating" through "The living conditions": Christopher Andersen, *Diana's Boys: William and Harry and the Mother They Loved* (New York: William Morrow, 2001), 302, 305, 306–7.

239 "William coped very well": Kayleigh Roberts, "Why Prince William Spent Three Months Scrubbing Toilets in Chile Before Going to College," *Marie Claire,* June 24, 2019.

239 "I don't like being treated": *William at 30,* Royalty Collection, ITV Studios, June 6, 2012, https://www.itvstudios.com/royalty-collection.

239 "To be honest, no one knew": Abbie Llewelyn, "Royal REBEL: How Prince William Nearly Did This SHOCKING Thing to His Appearance," *Express,* May 31, 2019.

239 "William's like one of the lads": *William at 30.*

239 "Wills is good fun" and "Hello all you groove jets": Andersen, *Diana's Boys,* 310, 308.

239 "For any of you people": *William at 30.*

239 "This is 'Tortel Love'": Andersen, *Diana's Boys,* 308.

239 "He'd still be there": Llewelyn, "Royal REBEL."

239 "It was probably the last time": Penny Junor, *Prince William: The Man Who Will Be King,* repr. ed. (New York: Pegasus Books, 2013), 168.

Chapter 84

240 "Silly old father": NBC News, "Three Princes," *Dateline,* May 21, 2006, https://www.nbcnews.com/dateline/video/three-princes-460342851671.

240 *I really want to win*: Kate Nicholson, "Charles' Terrible Accident in Front of Harry and William Revealed—'I Was Quietly Dying!,'" *Express,* March 25, 2020.

240 "We work really well" and "But when someone": "Three Princes."

240 "This is just to show" and "ideal sons": Christopher Andersen, *Diana's Boys: William and Harry and the Mother They Loved* (New York: William Morrow, 2001), 278, 279.

240 *It is great fun*: "Three Princes."

241 "literally become right-handed": Andersen, *Diana's Boys,* 279.

241 "Oh, Papa's just snoring!": Nicholson, "Charles' Terrible Accident."

241 "The pony came down": "Three Princes."

241 "We don't think": "Prince Charles Takes a Tumble," ABC News, January 6, 2006.

241 "I finally woke up": "Three Princes."

241 "There I was" and "And the rest!": Nicholson, "Charles' Terrible Accident."

241 "It's awful" and "We won the game": "Three Princes."

Chapter 85

242 "The university": Anjali Kwatra, "Girls Rush in for Chance to Study with the Prince," *Express,* January 26, 2001.

242–43 "I wish the lad well" through "There are some gorgeous": Yvonne Ridley, "Enjoy! A Town Holds Its Breath for Britain's Number One Heart-Throb," *Express,* August 19, 2001.

243 "but the best bit" and "I loved my gap year": Ben Summerskill, "Welcome to Will's New World," *The Guardian,* September 23, 2001.

243 "I don't know what their game is" through "Now I understand": Christopher Andersen, *Diana's Boys: William and Harry and the Mother They Loved* (New York: William Morrow, 2001), 294, 288, 294.

244 "I want a bit of space": Ingrid Seward, *William & Harry* (New York: Arcade, 2003), 283.

244 "I think he was really nervous" and "He was very unsteady": Robert Lacey, *Battle of Brothers: William and Harry—The Inside Story of a Family in Tumult,* rev. ed. (New York: Harper, 2021), 197.

244 "wobble": Robert Jobson, "Hug of Love for Dad," *Express,* March 30, 2002.

244 "William was a long way" through "We chatted a lot": Lacey, *Battle of Brothers,* 201, 200–2.

244 "It's just fine": Jobson, "Hug of Love for Dad."

244 "I just hope I can meet": Summerskill, "Welcome to Will's New World."

245 *She's a knockout!* through "He was sitting": Sarah Grossbart, "Inside the Early Days of Prince William and Kate Middleton's Romance," *E!,* April 29, 2020.

245 "Wow, Fergus, Kate's hot!": Grossbart, "Inside the Early Days."

Chapter 86

246 "Put the country first": Hope Coke, "Unearthed Footage of the Queen Mother Advising Princes William and Harry to 'Put Their Country First,'" *Tatler,* January 21, 2020.

246 "quite simply the most magical": Penny Junor, *Prince William: The Man Who Will Be King,* repr. ed. (New York: Pegasus Books, 2013), 196.

246 "Gran-Gran": Ken Wharfe, *Diana: Closely Guarded Secret* (London: John Blake Publishing, 2016), 123.

246–47 "a good giggle" through "I knew full well": Bridget Harrison, "'Cursed' Crown Jewel Brightens Queen Mum Coffin," *New York Post,* April 7, 2002.

247 "unsure, lacking in confidence": Bridie Pearson-Jones, "Queen Mother Didn't Understand Why Prince Charles 'Couldn't Keep Camilla as a Mistress and Stay Married to Princess Diana,' New Documentary Claims," *Daily Mail,* June 7, 2021.

247 "the Prince of Wales": Anna Kretschmer, "Royal Snub: How Queen 'Shamed Charles for Putting Gratification Before Duty,'" *Express,* January 31, 2020.

Chapter 87

248 "I didn't enjoy school" through "the Glossy Posse": Katie Nicholl, *Harry and Meghan: Life, Loss, and Love,* rev. ed. (New York: Hachette Books, 2019), 28, 29.

248 "nightmare" and "Every now and then": Giles Sheldrick, "Exams? They're Not Really for Me, Says Prince Harry," *Express,* January 22, 2013.

248 "To this day": Lady Colin Campbell, *Meghan and Harry: The Real Story* (New York: Pegasus Books, 2020), 54.

249 "Excellence without arrogance" through "We believe in academic ability": Ray Moseley, "Young Prince William Takes 1st Step Toward Becoming 'Old Etonian,'" *Chicago Tribune,* September 3, 1995.

249 "He turned up at Eton" through "He was totally fearless": Katie Nicholl, *The Making of a Royal Romance: William, Kate, and Harry—A Look Behind the Palace Walls* (New York: Weinstein Books, 2010), 96, 95.

249 "People would see me": Nicholl, *Harry and Meghan,* 28.

249 "Harry knew what" and "He was very good": Nicholl, *The Making of a Royal Romance,* 95.

250 "You know, if I could have" through "Seeiso had just lost": Nicholl, *Harry and Meghan,* 40–41, 46, 36–37.

250 "I met so many children": Robert Lacey, *Battle of Brothers: William and Harry—The Inside Story of a Family in Tumult,* rev. ed. (New York: Harper, 2021), 254.

250–51 "This is a country" through "All I'm out here doing": Nicholl, *Harry and Meghan,* 38, 39.

251 "I'm not going": "Harry 'Loves Wonderful Camilla,'" BBC News, October 7, 2005.

251 "She had such warmth": Lacey, *Battle of Brothers,* 106.

251 "She got close to people": Nicholl, *Harry and Meghan,* 31.

251 "We came up with the name": Lacey, *Battle of Brothers,* 254.

Chapter 88

252 "Haz" and "Chedda": Phil Dampier, "Haz Been," *Royal Observer,* March 10, 2021.

252 "I would love" and "a bright and bouncy": Robert Lacey, *Battle of Brothers: William and Harry—The Inside Story of a Family in Tumult,* rev. ed. (New York: Harper, 2021), 262.

252 "a hand grenade of a girl": Sarah Sands, "Tina Brown Reveals the Diana We Never Knew," *Daily Mail,* June 9, 2007.

253 "Look, I'm only twenty-two": Lacey, *Battle of Brothers,* 215.

253 "We are both very happy": Katie Nicholl, *Harry and Meghan: Life, Loss, and Love,* rev. ed. (New York: Hachette Books, 2019), 44.

253 "made our father very": "CNN Live at Daybreak," CNN Transcripts, September 15, 2005.

253 "Very happy, very pleased" and "As long as I don't lose": Robert Jobson, *William & Kate: The Love Story—A Celebration of the Wedding of the Century* (London: John Blake Publishing, 2010), 95–96.

253 "The Duke of Edinburgh and I": Caroline Hallemann, "The Sentimental Story Behind Camilla's Engagement Ring from Prince Charles," *Town & Country,* May 23, 2020.

PART 7: CADETS WALES

Chapter 89

257 "I want to fight for my country": Richard Palmer, "Harry: I Want to Fight for My Country," *Express,* September 15, 2005.

257 "I remember saying": Katie Nicholl, *Harry and Meghan: Life, Loss, and Love,* rev. ed. (New York: Hachette Books, 2019), 40–41.

257 "She was explaining" and "That's what he wanted": Brian Dakss, "Prince Harry Hits Sandhurst," CBS News, May 9, 2005.

258 "Nobody's really supposed" through "Sick Note": Palmer, "Harry: I Want to Fight."

258 "I'm not having a party": Richard Palmer, "I'll Keep the 'Child Streak' in Me," *Express,* September 15, 2005.

258 "There's no way": Katie Nicholl, *The Making of a Royal Romance: William, Kate, and Harry—A Look Behind the Palace Walls* (New York: Weinstein Books, 2010), 235.

258 "I am absolutely delighted": Caroline Davies, "Prince William to Join His Brother at Sandhurst," *Telegraph,* October 22, 2005.

258–59 "raw intelligence test" through "good leadership skills": Sean Rayment, "William Beats Harry in Army Intelligence Test," *Telegraph,* November 6, 2005.

259 "But I am only too well aware": Davies, "Prince William to Join His Brother."

Chapter 90

260 "my adorable Kate" and "always in his thoughts": Richard Palmer, "Now Get Your Hair Cut, You 'Orrible Royal," *Express,* January 9, 2006.

261 "No doubt Prince Harry": Stephen Rigley, "Attenshun! One's in the Army Now," *Daily Star,* January 9, 2006.

261 "Bye, Pa": Palmer, "Now Get Your Hair Cut."
261 "The last thing I want": Robert Jobson, *Harry's War: The True Story of the Soldier Prince* (London: John Blake Publishing, 2008), 227.
261 "grade 3 haircut" and "short": Palmer, "Now Get Your Hair Cut."
262 "credible threats": Robert Jobson, *William & Kate: The Love Story—A Celebration of the Wedding of the Century* (London: John Blake Publishing, 2010), 165–67.
262 "Kate will receive": "Timetable of a Romance," *Express,* July 23, 2013.

Chapter 91

263 "Football is a game": Stephen Bates, "William, the Footballer Prince, to Become FA President," *The Guardian,* September 16, 2005.
263 "loads of free tickets" and "they must've been desperate": NBC News, "Three Princes," *Dateline,* May 21, 2006, https://www.nbcnews.com/dateline/video/three-princes-460342851671.
263 "got into football big time": Myriam Toua, "Prince William Football: What Football Team Does Prince William Support?," *Express,* June 17, 2020.
263 "give me more emotional": Emma Dibdin, "Prince William Sends a Personal Message to the English Football Team Ahead of the Euro 2021 Final," *Town & Country,* July 9, 2021.
263 "It was the first team": "Three Princes."
263 "I must have been about": "'I Didn't Want to Support Man Utd or Chelsea,'" *Goal,* July 28, 2020.
263–64 "It was fantastic": Frederica Miller, "Royal Revelation: The Real Reason Prince William Supports Aston Villa," *Express,* January 6, 2020.
264 "I liked the idea that": "'I Didn't Want to Support Man Utd.'"
264 "is a risk" and "as long as you've had sufficient": Robert Jobson, *William & Kate: The Love Story—A Celebration of the Wedding of the Century* (London: John Blake Publishing, 2010), 173–74.
264 "I just enjoy everything": Kayleigh Roberts, "Prince William's Motorcycling Hobby 'Frightened the Life Out of' Queen Elizabeth," *Maire Claire,* February 18, 2019.
264 "it does help being anonymous": Jobson, *William & Kate,* 173–74.
264 "constantly fleeing" and "her son using": Roberts, "Prince William's Motorcycling Hobby."
265 "My father is concerned": "Wills Takes Off with 175mph 'Superbike,'" *Hello!,* May 23, 2006.

Chapter 92

266 "passing out": Robert Jobson, *Harry's War: The True Story of the Soldier Prince* (London: John Blake Publishing, 2008), 141–43.
266 "He's determined not to": Richard Palmer, "Now Get Your Hair Cut, You 'Orrible Royal," *Express,* January 9, 2006.
266 "a moment which I": Christopher Andersen, *Brothers and Wives: Inside the Private Lives of William, Kate, Harry, and Meghan* (New York: Gallery, 2021), 185.
267 "The boy has come of age": "Salute to Our Harry," *Daily Star,* April 13, 2006.
267 "all things military": Laura Neil, "Harry's Got Dream Job," *Express,* July 10, 2006.
268 "Hello" and "On a riot-training": Robert Jobson, *William & Kate: The Love Story—A Celebration of the Wedding of the Century* (London: John Blake Publishing, 2010), 163, 211.

Chapter 93

269–70 "Listen, do you want" through "As far as I can": Robert Jobson, *William & Kate: The Love Story—A Celebration of the Wedding of the Century* (London: John Blake Publishing, 2010), 220, 215.
270 "There is no twitch": Robert Lacey, *Battle of Brothers: William and Harry—The Inside Story of a Family in Tumult,* rev. ed. (New York: Harper, 2021), 76.
270–71 "How are things going" and "It's finally over": Adapted from Jobson, *William & Kate,* 228–29.

Chapter 94

272   "If they can get a bomb" and "We planted our people": Jason Groves and Hilary Douglas, "Target Harry," *Express,* April 15, 2007.

272   "His troop will": Iain Burchell, "Harry: I'll Quit Army," *Daily Star,* April 27, 2007.

273   "these threats expose": Thomas Harding and Caroline Davies, "Iraq Is Too Dangerous for Harry, Says Army," *Telegraph,* May 17, 2007.

273   "The threat level changes": Richard Palmer and John Ingham, "Harry's Career in Tatters," *Express,* May 17, 2007.

273   "If I'm going to cause": Penny Junor, *Prince Harry: Brother, Soldier, Son* (New York: Grand Central, 2014), 181–82.

273   "We have always known" and "He's a posh boy": John Ingham and Richard Palmer, "Harry Will Fight on the Frontline," *Express,* May 18, 2007.

273   "You're coming to Afghanistan": Junor, *Prince Harry,* 181–82.

Chapter 95

274   "Hello, Wembley!": Robert Jobson, *William & Kate: The Love Story—A Celebration of the Wedding of the Century* (London: John Blake Publishing, 2010), 240.

274   "If it goes wrong" and "ginger Bob Geldof": Robert Jobson, *Harry's War: The True Story of the Soldier Prince* (London: John Blake Publishing, 2008), 169.

274–75   "This event is about" and "the best birthday present": Jobson, *William & Kate,* 240.

275   *My gift is my song*: Elton John, "Your Song," Genius, https://genius.com/Elton-john-your-song-lyrics.

275   "So beautiful" through "We miss you. Our princess": "Puff Diddy—I'll Be Missing You @ Concert for Princess Diana in Wembley 2007," posted by Orangevirus, April 8, 2021, https://www.youtube.com/watch?v=FsQqlXbsx-Y.

275   "Looks like it's on again": Arthur Edwards, "Class Act," *The Sun,* January 6, 2022.

275   "Thank you to all" and "For us this has been": Penny Junor, *Prince Harry: Brother, Soldier, Son* (New York: Grand Central, 2014), 189.

276   "I wish I was there": Jobson, *Harry's War,* 170.

276   "On reflection I believe": Sally Bedell Smith, *Prince Charles: The Passions and Paradoxes of an Improbable Life* (New York: Random House, 2017), 425.

276   "I want to speak" through "Oh yes, I suppose so": Adapted from Junor, *Prince Harry,* 190.

277   "to the excluded and forgotten": Smith, *Prince Charles,* 425.

277   "the right word": Sarah Lyall, "A Memorial for the World's Princess," *New York Times,* September 1, 2007.

277   "William and I can separate" through "And then there are": Junor, *Prince Harry,* 191–92.

277–78   "She will always be remembered" through "She told me": Jobson, *Harry's War,* 174.

278   "a bit of excitement" and "finally get the chance": Sarah Lyall, "Prince Harry Withdrawn from Afghanistan," *New York Times,* February 29, 2008.

Chapter 96

279   "a tragic accident": Sarah Lyall, "Inquiry Concludes Diana's Death Was an Accident," *New York Times,* December 14, 2006.

279   "Mohamed al-Fayed has maintained": Paul Majendie and Michael Holden, "Diana Inquest Opens, 10 Years After Her Death," Reuters, October 2, 2007.

280   "Some have compared Kate": Rebecca English and Rebecca Camber, "Deer Hunter Kate Under Fire for Going Shooting with Royals," *Daily Mail,* October 15, 2007.

280   "best Christmas of his life": Angela Levin, "William and Harry Act II: How They've Been Shaped by the Women They Married," *Telegraph,* March 13, 2021.

Chapter 97

281   "Just walking around": "Prince Goes on Patrol Near Taliban," Reuters, March 1, 2008.

281   "wary about the fact": Robert Jobson, *Harry's War: The True Story of the Soldier Prince* (London: John Blake Publishing, 2008), 200.

281   "great soldiers" and "as though I was just": Patrick Hill, "Prince Harry's Dream Job Was Serving with SAS—but He Has No Regrets Not Trying It Out," *Mirror*, February 23, 2014.

281–82   "It's bizarre" through "Hopefully she would be proud": Jobson, *Harry's War*, 204, 229–30.

282   "It was an amazing feeling" and "If you had a list": Adapted from Tony Jones, "The Royal Heir Force," *Daily Star*, January 18, 2008.

283   "to withdraw Prince Harry": Sarah Lyall, "Prince Harry Withdrawn from Afghanistan," *New York Times*, February 29, 2008.

283   "There's always someone" through "you do what you have to do": Jobson, *Harry's War*, 235–70.

283   "Thank you, the interview's over": Adapted from Penny Junor, *Prince Harry: Brother, Soldier, Son* (New York: Grand Central, 2014), 210.

Chapter 98

284   "battlefield helicopter crews": David Jarvis, "Outcry as William Pops Over to Kate's in His RAF Copter," *Express*, April 21, 2008.

285   "In theory any pilot": Aislinn Simpson, "Prince William Lands Helicopter at Kate Middleton's House," *Telegraph*, April 20, 2008.

285   "unlawful killing" and "caused, or contributed to": Alan Cowell, "Negligent Driving Killed Diana, Jury Finds," *New York Times*, April 8, 2008.

285   "We agree with their verdicts" and "The two of us would like": Penny Junor, *Prince Harry: Brother, Soldier, Son* (New York: Grand Central, 2014), 186–88.

285–86   "This helicopter came out" and "The RAF have": Camilla Tominey, "William Flies into New Spot of Turbulence," *Express*, April 20, 2008.

286   "Whether it can be considered": Simpson, "Prince William Lands Helicopter."

286   "I'm working on my license" through "but he was very nice": Richard Palmer, "William Tells of His Helicopter 'Joyriding,'" *Express*, May 9, 2008.

Chapter 99

287   "Hi, I'm the guy" through "It's more like talking": Robert Jobson, *Harry's War: The True Story of the Soldier Prince* (London: John Blake Publishing, 2008), 270–72.

288   "Why not think about" through "but it's actually": Adapted from Penny Junor, *Prince Harry: Brother, Soldier, Son* (New York: Grand Central, 2014), 212.

289   "big blonde fringe": Anna Kretschmer, "Prince William Confession: How Duke Revealed Real Reason Behind Diana Mannerism," *Express*, May 7, 2020.

289   "Oh my God!": Robert Jobson, *William & Kate: The Love Story—A Celebration of the Wedding of the Century* (London: John Blake Publishing, 2010), 19.

289   "The time I spent" and "I now want to build": Andrew Pierce, "Prince William to Become Pilot in RAF Search and Rescue Service," *Telegraph*, September 15, 2008.

289   "already proved his worth" and "By the time": "Harry Copts It," *Daily Star*, October 27, 2008.

Chapter 100

290   "We're both here": Associated Press, "Prince William Hopes for Some Combat Experience," CTV News, June 18, 2009.

290   "To get out to Afghanistan": Rebecca English, "Brothers in Arms: Prince William Says 'I Want to Fight in Afghanistan,' as Harry Reveals Ambition to Return to War Zone," *Daily Mail*, June 18, 2009.

290   "If Harry can do it": Richard Palmer, "William: I Want to Fight in Afghanistan," *Express,* June 19, 2009.

290   "in my mind" through "Oh the lies, all lies": English, "Brothers in Arms."

291   "the immense entrepreneurial energy" and "They have to feel it": Sally Bedell Smith, *Prince Charles: The Passions and Paradoxes of an Improbable Life* (New York: Random House, 2017), 442.

291   "inherited": Emily Ferguson, "William's Touching Tribute to Diana: Prince Recalls 'Lasting Impression' of Charity Visits," *Express,* November 13, 2019.

291   "example of selfless service": "Our Patron Prince William," Centrepoint, https://centrepoint.org.uk /about-us/who-we-are/our-patron/.

291   "no shielding": Emily Hall, "Down and Out Prince," *Daily Star,* December 23, 2009.

291   "I cannot, after one night" and "I hope that": "Our Patron Prince William."

Chapter 101

292   "a behind-the-scenes glance": "Princes William and Harry Pose in New Portrait," CNN, January 6, 2010.

292   "I'm a little bit more ginger": Steve Hughes, "I'm Hair to the Throne, Wills!," *Daily Star,* February 2, 2010.

292   "my easiest way" and "a bit of a Lynx lover": "Harry Set to Return to Battle Zone," *Express,* February 14, 2010.

293   "That's all I wanted" through "I want to go sit in a cockpit": Penny Junor, *Prince Harry: Brother, Soldier, Son* (New York: Grand Central, 2014), 214–17, 218, 219.

293   "There is still a huge mountain" and "I think it will be": Jerry Lawton, "Harry's on Cloud Nine," *Daily Star,* May 8, 2010.

293   "My brother did it" through "I think as future leader": Richard Peppiatt, "Wills: Let Me Fight Taliban," *Daily Star,* October 20, 2010.

Chapter 102

294   "went up a tree a princess": Jane Flanagan, "Treetops, the Kenyan Safari Lodge Where Princess Elizabeth Became Queen, Forced to Close," *The Times* (London), October 14, 2021.

294   "It was my mother's" through "I just hope I look after it": Robert Jobson, *William & Kate: The Love Story—A Celebration of the Wedding of the Century* (London: John Blake Publishing, 2010), 3.

295   "I remember when I held" through "Then one day": Kelly Wynne, "Princess Diana's Engagement Ring Belonged to Harry After Her Death," *Newsweek,* December 10, 2018.

295   "I had a wonderful" and "I love the warm fires": Jobson, *William & Kate,* 10, 14.

295   "The potential risk": "Prince's 'Kidnap' Shown," *Daily Star,* October 22, 2010.

295–96 "Even after death": His Royal Highness Prince William, "Prince William: I Am Humbled by Respect for Armed Forces," *Sunday Telegraph,* November 14, 2010.

Chapter 103

297   "The Prince of Wales is delighted": Melissa Castellanos, "Prince William Engagement Announced on Twitter," CBS News, November 16, 2010.

297   "I'm delighted that my brother": Robert Jobson, *William & Kate: The Love Story—A Celebration of the Wedding of the Century* (London: John Blake Publishing, 2010), 2.

297   "It's the most brilliant news" and "They've been practicing": Sally Bedell Smith, *Prince Charles: The Passions and Paradoxes of an Improbable Life* (New York: Random House, 2017), 459.

297   "got a naughty sense of humor" and "which really helps": Jobson, *William & Kate,* 7, 8.

297   "My main aim is not": Penny Junor, *Prince William: The Man Who Will Be King,* repr. ed. (New York: Pegasus Books, 2013), 363.

298   "It was very romantic": Jobson, *William & Kate,* 8.

298   "The timing is right" through "Hopefully I'll take that in my stride": "Timetable of a Romance," *Express,* July 23, 2013.

298   "Obviously, I would have loved" through "Like Kate said": Jobson, *William & Kate,* 17.

Chapter 104

299   "classic royal wedding": Robert Jobson, *William & Kate: The Love Story—A Celebration of the Wedding of the Century* (London: John Blake Publishing, 2010), 16.

299   "Listen, I've got this list" through "Start from your friends": Katie Nicholl, *Kate: The Future Queen* (New York: Hachette Books, 2015), 220.

299   "sharp and clean": Elizabeth Holmes, *HRH: So Many Thoughts on Royal Style* (New York: Celadon, 2020), 184.

299   "Prince of Wheels": Steve Hughes, "Prince of Wheels," *Daily Star,* July 27, 2009.

300   "It's about other cars": "Prince William and Charles' Tensions over Duke's Use of Motorbikes," *Express,* September 16, 2021.

300   "On the day": Nick Collins, "Royal Wedding: Military in Full-Scale Dress Rehearsal," *Telegraph,* April 27, 2011.

300   "I'm going to marry": Tina Brown, *The Diana Chronicles* (New York: Anchor Books, 2008), 169.

301   "look right at them": Christopher Andersen, *Brothers and Wives: Inside the Private Lives of William, Kate, Harry, and Meghan* (New York: Gallery, 2021), 147.

301   "We had a couple of discussions": Raf Sanchez, "Prince William: I'm Struggling to Balance Military Career with Royal Duty," *Telegraph,* May 30, 2012.

301   "disappoints": Tim Ross and Thomas Harding, "Royal Wedding: Prince William Marries in Irish Guards Red," *Telegraph,* April 29, 2011.

301   "Once you're in the military": Sanchez, "Prince William."

Chapter 105

302   "Christ! She looks stunning!" and "make one another": Anna Pukas, "You Look Beautiful (It's Supposed to Be Just a Small Family Affair)," *Express,* April 30, 2011.

303   "It's amazing" through "Princess Diana would have loved": Richard Palmer, "Shall We Do It Now…? And Then They Kissed," *Express,* April 30, 2011.

303   "Let's all pray for Harry": William Hickey, "Hickey," *Express,* April 30, 2011.

303   "Pippa?": Christopher Andersen, *Brothers and Wives: Inside the Private Lives of William, Kate, Harry, and Meghan* (New York: Gallery, 2021), 214.

304   "She valued her privacy": Mehera Bonner, "How Prince William and Kate Middleton Inspired Harry's Breakup with Chelsy Davy," *Cosmopolitan,* August 11, 2018.

304   "I still have feelings": Andersen, *Brothers and Wives,* 214.

304   "Now to the bit": Gary Nicks, "It's Mister and Kisses," *Daily Star,* April 30, 2011.

304   "I still remember" through "we even had to share": "Former Royal Chef Revisits Prince William's 'Chocolate Biscuit' Grooms Cake for the 10th Anniversary," posted by Darren McGrady, April 27, 2021, https://www.youtube.com/watch?v=_mR4Oxljq9E.

304   "William didn't have a romantic" and "Our Mother would be so proud": Chris Byfield, "Prince Harry's Best Man Speech for William Was 'Emotional' Tribute to Diana," *Express,* September 15, 2021.

PART 8: OFFICERS AND GENTLEMEN
Chapter 106

307   "I count myself very": "Top Gun-in-Training Prince Harry Arrives in California," *Radar,* October 7, 2011.

307–8   "an Ugly" through "It's a joy for me": Mark Reynolds, "I'm an Ugly and I Love It," *Express,* January 22, 2013.

308   "Harry can't pass an exam" through "a romantic": Penny Junor, *Prince William: The Man Who Will Be King,* rev. ed. (New York: Pegasus Books, 2013), 324.

308   "Always outnumbered, never outgunned": Reynolds, "I'm an Ugly."

308   "Everyone is hoping": Jonathan Beale, "Pilot Prince Harry to Train in El Centro, California," *BBC News,* October 7, 2011.

308 "When are you going" and "Not for a long time": Keyan Milanian, "When Harry Met Chelsy . . . ," *Daily Star,* December 3, 2011.

308–9 "It is not just the quality" and "semi finalists": "Army Colonel Instructs Junior Officers to Dress More Like Princes William and Harry," *Telegraph,* November 28, 2011.

309 "If in doubt": Ellie Krupnick, "Colonel Barry Jenkins of Royal Artillery Regiment: Dress Like Prince Harry," *HuffPost,* November 28, 2011.

309 "I am a young Army officer" through "I share many": Richard Palmer, "Classy Kate's Velvet Touch," *Express,* December 20, 2011.

309 "We will continue": Gary Nicks, "Target Harry," *Daily Star,* February 11, 2012.

309 "The thinking is that being": Max Foster, "CNN Exclusive: Prince Harry Moves Next Door to Wills and Kate," CNN, March 28, 2012.

Chapter 107

310 "Seriously, can't you" and "Yeah, let me": Meghan Keneally, "'It's Always Nice to Pop Around for Tea . . . I Can Be a Bit of a Cheeky Grandson,'" *Daily Mail,* May 24, 2012.

310 "never going to": Keith Kendrick, "Prince William Interview: 'I'm Very Keen to Have a Family,'" *HuffPost,* May 20, 2012.

310 "the one time since she's died": Keneally, "'It's Always Nice to Pop Around for Tea.'"

310 "I think she had the best seat": Thea Trachtenberg, Carolyn Durand, John Green, and Matt Lombardi, "Prince Harry Reflects on Queen Elizabeth II's Legacy, Missing His Mom," ABC News, May 29, 2012.

311 "I really enjoy my time" and "the pressures of my other life": Raf Sanchez, "Prince William: I'm Struggling to Balance Military Career with Royal Duty," *Telegraph,* May 30, 2012.

311 "What they do about a home": Richard Palmer, "Wills Won't Rush to Spend His £10m Inheritance, Say Friends," *Express,* May 15, 2012.

311 "selflessness and duty" and "my incredible role model": Roya Nikkhah, "Prince William's Personal Tribute to the Queen—'My Incredible Role Model,'" *Telegraph,* May 27, 2012.

311 "The future of the monarchy" and "She invested a great deal of time": Christopher Andersen, *Diana's Boys: William and Harry and the Mother They Loved* (New York: William Morrow, 2001), 273–74.

311 "I still think she's just" and "I'm probably a bit": Keneally, "'It's Always Nice to Pop Around for Tea.'"

311 "In a small room" and "It's only really sort of been": Trachtenberg, Durand, Green, and Lombardi, "Prince Harry Reflects on Queen Elizabeth II's Legacy."

312 "I will help out": Roya Nikkhah, "William and Harry's Military Missions Keep Them from First Day of Jubilee Celebrations," *Telegraph,* June 3, 2012.

312 "Prince Harry and Prince William" and "They are very loyal": Max Foster, "CNN Exclusive: Prince Harry Moves Next Door to Wills and Kate," CNN, March 28, 2012.

312 "she was very conscious" and "She was grooming": Andersen, *Diana's Boys,* 184.

312 "I've longed for kids" and "I'm waiting to find": Sarah Anne Hughes, "Katie Couric Talks to Princes William and Harry About Queen Elizabeth, Having Kids," *Washington Post,* May 30, 2012.

312 "Harry Hunters": Adrian Lee, "Roisterer to Royal," *Express,* August 14, 2012.

312 "I don't think you can" and "If you find the right": Richard Palmer, "I'm Thrilled About the Baby, I Can't Wait to Be an Uncle," *Express,* January 22, 2013.

312 "I'd rather like" and "So that's the key": Kendrick, "Prince William Interview."

Chapter 108

313 "taking flying exams" and "involved in pre-deployment": Roya Nikkhah, "William and Harry's Military Missions Keep Them from First Day of Jubilee Celebrations," *Telegraph,* June 3, 2012.

314 "will be forced" and "in an orderly": "The Queens Diamond Jubilee Concert—Paul McCartney Part 2," posted by surethom, June 5, 2012, https://www.youtube.com/watch?v=ZcuOfh6e-bY.

314 "Your Majesty—Mummy" through "The only sad thing": "Prince Philip in Hospital and Misses Diamond Jubilee Concert," *BBC News*, June 4, 2012.

314 "winding down" and "I reckon I've done my bit": Robert Jobson, *The New Royal Family: Prince George, William and Kate, the Next Generation* (London: John Blake Publishing, 2013), 171.

314 "Good evening, Mr. Bond": Stephanie Petit, "How Queen Elizabeth Put Her Own Spin on Her Cameo in 2012 Olympics James Bond Sketch," *People*, October 28, 2019.

314 "Never can Her Majesty": "James Bond and The Queen London 2012 Performance," posted by Olympics, July 27, 2012, https://www.youtube.com/watch?v=1AS-dCdYZbo.

315 "Both of us were slightly" through "In fact she did": Avril Ormsby, "Princes 'Kept in Dark' over Queen's 007 Film Role," *Reuters*, August 3, 2012.

315 "statesmanlike and regal": Adrian Lee, "Roisterer to Royal," *Express*, August 14, 2012.

315 "cemented his image": Paul Harris, "King of the Closing Ceremony: Prince Harry Is Joined by Kate as He Takes Centre Stage as the Top Royal," *Daily Mail*, August 14, 2012.

315 "the Royal Family's secret weapon": Catherine Ostler, "Wish You Were Here! Postcards from Prince Harry's Diamond Jubilee Tour of the Caribbean," *Daily Mail*, March 8, 2012.

315 "People used to say to me": Penny Junor, *Prince William: The Man Who Will Be King*, rev. ed. (New York: Pegasus Books, 2013), 406.

315 "Harry has learned" and "Harry's grown up": Lee, "Roisterer to Royal."

315 "boys' trip": Melanie Bromley, "The Reinvention of Prince Harry: How Those Naked Vegas Pictures Helped Turn His Life Around," *E!*, August 22, 2016.

315 "drink-fueled": Lee, "Roisterer to Royal."

316 "Diana had a sense of the media": Sarah Sands, "Tina Brown Reveals the Diana We Never Knew," *Daily Mail*, June 9, 2007.

316 "strip billiards" and "in the upstairs cabin": John F. Burns, "For Prince Harry, Vegas Exploits Didn't Stay There," *New York Times*, August 22, 2012.

316 "an interview without coffee" through "social misbehavior": Rowena Mason, "Prince Harry May Face 'Interview Without Coffee' over Naked Photos," *Telegraph*, August 22, 2012.

316 "My father's always trying" and "a classic example": "Naked Romp 'Let My Family Down,'" *Express*, January 22, 2013.

316 "At the end of the day": "Prince Harry 'Longs for Family Time' on Afghanistan Return," *BBC News*, January 23, 2013.

316 "The scandal would be": Sally Bedell Smith, *Prince Charles: The Passions and Paradoxes of an Improbable Life* (New York: Random House, 2017), 477.

Chapter 109

317–18 "pride and anticipation" through "You cannot put it any other way": Gordon Rayner, "Prince Harry Arrives in Afghanistan at Start of Four-Month Tour as Apache Helicopter Pilot," *Telegraph*, September 6, 2012.

318 "all their power to kill or capture": Marc Walker, "Taliban Vow to Take Out Pilot Prince," *Daily Star*, September 8, 2012.

318 "After swift action": Donna Bowater and Ben Farmer, "British Troops Help Fight Off Taliban Attack on Afghan Military Base Housing Prince Harry," *Telegraph*, September 14, 2012.

318 "No-one can say": Ross Kanuik, "Operation Kill Harry Launched," *Daily Star*, September 15, 2012.

318 "was all about me" and "bit of a reality check": Jonathan Beale, "Prince Harry's Time as 'Warrior Prince' in Helmand," *BBC News*, January 21, 2013.

318 "The prince was seen" and "To cover this shame": Bowater and Farmer, "British Troops Help Fight Off Taliban Attack."

318 "Insha'Allah": Kanuik, "Operation Kill Harry Launched."

Chapter 110

319–20 "It was the angriest": Penny Junor, *Prince William: The Man Who Will Be King*, rev. ed. (New York: Pegasus Books, 2013), 424.

320 "The incident is reminiscent" and "It is unthinkable": Meg Jorsh, "Kate's Being Hunted 'Like Princess Di,'" *Daily Star*, September 15, 2012.

320 "My wife and I" through "painful": Brittany Vonow, "Barefaced Cheek: What Are the Kate Middleton Topless Pictures and When Did France's Closer Magazine Publish the Photographs?," *The Sun*, September 20, 2018.

320 "a breach of private life": Jorsh, "Kate's Being Hunted Like Princess Di."

320 "I want the Queen": Junor, *Prince William*, 425, 426.

320 "There's a reason": Piers Morgan (@piersmorgan), "There's a reason...," Twitter, September 14, 2012, 8:25 a.m., https://twitter.com/piersmorgan/status/246585520581402626.

320 "I don't suppose": Junor, *Prince William*, 425, 426.

320 "Girls don't have the same": Robert Jobson, *The New Royal Family: Prince George, William and Kate, the Next Generation* (London: John Blake Publishing, 2013), 158.

321 "I am delighted": "Kate Pregnant: Celebs Tweet Congratulations to William and Kate on Their Exciting Royal Baby News," *Hello!*, December 3, 2012.

321 "The whole world is watching": Alessandra Ram, "Morning Sickness, Cryptic Smiles: How the Press Covers Royal Pregnancies," *The Atlantic*, December 5, 2012.

321 "Diana, funny enough" and "She was doing her duty": Mary Pflum, "Princess Diana Set Royal Motherhood Example for Kate Middleton," ABC News, December 4, 2012.

321–22 "I'm fed up" through "Now I can't wait": "Princess Diana, Who Had to Take a Few Days...," UPI Archives, November 12, 1981.

322 "It's about time" and "I just hope": Richard Palmer, "I'm Thrilled About the Baby, I Can't Wait to Be an Uncle," *Express*, January 22, 2013.

Chapter 111

323 "I really am longing" through "You get asked to do things": "Prince Harry 'Longs for Family Time' on Afghanistan Return," BBC News, January 23, 2013.

323 "fired a certain amount": Richard Palmer, "Harry: We Take a Life to Save a Life," *Express*, January 22, 2013.

323 "a very small office": "Prince Harry Explains the Controls of His Apache Helicopter," BBC News, January 21, 2013.

324 "Take a life to save a life" and "That's what we revolve around": Palmer, "Harry: We Take a Life."

324 "It's a fantastic job": Penny Junor, *Prince William: The Man Who Will Be King*, rev. ed. (New York: Pegasus Books, 2013), 319–20.

324 "I don't see why he couldn't" and "No one knows": Giles Sheldrick, "Wills Would Love to Be in War Zone," *Express*, January 22, 2013.

324 "We've got nothing like this": Gordon Rayner, "Prince Harry at Home Among Warriors," *Telegraph*, May 11, 2013.

325 "I didn't know you had Pimm's" through "You skipped that one": Deborah Sherwood, "Harry's Game," *Daily Star*, May 12, 2013.

325 "I love the royal family" and "All my friends can't believe": Rayner, "Prince Harry at Home Among Warriors."

325 "Thank you Prince Harry": "'Warrior' Prince Harry Rocks the Warrior Games in Colo.," *USA Today*, May 18, 2013.

325 "giving a focus": Rayner, "Prince Harry at Home Among Warriors."

325 "He knows what" and "He's been on the ground": Dan Elliott, "Prince Harry Attends Warrior Games in Colorado Springs," 4CBS Denver, May 12, 2013.

326 "I don't see how": Sherwood, "Harry's Game."

326 "He is a target" and "Harry's security team": Justin Penrose, "Prince Harry Murder Plot," *Mirror*, June 2, 2013.

326   "as a young boy" through "Harry will think": Deborah Sherwood, "Party's Over, Harry: Ex-Bodyguard Warns Prince over Death Threats," *Daily Star,* June 16, 2013.

Chapter 112

327–28   "Do you want Kate's baby" through "Morning, Granddad": Robert Jobson, *The New Royal Family: Prince George, William and Kate, the Next Generation* (London: John Blake Publishing, 2013), 187, 192.

328   "I am enormously proud": Penny Junor, *Prince William: The Man Who Will Be King,* rev. ed. (New York: Pegasus Books, 2013), 429.

328   "It's the first time" through "I think any parent": Jobson, *The New Royal Family,* 190.

328   "The first born is very special": Junor, *Prince William,* 433.

328   "He's got her looks": Jobson, *The New Royal Family,* 191.

328   "He's got way more": Junor, *Prince William,* 432.

328   "We are still working": Jobson, *The New Royal Family,* 191.

328   "has a good upbringing" and "I only hope": Lesley Messer, "Prince Harry on Being an Uncle: I'll 'Make Sure He Has Fun,'" ABC News, July 25, 2013.

Chapter 113

329   "I still do not know": Cindy Watts, "Prince William Recounts Following Taylor Swift on Stage 'Like a Puppy,'" CMT News, December 6, 2021.

329–30   "I try and be charming" through *I'm off-duty*: William, Duke of Cambridge, "Time to Walk with Prince William," *Time to Walk,* Apple Fitness+, https://fitness.apple.com/us/workout/time-to-walk-with-prince-william/1556119505.

330   "She puts her hand": Emily Kirkpatrick, "Prince William 'Cringes' Remembering Singing with Taylor Swift and Jon Bon Jovi," *Vanity Fair,* September 6, 2021.

330   "I got up like a puppy": Duke of Cambridge, "Time to Walk with Prince William."

330   *Am I standing on the stage* and *Well, if they're enjoying*: Kirkpatrick, "Prince William 'Cringes.'"

330   "At times, when you're taken": Duke of Cambridge, "Time to Walk with Prince William."

330   "There's so many pressures": Watts, "Prince William Recounts Following Taylor Swift."

330   "A half-day on Friday": "Prince Harry and Team Arrive at South Pole," BBC News, December 13, 2013.

330–31   "He knows what he's doing" through "We wouldn't let it be": "Prince Harry Trains for Charity Polar Trek in Freezer," BBC News, September 17, 2013.

331   "Prince Harry was never, ever shy" through "he would come around": Penny Junor, *Prince Harry: Brother, Soldier, Son* (New York: Grand Central, 2014), 256.

331   "just quite jealous": Roisin Kelly, "Prince Harry Begins Antarctic Trek," *Parade,* December 2, 2013.

331   "slightly mad" through "Occasionally you've got to put": Jessica Derschowitz, "Prince Harry: William 'Jealous' of South Pole Trek," CBS News, November 26, 2013.

331   "We decided to use" through "There was always something": Rebecca English, "'Harry Drank Champagne Out of a Prosthetic Leg and Told Filthy Jokes While Others Danced Naked,'" *Daily Mail,* January 21, 2014.

331–32   "I am so proud" and "raise awareness": Frank Gardner, "Prince Harry to Join Army Veterans in North Pole Trek," BBC News, January 12, 2011.

332   "to demonstrate to those": English, "'Harry Drank Champagne.'"

Chapter 114

333   "can't seem to get enough" through "the one that he wanted": Victoria Murphy, "William and Kate Middleton Tour: 6 of the Best Bits from Royal Trip to Australia and New Zealand," *Mirror,* April 25, 2014.

334 "It's all yours" through "do some 'popping'": Adapted from Richard Palmer, "Kate's Great, but Wills Is Just Not Up to Scratch," *Express*, April 24, 2014.

334 "I don't know what normal" and "There are three parts of me": Katie Nicholl, *Harry and Meghan: Life, Loss, and Love*, rev. ed. (New York: Hachette Books, 2019), 154.

334–35 "look at all the press" and "Harry will end up": Jerry Adler and Donna Foote, "Growing Up Without Her," *Newsweek*, September 15, 1997.

335 "It's challenging, you can't deny it" and "It's not something": Joshi Herrmann, "Cressida Bonas's Brother Jacobi on Why He's Bringing Ibiza to Camden," *Evening Standard*, November 23, 2013.

335 "nerves about everything" through "I was so nervous, I was shaking": Megan C. Hills, "Prince Harry Describes His 'Worst' Speech at the 2014 Invictus Games in Instagram Video," *Evening Standard*, September 11, 2019.

335 "I have no doubt": "Prince Harry's speech at the opening ceremony of the Invictus Games," posted by The Royal Family, September 11, 2014, https://www.youtube.com/watch?v=Im-5ey1-siY.

336 "Harry has been involved" and "He has pulled his sleeves up": Nicholl, *Harry and Meghan*, 152.

336 "We were underdogs" and "You are a legend": Ruth Styles, "'I Was Completely over the Moon,'" *Daily Mail*, September 18, 2014.

336 "goes out to all the heroes" and "Thank you very much": Kevin EG Perry, "Foo Fighters Perform in Front of Prince Harry at Closing of Invictus Games," *NME*, September 15, 2014.

336 "She just danced along" through "I was completely over the moon": Styles, "'I Was Completely over the Moon.'"

Chapter 115

337 "Red Heads RULE!" and "Being a red head": Jeff Farrell, "Harry Reddy for Oz Action," *Daily Star*, April 7, 2015.

337 "After a decade" and "The experiences I have had": Kate Stanton, "Prince Harry Quits British Army After 10 Years," UPI, March 17, 2015.

338 "William has spent eight years": Richard Eden, "Why the Duke of Cambridge Will Not Pay Back His 'Outstanding Training Costs' at the RAF," *Telegraph*, September 15, 2013.

338 "absolutely delighted": "Royal Baby: Duchess of Cambridge Gives Birth to Daughter," BBC News, May 2, 2015.

338 "I cannot believe": Emily Nash, "What It Was Like to Cover Princess Charlotte's Birth First-Hand," *Hello!*, May 2, 2020.

339 "Perfect names" and "My 2-year-old": "Royal Princess Named Charlotte Elizabeth Diana," BBC News, May 4, 2015.

339 "She's beautiful": Mariana Cerqueira, "Prince Harry Makes Sad Confession About the Birth of Princess Charlotte," *GoodtoKnow*, May 30, 2019.

339 "The reason I am now fifth" and "I think the key to that": Latifa Yedroudj, "Harry 'GREAT' with Royal Children George, Charlotte and Mia—'He Loves Playing with Them,'" *Express*, May 13, 2019.

339–40 "epic" through "But then, when I grew up": Nicola Harley, "Prince Harry Calls to Bring Back National Service," *Telegraph*, May 16, 2015.

340 "the offer out to his team" and "doesn't just want Harry": Charlotte Duck, "Tom Cruise Wants Prince Harry for Top Gun 2," *Glamour*, July 13, 2015.

340 "Not only is Harry qualified": James Ingham, "EXCLUSIVE: Tom Cruise Aims to Bring Prince Harry on Board for Top Gun Sequel," *Daily Star*, September 7, 2019.

340 "Are we going" through "but we can make that OK": Drew Weisholtz, "Kevin Costner Says Princess Diana Wanted to Star in 'The Bodyguard' Sequel," *Today*, July 2, 2019.

340 "very happy not having a girlfriend" and "I'm no Bridget Jones": Harley, "Prince Harry Calls to Bring Back National Service."

340 "I don't think you can force" and "It would be great": Katie Nicholl, *Harry and Meghan: Life, Loss, and Love*, rev. ed. (New York: Hachette Books, 2019), 158.

Chapter 116

341 "What's your secret?": Allison Pearson, "The Queen Turns 90: Allison Pearson on the World's Best Loved Monarch," *Telegraph,* April 21, 2016.

341 "Stand up, William": Jane Warren, "Prince Charming," *Express,* July 18, 2016.

342 "There were a lot of raised eyebrows" through "determined that other people's": Leah Sinclair, "'That P***ed Him Off': Friend Reveals What Really Annoyed Prince William After Verbier Ski Trip Controversy," *Evening Standard,* March 21, 2021.

342 "knows what he wants" and "assertive but cool": Christopher Andersen, *Diana's Boys: William and Harry and the Mother They Loved* (New York: William Morrow, 2001), 318.

342 "We were first on the scene": "Prince William Embarks on Final Day as a Helicopter Pilot," *Telegraph,* July 27, 2017.

342 "Workshy William" and "Will-not": Camilla Tominey, "Let's Give William a Break," *Express,* March 19, 2017.

342 "at some point": Christine Hauser, "Prince William Starts Job as Air Ambulance Pilot," *New York Times,* July 1, 2015.

343 "very peaceful": Bridie Wilkins, "Prince William and Kate Middleton's Peaceful Country Mansion They Ditched for London—Inside," *Hello!,* December 12, 2021.

343 "There's wonderful highs" through "I've struggled at times": Monica Sisavat, "Prince William Opens Up About His Struggles with Parenthood, Calls George a 'Little Rascal,'" *PopSugar,* November 19, 2016.

343 "a little joy from heaven": Hauser, "Prince William Starts Job as Air Ambulance Pilot."

343 "a right little rascal": Sisavat, "Prince William Opens Up."

343 "As far as we're concerned" and "There'll be a time and a place": Warren, "Prince Charming."

343–44 "Hey, Prince Harry" through "mic drop": Liam Stack, "Prince Harry, Justin Trudeau and the Obamas Compete for Laughs Before Invictus Games," *New York Times,* May 2, 2016.

344 "Oh, really? Please": "Prince Harry in Toronto for Invictus Games Launch Ceremony," *CityNews,* May 2, 2016.

344 "If you've got the ability" and "I certainly enjoyed": Katie Nicholl, *Harry and Meghan: Life, Loss, and Love,* rev. ed. (New York: Hachette Books, 2019), 169.

344 "I've been hugely honored" through "I'll see you in Toronto": Carolyn Durand, "Prince Harry Closes 2016 Invictus Games: 'Never Stop Fighting,'" ABC News, May 13, 2016.

344 "It's one of my very, very happy memories": Carolyn Durand, "Prince Harry Makes Private Visit to Disney World," ABC News, May 11, 2016.

344 "When you are that age": Diana Pearl, "Prince Harry Takes Late-Night Trip to Disney World—and Rides Splash Mountain!," *People,* May 11, 2016.

344–45 "It's a huge shame" and "I hope she'd be incredibly proud": Scott Stump, "Prince Harry: I Hope Princess Diana Would Be 'Incredibly Proud' of the Invictus Games," *Today,* May 9, 2016.

Chapter 117

346 "Never complain. Never explain": Frederica Miller, "The Queen's 'Never Complain, Never Explain' Motto—What It Means and Where It Comes From," *Express,* June 17, 2021.

346 "We realized no one": Andrea Park, "Prince William Says 'Not One Celebrity' Wanted to Help Launch the Royal Heads Together Mental Health Initiative," *W,* January 24, 2019.

346 "What my mother believed in": Hannah Furness, "How Prince Harry Has Turned His Pain into a Pathway to Help Others," *Telegraph,* April 16, 2017.

346 "We need to normalize": Jane Mendle, "How Princess Diana Changed Lives by Discussing Her Mental Health," *Time,* August 30, 2017.

346 "be upfront and": Naomi Gordon, "The Duke of Cambridge Addresses Princess Diana's Bulimia in New Documentary," *Harper's Bazaar,* August 22, 2017.

346 "There may be a time": Diana Pearl, "Prince William Says Brits Should Lose the 'Stiff Upper Lip' When It Comes to Mental Health," *People,* April 17, 2017.

346–47 "Heads Together wants to help everyone": Adapted from John Chapman, "Red-Hot Kate Really Is a Knockout in the Ring," *Express,* May 17, 2016.

347 "Everyone can suffer": "Prince Harry Regrets Not Talking Sooner About Diana's Death," Reuters, July 25, 2016.

347 "I can safely say" through "So from an emotional side": Stone, "Prince Harry Says He Was 'Close to a Complete Breakdown.'"

347 "I really regret not talking": "Prince Harry Regrets Not Talking Sooner."

347 "You have a reluctance" through "My personal life": William, Duke of Cambridge, "Time to Walk with Prince William," *Time to Walk,* Apple Fitness+, https://fitness.apple.com/us/workout/time-to-walk-with-prince-william/1556119505.

348 "From what I hear" through "I wouldn't be surprised": Sarah Sands, "Tina Brown Reveals the Diana We Never Knew," *Daily Mail,* June 9, 2007.

348 "My brother—God bless him": Cecilia Rodriguez, "Prince Harry Opens Up About His 20-Year Mental Struggle," *Forbes,* April 18, 2017.

348 "This is not right": Diana Pearl, "Prince Harry's Most Revealing Quotes About His Near Breakdown: 'I Refused to Ever Think About My Mom,'" *People,* April 17, 2017.

348 "I miss her so much" through "The important thing": Adapted from Richard Palmer, "I Miss My Mother Every Day, William Tells Bereaved Teen," *Express,* August 25, 2016.

348 "an easy one" through "I'll be in floods": Adapted from Will Stone, "Wills: My Torment over Sad 999 Calls," *Daily Star,* August 26, 2016.

348–49 "In Britain, we don't talk" through "He has shown the world": Bryony Gordon, "The Day Prince Harry Showed the World How to Talk About Our Problems," *Telegraph,* April 16, 2017.

PART 9: THE CAMBRIDGES AND THE SUSSEXES

Chapter 118

353 "Almost immediately they were almost obsessed": Catriona Harvey-Jenner, "The Moment Prince Harry Knew Meghan Markle Was the One," *Cosmopolitan,* July 30, 2020.

353 "like something I have never seen": Christopher Andersen, *Brothers and Wives: Inside the Private Lives of William, Kate, Harry, and Meghan* (New York: Gallery Books, 2021), p. 254.

354 "gutted": David Pilditch, "Harry Cancels Secret Trip to See 'New Love,'" *Express,* November 1, 2016.

354 "There's something so incredibly romantic" through "African-American mum": Camilla Tominey, "Sexy Meghan Is Harry's New Girl," *Daily Star Sunday,* October 30, 2016.

354 "the fact that Meghan": Katie Nicholl, *Harry and Meghan: Life, Loss, and Love,* rev. ed. (New York: Hachette Books, 2019), 184.

354 "Americans are different": Andrew Jameson, "Meghan Set for a Right Royal Xmas," *Daily Star,* December 16, 2016.

354 "Brit dunce" through "Prince Harry could marry": Louise Berwick, "One's Gone Gangst E II R," *Daily Star,* November 3, 2016.

355 "The past week" through "Prince Harry is worried": "Prince Harry's Statement Defending Girlfriend Meghan Markle in Full," *Telegraph,* November 8, 2016.

355 "heart to heart" and "the Duke of Cambridge absolutely": Gordon Rayner, "The Duke of Cambridge Approved Prince Harry's Plea to Trolls to Leave Meghan Markle Alone," *Telegraph,* November 26, 2016.

355 "I believe we are expecting": Kate Nelson, "Prince Harried," *Daily Star,* November 23, 2016.

355 "I've spent the last 33" through "It was very sweet": Victoria Ward, "Meghan Markle Has Already Charmed the Queen's Corgis, Harry Reveals," *Telegraph,* November 27, 2016.

356 "It was totally clear": Louise Berwick, "My Fir Lady!," *Daily Star,* December 14, 2016.

356 "I thought he'd go": Gemma Mullin, "Pining for Each Other: Prince Harry and Girlfriend Meghan Markle Spotted Christmas Tree Shopping in South London," *The Sun,* December 13, 2016.

356 "It's fun to be good" and "I want to do something": Camilla Tominey, "'It's Fun to Be Good...but You Can Be Naughty,'" *Express,* December 18, 2016.

356 "Being 'ethnically ambiguous'": Meghan Markle, "I'm More Than an 'Other,'" *Elle*, December 2016.

356 "I was fighting the system": Tominey, "'It's Fun to Be Good.'"

357 "camped out with each other": HRH Prince Harry and Meghan Markle, "Prince Harry and Meghan Markle: Engagement Interview in Full," interview by Mishal Husain, BBC News, November 27, 2017, https://www.bbc.com/news/av/uk-42139382.

357 "I have this love of Africa": Flora Drury, "Prince Harry and Meghan Markle: The Royal Love Affair with Africa," BBC News, November 29, 2017.

Chapter 119

359 "a coed school": Carolyn Durand and Katie Kindelan, "Prince George Heads to 1st Day of Primary School Hand in Hand with Prince William," ABC News, September 7, 2017.

359 "It went well" and "There was one other": Maria Puente, "Prince George Arrives for First Day of Big-Boy School," *USA Today*, September 7, 2017.

359 "We are all excited": Katey Rich, "See Prince George Arrive for His First Day of School," *Vanity Fair*, September 7, 2017.

359 "Diana is part of this": Chanel Vargas, "All the Details on the Green Dress Meghan Markle Wore for the Engagement Interview," *Town & Country*, November 27, 2017.

359–60 "Tell us about your ring" through "jumping up and down": HRH Prince Harry and Meghan Markle, "Prince Harry and Meghan Markle: Engagement Interview in Full," interview by Mishal Husain, BBC News, November 27, 2017, https://www.bbc.com/news/av/uk-42139382.

360 "Hip hip hooray!" through "I just FaceTimed her": Ellen Barry, "'A Royal Baby, a Prince!': Kate and William Welcome New Baby," *New York Times*, April 23, 2018.

360 "Thrice the worry now": Richard Palmer, "Hello World! New Prince Takes His First Bow," *Express*, April 24, 2018.

361 "Union Jack Man" and "It's fantastic": Lloyd Johnson, "Royal Baby Watchers Set Up Camp DAYS Before Birth as Patriotic Crowds Gather at Lindo Wing," *Express*, April 23, 2018.

361 "Now it's Harry's turn": Barry, "'A Royal Baby, a Prince!'"

361 "Harry just got demoted again": Palmer, "Hello World!"

361 "He hasn't asked" and "it may be a sensitive issue": Robert Jobson, *Harry & Meghan: The Wedding Album* (London: Regal Press, 2018), 40.

361 "Prince Harry has asked": The Duke and Duchess of Cambridge (@KensingtonRoyal), "Prince Harry has…," Twitter, April 26, 2018, 5:29 a.m., https://twitter.com/kensingtonroyal/status/989436382404849664?s=12.

362 "Harry has made no secret" through "fit and healthy": Caroline Hallemann, "Why Is Prince Harry and Meghan Markle's Wedding So Close to Prince Louis's Birth?," *Town & Country*, May 6, 2018.

362 "The Duke has amazing willpower" and "When he sets his mind": "You're One of Us Now, Meghan…," *Express*, May 20, 2018.

Chapter 120

363 "a very special place": Jack Hawke, "Royal Wedding: Inside St George's Chapel Where Prince Harry and Meghan Markle Will Marry," ABC News, May 13, 2018.

364 "All guests will be asked": Ian Gallagher, "The Army That Will Help Meghan Look Her Best on Her Big Day—and the Strict List of DO's and DON'Ts for Her Wedding Guests," *Daily Mail*, May 6, 2018.

364 "Iron Duke": Thomas Mackie, "'IRON DUKE': Prince Philip Attended Royal Wedding with CRACKED Rib After Falling in Bath," *Express*, May 25, 2018.

365 "You look lovely" and "Thank you, Pa": Camilla Tominey, "The Power of Love…," *Sunday Express*, May 20, 2018.

365–66 "There's power, power in love" through "Yes": Robert Jobson, *Harry & Meghan: The Wedding Album* (London: Regal Press, 2018), 23, 24.

366 "My darling old Harry": Maria Pasquini and Monique Jessen, "Prince Charles Gives Heartfelt Speech at Royal Wedding Reception: 'My Darling Old Harry,'" *People*, May 19, 2018.

366 "Does anyone here": Ruth Hughes, "Speech That Moved Many to Tears, a Singing Elton, Then It's Off to the Party," *Sunday Express*, May 20, 2018.

366 "I would like you to allocate": Tony Whitfield, "Harry's Moving Tribute to Diana," *Sunday Express*, May 20, 2018.

367 "It's not often" and "She was just a normal girl": Aimee Lewis, "A Day in Windsor When Everything Changed," CNN, May 20, 2018.

Chapter 121

368 "Meghan is pregnant": SJ (@southwestSJ), "Meghan is pregnant...," Twitter, October 15, 2018, 3:44 a.m., https://twitter.com/southwestSJ/status/1051740605922062336.

368 "Meg Mania": Katie Nicholl, *Harry and Meghan: Life, Loss, and Love*, rev. ed. (New York: Hachette Books, 2019), 256.

368 "We have been so happy": Maura Hohman, "7 Times Prince Harry Couldn't Contain His Excitement About Becoming a Dad," *People*, April 16, 2019.

368 "On a very personal note": Caroline Hallemann, "Meghan Markle Just Gave a Moving Speech About Being Welcomed into the Invictus Games Family," *Town & Country*, October 27, 2018.

368 "Queen of Hearts": Omid Scobie, "What It's Like to Go on Tour with Prince Harry and Duchess Meghan," *Harper's Bazaar*, November 2, 2018.

369 "Almighty God": John Sentamu (@JohnSentamu), "Almighty God...," Twitter, January 17, 2019, 1:20 p.m., https://mobile.twitter.com/johnsentamu/status/1085965052744744960.

369 "After a lifetime": Hannah Furness, "William and Harry Split Royal Households as Sussexes Hire ex-Clinton Adviser," *Telegraph*, March 14, 2019.

369 "Fab Four": Adrian Lee, "Duchess Difficult?," *Express*, December 10, 2018.

369 "All the work" through "Healthy disagreements": Clive Hammond, "William's Brutal Response to Harry's Probe on Whether Royal Rift Was Over," *Express*, May 12, 2021.

369 "thick and fast" and "Working as family": Sebastian Murphy-Bates, "Was This the Moment William Hinted at Royal Rift?," *Daily Mail*, February 12, 2019.

369 "There are disagreements": Robert Lacey, *Battle of Brothers: William and Harry—The Inside Story of a Family in Tumult* (New York: Harper, 2021), 1.

370 "Their Royal Highnesses" and "The Duke and Duchess": Caroline Hallemann, "Meghan Markle Gave Birth to Her Son Archie in a Hospital, Despite Rumors of a Home Birth," *Town & Country*, May 17, 2019.

370 "When any of them have babies": Conor Gogarty, "Prince Harry and Meghan Markle Superfan Travels...from Weston-Super-Mare to Windsor Hoping Royal Baby Will Arrive on His Birthday," *Bristol Live*, April 30, 2019.

370 "I'm very excited" through "It's been the most amazing": Rebecca English, "Revealed: Overdue Meghan's Home Birth Dream Was Dashed as She Was Secretly Whisked to a London Hospital on Sunday by Harry and His Scotland Yard Security Team Before Their 'to Die for' Baby Boy Was Born at 5.26am," *Daily Mail*, May 6, 2019.

370 "This little thing": Rebecca English, "'This Little Thing Is Absolutely to Die For!,'" *Daily Mail*, May 6, 2019.

370 "Still thinking about names": HRH Prince Harry, "Prince Harry Delightfully Announces Meghan Has Had a Baby Boy."

370 "slimmed-down monarchy": Camilla Tominey and Duarte Dias, "What Will the Monarchy Look Like When Prince Charles Becomes King?," *Telegraph*, December 9, 2021.

371 "He has the sweetest" through "two special people": Josh Boswell, "EXCLUSIVE: Meghan Markle Has Been Planning Tell-All Interview with Oprah for Two Years—Since the Palace's PR Team Squashed the Sussexes' Sit Down with Gayle King in 2019," *Daily Mail*, May 6, 2019.

371 "We have no new ranges": Roxanne Adamiyatt, "Royal Baby Sussex Probably Won't Get His Own Commemorative Merchandise," *Town & Country*, May 6, 2019.

372   "Having spent the last" through "If they do come": Katie Nicholl, "Harry and Meghan Might Have a 'Particularly Frosty' Christmas at the Queen's—If They Come at All," *Vanity Fair,* November 12, 2019.

373   "Two hundred years" through "The path, of course": Caroline Hallemann, "Queen Elizabeth's Christmas Message Reflects on the Royal Family's 'Bumpy' Year," *Town & Country,* December 25, 2019.

Chapter 122

374   "I couldn't see anyone's face" and "You definitely get a bit of anxiety": Mark Jefferies, "William: How Bad Eyes Helped Me Conquer My Anxiety over Speeches," *Express,* May 28, 2020.

374   "Every time I put a suit": Dan Sales, "Harry Reveals He Would 'Pour with Sweat' Due to Stress of Public Events and It Would Only Stop When He 'Bumped into Someone Sweating More than Him,'" *Daily Mail,* May 21, 2021.

374   "When I first met my now-husband": "Meghan, Duchess of Sussex, Says Friends Told Her Not to Marry Prince Harry," BBC News, October 21, 2019.

375   "Meghan does seem" through "It's a bit like 'Downton Abbey'": Rebecca Mead, "Prince Harry and Meghan Markle's Fractured Fairy Tale," *The New Yorker,* April 13, 2020.

375   "My deepest fear" and "I've seen what happens": Erin Hill, "Prince Harry Shares Fears for Meghan Markle: 'I Lost My Mother, Now I Watch My Wife Falling Victim," *People,* October 1, 2019.

375   "We intend to step back" and "carve out a progressive": sussexroyal, "After many months of reflection . . . ," Instagram, January 8, 2020, https://www.instagram.com/p/B7EaGS_Jpb9/.

375   "War of the Windsors" through "more red carpets, not fewer": Christopher Wilson, "Caught Between Love for Family and Love for Wife," *Express,* January 12, 2020.

375   "What is so shocking": "Prince Harry and Meghan to Step Back as Senior Royals," BBC News, January 8, 2020.

375   "insulted": Jon Coates, "Showdown at Sandringham," *Sunday Express,* January 12, 2020.

376   "hurt" through "days, not weeks": Kate Nelson, "Her Maj Is Mega Upset," *Express,* January 14, 2020.

376   "All we can do": Jon Coates, "Wills: I'm Sad About All This," *Sunday Express,* January 12, 2020.

376   "It's sometimes trying" and "We just need to deal": Richard Palmer, "William: We Need to Move Forward," *Express,* January 16, 2020.

376   "Like all the best families": Camilla Tominey, "Her Majesty Has Been the Epitome of Rudyard Kipling's 'If,' Once Again," *Telegraph,* January 19, 2020.

376   "to support Her Majesty the Queen": Victoria Ward, "The Chasm Between What the Sussexes Wanted and What They Got," *The Telegraph,* January 20, 2020.

377   "Duke of Hotness" and "I 🖤 a man": Danyal Hussain, "'I Love a Man in Uniform,'" *Daily Mail,* March 16, 2019.

377   "Signs of real, wistful sadness": Harry Mount, "Farewell to Prince Harry—But How Will He Get On Without Us?," *Telegraph,* March 10, 2010.

377   "If you get hold": Steve Myall, "Princess Diana's Funeral: Secrets Revealed as Tensions Mounted over Burial Plans," *Mirror,* August 31, 2018.

377   "Did you see": Mead, "Prince Harry and Meghan Markle's Fractured Fairy Tale."

378   "Royal firstborns may get": Robert Lacey, *Battle of Brothers: William and Harry—The Inside Story of a Family in Tumult* (New York: Harper, 2021), 101–2.

378   "Wherever you go" through "opening up a place": Mead, "Prince Harry and Meghan Markle's Fractured Fairy Tale."

378   "I was born into this life" and "We are taking": Camilla Tominey, "Exclusive: Prince Harry Misses the Army and Tells Friends His Life Has Been Turned Upside Down," *Telegraph,* April 29, 2020.

378   "William's told me": Charlie Pittock, "Prince William Told a 'Tearful' Princess Diana to Leave the UK," *Express,* February 13, 2022.

378–79   "new life" through "Think of the lifestyle": "Butler: Diana Planned Move to Malibu," ABC News, January 6, 2006.

379   "two-year-old Harry": Mount, "Farewell to Prince Harry."

379   "he is really missing the Army" and "he can't believe": Tominey, "Exclusive."

379   "Even when we can't all": Victoria Ward, "Royal Courtiers Refuse Prince Harry's Request to Lay Remembrance Sunday Wreath on His Behalf," *Telegraph*, November 8, 2020.

Chapter 123

380   "The Queen says she is delighted" and "Archie is going": Guy Rais, "September Baby for Princess: The Queen Says She Is Delighted," *Daily Telegraph*, February 14, 1984.

380   "Her Majesty, Duke of Edinburgh": Mark Duell, "Two VERY Different Royal Baby Announcements," *Daily Mail*, February 16, 2021.

380   "intimate" and "wide-ranging": Victoria Ward, "Buckingham Palace Ready for Final 'Megxit' Announcement on Harry and Meghan's Royal Patronages," *Telegraph*, February 16, 2021.

381   "to continue with the responsibilities": Victoria Ward, "Prince Harry's Sadness at Giving Up Military Roles," *Telegraph*, February 20, 2021.

381   "Do what your heart": Katie Nicholl, *Harry and Meghan: Life, Loss, and Love*, rev. ed. (New York: Hachette Books, 2019), 207.

381   "Time heals all things": Michelle Ruiz, "The Royal Family's Continental Rift," *Vanity Fair*, May 4, 2021.

381   "No, I haven't": Richard Palmer, "William: I Haven't Spoken . . . but I Will Do," *Express*, March 12, 2001.

381   "trapped" and "once he got over the anger": Cyril Dixon, "I'm NOT Trapped by Royal Role Says William," *Express*, March 22, 2021.

381   "I will miss" and "My grandpa": Camilla Tominey, "William and Harry's Tributes to the Duke of Edinburgh Show Just How Far Apart They Are," *Telegraph*, April 12, 2021.

382   "Just take the f—king picture!": Nicki Gostin, "Prince Philip's Most Infamous Gaffes: 'I Can't Believe He Just Said That,'" *Page Six*, April 9, 2021.

382   "Never, never shout": Ingrid Seward, *Prince Philip Revealed* (New York: Atria, 2020), 304.

382   "He is a romantic": Jonny Dymond, "Prince Philip: An Extraordinary Man Who Led an Extraordinary Life," BBC News, April 9, 2021.

382   "Operation London Bridge" through "Operation Forth Bridge": Leena Kim, "A Brief Primer on the Secret Codenames Used When Royals Die," *Town & Country*, April 9, 2021.

383   "She is the Queen" through "I think that must be a very, very profound thing": Danya Bazaraa, "Queen Will Have 'Profound Chance to Say Goodbye' at Philip's Funeral, Says Archbishop," *Mirror*, April 16, 2021.

384   "want to hand over": Robert Jobson, *The New Royal Family: Prince George, William and Kate, the Next Generation* (London: John Blake Publishing, 2013), 9.

Chapter 124

385   "Every day, we wish": Mark Landler, "Unveiling of Diana Statue Reunites William and Harry, Briefly," *New York Times*, July 1, 2021.

385   "Ready?": John Twomey, "Statue Will Be Symbol of Her Life and Legacy," *Express*, July 2, 2021.

386   "for some preliminary investigations": Jack Hardy and Hannah Furness, "The Queen Was Admitted to Hospital After Cancelling Northern Ireland Visit, Palace Says," *Telegraph*, October 21, 2021.

386   "stoical and mentally strong" and "her main concern": Stephanie Petit and Simon Perry, "Queen Elizabeth's Private Pain: Royal Family Scandal and COVID Are 'Going to Take a Toll,' Says Insider," *People*, February 22, 2022.

386   "Bringing the family together" and "we'd bring everyone": Richard Palmer, "Queen's 'Precautionary' Move Puts Family First," *Express*, December 17, 2021.

386   "really, really upset": Jennifer Newton, "Kate Middleton 'Really Upset' About Feud with Harry and Meghan Markle, Says Insider," *Mirror*, September 17, 2021.

Notes

387   "We've been through such a bleak time" and "But I suppose through separation": Stephanie Petit, "Kate Middleton Calls Pandemic 'Bleak Time' in Comforting Message Ahead of Christmas Concert," *People,* December 23, 2021.

387   "She picked it up so well" through "very talented musician": Ruth Kinane, "Watch Kate Middleton Perform with Tom Walker During Christmas Concert at Westminster Abbey," *Entertainment Weekly,* December 27, 2021.

387   "Happy holidays": Richard Palmer, "Giggling Lilibet Makes Her Debut," *Express,* December 24, 2021.

387   "offensive weapon": Karla Adam, "Britain Gets Glimpse of Queen in Christmas Message," *Washington Post,* December 25, 2021.

387   "None of us can slow": Richard Palmer, "Speech Is 'Particularly Personal,'" *Express,* December 24, 2021.

388   "Although it's a time of great happiness": Adam, "Britain Gets Glimpse of Queen."

388   "She knows William" through "She thinks the future": Matt Wilkinson, "Queen Urges Prince William to Stop Flying in Helicopters with Kate & Kids over Safety Fears," *The Sun,* December 18, 2021.

388   "for good": Olivia Rudgard, "The Queen Leaves Buckingham Palace for Good as She Moves Permanently to Windsor Castle," *Telegraph,* March 6, 2022.

388   "a disgrace to the Sovereign": Clive Irving and Tom Sykes, "Will the Queen Ever Live at Buckingham Palace Again?," *Daily Beast,* November 16, 2021.

389   "upkeep, both from": Tom Sykes, "Prince Charles Thinks Buckingham Palace Is a Dump—Because It Is," *Daily Beast,* September 23, 2017.

389   "will be a much more modest": Kate Mansey, "Prince Charles Will Live in 'Flat Above the Shop' and Buckingham Palace Will Be Thrown Open to the Public in a Radical Overhaul of the Royal Estate When He Becomes King," *Mail on Sunday,* October 2, 2021.

389   "neither William or Kate" through "can easily return": Jenny Proudfoot, "Here's Everything to Know About Prince William and Kate Middleton's Exciting Moving Plans," *Marie Claire,* January 31, 2022.

389   "no longer on the cards": Mansey, "Prince Charles Will Live in 'Flat Above the Shop.'"

389   "feature stories of hope": Tom Sykes, "Prince Harry and Meghan Markle Strike Gold In Hollywood," *Daily Beast,* December 18, 2020.

389–90   "planned to leverage" through "her plan sounds very like": Tina Brown, *The Palace Papers: Inside the House of Windsor—the Truth and the Turmoil* (New York: Crown, 2022), p. 215.

390   "does not feel safe": Phil Boucher, "Prince Harry Tells London Court He 'Does Not Feel Safe' Bringing Archie and Lilibet to the U.K.," *People,* February 18, 2022.

390   "my grandmother and I" and "lowkey visit": Alyssa Bailey, "Meghan Markle and Prince Harry Quietly Met with the Queen for First Time in 2 Years," *Elle,* April 14, 2022.

390   "Meghan and I had tea" through "I'm sure she is": Interview between Hoda Kotb and Prince Harry, "Prince Harry Talks Visit with Queen Elizabeth, Fatherhood in TODAY Exclusive," April 20, 2022, https://www.today.com/video/prince-harry-says-he-wants-right-people-around-queen -elizabeth-138115141871.

390–91   "My mother, she'd be driving along" through "You'll want to play it again": William, Duke of Cambridge, "Time to Walk with Prince William," *Time to Walk,* Apple Fitness+, https://fitness .apple.com/us/workout/time-to-walk-with-prince-william/1556119505.

Epilogue

392   *How many directors*: Adapted from Anita Singh, "Isolation and Sacrifice: What Prince Charles Told Kenneth Branagh About the Life of a Future King," *Telegraph,* March 1, 2022.

392   "For someone in my position" and "it's someone closer": Ingrid Seward, *William & Harry* (New York: Arcade, 2003), 167.

392   *People in authority*: Singh, "Isolation and Sacrifice."

392   "incredible insight": Seward, *William & Harry,* 166.

393   "It was invaluable" and "Also the sense of responsibility": Benedict Nightingale, "Henry V Returns as a Monarch for This Era," *New York Times*, November 5, 1989.

393   *For all the first-class* through "a genuine expression": Claire Toureille, "Sir Kenneth Branagh Reveals 'Softly Spoken' Prince Charles Admitted to Feeling 'Isolated' and Carrying the 'Burden of Expectation' When He Spoke to the Royal Ahead of Playing Henry V in 1989," *Daily Mail,* March 1, 2022.

394   "They were only keen" and "enjoyed it as much": Seward, *William & Harry,* 167.

394   "This play is summing": "Found: The Scribbled Notes on Shakespeare That Prove Diana Did Pay Attention in Class...but Discarded School Book Suggests Maths Was Not Among Her Gifts," *Daily Mail*, October 31, 2010.

394   "Shakespeare" and "confronts us": Seward, *William & Harry,* 166.

About the Authors

James Patterson is one of the best-known and biggest-selling writers of all time. His books have sold in excess of 400 million copies worldwide. He is the author of some of the most popular series of the past two decades – the Alex Cross, Women's Murder Club, Detective Michael Bennett and Private novels – and he has written many other number one bestsellers including non-fiction and stand-alone thrillers.

James is passionate about encouraging children to read. Inspired by his own son who was a reluctant reader, he also writes a range of books for young readers including the Middle School, Dog Diaries, Treasure Hunters and Max Einstein series. James has donated millions in grants to independent bookshops and has been the most borrowed author in UK libraries for the past thirteen years in a row. He lives in Florida with his family.

Chris Mooney is the international bestselling author of fourteen thrillers. The Mystery Writers of America nominated *Remembering Sarah* for an Edgar Award. He teaches creative writing at Harvard.

THE MOST ANTICIPATED MEMOIR OF 2022

'The master storyteller of our times takes us on a funny, poignant, and ultimately triumphant journey'

HILLARY RODHAM CLINTON

'The whole story of his truly astonishing life'

BOB WOODWARD

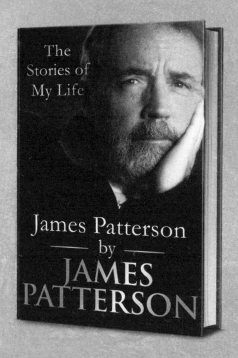

'The book was damn near addictive. I loved it'

RON HOWARD

'I love the pithy, bright anecdotes, and at times his poignant narrative will bring you to tears'

PATRICIA CORNWELL

hungry dogs run faster

THIS MORNING, I got up at quarter to six. Late for me. I made strong coffee and oatmeal with a sprinkle of brown sugar and a touch of cream. I leafed through the *New York Times, USA Today*, and the *Wall Street Journal*. Then I took a deep breath and started this ego-biography that you're reading.

My grandmother once told me, "You're lucky if you find something in life you like to do. Then it's a miracle if somebody'll pay you to do it." Well, I'm living a miracle. I spend my days, and many nights, writing stories about Alex Cross, the Women's Murder Club, Maximum Ride, the Kennedys, John Lennon, young Muhammad Ali, and now *this*.

My writing style is colloquial, which is the way we talk to one another, right? Some might disagree—some vehemently disagree—but I think colloquial storytelling is a valid form of expression. If you wrote down your favorite story to tell, there might not be any great sentences, but it still could be outstanding. Try it out. Write down a good story you tell friends—maybe starting with the line "Stop me if I've told you this one before"—and see how it looks on paper.

A word about my office. Come in. Look around. A well-worn,

1

hopelessly cluttered writing table sits at the center, surrounded by shelves filled to the brim with my favorite books, which I dip into all the time.

At the base of the bookshelves are counters. Today, there are thirty-one of my manuscripts on these surfaces. Every time journalists come to my office and see the thirty or so manuscripts in progress, they mutter something like "I had no idea." Right. *I had no idea how crazy you are, James.*

I got infamous writing mysteries, so here's the big mystery plot for this book: How did a shy, introspective kid from a struggling upstate New York river town who didn't have a lot of guidance or role models go on to become, at thirty-eight, CEO of the advertising agency J. Walter Thompson North America? How did this same person become the bestselling writer in the world? That's just not possible.

But it happened. In part because of something else my grandmother preached early and often—*hungry dogs run faster.*

And, boy, was I hungry.

One thing that I've learned and taken to heart about writing books or even delivering a good speech is to tell stories. Story after story after story. That's what got me here, so that's what I'm going to do. Let's see where storytelling takes us. This is just a fleeting thought, but try not to skim too much. If you do, it's the damn writer's fault. But I have a hunch there's something here that's worth a few hours. It has to do with the craft of storytelling.

One other thing. When I write, I pretend there's someone sitting across from me—and I don't want that person to get up until I'm finished with the story.

Right now, that person is you.

passion keeps you going...but it doesn't pay the rent

WHEN I FIRST arrived in New York, I would force myself to get up at five every morning to squeeze in a couple of hours of writing before I went to work at the ad factory. I was full of hope and big dreams but not enough confidence to quit my day job and write for my supper.

I'd play some music, maybe a little Harry Nilsson ("Gotta Get Up"), and do my first stint of scribbling sentences, cutting sentences, adding sentences, driving myself crazy.

The book's getting better, right?

The book's getting worse. Every sentence I write is inferior to the last.

I'm going to be the next Graham Greene.

Don't quit your day job, chump.

You start thinking you're a fraud, "a big fat failure." Okay, okay, so that's a line out of the movie *You've Got Mail*. So is "You are what you read."

As I said, I was driving myself crazy. It goes with the territory. I think that's what first-time novelists are supposed to do. Our rite of passage. Every night after work, I'd come home in a daze of jingle lyrics and cutesy catchphrases, sit in my kitchen, stare around at the tiny antiseptic space, then start writing again. I'd go till eleven or twelve. That's how I wrote *The Thomas Berryman Number*.

I did the first draft in pencil.

But then I typed. The two-finger minuet. I had to reach up to the counter to peck at the keys of my faithful Underwood Champion. Eventually, I hurt my back. That's when I stopped typing and started writing everything in pencil again.

I still write in pencil. I'm writing this with a number 2 pencil. The pencils were gifts from my old friend Tom McGoey. They each say *Alex Cross Lives Here*. My handwriting is impossible to read—even for me. Hell, *I'm* not sure what I just wrote.

After about a thousand revisions, when I thought the manuscript for *The Thomas Berryman Number* might be ready for human consumption, I mailed it out myself. No agent. No early readers. No compelling pitch letter.

I got rejections. Mostly form letters. A couple of handwritten notes from editors that were encouraging. One publisher, Morrow, held on to the manuscript for two months before rejecting it. With a form letter.

Then I read an article in the *New York Times Book Review* about the literary agency Sanford Greenburger Associates. Sanford Greenburger, the founder of the agency, had died in 1971. His son Francis took over the business. Francis was in his twenties, not much older than me. The article in the *Times* said they were accepting manuscripts from unpublished writers. That would be me.

I sent over the manuscript that had already been rejected thirty times. We're talking four hundred typewritten pages secured in a cardboard box. Two days later, I got a phone call from

Greenburger Associates. I'm thinking to myself, *I can't believe they turned my book down so fast!*

The caller turned out to be Francis himself. He said, "No, no, no, I'm not turning your novel down. Just the opposite. Come on over and see me. I want to sell this thing. I *will* sell your book."

So Francis hooked me up with Jay Acton, a hot young editor at Thomas Crowell, a small, family-owned New York publisher. Jay and I got along beautifully. He worked with me for about a month on the manuscript. He helped the book take shape and we cut some fat.

Then Jay rejected it. My thirty-first rejection.

But Francis Greenburger talked me down off a ledge of the thirty-story Graybar Building, where J. Walter Thompson had its offices. "Don't worry your pretty little head. I'm going to sell it this week."

And he sold it to Little, Brown. *That week.*

norman mailer and
james baldwin — fisticuffs

MY FIRST NEW YORK literary party taught me that, like a lot of secret societies, the inner world of literary people was borderline crazy and completely overrated.

That first lit party was at the home of Jay Acton, the editor who had helped me with but then rejected *The Thomas Berryman Number*. Jay and I had stayed friends and I liked him tremendously.

(Years later, the weirdest thing happened to Jay. He'd switched over to being a literary agent, and one of his clients was bestselling romance writer Helen Van Slyke. She was a friend and also a big moneymaker for Jay. Then Jay got the terrible news that Helen had died, suddenly and apparently without much warning. Next, Jay got some very different news. Helen Van Slyke had left Jay pretty much everything. Suddenly he was rich. I think he bought a minor-league baseball team and a radio station.)

I remember sitting in Jay's living room the night of that party. It was before *Berryman* was actually published. I was in the middle of a conversation with Wilfrid Sheed, whose novel *People Will Always Be Kind* I'd read and loved.

Sheed was, well, *kind*.

He gave me the best advice as I waited for *The Thomas Berryman Number* to be published. "Write another book. Start tonight. You can—" We were interrupted midsentence by some kind of hubbub happening elsewhere in the apartment. People were filing back into a rear hallway. I excused myself and followed the noise and the crowd.

I entered a large bedroom.

The room was packed with people. Noisy people. Sweating people. Tense people. *Fight fans!*

In the middle of the room stood these two small men. They were arguing loudly, fists clenched, looking like they were ready to rumble. The bedroom had become a pint-size boxing ring.

The men were Norman Mailer and James Baldwin. Two little guys who looked about as athletic as French poodles. Especially Baldwin. I remembered that Mailer had actually done some prizefighting, but he didn't look like much of a fighter to me. The two men were squared off at center ring.

Mailer and Baldwin were arguing about what should be considered good literature and what shouldn't. It seemed clear they weren't big fans of one another. Weird, because I was a fan of both of them, especially James Baldwin.

You could not have dragged me out of that noisy, stuffy, overcrowded bedroom. No fisticuffs yet, but lots of heated words. The literary crowd gathered in the room was *abuzz*. The pugilists were circling, looking for an opportunity to pounce, maybe throw the first punch, but definitely win the war of words.

I have to admit, I found the whole thing hilarious. But I knew I would never forget that scene, and obviously, I haven't.

It set the tone for the absurdity of literary warfare—which I've tried my best to avoid.

Wilfrid Sheed may have written *People Will Always Be Kind,* but I learned that wasn't always the case.

speaking of bookstore windows

OKAY, I AM walking along Broadway in New York City. I'm walking pretty quickly. I arrive at my local Barnes & Noble on the corner of Sixty-Seventh Street. I see three copies of my novel *Along Came a Spider* in the window. This is good stuff.

I've been pretty much waiting for this to happen since I first came to live in New York in the 1970s. It's now January of 1993.

I go inside the bookstore. I'm hyperventilating a little. I want to make this moment last.

It's a Sunday. I've just seen that *Along Came a Spider* is number 6 on the *New York Times* bestseller list. I don't think that could be a mistake, but I'm a little afraid it might be.

I walk toward the fiction section and I can already see the cover for *Along Came a Spider*. It features big type and an illustration of a spider hanging over a suburban-looking house.

Now here's what some writers do. We count the number of copies of our book in stock at the local bookstore.

I know there were twelve copies of *Along Came a Spider* here a few days ago. Now there are six copies.

So maybe the *New York Times* bestseller list is accurate. I'm feeling a little dizzy. I don't know how to handle this. I'm starting to get hopeful—and hope is not a strategy.

While I'm heading toward *Along Came a Spider,* a woman picks up a copy.

I stop walking.

Now, here's another thing that happens with some writers: If we see you pick up a copy of one of our books at the store, we watch you. If you buy the book, I swear, it makes our whole day. But if you put the book down, reject us, as it were, it breaks our hearts. Seriously. I think it hurts our souls.

So I'm watching this woman, practicing spy craft the way I've read about it in John le Carré mysteries.

She reads the flap copy, then she reads the author blurbs on the back cover. Then she puts *Along Came a Spider* under her arm.

I'm trying to be cool about this, but I want to go over and give her a big hug.

I watch this wonderful, wonderful person walk down a long, narrow aisle—and then she slides *Along Came a Spider* into her hobo bag.

She stole the book.

And all I can think is *Does that count as a sale?*

dolly, hello

I'LL TELL YOU one more love story, the most recent one. I fell head over heels in love with Dolly Parton the first time I met her in Nashville.

I had a half-baked but potentially really good idea for a story about a country singer. I suggested to Dolly's manager that she and I consider writing a novel together. Dolly was interested but she wanted to meet—face-to-face—before deciding. We needed to talk, to get to know one another, if we were going to be writing partners. That made perfect sense to me.

So I took a plane ride to Nashville, a city I've loved since I attended Vanderbilt. Her driver picked me up at the airport. You can tell a lot about rich or famous people by talking to the folks who work for them. The driver had been with Dolly for over twenty years. He told me she was the best, the kindest person on the planet. He loved her and said everybody did. I believed him because of the way he said it. Also because Dolly's reputation precedes her.

That day at her very homey office, I found her to be down-to-earth, genuine, thoughtful, smart as a whip, funny, and self-deprecating. Those are qualities that are right up my small-town alley. There's a line that was used to promote the *Friday*

Night Lights TV series that I like a lot: "clear eyes, full heart." That's Dolly Parton.

I guess she was okay with me too because we shook on a deal on the spot to write our book. No agents, no lawyers, nothing but a promise between the two of us. That's the way things should work, in my opinion. Get rid of the middlemen.

Dolly's one concern had been that there wouldn't be enough for her to contribute, and she refused to just put her name on the book. I told her that wasn't how this would work. I wanted her help with the outline and then the book itself. She would make our story authentic, because she knows *everything* about the music business. She would make the story strong, because that's what Dolly does best, tell stories. In fact, that's what country music is all about, storytelling.

Plus, there were a dozen or so songs in the novel. I needed a whole lot of help with those. Dolly said, "Jim, I've written thousands of songs. I can write a country song standing on my head. Want to see?"

Two days after I got home, I received an unbelievable surprise. Dolly already had some good ideas about the first draft of our outline. And she'd sent me the lyrics for *seven* original songs. She'd already written seven songs. Can you believe that? Well, it's how it happened.

I still remember sending her pages one Friday night and on *Saturday* getting back this note:

Hey Jimmy James,

Loving it, loving it, loving it!!! Love our red-headed twins and the community guitar at the Nashville

roadhouse. Nicely done. No notes on this batch—keep
it coming!

Love,
Dolly

Sue wants me to frame the damn note. She can't stop talking about "*Dolly's* novel."

Dolly and I became friends during our collaboration on *Run, Rose, Run*. She calls me "Jimmy James" or "JJ." For her birthday, I sent her one of those silver cups people give to a mom after she's had a baby. I had it inscribed HAPPY BIRTHDAY, BABY.

For my birthday, Dolly sang "Happy Birthday" to me over the phone. She also sent me a beautiful guitar. She inscribed it TO JIMMY JAMES, I WILL ALWAYS LOVE YOU.

How cool is that?

Also By James Patterson

ALEX CROSS NOVELS

Along Came a Spider • Kiss the Girls • Jack and Jill • Cat and Mouse • Pop Goes the Weasel • Roses are Red • Violets are Blue • Four Blind Mice • The Big Bad Wolf • London Bridges • Mary, Mary • Cross • Double Cross • Cross Country • Alex Cross's Trial (*with Richard DiLallo*) • I, Alex Cross • Cross Fire • Kill Alex Cross • Merry Christmas, Alex Cross • Alex Cross, Run • Cross My Heart • Hope to Die • Cross Justice • Cross the Line • The People vs. Alex Cross • Target: Alex Cross • Criss Cross • Deadly Cross • Fear No Evil

THE WOMEN'S MURDER CLUB SERIES

1st to Die (*with Andrew Gross*) • 2nd Chance (*with Andrew Gross*) • 3rd Degree (*with Andrew Gross*) • 4th of July (*with Maxine Paetro*) • The 5th Horseman (*with Maxine Paetro*) • The 6th Target (*with Maxine Paetro*) • 7th Heaven (*with Maxine Paetro*) • 8th Confession (*with Maxine Paetro*) • 9th Judgement (*with Maxine Paetro*) • 10th Anniversary (*with Maxine Paetro*) • 11th Hour (*with Maxine Paetro*) • 12th of Never (*with Maxine Paetro*) • Unlucky 13 (*with Maxine Paetro*) • 14th Deadly Sin (*with Maxine Paetro*) • 15th Affair (*with Maxine Paetro*) • 16th Seduction (*with Maxine Paetro*) • 17th Suspect (*with Maxine Paetro*) • 18th Abduction (*with Maxine Paetro*) • 19th Christmas (*with Maxine Paetro*) • 20th Victim (*with Maxine Paetro*) • 21st Birthday (*with Maxine Paetro*) • 22 Seconds (*with Maxine Paetro*)

DETECTIVE MICHAEL BENNETT SERIES

Step on a Crack (*with Michael Ledwidge*) • Run for Your Life (*with Michael Ledwidge*) • Worst Case (*with Michael Ledwidge*) • Tick Tock (*with Michael Ledwidge*) • I, Michael Bennett (*with Michael Ledwidge*) • Gone (*with Michael Ledwidge*) • Burn (*with Michael Ledwidge*) • Alert (*with Michael Ledwidge*) • Bullseye (*with Michael Ledwidge*) • Haunted (*with James O. Born*) • Ambush (*with James O. Born*) • Blindside (*with James O. Born*) • The Russian (*with James O. Born*) • Shattered (*with James O. Born*)

PRIVATE NOVELS

Private (*with Maxine Paetro*) • Private London (*with Mark Pearson*) • Private Games (*with Mark Sullivan*) • Private: No. 1 Suspect (*with Maxine Paetro*) • Private Berlin (*with Mark Sullivan*) • Private Down Under (*with Michael White*) • Private L.A. (*with Mark Sullivan*) • Private India (*with Ashwin Sanghi*) • Private Vegas (*with Maxine Paetro*) • Private Sydney (*with Kathryn Fox*) • Private Paris (*with Mark Sullivan*) • The Games (*with Mark Sullivan*) • Private Delhi (*with Ashwin Sanghi*) • Private Princess (*with Rees Jones*) • Private Moscow (*with Adam Hamdy*) • Private Rogue (*with Adam Hamdy*)

NON-FICTION

Torn Apart (*with Hal and Cory Friedman*) • The Murder of King Tut (*with Martin Dugard*) • All-American Murder (*with Alex Abramovich and Mike Harvkey*) • The Kennedy Curse (*with Cynthia Fagen*) • The Last Days of John Lennon (*with Casey Sherman and Dave Wedge*) • Walk in My Combat Boots (*with Matt Eversmann and Chris Mooney*) • ER Nurses: True stories from the frontline (*with Matt Eversmann*) • James Patterson by James Patterson: The Stories of My Life

MURDER IS FOREVER TRUE CRIME

Murder, Interrupted (*with Alex Abramovich and Christopher Charles*) • Home Sweet Murder (*with Andrew Bourelle and Scott Slaven*) • Murder Beyond the Grave (*with Andrew Bourelle and Christopher Charles*) • Murder Thy Neighbour (*with Andrew Bourelle and Max DiLallo*) • Murder of Innocence (*with Max DiLallo and Andrew Bourelle*) • Till Murder Do Us Part (*with Andrew Bourelle and Max DiLallo*)

COLLECTIONS

Triple Threat (*with Max DiLallo and Andrew Bourelle*) • Kill or Be Killed (*with Maxine Paetro, Rees Jones, Shan Serafin and Emily Raymond*) • The Moores are Missing (*with Loren D. Estleman, Sam Hawken and Ed Chatterton*) • The Family Lawyer (*with Robert Rotstein, Christopher Charles and Rachel Howzell Hall*) • Murder in Paradise (*with Doug Allyn, Connor Hyde and Duane Swierczynski*) • The House Next Door (*with Susan DiLallo, Max DiLallo and Brendan DuBois*) • 13-Minute Murder (*with Shan Serafin, Christopher Farnsworth and Scott Slaven*) • The River Murders (*with James O. Born*) • The Palm Beach Murders (*with James O. Born, Duane Swierczynski and Tim Arnold*) • Paris Detective

For more information about James Patterson's novels, visit www.penguin.co.uk.